O9-BUD-995

PENGUIN BOOKS
THE PORTABLE COLERIDGE

Each volume in The Viking Portable Library either presents a representative selection from the works of a single outstanding writer or offers a comprehensive anthology on a special subject. Averaging 700 pages in length and designed for compactness and readability, these books fill a need not met by other compilations. All are edited by distinguished authorities who have written introductory essays and included much other helpful material.

"The Viking Portables have done more for good reading and good writers than anything that has come along since I can remember."
—Arthur Mizener

PR4472 .R5 1978
C.3 CYP
The portable Coleridge /
33663001363148

DISCARD

Other Volumes in
THE VIKING PORTABLE LIBRARY

The Portable

COLERIDGE

EDITED, AND WITH AN INTRODUCTION, BY

I. A. RICHARDS

PENGUIN BOOKS

PENGUIN BOOKS
Published by the Penguin Group
Viking Penguin Inc., 40 West 23rd Street, New York, New York 10010, U.S.A.
Penguin Books Ltd, 27 Wrights Lane, London W8 5TZ, England
Penguin Books Australia Ltd, Ringwood, Victoria, Australia
Penguin Books Canada Ltd, 2801 John Street,
Markham, Ontario, Canada L3R 1B4
Penguin Books (N.Z.) Ltd, 182–190 Wairau Road,
Auckland 10, New Zealand

First published in the United States of America
by Viking Penguin Inc. 1950
Paperbound edition published 1961
Reprinted 1965, 1966, 1967, 1968, 1969,
1970, 1971, 1972, 1974, 1975
Published in Penguin Books 1977

15 17 19 20 18 16 14

Copyright 1950 by Viking Penguin Inc.
Copyright © renewed Viking Penguin Inc., 1978
All rights reserved

LIBRARY OF CONGRESS CATALOGING IN PUBLICATION DATA
Coleridge, Samuel Taylor, 1772-1834.
The portable Coleridge.
Reprint of the 1950 ed. published by The Viking Press,
New York, which was issued as no. 48 of the
Viking portable library.
Bibliography: p. 56. Includes index.
I. Richards, Ivor Armstrong, 1893– II. Title.
[PR4472.R5 1977]   821'.7   76-55363
ISBN 0 14 015.048 x

Printed in the United States of America
Set in Linotype Caledonia

Grateful acknowledgment is made to the following:
for excerpts from *Unpublished Letters of
Samuel Taylor Coleridge* to Earl Leslie Griggs and
the Yale University Press, New Haven; from *Coleridge's
Shakespearean Criticism* and *Coleridge's Miscellaneous
Criticism* to Thomas Middleton Raysor and the
Harvard University Press, Cambridge.

Except in the United States of America,
this book is sold subject to the condition
that it shall not, by way of trade or otherwise,
be lent, re-sold, hired out, or otherwise circulated
without the publisher's prior consent in any form of
binding or cover other than that in which it is
published and without a similar condition
including this condition being imposed
on the subsequent purchaser

Austin Community College
Learning Resources Center

Contents

LETTERS

NOTEBOOKS AND TABLE TALK

POLITICS

THEOLOGICO-METAPHYSICAL

CRITICISM

FROM BIOGRAPHIA LITERARIA

CONTENTS

Introduction

The story of Coleridge's life has been told many times, in outline and at length[1]—too often to an accompaniment of wrung hands, wry faces, shrugged shoulders, set frowns, and worse. It is very well documented; many parts of it can be told in great detail. Its hero offers a rarely equaled series of invitations to moralizing judgment: opportunities he himself is only too ready to exploit. But such comments really tell us less about Coleridge than about their authors. Our business is with him and still more with his work, not with some lesser man's opinions about his character and behavior. When in the last years of his life he himself notes, "A Friend of S. T. Coleridge's wrote under a portrait of him 'A glow-worm with a pin stuck thro' it, as seen in broad day-light,'"[2] that is an interesting fact about *him*—the more so if we suspect that the Friend may have been himself. But when his fullest biographer winds up a marvelously tight-packed account with a sentence ending, "a will-o'-the-wisp light for bemused thinkers," that presents only a fact about the biographer.

Those who are drawn to Coleridge by some affinity,

[1] See bibliography, pp. 56–57.
[2] "Or must we seek its *analogon* in the light of the glow-worm, that simply serves to distinguish one reptile from all the rest, and lighting, inch by inch, its mazy path through weeds and grass, leaves all else before, behind, and around it in darkness." ("Demosius and Mystes" in *Idea of the Christian Church.*)

1

by any one of those myriad elections by which his influ-
ence has spread, who sense in him a larger-than-life
resemblance to themselves, even in the utterances they
would least claim kinship with—his highest poetry or
his most maudlin prose, his philosophic summits or his
apologetic ditches—and who have this book in their
hands now for more than accidental reasons, will be
least resentful of some reachings toward the unsayable
in the last section of this introduction. We begin with
the facts of his outer life, turn then to facts about his
work, then to his poetry as the most important work he
had to do, and to his criticism as the clearest self-aware-
ness in him of the "each in all of human nature," and
come lastly to his philosophy as his transeendental con-
jecture as to what it all is and what it all is for.

Samuel Taylor Coleridge was born at Ottery St. Mary
in Devonshire, October 21, 1772, the son of a clergyman
and schoolmaster and youngest of a family of ten. His
own account of his early years will be found in the let-
ters here printed (pp. 217-27). His father died when he
was nine and about a year later he went to Christ's
Hospital in London, of which his younger schoolmates
Charles Lamb, in his Elia essay "Christ's Hospital Five-
and-Thirty Years Ago," and Leigh Hunt, in his *Auto-
biography*, give vivid accounts. Memories of these days
occur frequently in Coleridge's writings. (See "Frost at
Midnight," "Dejection" and *Biographia Literaria*, chap-
ter I, pp. 432 ff.) He was extremely successful in the
strict classical studies of the school, but the extent and
energy of his other interests were still more notable. An
early plunge into medical books (his brother Luke was a
surgeon at London Hospital) was followed by a passion-
ate immersion in metaphysics and theology, ranging from
Plotinus to Voltaire. It is significant that he was in the

sick ward for months, with jaundice and rheumatic fever, after bathing in his clothes in the New River and drying off in them.

He went up to Jesus College, Cambridge, at nineteen (October 1791). There was a year of steady reading and modest living and rheumatism. Then debts, due largely to carelessness, threw his whole being off balance. In a suicidal mood he wandered off to London and on a random impulse enlisted in the Light Dragoons (December 4, 1893) as Silas Tompkin Comberbach. He lived up to the name by failing too frequently to stay in the saddle. He was soon given orderly duties with smallpox patients and by early April his brothers had succeeded in buying him out and he returned to Cambridge. His college behaved very reasonably to him.

In June 1794 he walked to Oxford, where he met Southey, a decisive meeting. The two at once "struck out the leading features of a pantisocracy," Coleridge inventing the name. This was a noble and philosophic project for a group emigration to America. Twelve young men with their twelve wives were to settle there as an ideal community, an "experiment of human Perfectability." (See pp. 236–37 and 275 for the motives behind this.) Unfortunately Southey was in love with Edith Fricker, one of five daughters of a manufacturer of sugar pans whose business had vanished with the cessation of trade with America. Lovell, the earliest convert to their scheme, was engaged to another of the Fricker daughters. Why not a third, Sarah Fricker, for Coleridge? The chief impediment was a passion he had been nursing for Mary Evans, the sister of a school friend. A mild attachment to her had grown fervent in the crisis which sent him into the Dragoons. It was still painfully active throughout a walking tour in Wales (see p. 233) and another tour, with Southey, in Somerset. These feelings did not however prevent him from becoming engaged to Sarah in the interests of Pantisocracy before returning to Cambridge. All the Fricker girls and their mother were to go. During the winter the scheme, not surprisingly, collapsed. Southey's aunt, to whom they looked to finance the emigration, had shown him the door. Worse still, Southey had proposed introducing a servant class into the community. Mary Evans had written what she thought about it all, and in a following letter had answered Coleridge's prayer, "Indulge, Mary, this my first, my last request, and restore me to *reality*, however gloomy." (See letter, p. 240.)

The end of Pantisocracy should have put an end to his engagement. In spite of some struggles it did not. Coleridge left Cambridge, without taking his degree, before the end of the year, lingering in London till Southey came to fetch him to Bristol and Sarah. He married her in October 1795. Six weeks later Southey married his Edith, but not before a complete, though temporary, breach had occurred between the *ci-devant* Pantisocrats.

Married life began happily in the cottage at Clevedon described in "The Eolian Harp." The publisher Cottle had undertaken to buy Coleridge's verse (at a guinea and a half per hundred lines) and any prose works too. Lectures in the cause of civic liberties, anti-war pamphleteering, and some preaching as a Unitarian, led on to a venture with a periodical, *The Watchman*, addressed primarily to democrats. It failed after ten numbers, in part because Coleridge in the second number put at the head of his essay on fasts, "Wherefore my Bowels shall sound like an Harp" (Isaiah). Coleridge thought that cost him five hundred subscribers.

At this moment a group of admirers headed by

Thomas Poole put up a subsidy for him of about forty
pounds a year for seven years. "Reviews, the magazine
and other miscellaneous literary earnings—shilling-
scavenger employments," might provide another such
amount. But there was an allowance of twenty pounds to
be made to Mrs. Fricker, and other dependents to sup-
port, "five mouths opening and shutting as I pull the
string." And in September 1796 his first son, David
Hartley, was born. The search went on for some means
to deal with "the two giants leagued together, whose
most imperious commands I must obey, however re-
luctant—their names are BREAD and CHEESE."

At the end of the year he moved to a cottage at
Nether Stowey near to the most faithful and helpful of
all his friends, Thomas Poole, a prosperous tanner of
strong democratic views. And in the spring he began
to be in touch first with William Wordsworth and then
also with Dorothy. They were living at Racedown (some
forty miles away) and there Coleridge visited them
(June 5, 1797). Here is what Dorothy wrote to Wil-
liam's future wife, Mary Hutchinson, who had just left:

You had a great loss in not seeing Coleridge. He is a won-
derful man. His conversation teems with soul, mind, and
spirit. Then he is so benevolent, so good tempered and cheer-
ful, and, like William, interests himself so much about every
little trifle. At first I thought him very plain, that is, for
about three minutes: he is pale and thin, has a wide mouth,
thick lips, and not very good teeth, longish loose-growing
half-curling rough black hair. But if you hear him speak for
five minutes you think no more of them. His eye is large and
full, not dark but grey; such an eye as would receive from a
heavy soul the dullest expression; but it speaks every emotion
of his animated mind; it has more of the "poet's eye in a
fine frenzy rolling" than I ever witnessed. He has fine dark
eyebrows, and an overhanging forehead.

Much later she recalled that Coleridge "did not keep to the high road, but leapt over a gate and bounded down the pathless field by which he cut off an angle." (Cf. Aspheterism letter, p. 231.) With this pen portrait we may compare two others, Coleridge's own (see letter to Thelwall, pp. 250–51) and Hazlitt's:

> His complexion was at that time clear and even bright—
>
> "As are the children of yon azure sheen."

His forehead was broad and high, light as if built of ivory, with large projecting eyebrows, and his eyes rolling beneath them like a sea with darkened lustre. "A certain tender bloom his face o'erspread," a purple tinge as we see it in the pale thoughtful complexions of the Spanish portrait-painters, Murillo and Velasquez. His mouth was gross, voluptuous, open, eloquent; his chin good-humoured and round; but his nose, the rudder of the face, the index of the will, was small, feeble, nothing—like what he has done. . . . Coleridge, in his person, was rather above the common size, inclining to be corpulent, or, like Lord Hamlet, "somewhat fat and pursy." His hair (now, alas! grey) was then black and glossy as the raven's, and fell in smooth masses over his forehead.

On the smoothness of these masses, a member of his lecture audience in Bristol had remarked, "Mr. C—— would therefore do well to appear with cleaner stockings in public, and if his hair were combed out every time he appeared in public it would not depreciate him in the esteem of his friends." While we are thus visualizing, Coleridge's own portrait of Dorothy should be noted:

> Wordsworth & his exquisite Sister are with me— She is a woman indeed!—in mind, I mean, & heart—for her person is such, that if you expected to see a pretty woman, you would think her ordinary—if you expected to find an ordi-

nary woman, you would think her pretty!—But her manners are simple, ardent, impressive—

> In every motion her most innocent soul
> Outbeams so brightly, that who saw would say,
> Guilt was a thing impossible in her.

Her information various—her eye watchful in minutest observation of nature—and her taste a perfect electrometer—it bends, protrudes, and draws in, at subtlest beauties & most recondite faults. (To Cottle, July 1797)

The force of the attraction between Coleridge and the Wordsworths may be seen from some dates. He probably stayed at Racedown June 5 to 28, then back to Stowey and back again July 2 to fetch the Wordsworths to stay with him. On July 7 Lamb arrived for a visit. "This Lime Tree Bower My Prison" was written in Poole's garden while the Wordsworths and Lamb were out walking. "Dear Sarah" had upset some boiling milk over Coleridge's foot and he was unable to go with them. By the middle of July the Wordsworths had moved into a large vacant mansion at Alfoxden, three miles from the Nether Stowey cottage. Poole had arranged it, helpful as ever.

Soon came a visit from "Citizen Thelwall," a leading anti-Government democratic agitator. Coleridge had been disagreeing with him for some time in more and more friendly letters. His visit created local alarm. Wordsworth's coming had been bad enough, with his mysterious solitary walks toward the sea. (A French invasion, we must remember, was expected.) But now! Soon there was an agent observing and reporting on their doings, conversation, and visitors. He seems to have been a capable and sensible man, and in a conversation struck up on the road found Coleridge no friend to Jacobinism. On moving to Stowey Coleridge had written: "I have accordingly snapped my squeaking baby-trumpet of sedition, and have hung up its fragments in the chamber of Penitences." The influence of Nether Stowey worked on Thelwall too. (See p. 316.)

For Wordsworth Coleridge was soon head over heels in admiration. "Wordsworth is a very great man, the only man to whom *at all times* and *in all modes of excellence* I feel myself inferior." As with even Southey's verse before, admiration of others' work made him excessively diffident about his own, which at that date may well be thought to outweigh Wordsworth's. And, though no accountancy is possible with such deep interchanges and indebtednesses, Wordsworth seems undoubtedly the chief gainer from the strange poetic symbiosis which now began. It is arguable that as to many modes of excellence—by finding the style which Wordsworth was to advocate in the Preface to the *Lyrical Ballads,* by uttering a good half of the thoughts in that and in Wordsworth's later prose, by designing Wordsworth's major poems for him, and by discovering the philosophic seas on which they float[3]—Coleridge was Wordsworth's creator; or, since that is clearly too strong a word, that he first truly showed Wordsworth how to become his own poetic self.

As a minor example, here are Coleridge's reflections on a rivulet near Nether Stowey:

. . . I sought for a subject, that should give equal room and freedom for description, incident, and impassioned reflec-

[3] As De Selincourt remarked, "It is curious that whilst [*The Prelude*] pays a beautiful tribute to Wordsworth's love for his friend, so little acknowledgement is made of his incalculable intellectual debt to him. Yet it was through Coleridge that he came first to understand himself and his poetic aims." (*Wordsworthian and Other Studies,* London and New York: Oxford University Press, 1947.)

tions on men, nature, and society, yet supply in itself a natu-
ral connection to the parts, and unity to the whole. Such a
subject I conceived myself to have found in a stream, traced
from its source in the hills among the yellow-red moss and
conical glass-shaped tufts of bent, to the first break or fall,
where its drops become audible, and it begins to form a
channel; then to the peat and turf barn, itself built of the
same dark squares as it sheltered; to the sheepfold; to the
first cultivated plot of ground; to the lonely cottage and its
bleak garden won from the heath; to the hamlet, the villages,
the market-town, the manufactories, and the seaport. My
walks therefore were almost daily on the top of Quantock,
and among its sloping combes. With my pencil and memo-
randum book in my hand, I was *making studies,* as the artists
call them, and often moulding my thoughts into verse, with
the objects and imagery immediately before my senses.

Biographia Literaria, Chapter x

Twenty-two years after these studies Wordsworth's Son-
net Series, "The River Duddon," realizes the design.
In sonnet xxx there could be a memory of Coleridge:

> And oft-times he—who yielding to the force
> Of chance-temptation, ere his journey end,
> From chosen comrade turns, or faithful friend—
> In vain shall rue the broken intercourse.

What is certain is that Coleridge had been to Words-
worth what the Duddon may symbolize in the "After-
thought" which ends the Series:

> I thought of Thee, my partner and my guide,
> As being past away.—Vain sympathies!
> For, backward, Duddon, as I cast my eyes,
> I see what was, and is, and will abide;
> Still glides the Stream, and shall forever glide;
> The Form remains, the Function never dies;
> While we, the brave, the mighty, and the wise,
> We Men, who in our morn of youth defied

The elements, must vanish;—be it so!
Enough, if something from our hands have power
To live, and act, and serve the future hour.

Serve the future hour Coleridge's designs certainly
did—more often through Wordsworth's pen than his
own. Meanwhile the present hour itself was asking to be
served as endlessly as any other nursling. A tragedy
called then "Osorio"—to become, in 1813, the moder-
ately successful *Remorse*—was written for Sheridan and
rejected by him. Work for the *Morning Post* was under-
taken. Salaried posts as a Unitarian minister were con-
sidered—with much hesitation lest freedom of thought
should be impeded. By January 14 he was preaching a
trial sermon at Shrewsbury and almost resolved. Here
is Hazlitt's well-known description of his voice:

Mr. Coleridge rose and gave out his text, "And he went up
into the mountain to pray, HIMSELF, ALONE." As he gave
out this text, his voice "rose like a steam of rich distilled
perfumes"; and when he came to the two last words, which
he pronounced loud, deep, and distinct, it seemed to me, who
was then young, as if the sounds had echoed from the bot-
tom of the human heart, and as if that prayer might have
floated in solemn silence through the universe.

My First Acquaintance with Poets

The very next morning (January 15, 1798) came an
offer from Josiah and Tom Wedgwood of an annuity of
one hundred fifty pounds for life, without conditions. It
was to enable him to write rather than preach, however.
He accepted at once and resigned his Shrewsbury can-
didature.

At this point the voice of the moralizing biographer is
raised. "Perhaps the worst thing possible had happened
to him. He had talked long enough; sown enough wild
oats . . . it was time for him, in one way or another, to

take up his share of the economic burden which is, or ought to be, the common lot of humanity." [4] From another point of view, this may have equally been Coleridge's narrowest escape, and the Wedgwood brothers (Tom was a philosopher and original; Josiah an administrator; and a banker brother, John, lived near Bristol and entertained Coleridge) may deserve a grateful thought from everyone who owes anything to Coleridge. This voice of his had perilous powers. He was too much "a born preacher" to become one professionally.

There followed what may reasonably be considered a productive year, in spite of what look a little like other narrow escapes—this time from bodily dangers. Wordsworth remembered "a frightful internal pain" which sometimes caused Coleridge "when they walked together in Somerset, to throw himself down and writhe like a worm upon the ground." And there was a fever caused by an inflamed tooth. Soon after his recovery he walked over to Ottery (thirty-two or more miles) and on April 18 he walked back. In the next few days he wrote "The Nightingale" and "Fears in Solitude." In February he had written "Frost at Midnight" and "France: An Ode" (earlier named "Recantation").

On May 14 a son, Berkeley, was born in the midst

---

[4] E. K. Chambers, *Samuel Taylor Coleridge: A Biographical Study* (Oxford: The Clarendon Press, 1938, p. 90). He adds, "It is true that his first impulse was to recognize in full the moral obligation which it imposed upon him. 'Now I am enabled, as I have received freely, freely to give.' . . . The thought recurred to him from time to time for many years. But, unfortunately, the longer Coleridge looked at a moral obligation the more he became inclined in practice to shy away from it." The thought recurs in turning these pages: the deeper Chambers looked into Coleridge the more he became inclined to evade understanding him.

of a distracting embroilment with Charles Lloyd, Lamb, and Southey. Lloyd had been a most devout young disciple and for a time a paying guest-pupil in Bristol. And now (April 1798) he published a novel, *Edmund Oliver*, whose hero had a distressingly recognizable resemblance to Coleridge. "I have at all times," Edmund says, "a strange dreaminess about me which makes me indifferent to the future, if I can by any means fill the present with sensations—with that dreaminess I have gone on here from day to day: if at any time thought troubled, I have swallowed some spirits, or had recourse to my laudanum." Damaging reading—to the Wedgwoods, for example. So Coleridge spent some time, with the Wordsworths, chasing Lloyd, and more in correspondence which is often shrewd: ". . . You clothed my image with a suit of notions and feelings which could belong to nothing human." By July, however, this was in the main over and the summer, which came early that year, was in Wordsworth's memory:

> That summer when on Quantock's grassy Hills
> Far ranging, and amid her sylvan Coombs,
> Thou in delicious words, with happy heart,
> Didst speak the vision of that Ancient Man,
> The bright-eyed Mariner, and rueful woes
> Didst utter of the Lady Christabel.
> *The Prelude*, Book xiii, lines 395–400, 1805

These had been written in the late autumn of 1797, "Kubla Khan" probably in October 1797, though possibly it may have been in May 1798.

In September 1798 Coleridge, with a young Stowey admirer, John Chester, and the Wordsworths, left for Germany. There he remained till July 1799, learning German, writing affectionate letters to Sarah, plunging into German metaphysics, accumulating materials of all sorts, and planning a life of Lessing. In February the baby, Berkeley, died. The news threw Coleridge into deep ponderings of the grounds of belief: "I find it wise and human to believe, even on slight evidence, opinions, the contrary of which cannot be proved, and which promote our happiness without hampering our intellect." This may be compared, perhaps, to T. H. Huxley's assertion under a similar loss: "I know what I mean when I say I believe in the law of the inverse squares, and I will not rest my life and my hopes upon weaker convictions. I dare not if I would" (letter to Charles Kingsley).

Back at Stowey, Coleridge re-established relations, still not too cordial, with Southey; the Wordsworths had removed to Durham. Soon a false rumor of Wordsworth's ill health came and, with Cottle, he rushed in anxiety north. There, at Sockburn (October 1799), he met Sara Hutchinson, a friend of Dorothy's, and William's sister-in-law to be, and was seized with a passion which shaped ten years of his life (see p. 278). A later description by Coleridge's daughter Sara says, "She had fine, long, light brown hair, I think her only beauty, except a fair skin, for her features were plain and contracted, her figure dumpy, and devoid of grace and dignity. She was a plump woman, of little more than five feet." This passion probably explains why, after a walking tour with Wordsworth on which they saw Dove Cottage, Wordsworth's future home at Grasmere, he did not return to Stowey but took up work on the *Morning Post* in London (about November 27, 1799) and wrote to his wife to join him. She left after two months; but Coleridge remained, writing political articles, frequenting the theaters with dramatic reviewing in mind, reporting debates in Parliament, translating Schiller's *The Piccolomini* and *The Death of Wallenstein*, and consorting with Lamb. The great question, the Schiller job once done, was where to live. In the end he followed the Wordsworths to the Lake District; we may suppose Sara Hutchinson to have been a part of the attraction, but he was also fulfilling the promise made in lines 54–58 of "Frost at Midnight."

Greta Hall, Keswick, where Coleridge and his family took up residence July 24, 1800, was then a house with an outlook: "I question if there be a room in England which commands a view of mountains, and lakes, and woods and vales superior to that in which I am now sitting." "If impressions and ideas *constitute* our being, I shall have a tendency to become a god, so sublime and beautiful will be the series of my visual existence." (See pp. 283, 306, 307, 311.) For a while all this kept him up. There were many visits to the Wordsworths at Grasmere, which they returned. It was only a thirteen-mile walk over Dummail Raise. But Coleridge would sometimes add in Helvellyn or Fairfield—good mountain days. He even anticipated by more than a generation the modern taste for pure mountain adventure indulged for its own sake, making a solitary ascent (July 1802) of Scafell and down by Broad Stand into Eskdale, an expedition no tourist—as opposed to a shepherd—had ventured on before or was to repeat for another forty years. So integral may the pioneering spirit be.

In spite of this, ill health dogged him—rheumatisms which may have had as much to do with his teeth as with the weather and perhaps a good deal that would now be labeled psychosomatic. The winter of 1800–1801 saw him bedridden for weeks, and these pains drove him again to opium. As early as this the drug began to be a necessity to him. In the intervals between pain and the miraculous relief he took to yet another sort of pioneering, to experimental inquiry into sense

perception (see letters, pp. 267 and 271). "In the course
of these studies," he wrote to Poole, "I tried a multitude
of little experiments on my own sensations and on my
senses, and some of these (too often repeated) I have
reason to believe did injury to my nervous system. . . .
The disgust, the loathing that followed these fits, and
no doubt in part, too, the use of brandy and laudanum
which they rendered necessary!"

Much of this was an offshoot of his metaphysical
speculations which now became a sustained and pas-
sionate concern. It was in these two years that he re-
nounced and extricated himself from the associationism
of Hartley and the early Berkeley—the names of his
sons show how much they had meant to him. Hence-
forth for him the mind is to be activity. The great LOCK,
as he was to grow fond of calling the philosopher, had
been turned; and the key, though in parts it might seem
at times to have been cut and filed by Kant, was truly
what he had learned long ago from Plato and Plotinus
returning now in his own thought as power. The intel-
lectual excitement of the new world he feels that he is
creating for himself rings out gaily enough at times in
his letters. It is a mistake to take the mood of lines 89–
93 of "Dejection" and suppose this to have become
constantly the habit of his soul. Metaphysics and self-
observation, so indistinguishably interfused for him
henceforward, were very far from being a mere resource
against spiritual agony, "another anodyne." They were
a highly positive mode of spiritual adventure. No doubt
they did compensate him for some other things:

> viper thoughts that coil around my mind,
> Reality's dark dream!

But they were precisely his awakenings from that. By
1802 he has moved far from his early sentiments as a

preacher: "My philosophical refinements and metaphysi-cal theories lay by me in an hour of anguish, as toys by the bedside of a child deadly sick." (Letter to Benjamin Flower, Dec. 11, 1796.) He is thinking *with* rather than thinking *of* ideas: in these matters his opinions are turn-ing into that kind of knowledge which is a mode of being.

"Reality's dark dream," however, continued to be thwarting and destructive, and chiefly in scenes of domes-tic discord (see letter to Tom Wedgwood, pp. 284–85). These, perhaps, and the contrasts with the might-have-beens that thought of the other Sara called up, explain the stoppage for a while of Coleridge's poetry. And

> When two unequal Minds
> Meet in one House and two discordant Wills

the sight of the strong man Wordsworth, so much less in need of soothing support and so increasingly sur-rounded with it, must be less than a help. Wordsworth's cool and condescending attitude to Coleridge's poetry ("The Poem of my Friend has indeed great defects," he could write of "The Ancient Mariner") and his readiness to accept even the extremes of Coleridge's admiration as merely due may have contributed to the dejection. Coleridge's exaltation of Wordsworth's and depreciation of his own poetry had by now become fantastic. (See letter to Godwin, p. 277.) "If I die, and the booksellers will give you anything for my life, be sure to say: 'Wordsworth descended on him like the Γνῶθι σεαυτον from heaven; by showing him what true poetry was, he made him know that he himself was no Poet.' " The humor which pervades this letter should prevent us from taking it too tragically.

By the end of 1803 further ill health, and the con-tinued wear and tear of his remedy, made Coleridge seek another climate. After a tour in Scotland (see letter to Wedgwood, p. 289 ff) and a stay in London, he sailed to Malta (April 1804) and happened into a number of semi-official occupations there. His health improved at first—on a holiday he made two ascents of Mount Etna —but homesickness plagued him and it was with impatience that he awaited a chance to be sent back overland as a King's messenger. In the end he had to return at his own expense, via Naples and Rome, where he stayed some months, and, after many confused adventures, sailed from Leghorn, landing in August 1806 in worse shape even than when he left England.

He lingered in London making arrangements for his first course of lectures, and writing affectionately to his wife. There had been talk of a separation since 1801 and with the failure of great efforts towards improved harmony in 1802, the idea had grown stronger. The Wordsworths encouraged it and now, after a short visit in Keswick, Coleridge resolved upon a definitive step. Meanwhile he went with young Hartley, aged ten, to stay at Coleorton, where the Wordsworths and Sara Hutchinson were wintering. On January 7 he wrote "To William Wordsworth" in response to *The Prelude*. But in many ways he was now very seriously sick in mind and body, limp in will and swollen in flesh, irritable and neglectful, at odds with most people including Wordsworth and Josiah Wedgwood (Thomas had died leaving his share of the annuity to Coleridge by will). Only a visit to Poole at Stowey for a while restored him. It was in desperate condition that he tackled his first Royal Institute Lectures (January 15, 1808). Very mixed accounts exist of these. It is probable that the strain they put upon Coleridge still further impaired his condition and increased his opium addiction. To him lecturing seemed "still too histrionic, too like a retail trader in instruction and pastime, not to be depressing." But the lectures attracted wide attention. Coleridge by now was a major celebrity.

He returned to the Lake District in August 1808. The Southeys had since 1802 been installed in Greta Hall and Coleridge took up residence with the Wordsworths, now at Allan Bank, Grasmere. Here, with his boys in the holidays, he lived till early 1810, fighting "the fatal habit of taking enormous quantities of Laudanum, and latterly, of spirits too—the latter merely to keep the former on my revolting Stomach." In the hope that he could succeed in this fight he launched *The Friend*—a series of essays "on the Principles of Political Justice, of Morality and Taste and, in the light of Principles, the work of ancient and modern English Poets" to be published in periodical form. For the business side of this venture Coleridge was hardly the right man. It is no wonder that the Wordsworths were despairful. However, as a producer of copy, Coleridge was surprisingly successful. With Sara Hutchinson as his amanuensis, he managed to keep the series going through twenty-seven numbers. But when, after the twentieth number, the collection of subscriptions had to be attempted, the picture became grim. Coleridge thought he might have lost as much as two or three hundred pounds. And in March Sara Hutchinson left Allan Bank to live with a brother in Wales. That was the end. Coleridge moved in May to Keswick— "Poor Man!—I have not the least doubt but he is the most unhappy of the two," wrote Mrs. Coleridge—and after that to London to stay with Basil Montagu, an acquaintance since Stowey days. And here (October 28, 1810) "occasioned (in *great part*) by the wicked folly of the arch-fool Montagu," occurred that "compared with the sufferings of which all the

former afflictions of my life were less than flea-bites."
So Coleridge felt about it a year later. Montagu in a
quarrel passed on something that Wordsworth had told
him warningly about Coleridge's habits. The breach
thus confirmed was never more than superficially made
up.

From now on Coleridge's personal life is an uninviting
study. He resumed newspaper work for some months,
gave a more successful course of lectures on Shakespeare
and Milton, November 1811—January 1812, two more
in 1812; revisited the Lakes for copies of *The Friend,*
driving past the Wordsworths' house at Grasmere with-
out stopping; and rewrote his play, *Remorse,* which was
produced at Drury Lane in January 1813 and ran for
twenty nights. It brought him welcome financial relief,
since war losses had compelled Josiah Wedgwood to dis-
continue his annuity. This blow Coleridge took with dig-
nity and understanding. Much of the next year he was
in Bristol trying to help with the affairs of John Morgan,
who had housed and helped him often these last years.
(See "To Two Sisters.") Morgan seems to have been in
prison for debt. At Bristol he gave more lectures, in-
creasingly interrupted by opium trouble. He was making
efforts to escape—with and without the help of doctors
and attendants he could not help tricking. In the midst
of these he wrote *On the Principles of Genial Criticism
Concerning the Fine Arts.*

None of all this made money, and opium in these
quantities was not cheap; and by now Hartley was due
to go to college. Friends and family were concerned
about this, as he knew too well: "Oh! God! It is very
easy to say, Why does not Coleridge do this work or
that work? I declare to God, there is nothing I would
not do, consistent with my conscience, which was reg-

ular labour for a regular revenue. But to write such poetry or such philosophy as I would wish to write, or not to write at all, cannot be done amid distraction and anxiety for the day."

None the less, through a year (1815–16) with the Morgans in the country town of Calne, he busied himself in preparing an edition of his poems, with prefaces to contain "a disquisition on the powers of association and on the generic difference between the Fancy and the Imagination." *Biographia Literaria* was on the way. It is an extraordinary fact that Coleridge was able to write the best part of his most sustained prose work while in the full grasp of his malady.

Relief was at hand. In April 1816 it became only too clear again that strict measures were necessary. James Gillman, a Highgate physician, undertook them. In his devoted care, and for a time monetarily much in his debt, Coleridge spent the last eighteen years of his life. His supervision was broken only by short visits to reliable friends and a continental tour with Wordsworth in 1828. Even on his visits to the coasts for sea bathing, Gillman or Mrs. Gillman went along. How complete the cure finally became is a disputed question. But the result of control was apparent before long in production. First came *The Statesman's Manual, or the Bible the Best Guide to Political Skill and Foresight*, a "Lay Sermon" addressed to the governing classes. Then the *Biographia* could be finished off, largely with stuffing, but with Chapter xxii as well, to make up two volumes. Next came his "Treatise on Method," the introductory Essay to the *Encyclopedia Metropolitana*, editor of which he had become. He soon withdrew and made the "Treatise" over into a portion of the revised *Friend*, which was in print by the end of 1818. All this writing, moreover, did not prevent him from delivering lectures upon Shakespeare and much else (January to March 1818) and a new course on the history of philosophy (December 1818—March 1819) along with concurrent courses on literature.

These made little enough profit, however. And at this moment his publishers—the publishers of *Zapolya,* the *Lay Sermons, Sibylline Leaves, Biographia Literaria,* and *The Friend*—failed. There followed a dreary time in which numbers of Great Works had to be laid aside in favor of hack work. Rather too much of his energy went into angry complaints of critical and other ill-usage. Through 1824 he was writing *Aids to Reflection,* which earned him no money but won him a wide new group of admirers. After that an extensive circle formed, meeting in Coleridge's parlor on Thursday evenings. Its visitors have recorded—to an extent which is itself the best witness—the wonders of the performance they came to hear.

And yet this is not the impression with which a reader of Coleridge should turn to his work. Thanks to the fascination of the phosphorescent, these sketches gain an exaggerated importance. But fifteen years divide the sage of Highgate from the author of *Biographia Literaria* and as many divide *him* from the poet of 1798 and the thinker of 1801. And it is these last, and the laborious addict of 1815, not the eloquent old man of 1830, who speak most clearly to us. It is noteworthy, moreover, that whereas his prose (and prose discourse) tended to become more relaxed and diffuse, his *poetry* (some occasional verse apart) becomes more taut and self-sustaining. Consider "Youth and Age," "Phantom and Fact," "Self-Knowledge," and "Epitaph." It is with these that a sketch of Coleridge's life should close.

THE WORK

The Coleridge legend is well established and wide-spread. Carlyle's first impression on meeting him will state it for us: "His cardinal sin is that he wants *will*. He has no resolution. He shrinks from pain or labour in any of its shapes . . . sunk inextricably in the depths of putrescent idleness." Nobody did more than Coleridge to inculcate this view of himself. It is one of the most successful of his teachings. On this task, at least, he shrank not from labor. He began as a schoolboy and was busy with it till his last days. Friends early took it up. Eager audiences noted it down and correspondents who treasured the letters in which he voluminously developed it carried it on. His biographers all but agree over it. None the less this short account of the man and his work may well take a cool look at the legend.

In his own account of his childhood, written before he was twenty-five (see pp. 220–21) Coleridge has already said against himself most of the things which unfriendly critics have been at pains to stress in the record. "Before I was eight years old I was a *character*. Sensibility, imagination, vanity, sloth, and feelings of deep and bitter contempt for all who traversed the orbit of my understanding, were even then prominent and manifest." It should be added at once that he had an enviable number of most devoted friends, that this is written to amuse the closest of them, and that of all who traversed that prodigious orbit almost the only person for whom he expressed contempt was himself. He was joking here, in a letter to Tom Poole, a man who would well know how much to believe in this contempt. Few in fact have been freer from this "concentrated vinegar of egotism." (See *Anima Poetae,* January 1801, and letter

to Thelwall, p. 252–53.) And it is only the rest of
the picture that has become traditional. In it he is
the Great Disappointment; the man who might have
but didn't; the waster of unparalleled talents; the type
specimen of self-frustrating genius; the procrastinator,
the alibi fabricator and the idler. There is enough, fac-
tually, in his biography to account for this judgment;
but do not let us forget that any remarks about his will
or his idleness are diagnosis and interpretation. They
may be right; but they are no more than speculation,
and with the "idleness" theory at least we ought to bal-
ance its source against the facts which might support
it.

The source, I have suggested, was Coleridge's own
words. From his schoolboy verses onwards (see "*Quae
Nocent Docent*") he was fond of lamenting his lack of
industry:

> Should Sloth around me throw
> Her soul-enslaving, leaden chain!

He went up to Cambridge, however, about the best-read
boy of the year. His letters early become wearidful with
such complainings, and with morbidly elaborate anal-
yses of their causes. At its height, it is true, his poetry
could transform this depressant:

> And fears self-willed, that shunned the eye of Hope;
> And Hope that scarce would know itself from Fear;
> Sense of past Youth, and Manhood come in vain
> And Genius given, and Knowledge won in vain. . . .

> That way no more! and ill beseems it me,
> Who came a welcomer in herald's guise,
> Singing of Glory, and Futurity,
> To wander back on such unhealthful road,
> Plucking the poisons of self-harm!

But as a rule his abnormal consciousness of this failing was its own exacerbant. His demands upon himself might have been expressly calculated to prevent their fulfillment. And naturally these demands mounted with the occasion. At his lectures De Quincey remarked, "the entire absence of his own peculiar and majestic intellect," his failure to exhibit "that free and eloquent movement of thought which he could command at any time in a private company." And so too with formal essay writing. *The Friend* moved Charles Lloyd, who had been very close to him in earlier days, to observe, almost in his master's voice:

Coleridge has such a lamentable want of voluntary power. If he is excited by a remark in company, he will pour forth, in an evening, without the least apparent effort, what would furnish matter for a hundred essays—but the moment that he is to write, not from present impulse but from preordained deliberation, his powers fail him. He is one of those minds who, except in inspired moods, can do nothing—and his inspirations are all *oral*, and not *scriptural*. And when he is inspired he surpasses, in my opinion, all that could be thought or imagined of a human being.

His letters, however, and the scribblings with which he crowded the margins of countless books, show that this "oral" theory is wrong. Coleridge certainly was a monologist of superlative scope and power; but his random jottings often surpass even the best of his recorded talk. He was freest then. What he wrote was for his own eyes only. The unseen audience and the need to exert his powers worthily could fade out of mind. And in his formal writing the excursions, the indulgences, the footnotes in which he runs away from his theme—the pages of which he could have doubted, as he wrote them, whether they really belonged and would in fact be used—these commonly outweigh the rest. He is most often at his best when he has turned his back, for the moment, on his many times announced, his expected and overmuch challenging goal. The chief exception is the "Essay on Method" reprinted here from the third volume of *The Friend*, 1818; and even this is but a sketch towards the *magnum opus* which was always to be.

So too his best poetry is occasional or fragmentary. Apart from "The Ancient Mariner," if even that is, or could be, really finished, he has no completed poem to match his fragments. And some of the best of these come forward as metrical experiments ("A Sunset," "The Knight's Tomb"), as exercises ("A Tombless Epitaph"), as "a schoolboy poem" ("Time, Real and Imaginary") under the shelter in fact of any excuse which will free the poet from pen-fright. Uncompleted "Christabel" will serve as an example: "The reason of my not finishing 'Christabel' is not that I don't know how to do it—for I have, as I always had, the whole plan entire from beginning to end in my mind; but I fear I could not carry on with equal success the execution of the idea, an extremely subtle and difficult one." (*Table Talk*, July 6, 1833.) We need not take this original entirety of the plan more seriously than Wordsworth did. But Part One (1797) had been much admired in manuscript before Coleridge's struggles to continue it in 1800 and when at last he succeeded in adding Part Two, there was a releasing circumstance:

I tried and tried, and nothing would come of it. I desisted with a deeper dejection than I am willing to remember. The wind from the Skiddaw and Borrowdale was often as loud as wind need be—and many a walk in the clouds on the mountains did I take; but all would not do—till one day I dined out at the house of a neighbouring clergyman, and somehow or other drank so much wine, that I found some effort and dexterity requisite to balance myself on the hither side of sobriety. The next day my verse making faculties returned to me, and I proceeded successfully.

Unfortunately the use of wine had in general no such happy effect, it indeed it had any real relevance here. The secrets of inspiration are not so simple. Nor had the use of spirits or opium. This last, we should remember, was quite commonly prescribed in those days for troubles which would now send us to the dentist. As early as his first term at Cambridge we find him referring to it as to a familiar aid. "I am not however certain, that I do not owe my rheumatism to the dampness of my rooms. Opium never used to have any disagreeable effects on me—but it has on many." Later, the remedy (with the pains) was to fasten crushingly upon him (see letter to Poole, pp. 248 ff). Its effect then was to increase his self-reproaching and self-excusing beyond all endurance. We should remember that he was a sick man and that this is a symptom.

It is against this background—which should not be, for most people, very hard to imagine—a background of "such a dreadful *falling-abroad*, as it were, of my whole frame," of "an utter impotence of the Volition, the faculty *instrumental* to the Will . . . (its Hands, Legs, and Feet, as it were), in the state in which you may have seen paralytic Persons, who attempting to push a step forward in one direction are violently forced round to the opposite," in which "tho' there was no prospect, no gleam of Light before, an indefinite indescribable Terror as with a scourge of ever restless, ever coiling and uncoiling serpents, drove me on from behind. The worst was, that in the *exact proportion* to the importance and urgency of any Duty was it, as of a fatal necessity, sure to be neglected: because it added to the

Terror above described"—it is against such a back-
ground that we must consider the daunting amount and
variety of *work* which Coleridge in cold fact actually
did.

His poetry succeeds in more modes than most poets
have attempted. In several, moreover, it is highly dis-
tinctive. No one else has anything like "Kubla Khan,"
anything like "Phantom and Fact," anything like "Con-
stancy to an Ideal Object." As to amount, it seems more
impressive now than in the years when it was being
measured against the output levels of Tennyson, Brown-
ing, or Swinburne. The general impression that he dried
up comes in part from his own self-upbraidings, in part
from his readers' refusal to let any but Christabels count.
In spite of all the celebrated weakness of his personality
something in him kept him from imitating his own
poetry. Few of his contemporaries or of their descend-
ants showed equal integrity; the temptation to which
this will-less man could not yield overcame them.

This poet, moreover, was a critic who, in the range of
his reading, in the fertility of his comments upon writers
of every degree of difference from himself, in the span of
his admirations and their depth, as well as in the origina-
tive independence of his perceptions, surpasses all fore-
runners and, with due respect to later and better
equipped "library cormorants," all successors. In schol-
arship, by modern standards he is of course weak. But
there are aspects to this work—of being curator to the
culture—on which Coleridge's "Psyche" (see pp. 197
and 472) will serve as a comment. We should not forget
too that while the techniques of scholarship have ad-
vanced since Coleridge's time as much as those of medi-
cine, current conceptions of what all this knowledge is
for can claim no similar advances.

But this great critic was furthermore a philosopher,

immersed from his teens in this very inquiry, busied his life through in maintaining, with an eloquence unmatched since, that *all* judgment of literature, all preference and choice everywhere indeed, must be grounded "in the component faculties of the human mind itself, and their comparative dignity and importance" (*Biographia Literaria*, Chapter I, see p. 445), and that for the highest of these faculties—call it Reason or Imagination—that on which all the rest should and can depend, the source and sanction of all else, "the rules are themselves the very powers of growth and production" (*Biographia Literaria*, Chapter XVIII). This is hard doctrine for some present-day psychologists to translate into their own languages. The faculty to which as psychologists they have sworn fealty—call it Science; Coleridge called it Understanding—is in lively revolt today, as he prophesied, against any overlord whatsoever. It claims autonomy—a claim which Reason can grant to it *within the territory of Science.* But the territory of Science is not and cannot be the globe. There are other knowledges than those which Science can order. There is Morality, there is Politics, there is Poetry, there is Religion. What authorities govern these? And what supreme Authority sustains them all, would protect them from one another, prevent their trespasses, and heal their perennial warfare? These problems, which Science has made into *world-killers* today, were Coleridge's lifelong and overwhelming questions, truly the fountain-light of all his day and master-light of all his seeing. And though he frequented the philosophers of all the ages and borrowed varied makes of lantern from them, what led him at heart was a peculiar knowledge of himself, a unique awareness of the comings forth and holdings back, of the goings on, in particular and in general, of his own mind. This speculative genius—"the most systematic thinker of our time," John Stuart Mill called him—is primarily a psychologist "by the power of imagination proceeding on the *all in each* of human nature. By *meditation* rather than by *observation?* And by the later in consequence only of the former? As eyes, for which the former has predetermined their field of vision and to which, as to *its* organ, it communicates a microscopic power?" (*Biographia Literaria*, Chapter xviii.) He was to say in many ways: "An idea in mind is to a Law in nature as the power of seeing is to Light" (see p. 410). It is true that he very often failed to apply the knowledge so gained in his dealings with others. He was the typical Returner to the Cave, "slow in getting used to seeing in the dark." (*The Republic*, 517.)

But this muser on such recondite themes was also an active if intermittent journalist-commentator, contributing through very stormy times opinion-forming articles to which he could later look back (and it may be doubted whether many commentators can) with deep satisfaction.

To have lived in vain must be a painful thought to any man, and especially so to him who has made literature his profession. I should therefore rather condole than be angry with the mind, which could attribute to no worthier feelings, than those of vanity or self-love, the satisfaction which I acknowledged myself to have enjoyed from the re-publication of my political essays (either whole or as extracts) not only in many of our own provincial papers, but in the federal journals throughout America. I regarded it as some proof of my not having laboured altogether in vain, that from the articles written by me shortly before and at the commencement of the late unhappy war with America, not only the sentiments were adopted, but in some instances the very language, in several of the Massachusetts state-papers.

Biographia Literaria, Chapter x

It was perhaps easier then than now to oppose warlike feelings. However this may be, Coleridge, we must note, was an independent in his politics. He was accused of being a turncoat. To which he could reply that he had kept true to *principles,* others only to parties or countries. We would all like to think so of ourselves. But later students, with historical perspective to help them, endorse his claim. As Harold Beeley acutely remarks, "Thus he became a Tory, and yet his essential faith was unchanged. For he demanded of Toryism what he had previously demanded of Radicalism—government according to ethical principles, the conduct of secular affairs *sub specie aeternitatis.* So far from deserting his cause, he became a missionary for it and exercised a profound influence on English Conservatism." [5] His political principles, be it noted, were no airy abstractions. They were embodied through a searching knowledge of contemporary affairs animated by a down-to-earth sense of present dangers and made practical by a rather hardheaded concern with expediency. There is nothing in the least dreamy about them. The Pantisocratic phase got rid of that. "Governments are more the effect than the cause of that which we are." The two essays printed here will, I think, be found highly relevant to our present problems. For example, "A constitution equally suited to China and America, or to Russia and Great Britain, must surely be equally unfit for both, and deserve as little respect in political, as a quack's panacea in medical, practice" (see p. 333).

Last—but Coleridge in his later days put it first—

[5] "The Political Thought of Coleridge," in *Coleridge, Studies by Several Hands on the Hundredth Anniversary of His Death,* edited by Edmund Blunden and Earl Leslie Griggs. (London: Constable, 1934, p. 161.)

this political realist was a theologian whose discernment and courage won him pervasive and continuing influence. This came, in part, from superior insight into the nature of persuasion, as when he exposes the "theological utilitarianism" of Paley:

There are spiritual truths which must derive their evidence from within, which whoever rejects "neither will he believe though a man were to rise from the dead" to confirm them. . . What then can we think of a theological theory, which adopting a scheme of prudential legality common to it with "the sty of Epicurus," as far at least as the springs of action are concerned, makes its whole religion consist in the belief of miracles?

The Friend, II, ii

To many his distinction of the Understanding from the Reason offered a freedom which they recognized as veridical. What Reason beheld could be supremely trusted because "Reason is the Power of Universal and necessary Convictions, the Source and Substance of Truths above Sense, and having their evidence in themselves . . . the fountain of Ideas and the *Light* of the Conscience." (*Aids to Reflection,* CVI.) To use an aphorism Coleridge himself chose from Henry More:

The more imperious Sects having put such unhandsome vizards on Christianity, and the sincere Milk of the *Word* having been everywhere so sophisticated by the humours and inventions of men, it has driven these anxious Melancholists to seek for *a Teacher* that cannot deceive, the Voice of the *eternal* Word within them; to which, if they be faithful, they assure themselves it will be faithful to them in return. Nor would this be a groundless Presumption, if they had sought this Voice in the Reason and the Conscience, with the Scripture articulating the same.

Aids to Reflection, XCIV

On how the Scripture could articulate the same, Coleridge was not only among the first to protest, in detail and at length, against the contradictions and absurdities of supposing inerrant verbal inspiration, and against the practice, for example, of taking Bildad and Job as equally voices of the Lord; but he showed how to combine a radically historical view of the documents with a belief in their unique inspiration (*Confessions of an Inquiring Spirit*, Letter IV). In much of this he was a generation or more ahead of his time. And these were but a small portion of his theological labors. And as a make-weight, he was a copious and indefatigable letter-writer, always ready to write many pages on the obstacles to getting on with the job.

In the face of all this activity and achievement, so much self-reproach on the ground of Sloth takes on a queer air and tempts speculation. Could it be that his peculiar combination of gifts ("Never saw I his likeness, nor probably the world can see again,"—Charles Lamb. "The most wonderful man that he had ever known."—Wordsworth) *had* to set him superhuman tasks? A Jonathan Edwards—to take a not too unlike figure—can cherish an impossible enterprise life-long without knowing. But in Coleridge, until his last years, something seems to have known the impossibility as soon as he came near enough to it. It did not prevent him planning conquests from afar, but it did stop him, by one device or another, when he came to the point, and it kept him from thinking *then* and *there* that he was succeeding when he was not. He could, in brief, use his own criticism where it was most needed. The devices, the ways out, the preliminaries to the approaches to the preparations, into which this super-sanity forced him were often absurd, usually miserable, and sometimes agonizing. They could look like insanity. His unruly volition could and did martyrize him. Whether or not he saw the real causes of his troubles through the thick clouds of his excuses, there is no knowing. He comes through a thick and physiological bank of them with the following: "I dare believe that in the mind of a competent Judge what I have performed will excite more surprise than what I have omitted to do, or failed in doing" (see p. 303). The general contrary impression is good evidence only of the hunger he had known how to arouse. "By what I *have* effected, am I to be judged by my fellow men; what I *could* have done, is a question for my own conscience" (*Biographia Literaria,* Chapter x).

THE POETRY

An account, and still more, an appraisal, of Coleridge's poetry is made difficult by the degree to which one kind in it—the magical—has, nearly from the first, overshadowed the others. He has been the poet of "The Ancient Mariner," "Kubla Khan," and "Christabel." Thousands know these for each reader who can name another three of his poems. This in itself is some sort of evidence of their pre-eminence. They have held their place through a century despite violent oscillations in taste. It has been claimed for them that they have been more *constantly,* and more widely, enjoyed and admired than any other poems of their age. It may be so. They are in a mode of poetry less exposed than others to the more abrupt ups and downs of critical fashion. It would be Coleridgian, however, to ask whether this crest-and-trough movement does not spring from necessary shiftings in taste and whether insusceptibility to it is the best proof of strength. He always had much reserve himself in his attitude to these poems and thought the "expressions of admiration" for "Christabel" "from almost all of

our most celebrated Poets, . . . utterly disproportion-
ate to a work that pretended to be nothing more than a
common Faery Tale." (*Biographia Literaria,* Chapter
xxiv.) We can understand his doubts. "The Ancient
Mariner" and "Christabel" are far away in worlds of
their own. Their supernatural contrivances and the
"ancientness" in their diction protect an inner structure
obviously more like that of dream than waking life.
Structure may even be a misleading word here. They
are held together, if held they are, in ways we do well,
in *poetic* reading, not to inquire about, however much
our psychological curiosity, which Coleridge did so
much to develop, may make us wonder. We can guess
that this very incoherence, this absence of a moral or
intellectual core, helps them to their breath-taking
vividness. In reading them the more comprehending
parts of our minds should go to sleep. And "Kubla
Khan," that fragment, shares for analogous reasons the
same remoteness and freedom from implication.

A quite equal vividness, however, as some of Cole-
ridge's other poems will show us, can go along with a
much more "whole-soul'd" activity in the poet and the
reader. And it is to the point to recall that the poet
"described in *ideal* perfection, brings the whole soul of
man into activity." (*Biographia Literaria,* Chapter xiv,
and see p. 332.) But here is an opportunity for a need-
less mistake from which Coleridge can preserve us. "Do
not let us introduce an Act of Uniformity against Poets."
(Letter to Thelwall, p. 252.) Nothing more liberating
can be said. It applies as between poets and as between
varying work of one poet. Or, to quote from a fuller
statement, "We call, for we see and feel, the swan and
the dove both transcendently beautiful . . . if, having
first seen the dove, we abstracted its outlines, gave them
a false generalization, called them principles or ideal of

bird-beauty and then proceeded to criticise the swan or the eagle—not less absurd is it to pass judgment on the works of a poet . . . on any ground indeed save that of their inappropriateness to their own end or being, their want of significance, as symbol and physiognomy." There are times when criticism seems to be doing nothing else. Don't damn the dog for being such a poor sort of cat. We should be doing this if we let fondness for "The Ancient Mariner" blind us to the other sorts of poetry Coleridge wrote; or if increased attention to these other poems cast any shadow or suspicion upon the familiar three as to "their want of significance, as symbol and physiognomy." We should not think less well of them because we think better of others. What they have done they will do none the less because we recognize elsewhere "new organs of power and action appropriate to the new sphere of . . . motion and activity."

To be concrete, any new reader, I believe, who comes to "The Eolian Harp," "Dejection," "Limbo," "Constancy to an Ideal Object," or, more easily perhaps, to "Inscription for a Fountain on a Heath," "The Nightingale," "The Picture"; to "The Wandering of Cain," "Phantom or Fact"; or even to "A Character," or "A Sunset," taking them without expectations based on "Kubla Khan," will feel, with some of them at least, that new Coleridges are coming up over the horizon.

The group of descriptive-reflective poems, of which "Frost at Midnight" is the best known and perhaps the best, needs little comment. He is shaking himself free from the swelling, emphatic, declamatory diction of "Religious Musings," finding ways to make his language transparent to the scenes and thoughts it has to carry, helping, in fact, to get a medium ready for Wordsworth's use in "Tintern Abbey," to which, not least in certain

clumsinesses, these poems have much resemblance. At
this stage in these poets' growth, double negatives must
not daunt us:

> Nor perchance
> If I were not thus taught, should I the more
> Suffer my genial spirits to decay.
>> Tintern Abbey

> Nor dost not thou sometimes recall those hours
>> To the Rev. George Coleridge

> nor such thoughts
> Dim and unhallowed dost thou not reject
>> The Eolian Harp

But these are trivial opacities,[6] mentioned only that the
clarity of these poems at their best may be the more
apparent:

> the dell,
> Bathed by the mist, is fresh and delicate
> As vernal corn-field, or the unripe flax,
> When through its half transparent stalks, at eve
> The level sunshine glimmers with green light.
>> Fears in Solitude

> Therefore all seasons shall be sweet to thee,
> Whether the summer clothe the general earth
> With greenness, or the redbreast sit and sing
> Betwixt the tufts of snow on the bare branch
> Of mossy apple tree, while the nigh thatch

[6] Coleridge grew out of such things sooner, I think, than
did Wordsworth, whose finest specimen,

> Nor can I not believe but that hereby
> Great gains are mine;

as the opening of a sonnet on "Personal Talk" in *Poems of
Sentiment and Reflection,* may be several years later.

Smokes in the sun-thaw; whether the eave-drop fall
Heard only in the trances of the blast,
Or if the secret ministry of frost
Shall hang them up in silent icicles,
Quietly shining to the quiet Moon.

Frost at Midnight

Pale beneath the blaze
Hung the transparent foliage; and I watch'd
Some broad and sunny leaf, and lov'd to see
The shadow of the leaf and stem above
Dappling its sunshine!

This Lime-Tree Bower My Prison

These, in separation, will illustrate the freshness of Coleridge's observation. What they cannot illustrate is the deep consonance and unity of the descriptions with the accompanying reflections. It is no paradox to say that what Coleridge most admired in Wordsworth was what Wordsworth could have learned from these poems. Already, in practice, Coleridge had found

That outward forms, the loftiest, still receive
Their finer influence from the Life within.

Lines Written in the Album at Elbingerode

Round the thought in these last two lines Coleridge's deepest meditative poems may be grouped. They begin with "The Eolian Harp," reach their height in "Dejection" and "To William Wordsworth" and are supported, in various ways, by "Constancy to an Ideal Object," "Recollections of Love," "The Two Sisters," "Phantom," and "Limbo." To trace some conjectural links between them is a way to bring out something in Coleridge's thinking (if that is here its due name) which in his more expansive, "theologico-metaphysical" prose he dodges away from, muttering, "But this speculation would take us too far." In his poetry he is ready to go farther, "the whole soul" there having the arrogant Understanding under better control.

In "The Eolian Harp" his "pensive Sara" utters the Understanding's rebuke. The lines which provoked it Coleridge was fond of repeating and admiring *out of context:*

> And what if all of animated nature
> Be but organic Harps diversely fram'd,
> That tremble into thought, as o'er them sweeps
> Plastic and vast, one intellectual breeze,
> At once the Soul of each, and God of all?

Within the context they belong with "idle flitting phantasies," traverse a brain "indolent and passive" and are

> As wild and various as the random gales.

This is a highly disparaging introduction. And after Sara's "mild reproof," "such thoughts" become still worse. They are

> shapings of the unregenerate mind;
> Bubbles that glitter as they rise and break
> On vain Philosophy's aye-babbling spring.

It looks as if, in this brief, strange interlude of uncharacteristic happiness, enraptured with a bride whom shortly before and not long after he could be very sure he did not love, Coleridge is being resolutely submissive. However that may be, this bubble-gum view of Philosophy was not slow, itself, to break. Nothing more contrary to his general prose view of Philosophy, and to most of his poetic views, could be invented. And no such conflict between Philosophy and Theology could be anything but fugacious, "uncall'd and undetain'd," in Coleridge's mind. It happens to have left nice footprints in these verses, that is all. But this Wind Harp image, which *in the poem* occasions such mock penitence, is a constant and welcome visitor in his poetry for years. He was as attached to it as to his Aeolian lute itself (he spells it both ways) which for a time went with him everywhere. He could, I believe, have said of it, as he said later (see pp. 392–93) of a flowery meadow:

I seem to myself to behold in the quiet objects, on which I am gazing, more than an arbitrary illustration, more than a mere *simile*, the work of my own fancy. I feel an awe, as if there were before my eyes the same power as that of the reason—the same power in a lower dignity, and therefore a symbol established in the truth of things.

The Wind Harp, though it is a far humbler responsive system, can "say" for him nearly as much as a plant can. It bursts into "The Nightingale" at line 80, quivers gently in "Fears in Solitude" at line 21, and supplies the return or resolution to "France: An Ode," to take three instances only. We will do well to linger a moment to try to realize its scope.

As the intellectual breeze plays on the organic harp, the music which arises orders all perception. It orders therefore the harp and the breeze as well; "all of animated nature" and unanimated nature too, if there be any. Whatever it is which responds—and, in responding, perceives—gives the perceived form, through its response, to whatever is perceived. This itself, of course, is Coleridge's response to Berkeley, a strong influence upon him at this time. He does not seem to have been willing, though, ever to suppose—for more than a moment—that the *being* of things was that they were perceived. The problem for him was rather: How much that we seem to find in things is put there by the mode in which we perceive them? But we must widen "perceive" to do full justice to all the activity in the response. We must put in far more than "thought" narrowly taken.

> O yearning Thought! That liv'st but in the brain?

We must encompass even what is offered in the final lines of "To William Wordsworth":

> my being blended in one thought
> (Thought was it? or aspiration? or resolve?)
> Absorbed, yet hanging still upon the sound . . .

All the faculties of the soul are in activity in all perception, whether or not "with the subordination . . . to each other, according to their relative worth and dignity" (see p. 524). And we should not picture this projection in terms of knowledge only and not of love also. When, in the last stanza of "France: An Ode," Liberty, speeding

> Alike from Priestcraft's harpy minions
> And factious Blasphemy's obscener slaves,

comes at last to the poet

> —on that sea-cliff's verge,
> Whose pines, scarce travelled by the breeze above,
> Had made one murmur with the distant surge!
> Yes, while I stood and gazed, my temples bare,
> *And shot my being through earth, sea and air,*
> *Possessing all things with intensest love,*
> O Liberty! my spirit felt thee there.

I have italicized the lines which most concern us. Much of the being even of earth, sea, and air, as we behold them, comes to them from this all-possessing love. What *else* is in them—even the physicists seem now to insist—is only the physicists' problem.

This transference of a life from the poet's own spirit and its connection with the Wind Harp image is most fully and clearly described, and in the best poetry, in "Dejection: An Ode." The poem has, of course, the greatest autobiographical interest—especially now that the original text is available.[7] The revised versions, however, carry the philosophic meaning fully, though the new details now known sharpen the reader's sympathy for the poet. Coleridge had committed himself to marrying Sarah Fricker largely because her sister was to marry Southey. Then (October 26, 1799) he meets Sara Hutchinson whose sister, Mary, is to marry Wordsworth. There is a nightmare sort of pattern about this, as though Fate had just mistaken Southey for Wordsworth. Of this impact "Love" is the first record. Thenceforward Sara Hutchinson was often with the Wordsworths at Grasmere and went with them to stay with the Coleridges at Greta Hall several times, and Coleridge visited the Hutchinsons at Sockburn and Gallow Hill again and again. On April 4, 1802, while Wordsworth was staying with him on his way to see Mary about the marriage, Coleridge wrote a long verse letter to Sara containing the Ode as well as much sad personal matter of less value. On April 21, 1802, Dorothy Wordsworth records, "William and I sauntered in the garden. Coleridge came to us and repeated the verses he wrote to Sara. I was affected with them, and in miserable spirits. The sunshine, the green fields and the fair sky made me sadder; even the little happy sporting lambs seemed but sorrowful to me. . . . I went to bed after dinner, could not sleep." A revised version addressed to "Edmund" he published in the *Morning Post,* October 4, Wordsworth's wedding day.

Once the symbolism of the lute has been recognized, stanzas IV, V, and VIII are line by line a concrete poetic

[7] See *Wordsworthian and Other Studies* by Ernest De Selincourt, op. cit., pp. 56–76.

account of imagination—and of how it wanes when un-
visited by joy. They are also a concrete poetic account
of how the worlds we live in come about, and of why
they may differ—all the way from

> that inanimate cold world allowed
> To the poor loveless ever-anxious crowd.

to that other in which

> To thee do all things live from pole to pole
> Their life the eddying of thy living soul!

I have stressed the words "concrete poetic account."
It will be of little help to interrogate it as if it were an
abstract prose theory.[8] To do so would show that we had
not taken to heart the first lines of stanza IV:

> O Wordsworth! we receive but what we give
> And in our life alone does Nature live.

It is more to the point to put beside them these lines
which Coleridge wrote on the night five years later after
Wordsworth had read *The Prelude* aloud to him:

> moments awful
> Now in thy inner life, and now abroad
> When power streamed from thee, and thy soul received
> The light reflected, as a light bestowed.

Here Coleridge has changed to another image, paral-
lel in effect to the Wind Harp. As the Harp emits the
world (under the play of the intellectual breeze) yet
may equally seem but a passive toy; so this light may

[8] Those interested in the questions which come up if we
do may be referred to my *Coleridge on Imagination* (New
York: Norton, 1950), in which the complexities of the Wind
Harp image and its place in Coleridge's philosophy are ex-
plored at length.

seem to create (or to apparel [9]) every common sight
or equally to proceed from them. Turn now to the end
of "Constancy to an Ideal Object," a poem which fully
lives up to its Platonic title.

> And art thou nothing? Such thou art, as when
> The woodman winding westward up the glen
> At wintry dawn, where o'er the sheep-track's maze
> The viewless snow-mist weaves a glist'ning haze,
> Sees full before him, gliding without tread,
> An image with a glory round its head;
> The enamoured rustic worships its fair hues,
> Nor knows he *makes* the shadow, he pursues!

This is a yet more explicit utterance which becomes the
more alluring in its implications as we realize that the
Thou addressed is nothing less than an Idea in the full
sense—of such supreme consequence in Coleridge's the-
ology—in which Reason is the fountain of ideas and the
light of the Conscience. Once again here we must keep
our Understanding duly reminded of "its relative worth
and dignity." Perhaps the best way will be to busy it
with the reflection that the poet here is trying to exor-
cise Sara Hutchinson.[10] After two of the finest lines in
his work he has this:

> Yet still thou haunt'st me: and though well I see
> She is not thou, and only thou art she,
> Still, still as though some dear *embodied* Good
> Some *living* Love before my eyes there stood.

[9] Wordsworth's Ode, "Intimations of Immortality," is in
many ways a mate to "Dejection" which twice echoes its
opening stanzas.

[10] With this Ideal Object in mind two other poems gain
interest and intelligibility: "Recollections of Love" with its
Hardyesque last verse and "To Two Sisters," which might
better have stopped fourteen lines sooner.

It is interesting that he took the italics out in the last edition, as well as those at *makes* in the last line.

All these images present an idealism, Platonic-Kantian in origins but very distinctively Coleridgian in actuality. Two extremes will round the sequence off. How can a being freed from the temporal be presented?

> All look and likeness caught from earth,
> All accident of kin and birth,
> Had pass'd away. There was no trace
> Of aught on that illumined face
> Uprais'd beneath the rifted stone
> But of one spirit all her own;—
> She, she herself, and only she,
> Shone through her body visibly.

This in the Platonic sense is all Form, all Idea—as nearly as anything may be. At the opposite is that queer Ultimate: formless matter, the subject of the powerful and terrifying poem "Limbo." Sheer matter is ineffable in itself; but its neighbors, which are, increasingly, all that can be known to "the partisans of a crass and sensual materialism," are in Limbo. (Compare "Self-Knowledge.") Time and Space are the last things this "Sole true Something" can let go. With less it becomes nothing; with more it grows into anthropomorphic illusion—to the materialist. But to Coleridge this very "illusion," the music of the Wind Harp, is his being: What Man is, what his world is, and what his God is, are parts but of one just answer. But the just answer requires justice in that which gives it.

THE PHILOSOPHIC CRITIC

Not the ideas we think *of* but those we think *with*: "That only I count as *genuine knowledge* which returns again as power." Coleridge's power as a critic comes not

only, or even chiefly, from the width of his awareness
and curiosity, but from the depth of operation of his ac-
quisitions. Of all the knowledge with which Coleridge
worked none went deeper or did more than what he had
learned from Plato.

He could write and talk disengagedly enough about
Plato (see letter to Thelwall, p. 254, and *Table Talk*,
April 1830, p. 315). But it is not his references to "This
plank from the wreck of Paradise thrown on the shores
of idolatrous Greece" [11] or his acknowledgments, as in
Appendix B to *The Statesman's Manual* (see p. 390),
which show Coleridge's discipleship. It is the action of
thinking derived from Plato at the heart of his greatest
passages of theory and of application alike. More per-
haps than any other thinker, he illustrates that daunting
imitation-Greek epigram: "Wherever I go in my mind,
I meet Plato on his way back."

The only way to bring this out is to study an example,
and see as fully as we can, what the instruments he is
working with are. Let me take his account of "the poet
described in *ideal* perfection" which ends Chapter xiv
of *Biographia Literaria* and is the master key to all his
critical thinking:

The poet, described in ideal *perfection, brings the whole
soul of man into activity, with the subordination of its
faculties to each other, according to their relative worth
and dignity. He diffuses a tone and spirit of unity, that
blends, and (as it were) fuses, each into each, by that
synthetic and magical power, to which we have exclu-
sively appropriated the name of imagination. This power,
first put in action by the will and understanding, and
retained under their irremissive, though gentle and un-
noticed, controul* (laxis effertur habenis) *reveals itself*

[11] *Aids to Reflection*, xxxii.

in the balance or reconciliation of opposite or discordant qualities: of sameness, with difference; the individual, with the representative; the sense of novelty and freshness, with old and familiar objects; a more than usual state of emotion, with more than usual order; judgement ever awake and steady self-possession, with enthusiasm and feeling profound or vehement. . . .

The poet, described in ideal *perfection,*

Sir Richard Livingstone, I think, remarked that whenever we see a can of Ideal Milk, Plato is present. Here is a more complete presence. The word "ideal" is used and emphasized both to guard us from supposing that any actual poet achieves this perfection *and* to mark that we are concerned here with the Idea of a poem, with what makes poetry. (Compare *The Republic,* 476, 505; *Phaedo,* 100.)

brings the whole soul of man into activity,

What is a whole has components: here the faculties. Poetry is no exercise of one faculty, but of many—ideally of them all. And it is *activity:* poetry is something the poet does, not something done to him—this in direct rebuttal of Plato's view, in *Apology,* 22, and elsewhere, that "The poets are like diviners or soothsayers, who also say many fine things, but do not understand the meaning of them."

with the subordination of its faculties to each other,

We comprehend what the soul is only in so far as we comprehend what its faculties are and how they work together. The pattern for their cooperation is that outlined in *The Republic:* Reason being supreme; beneath it Understanding and Will ordering the emotions; beneath them again the desires and the senses.

according to their relative worth and dignity.

The rank of a faculty is the reflex of its responsibilities, its virtue or what it has to do within the pattern of co-operation. Thus the duty of Reason is to know, and its virtue or excellence is Wisdom; the duty of the middle order, the Executive (see pp. 389–90), is to arrange, direct, and protect, and its virtue is Courage; the duty of the third order, the base which supports all else, is to supply. It contains the energy-intake and productive organs. As such it has no distinctive virtue. It shares the two over-all virtues of the organism: Temperance and Justice themselves. As to Temperance, its English uses and popular travesties of Plato have been misleading. "If Wisdom belongs to the ruler (knowledge is power), and Courage is useful in the police, what is left over for the workers? Why not Temperance? Let them make a virtue of being content with little!" But in Plato and in Coleridge Temperance is nothing of this sort. It is the mutual responsibility uniting all the faculties and making them in agreement or harmony as to how all is to be ordered. Similarly Justice is an absence of infringement, a keeping to its own work or duty by each one of the faculties.[12]

Without some such gloss as this, what Coleridge meant by "the subordination of its faculties to each other" remains vague and uninstructive. With it we have a concrete enough view of "the whole soul" to follow what he goes on to say about what the poet does in a poem.

[12] Injustice, in this sense, is well exemplified by the funny pronouncements of many editors and scholars—Mackail and Lowes among them—on Coleridge's philosophy. They send us back to Coleridge's *golden rule* (*Biographia Literaria*, Chapter XII).

He diffuses a tone or spirit of unity,

Here, what has just been said about Temperance is applied. *Tone* has probably the general sense "healthy elasticity" as well as the medical sense "readiness to function." On *spirit*, see *Biographia Literaria,* Chapter xii, "Herein consists the essence of a spirit that it is self-representative."

that blends, and (as it were) fuses, each into each,

What these "eaches" may stretch to is the problem. At the lowest level they may be separate sense items, the hardness and coldness which are somehow *seen* in a slab of marble, for example. (Compare "The primary imagination," etc., *Biographia Literaria,* end of Chapter xiii.) But in his other descriptions of Imagination, Coleridge supposes the fusion of far more disparate things: of motions with stationary objects; of feelings with the things they are felt toward; of life with the lifeless. (See pp. 414, 529.) I doubt if he could or would have set any limits as to what might, on due occasion, be fused with what, except by appeal to that *unity* which he enshrined in his words "esemplastic" and "co-adunative," words coined to be technical substitutes for "imaginative." Whether the faculties, temporarily surpassing Justice, can swap jobs, and whether enough Temperance could justify even such trespassing, I am fairly sure he would say, "can be learned only by the fact." A poet who is poet *enough* can do anything. Even at this highest level, I think, we can apply his great dictum: "Could a rule be given from *without,* poetry would cease to be poetry, and sink into a mechanical art. It would be μόρφωσις not ποίησις. The rules of the IMAGINATION are themselves the very powers of growth and production." (*Biographia Literaria,* Chapter xvii.) Thus *each into each* and *to each other* should be studied together and along with Coleridge's remarks on "the concentration of all in each" and estrangement "from the one in all" in Appendix B to *The Statesman's Manual* (see p. 390).

by that synthetic and magical power to which we have exclusively appropriated the name of imagination

Synthetic not only as putting together but as unifying; and *magical* as being an operation and achievement beyond the account of what we now call science.

This power, first put in action by the will and understanding and retained under their irremissive, though gentle and unnoticed controul (laxis effertur habenis)[13]

A firm denial again of Plato's theory of inspiration. The poet is not seized or carried away. His two ruling faculties—subject only to Reason, in which their quarrels can be resolved—instigate and direct the work throughout.

reveals itself in the balance or reconciliation of opposite or discordant qualities:

Or is playing its subtlest tricks here. *Balance* and *reconciliation* have senses in which they may be only two words for the same thing, two metaphors, two vehicles whose tenors are the same: the *balance* of a skater whose movement is a resultant, a *reconciliation* of forces otherwise antagonistic. But these two words also have senses in which they are exclusive alternatives to each other—*either-or*: as in a *balance* of power (between U.S.A. and U.S.S.R.) to be contrasted with a *reconciliation*, a reunion of opponents. Similarly with *opposite* or *discordant*. An immense range of different possibilities is glanced over in these phrases. This power is revealed in, operates

---

[13] Would it be extravagant to see in this a reflection of the divine charioteers in *Phaedrus*, 247?

through, is exemplified in, them all. The list of instances which follows shows the variety of the situations covered. The first four offer us different formulations of the fundamental problem which Plato tackled with the doctrine of the Ideas:

of sameness with difference; of the general with the concrete; the idea with the image; the individual with the representative;

We may take these as four ways of talking about the same crux *and* as four approaches to it from which different aspects can be seen. Much of Coleridge's criticism of Shakespeare is an exploration of their uses (see pp. 347 and 410), and such examples do far more to show what this is all about than any discussion in technical language. None the less, since the imagination is the prime unifying and creative activity, its connection with the theory of the One and the Many deserves the stress.

the sense of novelty and freshness, with old and familiar objects;

Coleridge is moving here from the One and the Many, which this still touches upon, to the outcomes of imagination in "awakening the mind's attention from the lethargy of custom." (*Biographia Literaria,* Chapter xiv, p. 518.)

a more than usual state of emotion, with more than usual order;

Emotion and order are customarily regarded as opposites. Coleridge held that for *the whole soul,* a truly integral order, as contrasted with a local, departmental order, requires strong emotion. (See pp. 273, 305.)

judgement ever awake and steady self-possession, with enthusiasm and feeling profound or vehement. . . .

Above the emotions are the Will and Understanding.

However strong the emotion, in imagination there is no insurrection or carrying away. He is rescuing enthusiasm from the contempt of the eighteenth century, while firmly keeping it to its just limits. *Profound or vehement* offers us another reconciliation. He may have remembered Wordsworth's recent lines in "Laodamia":

> the Gods approve
> The depth, and not the tumult, of the soul;
> A fervent, not ungovernable, love.

Vehement, with its suggestion of carrying away, balances *profound.* In the positive darkness of Coleridge's most horrific and puzzling poem, "Ne plus ultra," we may find a hint that a certain sort of profundity:

> Condenséd blackness and abysmal storm
> Compacted to one sceptre . . .
> Ah sole despair
> Of both th' eternities of Heaven!

could be "a fear far worse" than any tumult. The two eternities[14] here seem to be Love and Knowledge—higher parallels to Will and Understanding—between

[14] LUCIFER. And if the higher knowledge quenches love,
What must *he be* you cannot love when known?
Since the all-knowing Cherubim love least,
The Seraph's love can be but ignorance . . .
Choose between Love and Knowledge—since there is
No other choice.

Byron, *Cain,* I, 432

Compare Coleridge: "In the state of perfection, perhaps, all other faculties may be swallowed up in Love, or superseded by immediate vision; but it is on the wings of the CHER-UBIM, *i.e.* (according to the interpretation of the ancient Hebrew doctors) the *intellectual* powers and energies, that we must first be borne up to the 'pure empyrean.' It must be seraphs, and not the hearts of imperfect mortals, that can burn unfuelled and self-fed." (*Aids to Reflection,* xv.)

which again Reason, the analogue of the fusing power of imagination, must mediate.

At the uttermost extreme from life and light and that Reason of which each individual must bear witness "to his own mind, even as he describes life and light: and with the silence of light it describes itself, and dwells in us only as far as we dwell in it" (see p. 378) is their equally unthinkable negation: sheer matter, nothingness. In between are all the modes and degees of being. Coleridge is a thinker who took creation, the process as well as the product, to be *explorable*, pre-eminently in such an instance as Shakespeare. In the individual poet, or maker, it could be studied as Imagination—to be as clearly as possible distinguished from the mere manipulation of fixities and definites—but, since he holds it to be "the repetition in the finite mind of the eternal act of creation in the infinite I AM," thought upon it cannot rest short of thought addressed to that eternal act itself. For all its imperfection, each *activity* through which we perceive anything whatever, is in its measure, however minute, a participation in that. But there are inactivities which can be masked as activities and one activity can attempt the part of another; there is Injustice; the molds of the Understanding can profess the tasks of life; and the Will is capable of every degree of revolt against Reason (see p. 391).

Coleridge is a philosophic critic because while studying these things in the concrete and on every scale from the single word or phrase up, he could see them more constantly than other men, and more clearly, as instances or illustrations of what he so carefully called *principles*. "Few men, I will be bold to say, put more meaning into their words than I." Into none of his words did he put more. "Every principle is actualized by an idea; and every idea is living, productive, partaketh of infinity, and (as Bacon has sublimely observed) containeth an endless power of semination. Hence it is, that science, which consists wholly in ideas and principles, is power" (see p. 387). In this again we may hear, if we wish, echoes, in Bacon and in Coleridge, of *Phaedrus, 277.* Coleridge would put all possible biologic meaning into this word "semination."

What Coleridge is seeking in all this is *authority:* alike for his all-encompassing philosophic position and for his most local act of critical choice. And he is finding it, where Plato found it,[15] in the dependence of all observations and of observation itself, of all inductions and of induction itself, of all that is understood and of understanding itself, upon that which makes and sustains them. He calls this, perhaps unfortunately, Reason, a name which delays and misleads many. By recourse to this dependence[16] Coleridge like Plato solves the paradox in every account of authority—that it derives from those who should be subject to it. He shows how it can be so derived without being dissipated or diminished. We know this paradox well: What should rule, in the individual—torn between Science and Poetry or between

[15] This is no inquiry into what Plato meant, but into what he had meant to Coleridge.

[16] "By the higher division of the intelligible I mean that which reason itself lays hold of, by the power of dialectic— treating its assumptions not as unquestioned starting points but as underpinnings or footholds or springboards by which it can rise to something which needs no assuming and is the starting point of all—and after reaching *that,* it takes hold of the first things which depend upon that and so goes downward to the conclusion." (*The Republic,* VI, 511. See my *How to Read a Page,* and my simplified version of *The Republic,* on these interpretations of Plato.)

It is odd that Coleridge nowhere, I think, refers to this passage, but takes a roundabout route in attributing this to Plato as esoteric doctrine (see pp. 351–52).

any others of the warring "subjects"—and in a world of Nations so unable to become United? "The perfect frame of a man is the perfect frame of a state" (p. 389).

Coleridge's ensuing remarks contain, I think, his clearest, shrewdest and most inclusive account of the whole soul of man and the subordination of its faculties to one another, and thereby of the practice and principles of critical choice and judgment. But the very word "inclusive" should warn us not to forget a releasing last word:

"As every faculty, with every the minutest organ of our nature, owes its whole reality and comprehensibility to an existence incomprehensible and groundless, because the ground of all comprehension; not without the union of all that is essential in all the functions of our spirit, not without an emotion tranquil from its very intensity, shall we worthily contemplate in the magnitude and integrity of the world that life-ebullient stream which breaks through every momentary embankment, again, indeed, and evermore to embank itself, but within no banks to stagnate or be imprisoned."

A NOTE ON SELECTIONS

Any editor of selections from Coleridge soon realizes that for everything he puts in there will be something he must push out. I have tried to rule my choices by Coleridge's own principle, "On whatever subject I think, to endeavour to discover all the good that . . . can result." (Letter to George Coleridge, April 1789.) His work is charged with constructive powers, some of which have as yet no more than begun to act. I have therefore left relatively unrepresented his political journalism, which needs a study of its historical setting for just appraisal, and his marginalia, which ask you to have your bookshelves within arm's reach, and so seem less suited to a *Portable*. I have been able thus to include most of the discussion of Method, from the later essays of *The Friend*, which Coleridge later thought, and with justice, the best of his prose. And I have followed chronological order so far as possible within the various sections. On Coleridge's peculiarities in spelling and punctuation I have followed the majority view that they are sufficiently expressive of him to remain incompletely regularized.

As I close my list, I am naturally attacked by fears, not so much that I have put in the wrong things and left out the right—I remember the General Confession —but that some reader may suppose that this book contains all that he would enjoy or profit from in Coleridge. A dip in the oceanlike rest of those writings would be the best cure.

ACKNOWLEDGMENTS

My indebtedness is first to those editors who have made and are making Coleridge's writings accessible— to E. H. Coleridge, to J. Shawcross, to E. L. Griggs, to T. M. Raysor, to Miss Alice Snyder, and to Miss Kathleen Coburn. Secondly I have especial gratitude to express to Stephen Potter for *Coleridge and S. T. C.* with its critique of my *Coleridge on Imagination*, and for "On Editing Coleridge" (*The Bookman*, 1934), his reflections at the end of his work on the Nonesuch selections. On the present appeal of Coleridge's thought I have profited from Herbert Read's *Coleridge as Critic*.

I. A. R.

A PARTIAL BIBLIOGRAPHY

TEXTS

Poems. Edited by Ernest Hartley Coleridge. London: Oxford University Press, 1912.

Letters of Samuel Taylor Coleridge. Edited by Ernest Hartley Coleridge. London: Heinemann, 1895.

Unpublished Letters of Samuel Taylor Coleridge. Edited by Earl Leslie Griggs. New Haven: Yale University Press, 1933.

The Friend. London: Bell, 1884.

Biographia Literaria. Edited by J. Shawcross. London: Oxford University Press, 1907. 2 vols.

The Table Talk and Omniana. Notes made by H. N. Coleridge. New York: Oxford University Press, 1917.

Coleridge's Shakespearean Criticism. Edited by Thomas Middleton Raysor. Cambridge: Harvard University Press, 1930. 2 vols.

Coleridge's Miscellaneous Criticism. Edited by Thomas Middleton Raysor. Cambridge: Harvard University Press, 1936.

Aids to Reflection. London: Bell, 1884.

On the Constitution of the Church and State, with the Lay Sermons: The Statesman's Manual and "Blessed are ye that sow beside all waters." London: Pickering, 1839.

Anima Poetae: From the notebooks edited by E. H. Coleridge. Boston: Houghton Mifflin Company, 1895.

BIOGRAPHIES

Samuel Taylor Coleridge: A Narrative of the Events of His Life. James Dykes Campbell. London and New York: Macmillan, 1894. A fair and plain account.

Samuel Taylor Coleridge: A Biographical Study. E. K.
Chambers. Oxford: The Clarendon Press, 1938. Detailed
but unsympathetic.

A useful bibliography for students and teachers by Vir-
ginia Wadlow Kennedy was published by The Enoch Pratt
Free Library, Baltimore, 1935.

CHRONOLOGY

1772	October 21. Samuel Taylor Coleridge born.
1782	July. Entered at Christ's Hospital.
1791	October. To Jesus College, Cambridge.
1793	December 2. Enlisted in Light Dragoons.
1794	April 10. Discharged.
	Met Southey at Oxford.
	December. Left Cambridge.
1795	January. Lectures at Bristol.
	October 4. Married to Sarah Fricker.
	November. Break with Southey.
	Clevedon.
1796	March 1–May 13. *The Watchman.*
	September 19. Hartley Coleridge born.
	December 31. Nether-Stowey.
1797	July 14. Wordsworths to Alfoxden.
	November 13. "Ancient Mariner" begun.
	First part of "Christabel."
1798	January. Wedgwood annuity.
	September 16 (to July 1799). Germany.
1799	October–November. Lake District.
1800	Spring. "Wallenstein" translation.
	July 24. Greta Hall, Keswick.
	September 14. Birth of Derwent Coleridge.
	Autumn. Second part of "Christabel."
1802	December 23. Birth of Sara Coleridge.
1803	August. Scotch tour.

1804   April 9. To Malta.

1805   Left Malta, September 21, 1805.

1806   January–May. Rome.
        August. England.
        December. To Wordsworths at Coleorton.

1808   January. First lectures at Royal Institution.
        September (to May 1810). Alan Bank, Grasmere.

1809   June (to March 1810). *The Friend.*
        May–October. Greta Hall.

1810   October 28. Break with Wordsworth.

1811   November. Lectures at London Philosophical Society.

1812   May. Lectures at Willis's Rooms.
        November. Lectures at Surrey Institution.

1813   January 23. *Remorse* at Drury Lane.
        October. To Bristol.
        October (to April 1814). Lectures at Bristol.

1814   November. With the Morgans to Calme.

1816   April 16. To Gilmans at Highgate.
        June. "Christabel," "Kubla Khan," published.

1817   *Lay Sermons, Biographia Literaria.*

1818   December (to March 1819). Lectures on History of
            Philosophy.

1825   *Aids to Reflection.*

1828   *Poetical Works.*

1830   *Church and State.*

1834   July 25. Died.

The Portable

COLERIDGE

POEMS

Sonnet

TO THE AUTUMNAL MOON

Mild Splendour of the various-vested Night!
    Mother of wildly-working visions! hail!
I watch thy gliding, while with watery light
    Thy weak eye glimmers through a fleecy veil;
And when thou lovest thy pale orb to shroud   5
    Behind the gather'd blackness lost on high;
And when thou dartest from the wind-rent cloud
    Thy placid lightning o'er the awaken'd sky.

Ah such is Hope! as changeful and as fair!
    Now dimly peering on the wistful sight;   10
Now hid behind the dragon-wing'd Despair:
    But soon emerging in her radiant might
She o'er the sorrow-clouded breast of Care
    Sails, like a meteor kindling in its flight.

1788

Quae Nocent Docent

[IN CHRIST'S HOSPITAL BOOK]

O! mihi praeteritos referat si Jupiter annos!

Oh! might my ill-past hours return again!
No more, as then, should Sloth around me throw
    Her soul-enslaving, leaden chain!

61

No more the precious time would I employ
In giddy revels, or in thoughtless joy,   5
A present joy producing future woe.

But o'er the midnight Lamp I'd love to pore,
I'd seek with care fair Learning's depths to sound,
   And gather scientific Lore:
Or to mature the embryo thoughts inclin'd,   10
That half-conceiv'd lay struggling in my mind,
The cloisters' solitary gloom I'd round.

'Tis vain to wish, for Time has ta'en his flight—
For follies past be ceas'd the fruitless tears:
   Let follies past to future care incite.   15
Averse maturer judgements to obey
Youth owns, with pleasure owns, the Passions' sway,
But sage Experience only comes with years.

                 1789 (first published in 1893)

Sonnet

TO THE RIVER OTTER

Dear native Brook! wild Streamlet of the West!
   How many various-fated years have past,
   What happy and what mournful hours, since last
I skimm'd the smooth thin stone along thy breast,
Numbering its light leaps! yet so deep imprest   5
Sink the sweet scenes of childhood, that mine eyes
   I never shut amid the sunny ray,
But straight with all their tints thy waters rise,
   Thy crossing plank, thy marge with willows grey,
And bedded sand that vein'd with various dyes   10
Gleam'd through thy bright transparence! On my way,

Visions of Childhood! oft have ye beguil'd
Lone manhood's cares, yet waking fondest sighs:
Ah! that once more I were a careless Child!

1793(?)

Pantisocracy

No more my visionary soul shall dwell
On joys that were; no more endure to weigh
The shame and anguish of the evil day,
Wisely forgetful! O'er the ocean swell
Sublime of Hope, I seek the cottag'd dell   5
Where Virtue calm with careless step may stray,
And dancing to the moonlight roundelay,
The wizard Passions weave an holy spell.
Eyes that have ach'd with Sorrow! Ye shall weep
Tears of doubt-mingled joy, like theirs who start   10
From Precipices of distemper'd sleep,
On which the fierce-eyed Fiends their revels keep,
And see the rising Sun, and feel it dart
New rays of pleasance trembling to the heart.

1794

To a Young Ass

ITS MOTHER BEING TETHERED NEAR IT

Poor little Foal of an oppressèd race!
I love the languid patience of thy face:
And oft with gentle hand I give thee bread,
And clap thy ragged coat, and pat thy head.
But what thy dulled spirits hath dismay'd,   5
That never thou dost sport along the glade?
And (most unlike the nature of things young)

That earthward still thy moveless head is hung?
Do thy prophetic fears anticipate,
Meek Child of Misery! thy future fate?   10
The starving meal, and all the thousand aches
"Which patient Merit of the Unworthy takes"?
Or is thy sad heart thrill'd with filial pain
To see thy wretched mother's shorten'd chain?
And truly, very piteous is *her* lot—   15
Chain'd to a log within a narrow spot,
Where the close-eaten grass is scarcely seen,
While sweet around her waves the tempting green!

Poor Ass! thy master should have learnt to show
Pity—best taught by fellowship of Woe!   20
For much I fear me that *He* lives like thee,
Half famish'd in a land of Luxury!
How *askingly* its footsteps hither bend?
It seems to say, "And have I then *one* friend?"
Innocent foal! thou poor despis'd forlorn!   25
I hail thee *Brother*—spite of the fool's scorn!
And fain would take thee with me, in the Dell
Where high-soul'd Pantisocracy shall dwell!
Where Mirth shall tickle Plenty's ribless side,[1]
And smiles from Beauty's Lip on sunbeams glide,   30
Where Toil shall wed young Health that charming Lass!
And use his sleek cows for a looking-glass—
Where Rats shall mess with Terriers hand-in-glove
And Mice with Pussy's Whiskers sport in Love
How thou wouldst toss thy heels in gamesome play,   35
And frisk about, as lamb or kitten gay!
Yea! and more musically sweet to me
Thy dissonant harsh bray of joy would be,

[1] This is a truly poetical line of which the author has as-
sured us that he did not *mean* it to have any *meaning*.
—Note by Ed. of MS. Oct. 1794.—E. H. Coleridge.

Than warbled melodies that soothe to rest
The aching of pale Fashion's vacant breast!   40
                                                      1794

The Eolian Harp

Composed at Clevedon, Somersetshire

My pensive Sara! thy soft cheek reclined
Thus on mine arm, most soothing sweet it is
To sit beside our Cot, our Cot o'ergrown
With white-flower'd Jasmin, and the broad-leav'd
      Myrtle,
(Meet emblems they of Innocence and Love!)   5
And watch the clouds, that late were rich with light,
Slow saddening round, and mark the star of eve
Serenely brilliant (such should Wisdom be)
Shine opposite! How exquisite the scents
Snatch'd from yon bean-field! and the world *so*
      hush'd!   10
The stilly murmur of the distant Sea
Tells us of silence.
                    And that simplest Lute,
Placed length-ways in the clasping casement, hark!
How by the desultory breeze caress'd,
Like some coy maid half yielding to her lover,   15
It pours such sweet upbraiding, as must needs
Tempt to repeat the wrong! And now, its strings
Boldlier swept, the long sequacious notes
Over delicious surges sink and rise,
Such a soft floating witchery of sound   20
As twilight Elfins make, when they at eve
Voyage on gentle gales from Fairy-Land,
Where Melodies round honey-dropping flowers,

Footless and wild, like birds of Paradise,
Nor pause, nor perch, hovering on untam'd wing!   25
O! the one Life within us and abroad,
Which meets all motion and becomes its soul,
A light in sound, a sound-like power in light,
Rhythm in all thought, and joyance every where—
Methinks, it should have been impossible   30
Not to love all things in a world so fill'd;
Where the breeze warbles, and the mute still air
Is Music slumbering on her instrument.

And thus, my Love! as on the midway slope
Of yonder hill I stretch my limbs at noon,   35
Whilst through my half-clos'd eye-lids I behold
The sunbeams dance, like diamonds, on the main,
And tranquil muse upon tranquillity;
Full many a thought uncall'd and undetain'd,
And many idle flitting phantasies,   40
Traverse my indolent and passive brain,
As wild and various as the random gales
That swell and flutter on this subject Lute!
And what if all of animated nature
Be but organic Harps diversely fram'd,   45
That tremble into thought, as o'er them sweeps
Plastic and vast, one intellectual breeze,
At once the Soul of each, and God of all?
But thy more serious eye a mild reproof
Darts, O belovéd Woman! nor such thoughts   50
Dim and unhallow'd dost thou not reject,
And biddest me walk humbly with my God.
Meek Daughter in the family of Christ!
Well hast thou said and holily disprais'd
These shapings of the unregenerate mind;   55
Bubbles that glitter as they rise and break
On vain Philosophy's aye-babbling spring.

For never guiltless may I speak of him,
The Incomprehensible! save when with awe
I praise him, and with Faith that inly *feels;*   60
Who with his saving mercies healéd me,
A sinful and most miserable man,
Wilder'd and dark, and gave me to possess
Peace, and this Cot, and thee, heart-honour'd Maid!

1795 August 20

Reflections on Having Left a Place of Retirement

Sermoni propriora.—Horace

Low was our pretty Cot: our tallest Rose
Peep'd at the chamber-window. We could hear
At silent noon, and eve, and early morn,
The Sea's faint murmur. In the open air
Our Myrtles blossom'd; and across the porch   5
Thick Jasmins twined: the little landscape round
Was green and woody, and refresh'd the eye.
It was a spot which you might aptly call
The Valley of Seclusion! Once I saw
(Hallowing his Sabbath-day by quietness)   10
A wealthy son of Commerce saunter by,
Bristowa's citizen: methought, it calm'd
His thirst of idle gold, and made him muse
With wiser feelings: for he paus'd, and look'd
With a pleas'd sadness, and gaz'd all around,   15
Then eyed our Cottage, and gaz'd round again,
And sigh'd, and said, it was a Blesséd Place.
And we *were* bless'd. Oft with patient ear
Long-listening to the viewless sky-lark's note

(Viewless, or haply for a moment seen   20
Gleaming on sunny wings) in whisper'd tones
I've said to my Belovéd, "Such, sweet Girl!
The inobtrusive song of Happiness,
Unearthly minstrelsy! then only heard
When the Soul seeks to hear; when all is hush'd,   25
And the Heart listens!"

                        But the time, when first
From that low Dell, steep up the stony Mount
I climb'd with perilous toil and reach'd the top,
Oh! what a goodly scene! *Here* the bleak mount,
The bare bleak mountain speckled thin with sheep;   30
Grey clouds, that shadowing spot the sunny fields;
And river, now with bushy rocks o'er-brow'd,
Now winding bright and full, with naked banks;
And seats, and lawns, the Abbey and the wood,
And cots, and hamlets, and faint city-spire;   35
The Channel *there,* the Islands and white sails,
Dim coasts, and cloud-like hills, and shoreless Ocean—
It seem'd like Omnipresence! God, methought,
Had built him there a Temple: the whole World
Seem'd *imag'd* in its vast circumference: 40
No *wish* profan'd my overwhelméd heart.
Blest hour! It was a luxury,—to be!

Ah! quiet Dell! dear Cot, and Mount sublime!
I was constrain'd to quit you. Was it right,
While my unnumber'd brethren toil'd and bled,   45
That I should dream away the entrusted hours
On rose-leaf beds, pampering the coward heart
With feelings all too delicate for use?
Sweet is the tear that from some Howard's eye
Drops on the cheek of one he lifts from earth: 50
And he that works me good with unmov'd face,

Does it but half: he chills me while he aids,
My benefactor, not my brother man!
Yet even this, this cold beneficence
Praise, praise it, O my Soul! oft as thou scann'st   55
The sluggard Pity's vision-weaving tribe!
Who sigh for Wretchedness, yet shun the Wretched,
Nursing in some delicious solitude
Their slothful loves and dainty sympathies!
I therefore go, and join head, heart, and hand,   60
Active and firm, to fight the bloodless fight
Of Science, Freedom, and the Truth in Christ.

Yet oft when after honourable toil
Rests the tir'd mind, and waking loves to dream,
My spirit shall revisit thee, dear Cot!   65
Thy Jasmin and thy window-peeping Rose,
And Myrtles fearless of the mild sea-air.
And I shall sigh fond wishes—sweet Abode!
Ah!—had none greater! And that all had such!
It might be so—but the time is not yet.   70
Speed it, O Father! Let thy Kingdom come!

                                                          1795

To a Young Friend

ON HIS PROPOSING TO DOMESTICATE
WITH THE AUTHOR

A mount, not wearisome and bare and steep,
   But a green mountain variously up-piled,
Where o'er the jutting rocks soft mosses creep,
Or colour'd lichens with slow oozing weep;
   Where cypress and the darker yew start wild;   5
And, 'mid the summer torrent's gentle dash

Dance brighten'd the red clusters of the ash;
   Beneath whose boughs, by those still sounds beguil'd,
Calm Pensiveness might muse herself to sleep;
   Till haply startled by some fleecy dam,   10
That rustling on the bushy cliff above
With melancholy bleat of anxious love,
   Made meek enquiry for her wandering lamb:
   Such a green mountain 'twere most sweet to climb,
E'en while the bosom ach'd with loneliness—   15
How more than sweet, if some dear friend should bless
   The adventurous toil, and up the path sublime
Now lead, now follow: the glad landscape round,
Wide and more wide, increasing without bound!

   O then 'twere loveliest sympathy, to mark   20
The berries of the half-uprooted ash
Dripping and bright; and list the torrent's dash,—
   Beneath the cypress, or the yew more dark,
Seated at ease, on some smooth mossy rock;
In social silence now, and now to unlock   25
The treasur'd heart; arm linked in friendly arm,
Save if the one, his muse's witching charm
Muttering brow-bent, at unwatch'd distance lag;
   Till high o'er head his beckoning friend appears,
And from the forehead of the topmost crag   30
   Shouts eagerly: for haply *there* uprears
That shadowing Pine its old romantic limbs,
   Which latest shall detain the enamour'd sight
Seen from below, when eve the valley dims,
   Tinged yellow with the rich departing light;   35
   And haply, bason'd in some unsunn'd cleft,
A beauteous spring, the rock's collected tears,
Sleeps shelter'd there, scarce wrinkled by the gale!
   Together thus, the world's vain turmoil left,
Stretch'd on the crag, and shadow'd by the pine,   40

And bending o'er the clear delicious fount,
Ah! dearest youth! it were a lot divine
To cheat our noons in moralising mood,
While west-winds fann'd our temples toil-bedew'd:
    Then downwards slope, oft pausing, from the
        mount,   45
To some lone mansion, in some woody dale,
Where smiling with blue eye, Domestic Bliss
Gives *this* the Husband's, *that* the Brother's kiss!

    Thus rudely vers'd in allegoric lore,
The Hill of Knowledge I essayed to trace;   50
That verdurous hill with many a resting-place,
And many a stream, whose warbling waters pour
    To glad, and fertilise the subject plains;
That hill with secret springs, and nooks untrod,
And many a fancy-blest and holy sod   55
    Where Inspiration, his diviner strains
Low-murmuring, lay; and starting from the rock's
Stiff evergreens, (whose spreading foliage mocks
Want's barren soil, and the bleak frosts of age,
And Bigotry's mad fire-invoking rage!)   60
O meek retiring spirit! we will climb,
Cheering and cheered, this lovely hill sublime;
    And from the stirring world up-lifted high
(Whose noises, faintly wafted on the wind,
To quiet musings shall attune the mind,   65
    And oft the melancholy *theme* supply),
    There, while the prospect through the gazing eye
    Pours all its healthful greenness on the soul,
We'll smile at wealth, and learn to smile at fame,
Our hopes, our knowledge, and our joys the same,   70
    As neighbouring fountains image each the whole:
Then when the mind hath drunk its fill of truth
    We'll discipline the heart to pure delight,

Rekindling sober joy's domestic flame.
They whom I love shall love thee, honour'd youth!   75
  Now may Heaven realise this vision bright!

1796

Addressed to a Young Man of Fortune

WHO ABANDONED HIMSELF TO AN INDOLENT AND CAUSELESS MELANCHOLY

[C. Lloyd]

Hence that fantastic wantonness of woe,
  O Youth to partial Fortune vainly dear!
To plunder'd Want's half-shelter'd hovel go,
  Go, and some hunger-bitten infant hear
  Moan haply in a dying mother's ear: 5
Or when the cold and dismal fog-damps brood
O'er the rank church-yard with sear elm-leaves strew'd,
Pace round some widow's grave, whose dearer part
  Was slaughter'd, where o'er his uncoffin'd limbs
The flocking flesh-birds scream'd! Then, while thy heart   10
  Groans, and thine eye a fiercer sorrow dims,
Know (and the truth shall kindle thy young mind)
What Nature makes thee mourn, she bids thee heal!
  O abject! if, to sickly dreams resign'd,
All effortless thou leave Life's commonweal   15
  A prey to Tyrants, Murderers of Mankind.

1796

To the Rev. George Coleridge[1]

OF OTTERY ST. MARY, DEVON

With Some Poems

Notus in fratres animi paterni.
HORACE, *Carmina*, II, 2

A blessèd lot hath he, who having passed
His youth and early manhood in the stir
And turmoil of the world, retreats at length,
With cares that move, not agitate the heart,
To the same dwelling where his father dwelt;   5
And haply views his tottering little ones
Embrace those agèd knees and climb that lap,
On which first kneeling his own infancy
Lisp'd its brief prayer. Such, O my earliest Friend!
Thy lot, and such thy brothers too enjoy.   10
At distance did ye climb Life's upland road,
Yet cheer'd and cheering: now fraternal love
Hath drawn you to one centre. Be your days
Holy, and blest and blessing may ye live!

To me the Eternal Wisdom hath dispens'd   15
A different fortune and more different mind—
Me from the spot where first I sprang to light

[1] First published as the Dedication to the *Poems* of 1797.
In a copy of the *Poems* of 1797, formerly in the possession
of the late Mr. Frederick Locker-Lampson, Coleridge affixed
the following note to the Dedication—"N.B. If this volume
should ever be delivered according to its direction, *i.e.* to
Posterity, let it be known that the Reverend George Cole-
ridge was displeased and thought his character endangered
by the Dedication."—S. T. Coleridge.—*E. H. Coleridge*

Too soon transplanted, ere my soul had fix'd
Its first domestic loves; and hence through life
Chasing chance-started friendships. A brief while   20
Some have preserv'd me from life's pelting ills;
But, like a tree with leaves of feeble stem,
If the clouds lasted, and a sudden breeze
Ruffled the boughs, they on my head at once
Dropped the collected shower; and some most false,   25
False and fair-foliag'd as the Manchineel,
Have tempted me to slumber in their shade
E'en mid the storm; then breathing subtlest damps,
Mix'd their own venom with the rain from Heaven,
That I woke poison'd! But, all praise to Him   30
Who gives us all things, more have yielded me
Permanent shelter; and beside one Friend,
Beneath the impervious covert of one oak,
I've rais'd a lowly shed, and know the names
Of Husband and of Father; not unhearing   35
Of that divine and nightly-whispering Voice,
Which from my childhood to maturer years
Spake to me of predestinated wreaths,
Bright with no fading colours!

                                        Yet at times
My soul is sad, that I have roam'd through life   40
Still most a stranger, most with naked heart
At mine own home and birth-place: chiefly then,
When I remember thee, my earliest Friend!
Thee, who didst watch my boyhood and my youth;
Didst trace my wanderings with a father's eye;   45
And boding evil yet still hoping good,
Rebuk'd each fault, and over all my woes
Sorrow'd in silence! He who counts alone
The beatings of the solitary heart,
That Being knows, how I have lov'd thee ever,   50

Lov'd as a brother, as a son rever'd thee!
Oh! 'tis to me an ever new delight,
To talk of thee and thine: or when the blast
Of the shrill winter, rattling our rude sash,
Endears the cleanly hearth and social bowl;   55
Or when, as now, on some delicious eve,
We in our sweet sequester'd orchard-plot
Sit on the tree crook'd earth-ward; whose old boughs,
That hang above us in an arborous roof,
Stirr'd by the faint gale of departing May,   60
Send their loose blossoms slanting o'er our heads!

Nor dost not thou sometimes recall those hours,
When with the joy of hope thou gavest thine ear
To my wild firstling-lays. Since then my song
Hath sounded deeper notes, such as beseem   65
Or that sad wisdom folly leaves behind,
Or such as, tuned to these tumultuous times,
Cope with the tempest's swell!

                              These various strains,
Which I have fram'd in many a various mood,
Accept, my Brother! and (for some perchance   70
Will strike discordant on thy milder mind)
If aught of error or intemperate truth
Should meet thine ear, think thou that riper Age
Will calm it down, and let thy love forgive it!
                    Nether-Stowey, Somerset, *May* 26, 1797

This Lime-Tree Bower My Prison

[ADDRESSED TO CHARLES LAMB, OF THE
INDIA HOUSE, LONDON]

*In the June of 1797 some long-expected friends paid a visit to
the author's cottage; and on the morning of their arrival, he
met with an accident, which disabled him from walking dur-
ing the whole time of their stay. One evening, when they had
left him for a few hours, he composed the following lines in
the garden-bower.[1]*

Well, they are gone, and here must I remain,
This lime-tree bower my prison! I have lost
Beauties and feelings, such as would have been
Most sweet to my remembrance even when age
Had dimm'd mine eyes to blindness! They, mean-
    while,   5
Friends, whom I never more may meet again,
On springy heath, along the hill-top edge,
Wander in gladness, and wind down, perchance,
To that still roaring dell, of which I told;
The roaring dell, o'erwooded, narrow, deep,   10
And only speckled by the mid-day sun;
Where its slim trunk the ash from rock to rock
Flings arching like a bridge;—that branchless ash,
Unsunn'd and damp, whose few poor yellow leaves
Ne'er tremble in the gale, yet tremble still,   15
Fann'd by the water-fall! and there my friends

---

[1] "Ch. and Mary Lamb—dear to my heart, yea, as it were
my Heart.—S. T. C. Æt. 63; 1834—1797–1834 = 37 years!"
(Marginal note written by S. T. Coleridge over against the
introductory note to "This Lime-Tree Bower My Prison," in
a copy of the *Poetical Works,* 1834.)—E. H. Coleridge

Behold the dark green file of long lank weeds,
That all at once (a most fantastic sight!)
Still nod and drip beneath the dripping edge
Of the blue clay-stone.

              Now, my friends emerge   20
Beneath the wide wide Heaven—and view again
The many-steepled tract magnificent
Of hilly fields and meadows, and the sea,
With some fair bark, perhaps, whose sails light up
The slip of smooth clear blue betwixt two Isles   25
Of purple shadow! Yes! they wander on
In gladness all; but thou, methinks, most glad,
My gentle-hearted Charles! for thou hast pined
And hunger'd after Nature, many a year,
In the great City pent, winning thy way   30
With sad yet patient soul, through evil and pain
And strange calamity! Ah! slowly sink
Behind the western ridge, thou glorious Sun!
Shine in the slant beams of the sinking orb,
Ye purple heath-flowers! richlier burn, ye clouds!   35
Live in the yellow light, ye distant groves!
And kindle, thou blue Ocean! So my friend
Struck with deep joy may stand, as I have stood,
Silent with swimming sense; yea, gazing round
On the wide landscape, gaze till all doth seem   40
Less gross than bodily; and of such hues
As veil the Almighty Spirit, when yet he makes
Spirits perceive his presence.

              A delight
Comes sudden on my heart, and I am glad
As I myself were there! Nor in this bower,   45
This little lime-tree bower, have I not mark'd

Much that has sooth'd me. Pale beneath the blaze
Hung the transparent foliage; and I watch'd
Some broad and sunny leaf, and lov'd to see
The shadow of the leaf and stem above   50
Dappling its sunshine! And that walnut-tree
Was richly ting'd, and a deep radiance lay
Full on the ancient ivy, which usurps
Those fronting elms, and now, with blackest mass
Makes their dark branches gleam a lighter hue   55
Through the late twilight: and though now the bat
Wheels silent by, and not a swallow twitters,
Yet still the solitary humble-bee
Sings in the bean-flower! Henceforth I shall know
That Nature ne'er deserts the wise and pure;   60
No plot so narrow, be but Nature there,
No waste so vacant, but may well employ
Each faculty of sense, and keep the heart
Awake to Love and Beauty! and sometimes
'Tis well to be bereft of promis'd good,   65
That we may lift the soul, and contemplate
With lively joy the joys we cannot share.
My gentle-hearted Charles! when the last rook
Beat its straight path along the dusky air
Homewards, I blest it! deeming its black wing   70
(Now a dim speck, now vanishing in light)
Had cross'd the mighty Orb's dilated glory,
While thou stood'st gazing; or, when all was still,
Flew creeking o'er thy head, and had a charm[1]

[1] Some months after I had written this line, it gave me
pleasure to find that Bartram had observed the same cir-
cumstance of the Savanna Crane. "When these Birds move
their wings in flight, their strokes are slow, moderate and
regular; and even when at a considerable distance or high
above us, we plainly hear the quill-feathers: their shafts and
webs upon one another creek as the joints or working of a
vessel in a tempestuous sea."—S. T. C.

For thee, my gentle-hearted Charles, to whom   75
No sound is dissonant which tells of Life.

1797

The Dungeon

[From *Osorio*, Act V; and *Remorse*, Act V, Scene i.]

And this place our forefathers made for man!
This is the process of our love and wisdom,
To each poor brother who offends against us—
Most innocent, perhaps—and what if guilty?
Is this the only cure? Merciful God!   5
Each pore and natural outlet shrivell'd up
By Ignorance and parching Poverty,
His energies roll back upon his heart,
And stagnate and corrupt; till chang'd to poison,
They break out on him, like a loathsome plague-
    spot;   10
Then we call in our pamper'd mountebanks—
And this is their best cure! uncomforted
And friendless solitude, groaning and tears,
And savage faces, at the clanking hour,
Seen through the steams and vapour of his dun-
    geon,   15
By the lamp's dismal twilight! So he lies
Circled with evil, till his very soul
Unmoulds its essence, hopelessly deform'd
By sights of ever more deformity!

With other ministrations thou, O Nature!   20
Healest thy wandering and distemper'd child:
Thou pourest on him thy soft influences,
Thy sunny hues, fair forms, and breathing sweets,

Thy melodies of woods, and winds, and waters,
Till he relent, and can no more endure   25
To be a jarring and a dissonant thing,
Amid this general dance and minstrelsy;
But, bursting into tears, wins back his way,
His angry spirit heal'd and harmoniz'd
By the benignant touch of Love and Beauty.   30
                                                         1797

The Rime of the Ancient Mariner

IN SEVEN PARTS

*Facile credo, plures esse Naturas invisibiles quam visibiles
in rerum universitate. Sed horum omnium familiam quis
nobis enarrabit? et gradus et cognationes et discrimina et
singulorum munera? Quid agunt? quae loca habitant? Harum
rerum notitiam semper ambivit ingenium humanum, nun-
quam attigit. Juvat, interea, non diffiteor, quandoque in
animo, tanquam in tabulâ, majoris et melioris mundi im-
aginem contemplari: ne mens assuefacta hodiernae vitae
minutiis se contrahat nimis, et tota subsidat in pusillas cogi-
tationes. Sed veritati interea invigilandum est, modusque ser-
vandus, ut certa ab incertis, diem a nocte, distinguamus.—*
T. BURNET, *Archaeol. Phil.* p. 68.

ARGUMENT

*How a Ship having passed the Line was driven by storms to
the cold Country towards the South Pole; and how from
thence she made her course to the tropical Latitude of the
Great Pacific Ocean; and of the strange things that befell;
and in what manner the Ancyent Marinere came back to his
own Country.*

PART I

An ancient Mariner meeteth three Gallants bidden to a wedding-feast, and detaineth one.

It is an ancient Mariner,
And he stoppeth one of three.
"By thy long grey beard and glittering
    eye,
Now wherefore stopp'st thou me?

The Bridegroom's doors are opened
    wide,   5
And I am next of kin;
The guests are met, the feast is set:
May'st hear the merry din."

He holds him with his skinny hand,
"There was a ship," quoth he.   10
"Hold off! unhand me, grey-beard loon!"
Eftsoons his hand dropt he.

The Wedding-Guest is spell-bound by the eye of the old seafaring man, and constrained to hear his tale.

He holds him with his glittering eye—
The Wedding-Guest stood still,
And listens like a three years' child: 15
The Mariner hath his will.

The Wedding-Guest sat on a stone:
He cannot choose but hear;
And thus spake on that ancient man,
The bright-eyed Mariner.   20

"The ship was cheered, the harbour
    cleared,
Merrily did we drop

Below the kirk, below the hill,

*The Mariner tells
how the ship
sailed southward
with a good wind
and fair weather,
till it reached the
Line.*
Below the lighthouse top.

The Sun came up upon the left,   25
Out of the sea came he!
And he shone bright, and on the right
Went down into the sea.

Higher and higher every day,
Till over the mast at noon—"   30
The Wedding-Guest here beat his breast,
For he heard the loud bassoon.

*The Wedding-
Guest heareth
the bridal music;
but the Mariner
continueth his
tale.*
The bride hath paced into the hall,
Red as a rose is she;
Nodding their heads before her goes   35
The merry minstrelsy.

The Wedding-Guest he beat his breast,
Yet he cannot choose but hear;
And thus spake on that ancient man,
The bright-eyed Mariner.   40

*The ship driven
by a storm to-
ward the south
pole.*
"And now the STORM-BLAST came, and he
Was tyrannous and strong;
He struck with his o'ertaking wings,
And chased us south along.

With sloping masts and dipping
      prow,   45
As who pursued with yell and blow
Still treads the shadow of his foe,
And forward bends his head,
The ship drove fast, loud roared the blast,
And southward aye we fled.   50

And now there came both mist and snow,
And it grew wondrous cold:
And ice, mast-high, came floating by,
As green as emerald.

*The land of ice,
and of fearful
sounds where no
living thing was
to be seen.*

And through the drifts the snowy
   clifts   55
Did send a dismal sheen:
Nor shapes of men nor beasts we ken—
The ice was all between.

The ice was here, the ice was there,
The ice was all around: 60
It cracked and growled, and roared and
   howled,
Like noises in a swound!

*Till a great sea-
bird, called the
Albatross, came
through the
snow-fog, and
was received
with great joy
and hospitality.*

At length did cross an Albatross,
Thorough the fog it came;
As if it had been a Christian soul,   65
We hailed it in God's name.

It ate the food it ne'er had eat,
And round and round it flew.
The ice did split with a thunder-fit;
The helmsman steered us through!   70

*And lo! the Al-
batross proveth
a bird of good
omen, and fol-
loweth the ship
as it returned
northward
through fog and
floating ice.*

And a good south wind sprung up be-
   hind;
The Albatross did follow,
And every day, for food or play,
Came to the mariners' hollo!

In mist or cloud, on mast or shroud,   75
It perched for vespers nine;

Whiles all the night, through fog-smoke
    white,
Glimmered the white Moon-shine."

*The ancient
Mariner inhospi-
tably killeth the
pious bird of
good omen.*

"God save thee, ancient Mariner!
From the fiends, that plague thee
    thus!—   80
Why look'st thou so?"—"With my cross-
    bow
I shot the ALBATROSS.

PART II

The Sun now rose upon the right:
Out of the sea came he,
Still hid in mist, and on the left   85
Went down into the sea.

And the good south wind still blew be-
    hind,
But no sweet bird did follow,
Nor any day for food or play
Came to the mariners' hollo!   90

*His shipmates
cry out against
the ancient Mar-
iner, for killing
the bird of good
luck.*

And I had done a hellish thing,
And it would work 'em woe:
For all averred, I had killed the bird
That made the breeze to blow.
Ah wretch! said they, the bird to slay,   95
That made the breeze to blow!

*But when the
fog cleared off,
they justify the
same, and thus
make themselves
accomplices in
the crime.*

Nor dim nor red, like God's own head,
The glorious Sun uprist:
Then all averred, I had killed the bird
That brought the fog and mist.   100

'Twas right, said they, such birds to slay,
That bring the fog and mist.

The fair breeze continues; the ship enters the Pacific Ocean, and sails northward, even till it reaches the Line.

The fair breeze blew, the white foam
    flew,
The furrow followed free;
We were the first that ever burst   105
Into that silent sea.

The ship hath been suddenly becalmed.

Down dropt the breeze, the sails dropt
    down,
'Twas sad as sad could be;
And we did speak only to break
The silence of the sea!   110

All in a hot and copper sky,
The bloody Sun, at noon,
Right up above the mast did stand,
No bigger than the Moon.

Day after day, day after day,   115
We stuck, nor breath nor motion;
As idle as a painted ship
Upon a painted ocean.

And the Albatross begins to be avenged.

Water, water, every where,
And all the boards did shrink;   120
Water, water, every where,
Nor any drop to drink.

The very deep did rot: O Christ!
That ever this should be!
Yea, slimy things did crawl with legs   125
Upon the slimy sea.

About, about, in reel and rout
The death-fires danced at night;
The water, like a witch's oils,
Burnt green, and blue and white.   130

And some in dreams assuréd were
Of the Spirit that plagued us so;
Nine fathom deep he had followed us
From the land of mist and snow.

*A Spirit had
followed them;
one of the invis-
ible inhabitants
of this planet,
neither departed souls nor angels; concerning whom the learned Jew,
Josephus, and the Platonic Constantinopolitan, Michael Psellus, may
be consulted. They are very numerous, and there is no climate or ele-
ment without one or more.*

And every tongue, through utter
    drought,   135
Was withered at the root;
We could not speak, no more than if
We had been choked with soot.

*The shipmates,
in their sore dis-
tress, would fain
throw the whole
guilt on the an-
cient Mariner: in*
Ah! well a-day! what evil looks
Had I from old and young!   140
Instead of the cross, the Albatross
About my neck was hung.
sign whereof they hang the dead sea-bird round his neck.

PART III

There passed a weary time. Each throat
Was parched, and glazed each eye.
A weary time! a weary time!   145
How glazed each weary eye,
*The ancient Mar-
iner beholdeth a
sign in the ele-
ment afar off.*
When looking westward, I beheld
A something in the sky.

At first it seemed a little speck,
And then it seemed a mist;   150
It moved and moved, and took at last
A certain shape, I wist.

A speck, a mist, a shape, I wist!
And still it neared and neared:
As if it dodged a water-sprite,   155
It plunged and tacked and veered.

At its nearer approach; it seemeth him to be a ship; and at a dear ransom he freeth his speech from the bonds of thirst.

With throats unslaked, with black lips
    baked,
We could nor laugh nor wail;
Through utter drought all dumb we
    stood!
I bit my arm, I sucked the blood,   160
And cried, A sail! a sail!

With throats unslaked, with black lips
    baked,
Agape they heard me call:

A flash of joy;

Gramercy! they for joy did grin,
And all at once their breath drew in,   165
As they were drinking all.

And horror follows. For can it be a ship that comes onward without wind or tide?

See! see! (I cried) she tacks no more!
Hither to work us weal;
Without a breeze, without a tide,
She steadies with upright keel!   170

The western wave was all a-flame.
The day was well nigh done!
Almost upon the western wave
Rested the broad bright Sun;

When that strange shape drove sud-
   denly   175
Betwixt us and the Sun.

*It seemeth him
but the skeleton
of a ship.*

And straight the Sun was flecked with
   bars,
(Heaven's Mother send us grace!)
As if through a dungeon-grate he peered
With broad and burning face.   180

Alas! (thought I, and my heart beat loud)

*And its ribs are
seen as bars on
the face of the
setting Sun.*

How fast she nears and nears!
Are those *her* sails that glance in the Sun,
Like restless gossameres?

*The Spectre-
Woman and her
Deathmate, and
no other on
board the skele-
ton ship.
Like vessel, like
crew!*

Are those *her* ribs through which the
   Sun   185
Did peer, as through a grate?
And is that Woman all her crew?
Is that a DEATH? and are there two?
Is DEATH that woman's mate?

Her lips were red, *her* looks were
   free,   190
Her locks were yellow as gold:
Her skin was as white as leprosy,
The Night-mare LIFE-IN-DEATH was she,
Who thicks man's blood with cold.

*Death and Life-
in-Death have
diced for the
ship's crew, and
she (the latter)
winneth the an-
cient Mariner.*

The naked hulk alongside came,   195
And the twain were casting dice;
'The game is done! I've won! I've won!'
Quoth she, and whistles thrice.

No twilight within the courts of the Sun.

The Sun's rim dips; the stars rush out:
At one stride comes the dark;   200
With far-heard whisper, o'er the sea,
Off shot the spectre-bark.

At the rising of the Moon,

We listened and looked sideways up!
Fear at my heart, as at a cup,
My life-blood seemed to sip!   205
The stars were dim, and thick the night,
The steersman's face by his lamp gleamed
        white;

From the sails the dew did drip—
Till clomb above the eastern bar
The hornéd Moon, with one bright
        star   210
Within the nether tip.

One after another,

One after one, by the star-dogged Moon,
Too quick for groan or sigh,
Each turned his face with ghastly pang,
And cursed me with his eye.   215

His shipmates drop down dead.

Four times fifty living men,
(And I heard nor sigh nor groan)
With heavy thump, a lifeless lump,
They dropped down one by one.

But Life-in-Death begins her work on the ancient Mariner.

The souls did from their bodies
        fly,—   220
They fled to bliss or woe!
And every soul, it passed me by,
Like the whizz of my cross-bow!"

PART IV

The Wedding-Guest feareth that a Spirit is talking to him;

"I fear thee, ancient Mariner!
I fear thy skinny hand!   225
And thou art long, and lank, and brown,
As is the ribbed sea-sand.[1]

I fear thee and thy glittering eye,
And thy skinny hand, so brown."—

But the ancient Mariner assureth him of his bodily life, and proceedeth to relate his horrible penance.

"Fear not, fear not, thou Wedding-
    Guest!   230
This body dropt not down.

Alone, alone, all, all alone,
Alone on a wide wide sea!
And never a saint took pity on
My soul in agony.   235

He despiseth the creatures of the calm,

The many men, so beautiful!
And they all dead did lie:
And a thousand thousand slimy things
Lived on; and so did I.

And envieth that they should live, and so many lie dead.

I looked upon the rotting sea,   240
And drew my eyes away;
I looked upon the rotting deck,
And there the dead men lay.

I looked to heaven, and tried to pray;
But or ever a prayer had gusht,   245
A wicked whisper came, and made
My heart as dry as dust.

[1] For the last two lines of this stanza, I am indebted to Mr. Wordsworth. It was on a delightful walk from Nether Stowey to Dulverton, with him and his sister, in the Autumn of 1797, that this Poem was planned, and in part composed. —S. T. C.

I closed my lids, and kept them close,
And the balls like pulses beat;
For the sky and the sea, and the sea and
    the sky   250
Lay like a load on my weary eye,
And the dead were at my feet.

But the curse liveth for him in the eye of the dead men.

The cold sweat melted from their limbs,
Nor rot nor reek did they:
The look with which they looked on
    me   255
Had never passed away.

An orphan's curse would drag to hell
A spirit from on high;
But oh! more horrible than that
Is the curse in a dead man's eye!   260
Seven days, seven nights, I saw that curse,
And yet I could not die.

In his loneliness and fixedness he yearneth towards the journeying Moon, and the stars that still sojourn, yet still move onward; and everywhere the blue sky belongs to them, and is their appointed rest, and their native country and their own natural homes, which they enter unannounced, as lords that are certainly expected and yet there is a silent joy at their arrival.

The moving Moon went up the sky,
And no where did abide:
Softly she was going 'up,   265
And a star or two beside—

Her beams bemocked the sultry main,
Like April hoar-frost spread;
But where the ship's huge shadow lay,
The charméd water burnt alway   270
A still and awful red.

By the light of the Moon he beholdeth God's

Beyond the shadow of the ship,
I watched the water-snakes:

creatures of the
great calm.

They moved in tracks of shining white,
And when they reared, the elfish
    light   275
Fell off in hoary flakes.

Within the shadow of the ship
I watched their rich attire:
Blue, glossy green, and velvet black,
They coiled and swam; and every
    track   280
Was a flash of golden fire.

Their beauty
and their happi-
ness.

O happy living things! no tongue
Their beauty might declare:
A spring of love gushed from my heart,

He blesseth them
in his heart.

And I blessed them unaware: 285
Sure my kind saint took pity on me,
And I blessed them unaware.

The spell begins
to break.

The self-same moment I could pray;
And from my neck so free
The Albatross fell off, and sank   290
Like lead into the sea.

PART V

Oh sleep! it is a gentle thing,
Beloved from pole to pole!
To Mary Queen the praise be given!
She sent the gentle sleep from
    Heaven,   295
That slid into my soul.

By grace of the
holy Mother, the
ancient Mariner

The silly buckets on the deck,
That had so long remained,

is refreshed with rain.

I dreamt that they were filled with dew;
And when I awoke, it rained.   300

My lips were wet, my throat was cold,
My garments all were dank;
Sure I had drunken in my dreams,
And still my body drank.

I moved, and could not feel my
          limbs: 305
I was so light—almost
I thought that I had died in sleep,
And was a blessèd ghost.

He heareth sounds and seeth strange sights and commotions in the sky and the element.

And soon I heard a roaring wind:
It did not come anear;   310
But with its sound it shook the sails,
That were so thin and sere.

The upper air burst into life!
And a hundred fire-flags sheen,
To and fro they were hurried about!   315
And to and fro, and in and out,
The wan stars danced between.

And the coming wind did roar more loud,
And the sails did sigh like sedge;
And the rain poured down from one black
          cloud;   320
The Moon was at its edge.

The thick black cloud was cleft, and still
The Moon was at its side:
Like waters shot from some high crag,
The lightning fell with never a jag, 325
A river steep and wide.

The bodies of the ship's crew are inspirited, and the ship moves on;

The loud wind never reached the ship,
Yet now the ship moved on!
Beneath the lightning and the Moon
The dead men gave a groan.   330

They groaned, they stirred, they all up-
    rose,
Nor spake, nor moved their eyes;
It had been strange, even in a dream,
To have seen those dead men rise.

The helmsman steered, the ship moved
    on;   335
Yet never a breeze up-blew;
The mariners all 'gan work the ropes,
Where they were wont to do;
They raised their limbs like lifeless tools—
We were a ghastly crew.   340

The body of my brother's son
Stood by me, knee to knee:
The body and I pulled at one rope,
But he said nought to me."

"I fear thee, ancient Mariner!"   345
"Be calm, thou Wedding-Guest!
'Twas not those souls that fled in pain,
Which to their corses came again,
But a troop of spirits blest:

But not by the souls of the men, nor by dæmons of earth or middle air, but by a blessed troop of angelic spirits, sent down by the invocation of the guardian saint.

For when it dawned—they dropped their
    arms,   350
And clustered round the mast;

Sweet sounds rose slowly through their
   mouths,
And from their bodies passed.

Around, around, flew each sweet sound,
Then darted to the Sun;   355
Slowly the sounds came back again,
Now mixed, now one by one.

Sometimes a-dropping from the sky
I heard the sky-lark sing;
Sometimes all little birds that are,   360
How they seemed to fill the sea and air
With their sweet jargoning!

And now 'twas like all instruments,
Now like a lonely flute;
And now it is an angel's song,   365
That makes the heavens be mute.

It ceased; yet still the sails made on
A pleasant noise till noon,
A noise like of a hidden brook
In the leafy month of June,   370
That to the sleeping woods all night
Singeth a quiet tune.

Till noon we quietly sailed on,
Yet never a breeze did breathe:
Slowly and smoothly went the ship,   375
Moved onward from beneath.

The lonesome Spirit from the south-pole carries on the ship

Under the keel nine fathom deep,
From the land of mist and snow,
The spirit slid: and it was he

*as far as the
Line, in obedi-
ence to the an-
gelic troop, but
still requireth
vengeance.*

That made the ship to go.   380
The sails at noon left off their tune,
And the ship stood still also.

The Sun, right up above the mast,
Had fixed her to the ocean:
But in a minute she 'gan stir,   385
With a short uneasy motion—
Backwards and forwards half her length
With a short uneasy motion.

Then like a pawing horse let go,
She made a sudden bound: 390
It flung the blood into my head,
And I fell down in a swound.

*The Polar
Spirit's fellow-
dæmons, the in-
visible inhabit-
ants of the ele-
ment, take part
in his wrong;
and two of them
relate, one to the
other, that pen-
ance long and
heavy for the
ancient Mariner
hath been ac-
corded to the
Polar Spirit, who
returneth south-
ward.*

How long in that same fit I lay,
I have not to declare;
But ere my living life returned,   395
I heard and in my soul discerned
Two voices in the air.

'Is it he?' quoth one, 'Is this the man?
By him who died on cross,
With his cruel bow he laid full low   400
The harmless Albatross.

The spirit who bideth by himself
In the land of mist and snow,
He loved the bird that loved the man
Who shot him with his bow.'   405

The other was a softer voice,
As soft as honey-dew:
Quoth he, 'The man hath penance done,
And penance more will do.'

PART VI

FIRST VOICE

'But tell me, tell me! speak again,   410
Thy soft response renewing—
What makes that ship drive on so fast?
What is the ocean doing?'

SECOND VOICE

'Still as a slave before his lord,
The ocean hath no blast;   415
His great bright eye most silently
Up to the Moon is cast—

If he may know which way to go;
For she guides him smooth or grim.
See, brother, see! how graciously   420
She looketh down on him.'

FIRST VOICE

The Mariner hath been cast into a trance; for the angelic power causeth the vessel to drive northward faster than human life could endure.

'But why drives on that ship so fast,
Without or wave or wind?'

SECOND VOICE

'The air is cut away before,
And closes from behind.   425

Fly, brother, fly! more high, more high!
Or we shall be belated:

For slow and slow that ship will go,
When the Mariner's trance is abated.'

*The supernatural
motion is re-
tarded; the
Mariner awakes,
and his penance
begins anew.*

I woke, and we were sailing on   430
As in a gentle weather:
'Twas night, calm night, the moon was
      high;
The dead men stood together.

All stood togther on the deck,
For a charnel-dungeon fitter: 435
All fixed on me their stony eyes,
That in the Moon did glitter.

The pang, the curse, with which they
      died,
Had never passed away:
I could not draw my eyes from
      theirs,   440
Nor turn them up to pray.

*The curse is
finally expiated.*

And now this spell was snapt: once more
I viewed the ocean green,
And looked far forth, yet little saw
Of·what had else been seen—   445

Like one, that on a lonesome road
Doth walk in fear and dread,
And having once turned round walks on,
And turns no more his head;
Because he knows, a frightful fiend   450
Doth close behind him tread.

But soon there breathed a wind on me,
Nor sound nor motion made:

Its path was not upon the sea,
In ripple or in shade.   455

It raised my hair, it fanned my cheek
Like a meadow-gale of spring—
It mingled strangely with my fears,
Yet it felt like a welcoming.

Swiftly, swiftly flew the ship,   460
Yet she sailed softly too:
Sweetly, sweetly blew the breeze—
On me alone it blew.

*And the ancient
Mariner behold-
eth his native
country.* Oh! dream of joy! is this indeed
The light-house top I see?   465
Is this the hill? is this the kirk?
Is this mine own countree?

We drifted o'er the harbour-bar,
And I with sobs did pray—
O let me be awake, my God!   470
Or let me sleep alway.

The harbour-bay was clear as glass,
So smoothly it was strewn!
And on the bay the moonlight lay,
And the shadow of the Moon.   475

The rock shone bright, the kirk no less,
That stands above the rock:
The moonlight steeped in silentness
The steady weathercock.

And the bay was white with silent
    light,   480

Till rising from the same,
*The angelic
spirits leave the
dead bodies,*
Full many shapes, that shadows were,
In crimson colours came.

A little distance from the prow
*And appear in
their own forms
of light.*
Those crimson shadows were: 485
I turned my eyes upon the deck—
Oh, Christ! what saw I there!

Each corse lay flat, lifeless and flat,
And, by the holy rood!
A man all light, a seraph-man,   490
On every corse there stood.

This seraph-band, each waved his hand:
It was a heavenly sight!
They stood as signals to the land,
Each one a lovely light;   495

This seraph-band, each waved his hand,
No voice did they impart—
No voice; but oh! the silence sank
Like music on my heart.

But soon I heard the dash of oars,   500
I heard the Pilot's cheer;
My head was turned perforce away
And I saw a boat appear.

The Pilot and the Pilot's boy,
I heard them coming fast: 505
Dear Lord in Heaven! it was a joy
The dead men could not blast.

I saw a third—I heard his voice:
It is the Hermit good!
He singeth loud his godly hymns   510
That he makes in the wood.
He'll shrieve my soul, he'll wash away
The Albatross's blood.

PART VII

The Hermit of the Wood,

This Hermit good lives in that wood
Which slopes down to the sea.   515
How loudly his sweet voice he rears!
He loves to talk with marineres
That come from a far countree.

He kneels at morn, and noon, and eve—
He hath a cushion plump: 520
It is the moss that wholly hides
The rotted old oak-stump.

The skiff-boat neared: I heard them talk,
'Why, this is strange, I trow!
Where are those lights so many and
    fair,   525
That signal made but now?'

Approacheth the ship with wonder.

'Strange, by my faith!' the Hermit said—
'And they answered not our cheer!
The planks looked warped! and see those
    sails,
How thin they are and sere!   530
I never saw aught like to them,
Unless perchance it were

Brown skeletons of leaves that lag
My forest-brook along;
When the ivy-tod is heavy with
    snow,   535
And the owlet whoops to the wolf below,
That eats the she-wolf's young.'

'Dear Lord! it hath a fiendish look—
(The Pilot made reply)
I am a-feared'—'Push on, push on!'   540
Said the Hermit cheerily.

The boat came closer to the ship,
But I nor spake nor stirred;
The boat came close beneath the ship,
And straight a sound was heard.   545

*The ship sud-
denly sinketh.*

Under the water it rumbled on,
Still louder and more dread:
It reached the ship, it split the bay;
The ship went down like lead.

*The ancient
Mariner is saved
in the Pilot's
boat.*

Stunned by that loud and dreadful
    sound,   550
Which sky and ocean smote,
Like one that hath been seven days
    drowned
My body lay afloat;
But swift as dreams, myself I found
Within the Pilot's boat: 555

Upon the whirl, where sank the ship,
The boat spun round and round;
And all was still, save that the hill
Was telling of the sound.

I moved my lips—the Pilot shrieked 560
And fell down in a fit;
The holy Hermit raised his eyes,
And prayed where he did sit.

I took the oars: the Pilot's boy,
Who now doth crazy go,   565
Laughed loud and long, and all the while
His eyes went to and fro.
'Ha! ha!' quoth he, 'full plain I see,
The Devil knows how to row.'

And now, all in my own countree, 570
I stood on the firm land!
The Hermit stepped forth from the boat,
And scarcely he could stand.

The ancient Mariner earnestly entreateth the Hermit to shrieve him; and the penance of life falls on him.

'O shrieve me, shrieve me, holy man!'
The Hermit crossed his brow.   575
'Say quick,' quoth he, 'I bid thee say—
What manner of man art thou?'

Forthwith this frame of mine was
    wrenched
With a woful agony,
Which forced me to begin my tale; 580
And then it left me free.

And ever and anon throughout his future life an agony constraineth him to travel from land to land;

Since then, at an uncertain hour,
That agony returns:
And till my ghastly tale is told,
This heart within me burns.   585

I pass, like night, from land to land;
I have strange power of speech;

That moment that his face I see,
I know the man that must hear me:
To him my tale I teach.   590

What loud uproar bursts from that door!
The wedding-guests are there:
But in the garden-bower the bride
And bride-maids singing are:
And hark the little vesper bell,   595
Which biddeth me to prayer!

O Wedding-Guest! this soul hath been
Alone on a wide wide sea:
So lonely 'twas, that God himself
Scarce seeméd there to be.   600

O sweeter than the marriage-feast,
'Tis sweeter far to me,
To walk together to the kirk
With a goodly company!—

To walk together to the kirk,   605
And all together pray,
While each to his great Father bends,
Old men, and babes, and loving friends
And youths and maidens gay!

And to teach, by his own example, love and reverence to all things that God made and loveth.

Farewell, farewell! but this I tell   610
To thee, thou Wedding-Guest!
He prayeth well, who loveth well
Both man and bird and beast.

He prayeth best, who loveth best
All things both great and small;   615

For the dear God who loveth us,
He made and loveth all."

The Mariner, whose eye is bright,
Whose beard with age is hoar,
Is gone: and now the Wedding-
    Guest   620
Turned from the bridegroom's door.

He went like one that hath been stunned,
And is of sense forlorn:
A sadder and a wiser man,
He rose the morrow morn.   625
                                    1797–1798

Christabel

PREFACE

*The first part of the following poem was written in the year
1797, at Stowey, in the county of Somerset. The second part,
after my return from Germany, in the year 1800, at Keswick,
Cumberland. It is probable that if the poem had been fin-
ished at either of the former periods, or if even the first and
second part had been published in the year 1800, the impres-
sion of its originality would have been much greater than
I dare at present expect. But for this I have only my own
indolence to blame. The dates are mentioned for the exclu-
sive purpose of precluding charges of plagiarism or servile
imitation from myself. For there is amongst us a set of critics,
who seem to hold, that every possible thought and image is
traditional; who have no notion that there are such things as
fountains in the world, small as well as great; and who would
therefore charitably derive every rill they behold flowing,
from a perforation made in some other man's tank. I am con-*

fident, however, that as far as the present poem is concerned, the celebrated poets whose writings I might be suspected of having imitated, either in particular passages, or in the tone and the spirit of the whole, would be among the first to vindicate me from the charge, and, on any striking coincidence, would permit me to address them in this doggerel version of two monkish Latin hexameters.

> 'Tis mine and it is likewise yours;
> But an if this will not do;
> Let it be mine, good friend! for *I*
> Am the poorer of the two.

I have only to add that the metre of Christabel is not, properly speaking, irregular, though it may seem so from its being founded on a new principle: namely, that of counting in each line the accents, not the syllables. Though the latter may vary from seven to twelve, yet in each line the accents will be found to be only four. Nevertheless, this occasional variation in number of syllables is not introduced wantonly, or for the mere ends of convenience, but in correspondence with some transition in the nature of the imagery or passion.

PART I

'Tis the middle of night by the castle clock,
And the owls have awakened the crowing cock;
Tu—whit!——Tu—whoo!
And hark, again! the crowing cock,
How drowsily it crew.   5
Sir Leoline, the Baron rich,
Hath a toothless mastiff bitch;
From her kennel beneath the rock
She maketh answer to the clock,
Four for the quarters, and twelve for the hour;   10
Ever and aye, by shine and shower,
Sixteen short howls, not over loud;
Some say, she sees my lady's shroud.

Is the night chilly and dark?
The night is chilly, but not dark.   15
The thin gray cloud is spread on high,
It covers but not hides the sky.
The moon is behind, and at the full;
And yet she looks both small and dull.
The night is chill, the cloud is gray: 20
'Tis a month before the month of May,
And the Spring comes slowly up this way.

The lovely lady, Christabel,
Whom her father loves so well,
What makes her in the wood so late,   25
A furlong from the castle gate?
She had dreams all yesternight
Of her own betrothéd knight;
And she in the midnight wood will pray
For the weal of her lover that's far away.   30

She stole along, she nothing spoke,
The sighs she heaved were soft and low,
And naught was green upon the oak
But moss and rarest misletoe:
She kneels beneath the huge oak tree,   35
And in silence prayeth she.

The lady sprang up suddenly,
The lovely lady, Christabel!
It moaned as near, as near can be,
But what it is she cannot tell.—   40
On the other side it seems to be,
Of the huge, broad-breasted, old oak tree.

The night is chill; the forest bare;
Is it the wind that moaneth bleak?

There is not wind enough in the air   45
To move away the ringlet curl
From the lovely lady's cheek—
There is not wind enough to twirl
The one red leaf, the last of its clan,
That dances as often as dance it can,   50
Hanging so light, and hanging so high,
On the topmost twig that looks up at the sky.

Hush, beating heart of Christabel!
Jesu, Maria, shield her well!
She folded her arms beneath her cloak,   55
And stole to the other side of the oak.
        What sees she there?

There she sees a damsel bright,
Drest in a silken robe of white,
That shadowy in the moonlight shone: 60
The neck that made that white robe wan,
Her stately neck, and arms were bare;
Her blue-veined feet unsandal'd were,
And wildly glittered here and there
The gems entangled in her hair.   65
I guess, 'twas frightful there to see
A lady so richly clad as she—
Beautiful exceedingly!

Mary mother, save me now!
(Said Christabel,) And who art thou?   70

The lady strange made answer meet,
And her voice was faint and sweet:—
Have pity on my sore distress,
I scarce can speak for weariness:
Stretch forth thy hand, and have no fear!   75

Said Christabel, How camest thou here?
And the lady, whose voice was faint and sweet,
Did thus pursue her answer meet:—

My sire is of a noble line,
And my name is Geraldine: 80
Five warriors seized me yestermorn,
Me, even me, a maid forlorn:
They choked my cries with force and fright,
And tied me on a palfrey white.
The palfrey was as fleet as wind,   85
And they rode furiously behind.
They spurred amain, their steeds were white:
And once we crossed the shade of night.
As sure as Heaven shall rescue me,
I have no thought what men they be;   90
Nor do I know how long it is
(For I have lain entranced I wis)
Since one, the tallest of the five,
Took me from the palfrey's back,
A weary woman, scarce alive.   95
Some muttered words his comrades spoke:
He placed me underneath this oak;
He swore they would return with haste;
Whither they went I cannot tell—
I thought I heard, some minutes past,   100
Sounds as of a castle bell.
Stretch forth thy hand (thus ended she),
And help a wretched maid to flee.

Then Christabel stretched forth her hand,
And comforted fair Geraldine: 105
O well, bright dame! may you command
The service of Sir Leoline;
And gladly our stout chivalry

Will he send forth and friends withal
To guide and guard you safe and free   110
Home to your noble father's hall.

She rose: and forth with steps they passed
That strove to be, and were not, fast.
Her gracious stars the lady blest,
And thus spake on sweet Christabel: 115
All our household are at rest,
The hall as silent as the cell;
Sir Leoline is weak in health,
And may not well awakened be,
But we will move as if in stealth,   120
And I beseech your courtesy,
This night, to share your couch with me.

They crossed the moat, and Christabel
Took the key that fitted well;
A little door she opened straight,   125
All in the middle of the gate;
The gate that was ironed within and without,
Where an army in battle array had marched out.
The lady sank, belike through pain,
And Christabel with might and main   130
Lifted her up, a weary weight,
Over the threshold of the gate:
Then the lady rose again,
And moved, as she were not in pain.

So free from danger, free from fear,   135
They crossed the court: right glad they were.
And Christabel devoutly cried
To the lady by her side,
Praise we the Virgin all divine
Who hath rescued thee from thy distress!   140

Alas, alas! said Geraldine,
I cannot speak for weariness.
So free from danger, free from fear,
They crossed the court: right glad they were.

Outside her kennel, the mastiff old   145
Lay fast asleep, in moonshine cold.
The mastiff old did not awake,
Yet she an angry moan did make!
And what can ail the mastiff bitch?
Never till now she uttered yell   150
Beneath the eye of Christabel.
Perhaps it is the owlet's scritch:
For what can ail the mastiff bitch?

They passed the hall, that echoes still,
Pass as lightly as you will!   155
The brands were flat, the brands were dying,
Amid their own white ashes lying;
But when the lady passed, there came
A tongue of light, a fit of flame;
And Christabel saw the lady's eye,   160
And nothing else saw she thereby,
Save the boss of the shield of Sir Leoline tall,
Which hung in a murky old niche in the wall.
O softly tread, said Christabel,
My father seldom sleepeth well.   165

Sweet Christabel her feet doth bare,
And jealous of the listening air
They steal their way from stair to stair,
Now in glimmer, and now in gloom,
And now they pass the Baron's room,   170
As still as death, with stifled breath!
And now have reached her chamber door;

And now doth Geraldine press down
The rushes of the chamber floor.

The moon shines dim in the open air,   175
And not a moonbeam enters here.
But they without its light can see
The chamber carved so curiously,
Carved with figures strange and sweet,

All made out of the carver's brain,   180
For a lady's chamber meet:
The lamp with twofold silver chain
Is fastened to an angel's feet.

The silver lamp burns dead and dim;
But Christabel the lamp will trim.   185
She trimmed the lamp, and made it bright,
And left it swinging to and fro,
While Geraldine, in wretched plight,
Sank down upon the floor below.

O weary lady, Geraldine,   190
I pray you, drink this cordial wine!
It is a wine of virtuous powers;
My mother made it of wild flowers.

And will your mother pity me,
Who am a maiden most forlorn?   195
Christabel answered—Woe is me!
She died the hour that I was born.
I have heard the grey-haired friar tell
How on her death-bed she did say,
That she should hear the castle-bell   200
Strike twelve upon my wedding-day.
O mother dear! that thou wert here!

I would, said Geraldine, she were!
But soon with altered voice, said she—
"Off, wandering mother! Peak and pine!   205
I have power to bid thee flee."
Alas! what ails poor Geraldine?
Why stares she with unsettled eye?
Can she the bodiless dead espy?
And why with hollow voice cries she,   210
"Off, woman, off! this hour is mine—
Though thou her guardian spirit be,
Off, woman, off! 'tis given to me."

Then Christabel knelt by the lady's side,
And raised to heaven her eyes so blue—   215
Alas! said she, this ghastly ride—
Dear lady! it hath wildered you!
The lady wiped her moist cold brow,
And faintly said, " 'tis over now!"

Again the wild-flower wine she drank: 220
Her fair large eyes 'gan glitter bright,
And from the floor whereon she sank,
The lofty lady stood upright:
She was most beautiful to see,
Like a lady of a far countrée.   225

And thus the lofty lady spake—
"All they who live in the upper sky,
Do love you, holy Christabel!
And you love them, and for their sake
And for the good which me befel,   230
Even I in my degree will try,
Fair maiden, to requite you well.
But now unrobe yourself; for I
Must pray, ere yet in bed I lie."

Quoth Christabel, So let it be!   235
And as the lady bade, did she.
Her gentle limbs did she undress,
And lay down in her loveliness.

But through her brain of weal and woe
So many thoughts moved to and fro,   240
That vain it were her lids to close;
So half-way from the bed she rose,
And on her elbow did recline
To look at the lady Geraldine.

Beneath the lamp the lady bowed,   245
And slowly rolled her eyes around;
Then drawing in her breath aloud,
Like one that shuddered, she unbound
The cincture from beneath her breast:
Her silken robe, and inner vest,   250
Dropt to her feet, and full in view,
Behold! her bosom and half her side——
A sight to dream of, not to tell!
O shield her! shield sweet Christabel!

Yet Geraldine nor speaks nor stirs;   255
Ah! what a stricken look was hers!
Deep from within she seems half-way
To lift some weight with sick assay,
And eyes the maid and seeks delay;
Then suddenly, as one defied,   260
Collects herself in scorn and pride,
And lay down by the Maiden's side!——
And in her arms the maid she took,
            Ah wel-a-day!
And with low voice and doleful look   265
These words did say:

"In the touch of this bosom there worketh a spell,
Which is lord of thy utterance, Christabel!
Thou knowest to-night, and wilt know to-morrow,
This mark of my shame, this seal of my sorrow;   270
　　But vainly thou warrest,
　　　For this is alone in
　　Thy power to declare,
　　　That in the dim forest
　　Thou heard'st a low moaning,   275
And found'st a bright lady, surpassingly fair;
And didst bring her home with thee in love and in
　　　charity,
To shield her and shelter her from the damp air."

THE CONCLUSION TO PART I

It was a lovely sight to see
The lady Christabel, when she   280
Was praying at the old oak tree.
　　Amid the jaggéd shadows
　　Of mossy leafless boughs,
　　Kneeling in the moonlight,
　　To make her gentle vows;   285
Her slender palms together prest,
Heaving sometimes on her breast;
Her face resigned to bliss or bale—
Her face, oh call it fair not pale,
And both blue eyes more bright than clear,   290
Each about to have a tear.

With open eyes (ah woe is me!)
Asleep, and dreaming fearfully,
Fearfully dreaming, yet, I wis,
Dreaming that alone, which is—   295
O sorrow and shame! Can this be she,

The lady, who knelt at the old oak tree?
And lo! the worker of these harms,
That holds the maiden in her arms,
Seems to slumber still and mild,   300
As a mother with her child.

A star hath set, a star hath risen,
O Geraldine! since arms of thine
Have been the lovely lady's prison.
O Geraldine! one hour was thine—   305
Thou'st had thy will! By tairn and rill,
The night-birds all that hour were still.
But now they are jubilant anew,
From cliff and tower, tu—whoo! tu—whoo!
Tu—whoo! tu—whoo! from wood and fell!   310

And see! the lady Christabel
Gathers herself from out her trance;
Her limbs relax, her countenance
Grows sad and soft; the smooth thin lids
Close o'er her eyes; and tears she sheds—   315
Large tears that leave the lashes bright!
And oft the while she seems to smile
As infants at a sudden light!

Yea, she doth smile, and she doth weep,
Like a youthful hermitess,   320
Beauteous in a wilderness,
Who, praying always, prays in sleep.
And, if she move unquietly,
Perchance, 'tis but the blood so free
Comes back and tingles in her feet.   325
No doubt, she hath a vision sweet.
What if her guardian spirit 'twere,
What if she knew her mother near?

But this she knows, in joys and woes,
That saints will aid if men will call: 330
For the blue sky bends over all!

1797

PART II

Each matin bell, the Baron saith,
Knells us back to a world of death.
These words Sir Leoline first said,
When he rose and found his lady dead: 335
These words Sir Leoline will say
Many a morn to his dying day!

And hence the custom and law began
That still at dawn the sacristan,
Who duly pulls the heavy bell,   340
Five and forty beads must tell
Between each stroke—a warning knell,
Which not a soul can choose but hear
From Bratha Head to Wyndermere.

Saith Bracy the bard, So let it knell!   345
And let the drowsy sacristan
Still count as slowly as he can!
There is no lack of such, I ween,
As well fill up the space between.
In Langdale Pike and Witch's Lair,   350
And Dungeon-ghyll so foully rent,
With ropes of rock and bells of air
Three sinful sextons' ghosts are pent,
Who all give back, one after t'other,
The death-note to their living brother;   355
And oft too, by the knell offended,
Just as their one! two! three! is ended,

The devil mocks the doleful tale
With a merry peal from Borodale.

The air is still! through mist and cloud   360
That merry peal comes ringing loud;
And Geraldine shakes off her dread,
And rises lightly from the bed;
Puts on her silken vestments white,
And tricks her hair in lovely plight,   365
And nothing doubting of her spell
Awakens the lady Christabel.
"Sleep you, sweet lady Christabel?
I trust that you have rested well."

And Christabel awoke and spied   370
The same who lay down by her side—
O rather say, the same whom she
Raised up beneath the old oak tree!
Nay, fairer yet! and yet more fair!
For she belike hath drunken deep   375
Of all the blessedness of sleep!
And while she spake, her looks, her air
Such gentle thankfulness declare,
That (so it seemed) her girded vests
Grew tight beneath her heaving breasts.   380
"Sure I have sinn'd!" said Christabel,
"Now heaven be praised if all be well!"
And in low faltering tones, yet sweet,
Did she the lofty lady greet
With such perplexity of mind   385
As dreams too lively leave behind.

So quickly she rose, and quickly arrayed
Her maiden limbs, and having prayed
That He, who on the cross did groan,

Might wash away her sins unknown, 390
She forthwith led fair Geraldine
To meet her sire, Sir Leoline.

The lovely maid and the lady tall
Are pacing both into the hall,
And pacing on through page and groom, 395
Enter the Baron's presence-room.

The Baron rose, and while he prest
His gentle daughter to his breast,
With cheerful wonder in his eyes
The lady Geraldine espies, 400
And gave such welcome to the same,
As might beseem so bright a dame!

But when he heard the lady's tale,
And when she told her father's name,
Why waxed Sir Leoline so pale, 405
Murmuring o'er the name again,
Lord Roland de Vaux of Tryermaine?

Alas! they had been friends in youth;
But whispering tongues can poison truth;
And constancy lives in realms above; 410
And life is thorny; and youth is vain;
And to be wroth with one we love
Doth work like madness in the brain.
And thus it chanced, as I divine,
With Roland and Sir Leoline. 415
Each spake words of high disdain
And insult to his heart's best brother:
They parted—ne'er to meet again!
But never either found another
To free the hollow heart from paining— 420
They stood aloof, the scars remaining,

Like cliffs which had been rent asunder;
A dreary sea now flows between;—
But neither heat, nor frost, nor thunder,
Shall wholly do away, I ween,   425
The marks of that which once hath been.

Sir Leoline, a moment's space,
Stood gazing on the damsel's face:
And the youthful Lord of Tryermaine
Came back upon his heart again.   430

O then the Baron forgot his age,
His noble heart swelled high with rage;
He swore by the wounds in Jesu's side
He would proclaim it far and wide,
With trump and solemn heraldry,   435
That they, who thus had wronged the dame,
Were base as spotted infamy!
"And if they dare deny the same,
My herald shall appoint a week,
And let the recreant traitors seek   440
My tourney court—that there and then
I may dislodge their reptile souls
From the bodies and forms of men!"
He spake: his eye in lightning rolls!
For the lady was ruthlessly seized; and he kenned   445
In the beautiful lady the child of his friend!

And now the tears were on his face,
And fondly in his arms he took
Fair Geraldine, who met the embrace,
Prolonging it with joyous look.   450
Which when she viewed, a vision fell
Upon the soul of Christabel,
The vision of fear, the touch and pain!

She shrunk and shuddered, and saw again—
(Ah, woe is me! Was it for thee,   455
Thou gentle maid! such sights to see?)

Again she saw that bosom old,
Again she felt that bosom cold,
And drew in her breath with a hissing sound:
Whereat the Knight turned wildly round,   460
And nothing saw, but his own sweet maid
With eyes upraised, as one that prayed.

The touch, the sight, had passed away,
And in its stead that vision blest,
Which comforted her after-rest   465
While in the lady's arms she lay,
Had put a rapture in her breast,
And on her lips and o'er her eyes
Spread smiles like light!
                    With new surprise,
"What ails then my beloved child?"   470
The Baron said—His daughter mild
Made answer, "All will yet be well!"
I ween, she had no power to tell
Aught else: so mighty was the spell.

Yet he, who saw this Geraldine,   475
Had deemed her sure a thing divine:
Such sorrow with such grace she blended,
As if she feared she had offended
Sweet Christabel, that gentle maid!
And with such lowly tones she prayed   480
She might be sent without delay
Home to her father's mansion.
                    "Nay!
Nay, by my soul!" said Leoline.
"Ho! Bracy the bard, the charge be thine!

Go thou, with music sweet and loud,   485
And take two steeds with trappings proud,
And take the youth whom thou lov'st best
To bear thy harp, and learn thy song,
And clothe you both in solemn vest,
And over the mountains haste along,   490
Lest wandering folk, that are abroad,
Detain you on the valley road.

"And when he has crossed the Irthing flood,
My merry bard! he hastes, he hastes
Up Knorren Moor, through Halegarth Wood,   495
And reaches soon that castle good
Which stands and threatens Scotland's wastes.

"Bard Bracy! bard Bracy! your horses are fleet,
Ye must ride up the hall, your music so sweet,
More loud than your horses' echoing feet!   500
And loud and loud to Lord Roland call,
Thy daughter is safe in Langdale hall!
Thy beautiful daughter is safe and free—
Sir Leoline greets thee thus through me!
He bids thee come without delay   505
With all thy numerous array
And take thy lovely daughter home:
And he will meet thee on the way
With all his numerous array
White with their panting palfreys' foam: 510
And, by mine honour! I will say,
That I repent me of the day
When I spake words of fierce disdain
To Roland de Vaux of Tryermaine!—
—For since that evil hour hath flown,   515
Many a summer's sun hath shone;

Yet ne'er found I a friend again
Like Roland de Vaux of Tryermaine."

The lady fell, and clasped his knees,
Her face upraised, her eyes o'erflowing;   520
And Bracy replied, with faltering voice,
His gracious Hail on all bestowing!—
"Thy words, thou sire of Christabel,
Are sweeter than my harp can tell;
Yet might I gain a boon of thee,   525
This day my journey should not be,
So strange a dream hath come to me,
That I had vowed with music loud
To clear yon wood from thing unblest,
Warned by a vision in my rest!   530
For in my sleep I saw that dove,
That gentle bird, whom thou dost love,
And call'st by thy own daughter's name—
Sir Leoline! I saw the same
Fluttering, and uttering fearful moan,   535
Among the green herbs in the forest alone.
Which when I saw and when I heard,
I wonder'd what might ail the bird;
For nothing near it could I see,
Save the grass and green herbs underneath the old
            tree.   540

"And in my dream methought I went
To search out what might there be found;
And what the sweet bird's trouble meant,
That thus lay fluttering on the ground.
I went and peered, and could descry   545
No cause for her distressful cry;
But yet for her dear lady's sake
I stooped, methought, the dove to take,

When lo! I saw a bright green snake
Coiled around its wings and neck.   550
Green as the herbs on which it couched,
Close by the dove's its head it crouched;
And with the dove it heaves and stirs,
Swelling its neck as she swelled hers!
I woke; it was the midnight hour,   555
The clock was echoing in the tower;
But though my slumber was gone by,
This dream it would not pass away—
It seems to live upon my eye!
And thence I vowed this self-same day   560
With music strong and saintly song
To wander through the forest bare,
Lest aught unholy loiter there."

Thus Bracy said: the Baron, the while,
Half-listening heard him with a smile;   565
Then turned to Lady Geraldine,
His eyes made up of wonder and love;
And said in courtly accents fine,
"Sweet maid, Lord Roland's beauteous dove,
With arms more strong than harp or song,   570
Thy sire and I will crush the snake!"
He kissed her forehead as he spake,
And Geraldine in maiden wise
Casting down her large bright eyes,
With blushing cheek and courtesy fine   575
She turned her from Sir Leoline;
Softly gathering up her train,
That o'er her right arm fell again;
And folded her arms across her chest,
And couched her head upon her breast,   580
And looked askance at Christabel——
Jesu, Maria, shield her well!

A snake's small eye blinks dull and shy;
And the lady's eyes they shrunk in her head,
Each shrunk up to a serpent's eye,   585
And with somewhat of malice, and more of dread,
At Christabel she looked askance!—
One moment—and the sight was fled!
But Christabel in dizzy trance
Stumbling on the unsteady ground   590
Shuddered aloud, with a hissing sound;
And Geraldine again turned round,
And like a thing, that sought relief,
Full of wonder and full of grief,
She rolled her large bright eyes divine   595
Wildly on Sir Leoline.

The maid, alas! her thoughts are gone,
She nothing sees—no sight but one!
The maid, devoid of guile and sin,
I know not how, in fearful wise,   600
So deeply had she drunken in
That look, those shrunken serpent eyes,
That all her features were resigned
To this sole image in her mind:
And passively did imitate   605
That look of dull and treacherous hate!
And thus she stood, in dizzy trance,
Still picturing that look askance
With forced unconscious sympathy
Full before her father's view—   610
As far as such a look could be
In eyes so innocent and blue!

And when the trance was o'er, the maid
Paused awhile, and inly prayed:
Then falling at the Baron's feet,   615

"By my mother's soul do I entreat
That thou this woman send away!"
She said: and more she could not say:
For what she knew she could not tell,
O'er-mastered by the mighty spell.   620

Why is thy cheek so wan and wild,
Sir Leoline? Thy only child
Lies at thy feet, thy joy, thy pride,
So fair, so innocent, so mild;
The same, for whom thy lady died!   625
O by the pangs of her dear mother
Think thou no evil of thy child!
For her, and thee, and for no other,
She prayed the moment ere she died:
Prayed that the babe for whom she died,   630
Might prove her dear lord's joy and pride!
        That prayer her deadly pangs beguiled,
                Sir Leoline!
        And wouldst thou wrong thy only child,
                Her child and thine?   635

Within the Baron's heart and brain
If thoughts, like these, had any share,
They only swelled his rage and pain,
And did but work confusion there.
His heart was cleft with pain and rage,   640
His cheeks they quivered, his eyes were wild,
Dishonoured thus in his old age;
Dishonoured by his only child,
And all his hospitality
To the wronged daughter of his friend   645
By more than woman's jealousy
Brought thus to a disgraceful end—
He rolled his eye with stern regard

Upon the gentle minstrel bard,
And said in tones abrupt, austere—   650
"Why, Bracy! dost thou loiter here?
I bade thee hence!" The bard obeyed;
And turning from his own sweet maid,
The agéd knight, Sir Leoline,
Led forth the lady Geraldine!   655
                                                      1800

THE CONCLUSION TO PART II

A little child, a limber elf,
Singing, dancing to itself,
A fairy thing with red round cheeks,
That always finds, and never seeks,
Makes such a vision to the sight   660
As fills a father's eyes with light;
And pleasures flow in so thick and fast
Upon his heart, that he at last
Must needs express his love's excess
With words of unmeant bitterness.   665
Perhaps 'tis pretty to force together
Thoughts so all unlike each other;
To mutter and mock a broken charm,
To dally with wrong that does no harm.
Perhaps 'tis tender too and pretty   670
At each wild word to feel within
A sweet recoil of love and pity.
And what, if in a world of sin
(O sorrow and shame should this be true!)
Such giddiness of heart and brain   675
Comes seldom save from rage and pain,
So talks as it's most used to do.

                                                      1801

Frost at Midnight

The Frost performs its secret ministry,
Unhelped by any wind. The owlet's cry
Came loud—and hark, again! loud as before.
The inmates of my cottage, all at rest,
Have left me to that solitude, which suits   5
Abstruser musings: save that at my side
My cradled infant slumbers peacefully.
'Tis calm indeed! so calm, that it disturbs
And vexes meditation with its strange
And extreme silentness. Sea, hill, and wood,   10
This populous village! Sea, and hill, and wood,
With all the numberless goings-on of life,
Inaudible as dreams! the thin blue flame
Lies on my low-burnt fire, and quivers not;
Only that film, which fluttered on the grate,   15
Still flutters there, the sole unquiet thing.
Methinks, its motion in this hush of nature
Gives it dim sympathies with me who live,
Making it a companionable form,
Whose puny flaps and freaks the idling Spirit   20
By its own moods interprets, every where
Echo or mirror seeking of itself,
And makes a toy of Thought.

                              But O! how oft,
How oft, at school, with most believing mind,
Presageful, have I gazed upon the bars,   25
To watch that fluttering *stranger!* and as oft
With unclosed lids, already had I dreamt
Of my sweet birth-place, and the old church-tower,

Whose bells, the poor man's only music, rang
From morn to evening, all the hot Fair-day,   30
So sweetly, that they stirred and haunted me
With a wild pleasure, falling on mine ear
Most like articulate sounds of things to come!
So gazed I, till the soothing things, I dreamt,
Lulled me to sleep, and sleep prolonged my dreams!   35
And so I brooded all the following morn,
Awed by the stern preceptor's face, mine eye
Fixed with mock study on my swimming book:
Save if the door half opened, and I snatched
A hasty glance, and still my heart leaped up,   40
For still I hoped to see the *stranger's* face,
Townsman, or aunt, or sister more beloved,
My play-mate when we both were clothed alike!

    Dear Babe, that sleepest cradled by my side,
Whose gentle breathings, heard in this deep calm,   45
Fill up the interspersèd vacancies
And momentary pauses of the thought!
My babe so beautiful! it thrills my heart
With tender gladness, thus to look at thee,
And think that thou shalt learn far other lore,   50
And in far other scenes! For I was reared
In the great city, pent 'mid cloisters dim,
And saw nought lovely but the sky and stars.
But *thou*, my babe! shalt wander like a breeze
By lakes and sandy shores, beneath the crags   55
Of ancient mountain, and beneath the clouds,
Which image in their bulk both lakes and shores
And mountain crags: so shalt thou see and hear
The lovely shapes and sounds intelligible
Of that eternal language, which thy God   60
Utters, who from eternity doth teach
Himself in all, and all things in himself.

Great universal Teacher! he shall mould
Thy spirit, and by giving make it ask.

Therefore all seasons shall be sweet to thee,   65
Whether the summer clothe the general earth
With greenness, or the redbreast sit and sing
Betwixt the tufts of snow on the bare branch
Of mossy apple-tree, while the nigh thatch
Smokes in the sun-thaw; whether the eave-drops fall   70
Heard only in the trances of the blast,
Or if the secret ministry of frost
Shall hang them up in silent icicles,
Quietly shining to the quiet Moon.

February, 1798

France: An Ode

ARGUMENT

"First Stanza. *An invocation to those objects in Nature the
contemplation of which had inspired the Poet with a devo-
tional love of Liberty. Second Stanza. The exultation of the
Poet at the commencement of the French Revolution, and
his unqualified abhorrence of the Alliance against the Repub-
lic. Third Stanza. The blasphemies and horrors during the
domination of the Terrorists regarded by the Poet as a tran-
sient storm, and as the natural consequence of the former
despotism and of the foul superstition of Popery. Reason,
indeed, began to suggest many apprehensions; yet still the
Poet struggled to retain the hope that France would make
conquests by no other means than by presenting to the obser-
vation of Europe a people more happy and better instructed
than under other forms of Government. Fourth Stanza.
Switzerland, and the Poet's recantation. Fifth Stanza. An
address to Liberty, in which the Poet expresses his convic-
tion that those feelings and that grand ideal of Freedom
which the mind attains by its contemplation of its individual*

nature, and of the sublime surrounding objects (see Stanza
the First) do not belong to men, as a society, nor can pos-
sibly be either gratified or realised, under any form of human
government; but belong to the individual man, so far as he is
pure, and inflamed with the love and adoration of God in
Nature."

I

Ye Clouds! that far above me float and pause,
   Whose pathless march no mortal may controul!
   Ye Ocean-Waves! that, wheresoe'er ye roll,
Yield homage only to eternal laws!
Ye Woods! that listen to the night-birds singing,   5
   Midway the smooth and perilous slope reclined,
Save when your own imperious branches swinging,
   Have made a solemn music of the wind!
Where, like a man beloved of God,
Through glooms, which never woodman trod,   10
     How oft, pursuing fancies holy,
My moonlight way o'er flowering weeds I wound,
     Inspired, beyond the guess of folly,
By each rude shape and wild unconquerable sound!
O ye loud Waves! and O ye Forests high!   15
   And O ye Clouds that far above me soared!
Thou rising Sun! thou blue rejoicing Sky!
   Yea, every thing that is and will be free!
   Bear witness for me, wheresoe'er ye be,
With what deep worship I have still adored   20
   The spirit of divinest Liberty.

II

When France in wrath her giant-limbs upreared,
   And with that oath, which smote air, earth, and sea,
   Stamped her strong foot and said she would be free,
Bear witness for me, how I hoped and feared!   25
With what a joy my lofty gratulation

Unawed I sang, amid a slavish band:
And when to whelm the disenchanted nation,
   Like fiends embattled by a wizard's wand,
     The Monarchs marched in evil day,   30
     And Britain joined the dire array;
   Though dear her shores and circling ocean,
Though many friendships, many youthful loves
   Had swoln the patriot emotion
And flung a magic light o'er all her hills and groves; 35
Yet still my voice, unaltered, sang defeat
   To all that braved the tyrant-quelling lance,
And shame too long delayed and vain retreat!
For ne'er, O Liberty! with partial aim
I dimmed thy light or damped thy holy flame;   40
   But blessed the paeans of delivered France,
And hung my head and wept at Britain's name.

III

"And what," I said, "though Blasphemy's loud scream
   With that sweet music of deliverance strove!
   Though all the fierce and drunken passions wove 45
A dance more wild than e'er was maniac's dream!
   Ye storms, that round the dawning East assembled,
The Sun was rising, though ye hid his light!"
   And when, to soothe my soul, that hoped and
      trembled,
The dissonance ceased, and all seemed calm and
      bright;   50
   When France her front deep-scarr'd and gory
   Concealed with clustering wreaths of glory;
     When, insupportably advancing,
   Her arm made mockery of the warrior's ramp;
     While timid looks of fury glancing,   55
   Domestic treason, crushed beneath her fatal stamp,
Writhed like a wounded dragon in his gore;

Then I reproached my fears that would not flee;
"And soon," I said, "shall Wisdom teach her lore
In the low huts of them that toil and groan!   60
And, conquering by her happiness alone,
    Shall France compel the nations to be free,
Till Love and Joy look round, and call the Earth their
    own."

IV

Forgive me, Freedom! O forgive those dreams!
    I hear thy voice, I hear thy loud lament,   65
    From bleak Helvetia's icy caverns sent—
I hear thy groans upon her blood-stained streams!
    Heroes, that for your peaceful country perished,
And ye that, fleeing, spot your mountain-snows
    With bleeding wounds; forgive me, that I cher-
        ished   70
One thought that ever blessed your cruel foes!
    To scatter rage, and traitorous guilt,
    Where Peace her jealous home had built;
        A patriot-race to disinherit
Of all that made their stormy wilds so dear;   75
    And with inexpiable spirit
To taint the bloodless freedom of the mountaineer—
O France, that mockest Heaven, adulterous, blind,
    And patriot only in pernicious toils!
Are these thy boasts, Champion of human kind?   80
    To mix with Kings in the low lust of sway,
Yell in the hunt, and share the murderous prey;
To insult the shrine of Liberty with spoils
    From freemen torn; to tempt and to betray?

V

    The Sensual and the Dark rebel in vain,   85
    Slaves by their own compulsion! In mad game

They burst their manacles and wear the name
 Of Freedom, graven on a heavier chain!
 O Liberty! with profitless endeavour
Have I pursued thee, many a weary hour;   90
 But thou nor swell'st the victor's strain, nor ever
Didst breathe thy soul in forms of human power.
 Alike from all, howe'er they praise thee,
 (Nor prayer, nor boastful name delays thee)
 Alike from Priestcraft's harpy minions,   95
 And factious Blasphemy's obscener slaves,
 Thou speedest on thy subtle pinions,
The guide of homeless winds, and playmate of the
  waves!
And there I felt thee!—on that sea-cliff's verge,
 Whose pines, scarce travelled by the breeze
  above,   100
Had made one murmur with the distant surge!
Yes; while I stood and gazed, my temples bare,
And shot my being through earth, sea, and air,
 Possessing all things with intensest love,
 O Liberty! my spirit felt thee there.   105

February, 1798

Lewti

OR THE CIRCASSIAN LOVE-CHAUNT

At midnight by the stream I roved,
To forget the form I loved.
Image of Lewti! from my mind
Depart; for Lewti is not kind.
The Moon was high, the moonlight gleam 5
 And the shadow of a star

Heaved upon Tamaha's stream;
　　But the rock shone brighter far,
The rock half sheltered from my view
By pendent boughs of tressy yew.—   10
So shines my Lewti's forehead fair,
Gleaming through her sable hair.
Image of Lewti! from my mind
Depart; for Lewti is not kind.

I saw a cloud of palest hue,   15
　　Onward to the moon it passed;
Still brighter and more bright it grew,
With floating colours not a few,
Till it reached the moon at last:
Then the cloud was wholly bright,   20
With a rich and amber light!
And so with many a hope I seek,
　　And with such joy I find my Lewti;
And even so my pale wan cheek
　　Drinks in as deep a flush of beauty!   25
Nay, treacherous image! leave my mind,
If Lewti never will be kind.

The little cloud—it floats away,
　　Away it goes; away so soon!
Alas! it has no power to stay: 30
Its hues are dim, its hues are grey—
　　Away it passes from the moon!
How mournfully it seems to fly,
　　Ever fading more and more,
To joyless regions of the sky—   35
　　And now 'tis whiter than before!
As white as my poor cheek will be,
　　When, Lewti! on my couch I lie,

A dying man for love of thee.
Nay, treacherous image! leave my mind—   40
And yet, thou didst not look unkind.

I saw a vapour in the sky,
Thin, and white, and very high;
I ne'er beheld so thin a cloud:
   Perhaps the breezes that can fly   45
   Now below and now above,
Have snatched aloft the lawny shroud
   Of Lady fair—that died for love.
For maids, as well as youths, have perished
From fruitless love too fondly cherished.   50
Nay, treacherous image! leave my mind—
For Lewti never will be kind.

Hush! my heedless feet from under
   Slip the crumbling banks for ever:
Like echoes to a distant thunder,   55
   They plunge into the gentle river.
The river-swans have heard my tread,
And startle from their reedy bed.
O beauteous birds! methinks ye measure
   Your movements to some heavenly tune!   60
O beauteous birds! 'tis such a pleasure
   To see you move beneath the moon,
I would it were your true delight
To sleep by day and wake all night.

I know the place where Lewti lies,   65
When silent night has closed her eyes:
   It is a breezy jasmine-bower,
The nightingale sings o'er her head:
   Voice of the Night! had I the power
That leafy labyrinth to thread,   70

And creep, like thee, with soundless tread,
I then might view her bosom white
Heaving lovely to my sight,
As these two swans together heave
On the gently-swelling wave.   75

Oh! that she saw me in a dream,
   And dreamt that I had died for care;
All pale and wasted I would seem,
   Yet fair withal, as spirits are!
I'd die indeed, if I might see   80
Her bosom heave, and heave for me!
Soothe, gentle image! soothe my mind!
To-morrow Lewti may be kind.

                                1798

Fears in Solitude

WRITTEN IN APRIL 1798, DURING THE
ALARM OF AN INVASION

A green and silent spot, amid the hills,
A small and silent dell! O'er stiller place
No singing sky-lark ever poised himself.
The hills are heathy, save that swelling slope,
Which hath a gay and gorgeous covering on,   5
All golden with the never-bloomless furze,
Which now blooms most profusely: but the dell,
Bathed by the mist, is fresh and delicate
As vernal corn-field, or the unripe flax,
When, through its half-transparent stalks, at eve, 10
The level sunshine glimmers with green light.
Oh! 'tis a quiet spirit-healing nook!
Which all, methinks, would love; but chiefly he,
The humble man, who, in his youthful years,

Knew just so much of folly, as had made   15
His early manhood more securely wise!
Here he might lie on fern or withered heath,
While from the singing lark (that sings unseen
The minstrelsy that solitude loves best),
And from the sun, and from the breezy air,   20
Sweet influences trembled o'er his frame;
And he, with many feelings, many thoughts,
Made up a meditative joy, and found
Religious meanings in the forms of Nature!
And so, his senses gradually wrapt   25
In a half sleep, he dreams of better worlds,
And dreaming hears thee still, O singing lark,
That singest like an angel in the clouds!

    My God! it is a melancholy thing
For such a man, who would full fain preserve   30
His soul in calmness, yet perforce must feel
For all his human brethren—O my God!
It weighs upon the heart, that he must think
What uproar and what strife may now be stirring
This way or that way o'er these silent hills—   35
Invasion, and the thunder and the shout,
And all the crash of onset; fear and rage,
And undetermined conflict—even now,
Even now, perchance, and in his native isle:
Carnage and groans beneath this blessed sun!   40
We have offended, Oh! my countrymen!
We have offended very grievously,
And been most tyrannous. From east to west
A groan of accusation pierces Heaven!
The wretched plead against us; multitudes   45
Countless and vehement, the sons of God,
Our brethren! Like a cloud that travels on,
Steamed up from Cairo's swamps of pestilence,

Even so, my countrymen! have we gone forth
And borne to distant tribes slavery and pangs,   50
And, deadlier far, our vices, whose deep taint
With slow perdition murders the whole man,
His body and his soul! Meanwhile, at home,
All individual dignity and power
Engulfed in Courts, Committees, Institutions,   55
Associations and Societies,
A vain, speech-mouthing, speech-reporting Guild,
One Benefit-Club for mutual flattery,
We have drunk up, demure as at a grace,
Pollutions from the brimming cup of wealth;   60
Contemptuous of all honourable rule,
Yet bartering freedom and the poor man's life
For gold, as at a market! The sweet words
Of Christian promise, words that even yet
Might stem destruction, were they wisely preached,   65
Are muttered o'er by men, whose tones proclaim
How flat and wearisome they feel their trade:
Rank scoffers some, but most too indolent
To deem them falsehoods or to know their truth.
Oh! blasphemous! the Book of Life is made   70
A superstitious instrument, on which
We gabble o'er the oaths we mean to break;
For all must swear—all and in every place,
College and wharf, council and justice-court;
All, all must swear, the briber and the bribed;   75
Merchant and lawyer, senator and priest,
The rich, the poor, the old man and the young;
All, all make up one scheme of perjury,
That faith doth reel; the very name of God
Sounds like a juggler's charm; and, bold with joy,   80
Forth from his dark and lonely hiding-place,
(Portentous sight!) the owlet Atheism,
Sailing on obscene wings athwart the noon,

Drops his blue-fringéd lids, and holds them close,
And hooting at the glorious sun in Heaven,   85
Cries out, "Where is it?"

                    Thankless too for peace,
(Peace long preserved by fleets and perilous seas)
Secure from actual warfare, we have loved
To swell the war-whoop, passionate for war!
Alas! for ages ignorant of all   90
Its ghastlier workings, (famine or blue plague,
Battle, or siege, or flight through wintry snows,)
We, this whole people, have been clamorous
For war and bloodshed; animating sports,
The which we pay for as a thing to talk of,   95
Spectators and not combatants! No guess
Anticipative of a wrong unfelt,
No speculation on contingency,
However dim and vague, too vague and dim
To yield a justifying cause; and forth,   100
(Stuffed out with big preamble, holy names,
And adjurations of the God in Heaven,)
We send our mandates for the certain death
Of thousands and ten thousands! Boys and girls,
And women, that would groan to see a child   105
Pull off an insect's leg, all read of war,
The best amusement for our morning meal!
The poor wretch, who has learnt his only prayers
From curses, who knows scarcely words enough
To ask a blessing from his Heavenly Father,   110
Becomes a fluent phraseman, absolute
And technical in victories and defeats,
And all our dainty terms for fratricide;
Terms which we trundle smoothly o'er our tongues
Like mere abstractions, empty sounds to which   115
We join no feeling and attach no form!

As if the soldier died without a wound;
As if the fibres of this godlike frame
Were gored without a pang; as if the wretch,
Who fell in battle, doing bloody deeds,   120
Passed off to Heaven, translated and not killed;
As though he had no wife to pine for him,
No God to judge him! Therefore, evil days
Are coming on us, O my countrymen!
And what if all-avenging Providence,   125
Strong and retributive, should make us know
The meaning of our words, force us to feel
The desolation and the agony
Of our fierce doings?

                    Spare us yet awhile,
Father and God! O! spare us yet awhile!   130
Oh! let not English women drag their flight
Fainting beneath the burthen of their babes,
Of the sweet infants, that but yesterday
Laughed at the breast! Sons, brothers, husbands, all
Who ever gazed with fondness on the forms   135
Which grew up with you round the same fire-side,
And all who ever heard the sabbath-bells
Without the infidel's scorn, make yourselves pure!
Stand forth! be men! repel an impious foe,
Impious and false, a light yet cruel race,   140
Who laugh away all virtue, mingling mirth
With deeds of murder; and still promising
Freedom, themselves too sensual to be free,
Poison life's amities, and cheat the heart
Of faith and quiet hope, and all that soothes,   145
And all that lifts the spirit! Stand we forth;
Render them back upon the insulted ocean,
And let them toss as idly on its waves
As the vile sea-weed, which some mountain-blast

Swept from our shores! And oh! may we return   150
Not with a drunken triumph, but with fear,
Repenting of the wrongs with which we stung
So fierce a foe to frenzy!

                    I have told,
O Britons! O my brethren! I have told
Most bitter truth, but without bitterness.   155
Nor deem my zeal or factious or mistimed;
For never can true courage dwell with them,
Who, playing tricks with conscience, dare not look
At their own vices. We have been too long
Dupes of a deep delusion! Some, belike,   160
Groaning with restless enmity, expect
All change from change of constituted power;
As if a Government had been a robe,
On which our vice and wretchedness were tagged
Like fancy-points and fringes, with the robe   165
Pulled off at pleasure. Fondly these attach
A radical causation to a few
Poor drudges of chastising Providence,
Who borrow all their hues and qualities
From our own folly and rank wickedness,   170
Which gave them birth and nursed them. Others, mean-
          while,
Dote with a mad idolatry; and all
Who will not fall before their images,
And yield them worship, they are enemies
Even of their country!

                    Such have I been deemed.—   175
But, O dear Britain! O my Mother Isle!
Needs must thou prove a name most dear and holy
To me, a son, a brother, and a friend,
A husband, and a father! who revere

All bonds of natural love, and find them all 180
Within the limits of thy rocky shores.
O native Britain! O my Mother Isle!
How shouldst thou prove aught else but dear and holy
To me, who from thy lakes and mountain-hills,
Thy clouds, thy qiuet dales, thy rocks and seas, 185
Have drunk in all my intellectual life,
All sweet sensations, all ennobling thoughts,
All adoration of the God in nature,
All lovely and all honourable things,
Whatever makes this mortal spirit feel 190
The joy and greatness of its future being?
There lives nor form nor feeling in my soul
Unborrowed from my country! O divine
And beauteous island! thou hast been my sole
And most magnificent temple, in the which 195
I walk with awe, and sing my stately songs,
Loving the God that made me!—

                         May my fears,
My filial fears, be vain! and may the vaunts
And menace of the vengeful enemy
Pass like the gust, that roared and died away 200
In the distant tree: which heard, and only heard
In this low dell, bowed not the delicate grass.

  But now the gentle dew-fall sends abroad
The fruit-like perfume of the golden furze:
The light has left the summit of the hill, 205
Though still a sunny gleam lies beautiful,
Aslant the ivied beacon. Now farewell,
Farewell, awhile, O soft and silent spot!
On the green sheep-track, up the heathy hill,
Homeward I wind my way; and lo! recalled 210
From bodings that have well-nigh wearied me,

I find myself upon the brow, and pause
Startled! And after lonely sojourning
In such a quiet and surrounded nook,
This burst of prospect, here the shadowy main,　　215
Dim-tinted, there the mighty majesty
Of that huge amphitheatre of rich
And elmy fields, seems like society—
Conversing with the mind, and giving it
A livelier impulse and a dance of thought!　　220
And now, belovéd Stowey! I behold
Thy church-tower, and, methinks, the four huge elms
Clustering, which mark the mansion of my friend;
And close behind them, hidden from my view,
Is my own lowly cottage, where my babe　　225
And my babe's mother dwell in peace! With light
And quickened footsteps thitherward I tend,
Remembering thee, O green and silent dell!
And grateful, that by nature's quietness
And solitary musings, all my heart　　230
Is softened, and made worthy to indulge
Love, and the thoughts that yearn for human kind.

Nether-Stowey, *April* 20, 1798

The Nightingale

A CONVERSATION POEM, APRIL 1798

No cloud, no relique of the sunken day
Distinguishes the West, no long thin slip
Of sullen light, no obscure trembling hues.
Come, we will rest on this old mossy bridge!
You see the glimmer of the stream beneath,　　5
But hear no murmuring: it flows silently,
O'er its soft bed of verdure. All is still,
A balmy night! and though the stars be dim,

Yet let us think upon the vernal showers
That gladden the green earth, and we shall find   10
A pleasure in the dimness of the stars.
And hark! the Nightingale begins its song,
"Most musical, most melancholy" bird!
A melancholy bird? Oh! idle thought!
In Nature there is nothing melancholy.   15
But some night-wandering man whose heart was pierced
With the remembrance of a grievous wrong,
Or slow distemper, or neglected love,
(And so, poor wretch! filled all things with himself,
And made all gentle sounds tell back the tale   20
Of his own sorrow) he, and such as he,
First named these notes a melancholy strain.
And many a poet echoes the conceit;
Poet who hath been building up the rhyme
When he had better far have stretched his limbs   25
Beside a brook in mossy forest-dell,
By sun or moon-light, to the influxes
Of shapes and sounds and shifting elements
Surrendering his whole spirit, of his song
And of his fame forgetful! so his fame   30
Should share in Nature's immortality,
A venerable thing! and so his song
Should make all Nature lovelier, and itself
Be loved like Nature! But 'twill not be so;
And youths and maidens most poetical,   35
Who lose the deepening twilights of the spring
In ball-rooms and hot theatres, they still
Full of meek sympathy must heave their sighs
O'er Philomela's pity-pleading strains.

My Friend, and thou, our Sister! we have learnt   40
A different lore: we may not thus profane
Nature's sweet voices, always full of love

And joyance! 'Tis the merry Nightingale
That crowds, and hurries, and precipitates
With fast thick warble his delicious notes,   45
As he were fearful that an April night
Would be too short for him to utter forth
His love-chant, and disburthen his full soul
Of all its music!
          And I know a grove
Of large extent, hard by a castle huge,   50
Which the great lord inhabits not; and so
This grove is wild with tangling underwood,
And the trim walks are broken up, and grass,
Thin grass and king-cups grow within the paths.
But never elsewhere in one place I knew   55
So many nightingales; and far and near,
In wood and thicket, over the wide grove,
They answer and provoke each other's song,
With skirmish and capricious passagings,
And murmurs musical and swift jug jug,   60
And one low piping sound more sweet than all—
Stirring the air with such a harmony,
That should you close your eyes, you might almost
Forget it was not day! On moonlight bushes,
Whose dewy leaflets are but half-disclosed,   65
You may perchance behold them on the twigs,
Their bright, bright eyes, their eyes both bright and full,
Glistening, while many a glow-worm in the shade
Lights up her love-torch.
              A most gentle Maid,
Who dwelleth in her hospitable home   70
Hard by the castle, and at latest eve
(Even like a Lady vowed and dedicate
To something more than Nature in the grove)
Glides through the pathways; she knows all their notes,
That gentle Maid! and oft, a moment's space,   75

What time the moon was lost behind a cloud,
Hath heard a pause of silence; till the moon
Emerging, hath awakened earth and sky
With one sensation, and those wakeful birds
Have all burst forth in choral minstrelsy,   80
As if some sudden gale had swept at once
A hundred airy harps! And she hath watched
Many a nightingale perch giddily
On blossomy twig still swinging from the breeze,
And to that motion tune his wanton song   85
Like tipsy Joy that reels with tossing head.

Farewell, O Warbler! till to-morrow eve,
And you, my friends! farewell, a short farewell!
We have been loitering long and pleasantly,
And now for our dear homes.—That strain again!   90
Full fain it would delay me! My dear babe,
Who, capable of no articulate sound,
Mars all things with his imitative lisp,
How he would place his hand beside his ear,
His little hand, the small forefinger up,   95
And bid us listen! And I deem it wise
To make him Nature's play-mate. He knows well
The evening-star; and once, when he awoke
In most distressful mood (some inward pain
Had made up that strange thing, an infant's
      dream—)   100
I hurried with him to our orchard-plot,
And he beheld the moon, and, hushed at once,
Suspends his sobs, and laughs most silently,
While his fair eyes, that swam with undropped tears,
Did glitter in the yellow moon-beam! Well!—   105
It is a father's tale: But if that Heaven
Should give me life, his childhood shall grow up
Familiar with these songs, that with the night

He may associate joy.—Once more, farewell,
Sweet Nightingale! once more, my friends! farewell.   110
                                                      1798

The Wanderings of Cain

PREFATORY NOTE

A prose composition, one not in metre at least, seems primâ
facie *to require explanation or apology. It was written in
the year 1798, near Nether Stowey, in Somersetshire, at
which place* (sanctum et amabile nomen! *rich by so many
associations and recollections) the author had taken up his
residence in order to enjoy the society and close neighbour-
hood of a dear and honoured friend, T. Poole, Esq. The work
was to have been written in concert with another [Words-
worth], whose name is too venerable within the precincts of
genius to be unnecessarily brought into connection with such
a trifle, and who was then residing at a small distance from
Nether Stowey. The title and subject were suggested by my-
self, who likewise drew out the scheme and the contents for
each of the three books or cantos, of which the work was to
consist, and which, the reader is to be informed, was to have
been finished in one night! My partner undertook the first
canto: I the second: and which ever had* done first, *was to set
about the third. Almost thirty years have passed by; yet at
this moment I cannot without something more than a smile
moot the question which of the two things was the more im-
practicable, for a mind so eminently original to compose
another man's thoughts and fancies, or for a taste so austerely
pure and simple to imitate the Death of Abel? Methinks I see
his grand and noble countenance as at the moment when hav-
ing despatched my own portion of the task at full finger-
speed, I hastened to him with my manuscript—that look of
humourous despondency fixed on his almost blank sheet of
paper, and then its silent mock-piteous admission of failure
struggling with the sense of the exceeding ridiculousness of*

*the whole scheme—which broke up in a laugh: and the An-
cient Mariner was written instead.*

*Years afterward, however, the draft of the plan and pro-
posed incidents, and the portion executed, obtained favour
in the eyes of more than one person, whose judgment on a
poetic work could not but have weighed with me, even
though no parental partiality had been thrown into the same
scale, as a make-weight: and I determined on commencing
anew, and composing the whole in stanzas, and made some
progress in realising this intention, when adverse gales drove
my bark off the "Fortunate Isles" of the Muses: and then
other and more momentous interests prompted a different
voyage, to firmer anchorage and a securer port. I have in vain
tried to recover the lines from the palimpsest tablet of my
memory: and I can only offer the introductory stanza, which
had been committed to writing for the purpose of procuring
a friend's judgment on the metre, as a specimen:—*

> *Encinctured with a twine of leaves,*
> *That leafy twine his only dress!*
> *A lovely Boy was plucking fruits,*
> *By moonlight, in a wilderness.*
> *The moon was bright, the air was free,*
> *And fruits and flowers together grew*
> *On many a shrub and many a tree:*
> *And all put on a gentle hue,*
> *Hanging in the shadowy air*
> *Like a picture rich and rare.*
> *It was a climate where, they say,*
> *The night is more belov'd than day.*
> *But who that beauteous Boy beguil'd,*
> *That beauteous Boy to linger here?*
> *Alone, by night, a little child,*
> *In place so silent and so wild—*
> *Has he no friend, no loving mother near?*

*I have here given the birth, parentage, and premature
decease of the "Wanderings of Cain, a poem",—intreating,
however, my Readers, not to think so meanly of my judgment*

*as to suppose that I either regard or offer it as any excuse for
the publication of the following fragment (and I may add, of
one or two others in its neighbourhood) in its primitive
crudity. But I should find still greater difficulty in forgiving
myself were I to record pro* taedio *publico a set of petty mis-
haps and annoyances which I myself wish to forget. I must
be content therefore with assuring the friendly Reader, that
the less he attributes its appearance to the Author's will,
choice, or judgment, the nearer to the truth he will be.*

S. T. COLERIDGE (1828).

CANTO II

"A little further, O my father, yet a little further, and
we shall come into the open moonlight." Their road was
through a forest of fir-trees; at its entrance the trees
stood at distances from each other, and the path was
broad, and the moonlight and the moonlight shadows
reposed upon it, and appeared quietly to inhabit that
solitude. But soon the path winded and became narrow;
the sun at high noon sometimes speckled, but never il-
lumined it, and now it was dark as a cavern.

"It is dark, O my father!" said Enos, "but the path
under our feet is smooth and soft, and we shall soon
come out into the open moonlight."

"Lead on, my child!" said Cain; "guide me, little
child!" And the innocent little child clasped a finger of
the hand which had murdered the righteous Abel, and
he guided his father. "The fir branches drip upon thee,
my son." "Yea, pleasantly, father, for I ran fast and
eagerly to bring thee the pitcher and the cake, and my
body is not yet cool. How happy the squirrels are that
feed on these fir-trees! they leap from bough to bough,
and the old squirrels play round their young ones in the
nest. I clomb a tree yesterday at noon, O my father, that

I might play with them, but they leaped away from the branches, even to the slender twigs did they leap, and in a moment I beheld them on another tree. Why, O my father, would they not play with me? I would be good to them as thou art good to me: and I groaned to them even as thou groanest when thou givest me to eat, and when thou coverest me at evening, and as often as I stand at thy knee and thine eyes look at me?" Then Cain stopped, and stifling his groans he sank to the earth, and the child Enos stood in the darkness beside him.

And Cain lifted up his voice and cried bitterly, and said, "The Mighty One that persecuteth me is on this side and on that; he pursueth my soul like the wind, like the sand-blast he passeth through me; he is around me even as the air! O that I might be utterly no more! I desire to die—yea, the things that never had life, neither move they upon the earth—behold! they seem precious to mine eyes. O that a man might live without the breath of his nostrils. So I might abide in darkness, and blackness, and an empty space! Yea, I would lie down. I would not rise, neither would I stir my limbs till I became as the rock in the den of the lion, on which the young lion resteth his head whilst he sleepeth. For the torrent that roareth far off hath a voice: and the clouds in heaven look terribly on me; the Mighty One who is against me speaketh in the wind of the cedar grove; and in silence am I dried up." Then Enos spake to his father, "Arise, my father, arise, we are but a little way from the place where I found the cake and the pitcher." And Cain said, "How knowest thou!" and the child answered— "Behold the bare rocks are a few of thy strides distant from the forest; and while even now thou wert lifting up thy voice, I heard the echo." Then the child took hold of his father, as if he would raise him: and Cain being faint

and feeble rose slowly on his knees and pressed himself against the trunk of a fir, and stood upright and followed the child.

The path was dark till within three strides' length of its termination, when it turned suddenly; the thick black trees formed a low arch, and the moonlight appeared for a moment like a dazzling portal. Enos ran before and stood in the open air; and when Cain, his father, emerged from the darkness, the child was affrighted. For the mighty limbs of Cain were wasted as by fire; his hair was as the matted curls on the bison's forehead, and so glared his fierce and sullen eye beneath: and the black abundant locks on either side, a rank and tangled mass, were stained and scorched, as though the grasp of a burning iron hand had striven to rend them; and his countenance told in a strange and terrible language of agonies that had been, and were, and were still to continue to be.

The scene around was desolate; as far as the eye could reach it was desolate: the bare rocks faced each other, and left a long and wide interval of thin white sand. You might wander on and look round and round, and peep into the crevices of the rocks and discover nothing that acknowledged the influence of the seasons. There was no spring, no summer, no autumn: and the winter's snow, that would have been lovely, fell not on these hot rocks and scorching sands. Never morning lark had poised himself over this desert; but the huge serpent often hissed there beneath the talons of the vulture, and the vulture screamed, his wings imprisoned within the coils of the serpent. The pointed and shattered summits of the ridges of the rocks made a rude mimicry of human concerns, and seemed to prophecy mutely of things that then were not; steeples, and battlements, and ships with naked masts. As far from the

wood as a boy might sling a pebble of the brook, there was one rock by itself at a small distance from the main ridge. It had been precipitated there perhaps by the groan which the Earth uttered when our first father fell. Before you approached, it appeared to lie flat on the ground, but its base slanted from its point, and between its point and the sands a tall man might stand upright. It was here that Enos had found the pitcher and cake, and to this place he led his father. But ere they had reached the rock they beheld a human shape: his back was towards them, and they were advancing unperceived, when they heard him smite his breast and cry aloud, "Woe is me! woe is me! I must never die again, and yet I am perishing with thirst and hunger."

Pallid, as the reflection of the sheeted lightning on the heavy-sailing night-cloud, became the face of Cain; but the child Enos took hold of the shaggy skin, his father's robe, and raised his eyes to his father, and listening whispered, "Ere yet I could speak, I am sure, O my father, that I heard that voice. Have not I often said that I remembered a sweet voice? O my father! this is it": and Cain trembled exceedingly. The voice was sweet indeed, but it was thin and querulous, like that of a feeble slave in misery, who despairs altogether, yet can not refrain himself from weeping and lamentation. And, behold! Enos glided forward, and creeping softly round the base of the rock, stood before the stranger, and looked up into his face. And the Shape shrieked, and turned round, and Cain beheld him, that his limbs and his face were those of his brother Abel whom he had killed! And Cain stood like one who struggles in his sleep because of the exceeding terribleness of a dream.

Thus as he stood in silence and darkness of soul, the Shape fell at his feet, and embraced his knees, and cried out with a bitter outcry, "Thou eldest born of Adam, whom Eve, my mother, brought forth, cease to torment me! I was feeding my flocks in green pastures by the side of quiet rivers, and thou killedst me; and now I am in misery." Then Cain closed his eyes, and hid them with his hands; and again he opened his eyes, and looked around him, and said to Enos, "What beholdest thou? Didst thou hear a voice, my son?" "Yes, my father, I beheld a man in unclean garments, and he uttered a sweet voice, full of lamentation." Then Cain raised up the Shape that was like Abel, and said:—"The Creator of our father, who had respect unto thee, and unto thy offering, wherefore hath he forsaken thee?" Then the Shape shrieked a second time, and rent his garment, and his naked skin was like the white sands beneath their feet; and he shrieked yet a third time, and threw himself on his face upon the sand that was black with the shadow of the rock, and Cain and Enos sate beside him; the child by his right hand, and Cain by his left. They were all three under the rock, and within the shadow. The Shape that was like Abel raised himself up, and spake to the child, "I know where the cold waters are, but I may not drink, wherefore didst thou then take away my pitcher?" But Cain said, "Didst thou not find favour in the sight of the Lord thy God?" The Shape answered, "The Lord is God of the living only, the dead have another God." Then the child Enos lifted up his eyes and prayed; but Cain rejoiced secretly in his heart. "Wretched shall they be all the days of their mortal life," exclaimed the Shape, "who sacrifice worthy and acceptable sacrifices to the God of the dead; but after death their toil ceaseth. Woe is me, for I was well beloved by the God of the living, and cruel wert thou, O my brother, who didst snatch me away from his power and his dominion." Having uttered these words, he rose suddenly, and fled over the sands: and Cain said in his

heart, "The curse of the Lord is on me; but who is the
God of the dead?" and he ran after the Shape, and the
Shape fled shrieking over the sands, and the sands rose
like white mists behind the steps of Cain, but the feet
of him that was like Abel disturbed not the sands. He
greatly outrun Cain, and turning short, he wheeled
round, and came again to the rock where they had been
sitting, and where Enos still stood; and the child caught
hold of his garment as he passed by, and he fell upon
the ground. And Cain stopped, and beholding him not,
said, "he has passed into the dark woods," and he
walked slowly back to the rocks; and when he reached
it the child told him that he had caught hold of his
garment as he passed by, and that the man had fallen
upon the ground: and Cain once more sate beside him,
and said, "Abel, my brother, I would lament for thee,
but that the spirit within me is withered, and burnt up
with extreme agony. Now, I pray thee, by thy flocks, and
by thy pastures, and by the quiet rivers which thou
lovedst, that thou tell me all that thou knowest. Who is
the God of the dead? where doth he make his dwelling?
what sacrifices are acceptable unto him? for I have
offered, but have not been received; I have prayed, and
have not been heard; and how can I be afflicted more
than I already am?" The Shape arose and answered, "O
that thou hadst had pity on me as I will have pity on
thee. Follow me, Son of Adam! and bring thy child with
thee!"

And they three passed over the white sands between
the rocks, silent as the shadows.

1798

Kubla Khan

OR, A VISION IN A DREAM

A FRAGMENT

The following fragment is here published at the request of a poet of great and deserved celebrity [Lord Byron], and, as far as the Author's own opinions are concerned, rather as a psychological curiosity, than on the ground of any supposed poetic merits.

In the summer of the year 1797, the Author, then in ill health, had retired to a lonely farm-house between Porlock and Linton, on the Exmoor confines of Somerset and Devonshire. In consequence of a slight indisposition, an anodyne had been prescribed, from the effects of which he fell asleep in his chair at the moment that he was reading the following sentence, or words of the same substance, in "Purchas's Pilgrimage": "Here the Khan Kubla commanded a palace to be built, and a stately garden thereunto. And thus ten miles of fertile ground were inclosed with a wall." The Author continued for about three hours in a profound sleep, at least of the external senses, during which time he has the most vivid confidence, that he could not have composed less than from two to three hundred lines; if that indeed can be called composition in which all the images rose up before him as things, with a parallel production of the correspondent expressions, without any sensation or consciousness of effort. On awaking he appeared to himself to have a distinct recollection of the whole, and taking his pen, ink, and paper, instantly and eagerly wrote down the lines that are here preserved. At this moment he was unfortunately called out by a person on business from Porlock, and detained by him above an hour, and on his return to his room, found, to his no small surprise and mortification, that though he still retained some vague and dim recollection of the general purport of the vision, yet, with the exception of some eight or ten scattered

lines and images, all the rest had passed away like the images
on the surface of a stream into which a stone has been cast,
but, alas! without the after restoration of the latter!

In Xanadu did Kubla Khan
A stately pleasure-dome decree:
Where Alph, the sacred river, ran
Through caverns measureless to man
   Down to a sunless sea.   5
So twice five miles of fertile ground
With walls and towers were girdled round:
And there were gardens bright with sinuous rills,
Where blossomed many an incense-bearing tree;
And here were forests ancient as the hills,   10
Enfolding sunny spots of greenery.

But oh! that deep romantic chasm which slanted
Down the green hill athwart a cedarn cover!
A savage place! as holy and enchanted
As e'er beneath a waning moon was haunted   15
By woman wailing for her demon-lover!
And from this chasm, with ceaseless turmoil seething.
As if this earth in fast thick pants were breathing,
A mighty fountain momently was forced:
Amid whose swift half-intermitted burst   20
Huge fragments vaulted like rebounding hail,
Or chaffy grain beneath the thresher's flail:
And 'mid these dancing rocks at once and ever
It flung up momently the sacred river.
Five miles meandering with a mazy motion   25
Through wood and dale the sacred river ran,
Then reached the caverns measureless to man,
And sank in tumult to a lifeless ocean:
And 'mid this tumult Kubla heard from far
Ancestral voices prophesying war!   30
   The shadow of the dome of pleasure

Floated midway on the waves;
Where was heard the mingled measure
From the fountain and the caves.
It was a miracle of rare device,   35
A sunny pleasure-dome with caves of ice!

A damsel with a dulcimer
In a vision once I saw:
It was an Abyssinian maid,
And on her dulcimer she played,   40
Singing of Mount Abora.
Could I revive within me
Her symphony and song,
To such a deep delight 'twould win me,
That with music loud and long,   45
I would build that dome in air,
That sunny dome! those caves of ice!
And all who heard should see them there,
And all should cry, Beware! Beware!
His flashing eyes, his floating hair!   50
Weave a circle round him thrice,
And close your eyes with holy dread,
For he on honey-dew hath fed,
And drunk the milk of Paradise.

1798

Fragment

Seaward, white gleaming thro' the busy scud
With arching Wings, the sea-mew o'er my head
Posts on, as bent on speed, now passaging
Edges the stiffer Breeze, now, yielding, drifts,
Now floats upon the air, and sends from far
A wildly-wailing Note.

Hexameters[1]

William, my teacher, my friend! dear William and dear
    Dorothea!
Smooth out the folds of my letter, and place it on desk or
    on table;
Place it on table or desk; and your right hands loosely
    half-closing,
Gently sustain them in air, and extending the digit
    didactic,
Rest it a moment on each of the forks of the five-forkéd
    left hand,   5
Twice on the breadth of the thumb, and once on the
    tip of each finger;
Read with a nod of the head in a humouring recitativo;
And, as I live, you will see my hexameters hopping be-
    fore you.
This is a galloping measure; a hop, and a trot, and a
    gallop!

All my hexameters fly, like stags pursued by the stag-
    hounds,   10
Breathless and panting, and ready to drop, yet flying still
    onwards,
I would full fain pull in my hard-mouthed runaway
    hunter;
But our English Spondeans are clumsy yet impotent
    curb-reins;
And so to make him go slowly, no way left have I but
    to lame him.

[1] The "Hexameters" were sent in a letter, written in the
winter of 1798–99 from Ratzeburg to the Wordsworths at
Goslar.—*E. H. Coleridge*

William, my head and my heart! dear Poet that feelest
    and thinkest!   15
Dorothy, eager of soul, my most affectionate sister!
Many a mile, O! many a wearisome mile are ye dis-
    tant,
Long, long comfortless roads, with no one eye that doth
    know us.
O! it is all too far to send you mockeries idle:
Yea, and I feel it not right! But O! my friends, my be-
    lovéd!   20
Feverish and wakeful I lie,—I am weary of feeling and
    thinking.
Every thought is worn *down*, I am weary yet cannot be
    vacant.
Five long hours have I tossed, rheumatic heats, dry and
    flushing,
Gnawing behind in my head, and wandering and throb-
    bing about me,
Busy and tiresome, my friends, as the beat of the boding
    night-spider.   25

I forget the beginning of the line:

. . . my eyes are a burthen,
Now unwillingly closed, now open and aching with
    darkness.
O! what a life is the eye! what a strange and inscrutable
    essence!
Him that is utterly blind, nor glimpses the fire that
    warms him;
Him that never beheld the swelling breast of his
    mother;   30
Him that smiled in his gladness as a babe that smiles in
    its slumber;
Even for him it exists, it moves and stirs in its prison;

Lives with a separate life, and "Is it a Spirit?" he mur-
   murs:
"Sure it has thoughts of its own, and to see is only a
   language."

*There was a great deal more, which I have forgotten.
. . . The last line which I wrote, I remember, and write
it for the truth of the sentiment, scarcely less true in
company than in pain and solitude:—*

William, my head and my heart! dear William and dear
   Dorothea!   35
You have all in each other; but I am lonely, and want
   you!

                                                   1798–99

Catullian Hendecasyllables

Hear, my belovéd, an old Milesian story!—
High, and embosom'd in congregated laurels,
Glimmer'd a temple upon a breezy headland;
In the dim distance amid the skiey billows
Rose a fair island; the god of flocks had blest it.   5
From the far shores of the bleat-resounding island
Oft by the moonlight a little boat came floating,
Came to the sea-cave beneath the breezy headland,
Where amid myrtles a pathway stole in mazes
Up to the groves of the high embosom'd temple.   10
There in a thicket of dedicated roses,
Oft did a priestess, as lovely as a vision,
Pouring her soul to the son of Cytherea,
Pray him to hover around the slight canoe-boat,
And with invisible pilotage to guide it   15

Over the dusk wave, until the nightly sailor
Shivering with ecstasy sank upon her bosom.

1799(?)

The Homeric Hexameter

DESCRIBED AND EXEMPLIFIED

Strongly it bears us along in swelling and limitless bil-
lows,
Nothing before and nothing behind but the sky and the
ocean.

1799(?)

The Ovidian Elegiac Metre

DESCRIBED AND EXEMPLIFIED

In the hexameter rises the fountain's silvery column;
In the pentameter aye falling in melody back.

1799

Lines Written in the Album
at Elbingerode

IN THE HARTZ FOREST

I stood on Brocken's sovran height, and saw
Woods crowding upon woods, hills over hills,
A surging scene, and only limited
By the blue distance. Heavily my way
Downward I dragged through fir groves evermore,   5
Where bright green moss heaves in sepulchral forms
Speckled with sunshine; and, but seldom heard,

The sweet bird's song became a hollow sound;
And the breeze, murmuring indivisibly,
Preserved its solemn murmur most distinct   10
From many a note of many a waterfall,
And the brook's chatter; 'mid whose islet-stones
The dingy kidling with its tinkling bell
Leaped frolicsome, or old romantic goat
Sat, his white beard slow waving. I moved on   15
In low and languid mood: for I had found
That outward forms, the loftiest, still receive
Their finer influence from the Life within;—
Fair cyphers else: fair, but of import vague
Or unconcerning, where the heart not finds   20
History or prophecy of friend, or child,
Or gentle maid, our first and early love,
Or father, or the venerable name
Of our adoréd country! O thou Queen,
Thou delegated Deity of Earth,
O dear, dear England! how my longing eye
Turned westward, shaping in the steady clouds
Thy sands and high white cliffs!

                                My native Land!
Filled with the thought of thee this heart was proud,
Yea, mine eye swam with tears: that all the view   30
From sovran Brocken, woods and woody hills,
Floated away, like a departing dream,
Feeble and dim! Stranger, these impulses
Blame thou not lightly; nor will I profane,
With hasty judgment or injurious doubt,   35
That man's sublimer spirit, who can feel
That God is everywhere! the God who framed
Mankind to be one mighty family,
Himself our Father, and the World our Home.
                                        May 17, 1799

Lines Composed in a Concert-Room

Nor cold, nor stern, my soul! yet I detest
   These scented Rooms, where, to a gaudy throng,
Heaves the proud Harlot her distended breast,
   In intricacies of laborious song.

These feel not Music's genuine power, nor deign   5
   To melt at Nature's passion-warbled plaint;
But when the long-breathed singer's uptrilled strain
   Bursts in a squall—they gape for wonderment.

Hark! the deep buzz of Vanity and Hate!
   Scornful, yet envious, with self-torturing sneer   10
My lady eyes some maid of humbler state,
   While the pert Captain, or the primmer Priest,
Prattles accordant scandal in her ear.

O give me, from this heartless scene released,
   To hear our old Musician, blind and grey,   15
(Whom stretching from my nurse's arms I kissed,)
   His Scottish tunes and warlike marches play,
By moonshine, on the balmy summer-night,
   The while I dance amid the tedded hay
With merry maids, whose ringlets toss in light.   20

Or lies the purple evening on the bay
Of the calm glossy lake, O let me hide
   Unheard, unseen, behind the alder-trees,
For round their roots the fisher's boat is tied,
   On whose trim seat doth Edmund stretch at ease,   25
And while the lazy boat sways to and fro,

Breathes in his flute sad airs, so wild and slow,
That his own cheek is wet with quiet tears.

But O, dear Anne! when midnight wind careers,
And the gust pelting on the out-house shed   30
  Makes the cock shrilly in the rainstorm crow,
  To hear thee sing some ballad full of woe,
Ballad of ship-wreck'd sailor floating dead,
  Whom his own true-love buried in the sands!
Thee, gentle woman, for thy voice remeasures   35
Whatever tones and melancholy pleasures
  The things of Nature utter; birds or trees,
Or moan of ocean-gale in weedy caves,
Or where the stiff grass mid the heath-plant waves,
  Murmur and music thin of sudden breeze.   40
                                  1799

Love

All thoughts, all passions, all delights,
Whatever stirs this mortal frame,
All are but ministers of Love,
    And feed his sacred flame.

Oft in my waking dreams do I   5
Live o'er again that happy hour,
When midway on the mount I lay,
    Beside the ruined tower.

The moonshine, stealing o'er the scene
Had blended with the lights of eve;   10
And she was there, my hope, my joy,
    My own dear Genevieve!

She leant against the arméd man,
The statue of the arméd knight;
She stood and listened to my lay,   15
    Amid the lingering light.

Few sorrows hath she of her own,
My hope! my joy! my Genevieve!
She loves me best, whene'er I sing
    The songs that make her grieve.   20

I played a soft and doleful air,
I sang an old and moving story—
An old rude song, that suited well
    That ruin wild and hoary.

She listened with a flitting blush,   25
With downcast eyes and modest grace;
For well she knew, I could not choose
    But gaze upon her face.

I told her of the Knight that wore   2½
Upon his shield a burning brand;   30
And that for ten long years he wooed
    The Lady of the Land.

I told her how he pined: and ah!
The deep, the low, the pleading tone
With which I sang another's love,   35
    Interpreted my own.

She listened with a flitting blush,
With downcast eyes, and modest grace;
And she forgave me, that I gazed
    Too fondly on her face!   40

But when I told the cruel scorn
That crazed that bold and lovely Knight,
And that he crossed the mountain-woods,
    Nor rested day nor night;

That sometimes from the savage den,   45
And sometimes from the darksome shade,
And sometimes starting up at once
    In green and sunny glade,—

There came and looked him in the face
An angel beautiful and bright;   ·   50
And that he knew it was a Fiend,
    This miserable Knight!

And that unknowing what he did,
He leaped amid a murderous band,
And saved from outrage worse than death   55
    The Lady of the Land!

And how she wept, and clasped his knees;
And how she tended him in vain—
And ever strove to expiate
    The scorn that crazed his brain;—   60

And that she nursed him in a cave;
And how his madness went away,
When on the yellow forest-leaves
    A dying man he lay;—

His dying words—but when I reached   65
That tenderest strain of all the ditty,
My faultering voice and pausing harp
    Disturbed her soul with pity!

All impulses of soul and sense
Had thrilled my guileless Genevieve;   70
The music and the doleful tale,
 The rich and balmy eye;

And hopes, and fears that kindle hope,
An undistinguishable throng,
And gentle wishes long subdued,   75
 Subdued and cherished long!

She wept with pity and delight,
She blushed with love, and virgin-shame;
And like the murmur of a dream,
 I heard her breathe my name.   80

Her bosom heaved—she stepped aside,
As conscious of my look she stepped—
Then suddenly, with timorous eye
 She fled to me and wept.

She half enclosed me with her arms,   85
She pressed me with a meek embrace;
And bending back her head, looked up,
 And gazed upon my face.

'Twas partly love, and partly fear,
And partly 'twas a bashful art,   90
That I might rather feel, than see,
 The swelling of her heart.

I calmed her fears, and she was calm,
And told her love with virgin pride;
And so I won my Genevieve,   95
 My bright and beauteous Bride.

1799

Dejection: An Ode
[WRITTEN APRIL 4, 1802]

> Late, late yestreen I saw the new Moon,
> With the old Moon in her arms;
> And I fear, I fear, my Master dear!
> We shall have a deadly storm.
>> *Ballad of Sir Patrick Spence.*

I

Well! If the Bard was weather-wise, who made
　The grand old ballad of Sir Patrick Spence,
　This night, so tranquil now, will not go hence
Unroused by winds, that ply a busier trade
Than those which mould yon cloud in lazy flakes,　5
Or the dull sobbing draft, that moans and rakes
Upon the strings of this Æolian lute,
　　Which better far were mute.
　For lo! the New-moon winter-bright!
　And overspread with phantom light,　　10
　(With swimming phantom light o'erspread
　But rimmed and circled by a silver thread)
I see the old Moon in her lap, foretelling
　The coming-on of rain and squally blast.
And oh! that even now the gust were swelling,　15
　And the slant night-shower driving loud and fast!
Those sounds which oft have raised me, whilst they
　　awed,
　　And sent my soul abroad,
Might now perhaps their wonted impulse give,
Might startle this dull pain, and make it move and
　　live!　　20

II

A grief without a pang, void, dark, and drear,
　A stifled, drowsy, unimpassioned grief,
　Which finds no natural outlet, no relief,
　　In word, or sigh, or tear—
O Lady! in this wan and heartless mood,　　　　　25
To other thoughts by yonder throstle woo'd,
　All this long eve, so balmy and serene,
Have I been gazing on the western sky,
　And its peculiar tint of yellow green:
And still I gaze—and with how blank an eye!　　30
And those thin clouds above, in flakes and bars,
That give away their motion to the stars;
Those stars, that glide behind them or between,
Now sparkling, now bedimmed, but always seen:
Yon crescent Moon, as fixed as if it grew　　　35
In its own cloudless, starless lake of blue;
I see them all so excellently fair,
I see, not feel, how beautiful they are!

III

　My genial spirits fail;
　　And what can these avail　　　　　40
To lift the smothering weight from off my breast?
　　It were a vain endeavour,
　　Though I should gaze for ever
On that green light that lingers in the west:
I may not hope from outward forms to win　　　45
The passion and the life, whose fountains are within.

IV

O Lady! we receive but what we give,
And in our life alone does Nature live:
Ours is her wedding garment, ours her shroud!

And would we aught behold, of higher worth,   50
Than that inanimate cold world allowed
To the poor loveless ever-anxious crowd,
   Ah! from the soul itself must issue forth
A light, a glory, a fair luminous cloud
      Enveloping the Earth—   55
And from the soul itself must there be sent
   A sweet and potent voice, of its own birth,
Of all sweet sounds the life and element!

V

O pure of heart! thou need'st not ask of me
What this strong music in the soul may be!   60
What, and wherein it doth exist,
This light, this glory, this fair luminous mist,
This beautiful and beauty-making power.
   Joy, virtuous Lady! Joy that ne'er was given,
Save to the pure, and in their purest hour,   65
Life, and Life's effluence, cloud at once and shower,
Joy, Lady! is the spirit and the power,
Which wedding Nature to us gives in dower
   A new Earth and new Heaven,
Undreamt of by the sensual and the proud—   70
Joy is the sweet voice, Joy the luminous cloud—
      We in ourselves rejoice!
And thence flows all that charms or ear or sight,
   All melodies the echoes of that voice,
All colours a suffusion from that light.   75

VI

There was a time when, though my path was rough,
   This joy within me dallied with distress,
And all misfortunes were but as the stuff
   Whence Fancy made me dreams of happiness:
For hope grew round me, like the twining vine,   80

And fruits, and foliage, not my own, seemed mine.
But now afflictions bow me down to earth:
Nor care I that they rob me of my mirth;
    But oh! each visitation
Suspends what nature gave me at my birth,   85
  My shaping spirit of Imagination.
For not to think of what I needs must feel,
  But to be still and patient, all I can;
And haply by abstruse research to steal
  From my own nature all the natural man—   90
  This was my sole resource, my only plan:
Till that which suits a part infects the whole,
And now is almost grown the habit of my soul.

VII

Hence, viper thoughts, that coil around my mind,
    Reality's dark dream!   95
I turn from you, and listen to the wind,
  Which long has raved unnoticed. What a scream
Of agony by torture lengthened out
That lute sent forth! Thou Wind, that rav'st without,
  Bare crag, or mountain-tairn, or blasted tree,   100
Or pine-grove whither woodman never clomb,
Or lonely house, long held the witches' home,
  Methinks were fitter instruments for thee,
Mad Lutanist! who in this month of showers,
Of dark-brown gardens, and of peeping flowers,   105
Mak'st Devils' yule, with worse than wintry song,
The blossoms, buds, and timorous leaves among.
  Thou Actor, perfect in all tragic sounds!
Thou mighty Poet, e'en to frenzy bold!
    What tell'st thou now about?   110
    'Tis of the rushing of an host in rout,
  With groans, of trampled men, with smarting
        wounds—

At once they groan with pain, and shudder with the
     cold!
But hush! there is a pause of deepest silence!
    And all that noise, as of a rushing crowd,   115
With groans, and tremulous shudderings—all is over—
    It tells another tale, with sounds less deep and loud!
       A tale of less affright,
       And tempered with delight,
As Otway's self had framed the tender lay,—   120
       'Tis of a little child
       Upon a lonesome wild,
Not far from home, but she hath lost her way:
And now moans low in bitter grief and fear,
And now screams loud, and hopes to make her mother
     hear.   125

VIII

'Tis midnight, but small thoughts have I of sleep:
Full seldom may my friend such vigils keep!
Visit her, gentle Sleep! with wings of healing,
    And may this storm be but a mountain-birth,
May all the stars hang bright above her dwelling,   130
    Silent as though they watched the sleeping Earth!
       With light heart may she rise,
       Gay fancy, cheerful eyes,
    Joy lift her spirit, joy attune her voice;
To her may all things live, from pole to pole,   135
Their life the eddying of her living soul!
    O simple spirit, guided from above,
Dear Lady! friend devoutest of my choice,
Thus mayest thou ever, evermore rejoice.

                  1802

Reality's Dark Dream

I know 'tis but a dream, yet feel more anguish
Than if 'twere truth. It has been often so:
Must I die under it? Is no one near?
Will no one hear these stifled groans and wake me?

1803(?)

The Picture

OR THE LOVER'S RESOLUTION

Through weeds and thorns, and matted underwood
I force my way; now climb, and now descend
O'er rocks, or bare or mossy, with wild foot
Crushing the purple whorts; while oft unseen,
Hurrying along the drifted forest-leaves,   5
The scared snake rustles. Onward still I toil,
I know not, ask not whither! A new joy,
Lovely as light, sudden as summer gust,
And gladsome as the first-born of the spring,
Beckons me on, or follows from behind,   10
Playmate, or guide! The master-passion quelled,
I feel that I am free. With dun-red bark
The fir-trees, and the unfrequent slender oak,
Forth from this tangle wild of bush and brake
Soar up, and form a melancholy vault   15
High o'er me, murmuring like a distant sea.

Here Wisdom might resort, and here Remorse;
Here too the love-lorn man, who, sick in soul,
And of this busy human heart aweary,

Worships the spirit of unconscious life   20
In tree or wild-flower.—Gentle lunatic!
If so he might not wholly cease to be,
He would far rather not be that he is;
But would be something that he knows not of,
In winds or waters, or among the rocks!   25

But hence, fond wretch! breathe not contagion here!
No myrtle-walks are these: these are no groves
Where Love dare loiter! If in sullen mood
He should stray hither, the low stumps shall gore
His dainty feet, the briar and the thorn   30
Make his plumes haggard. Like a wounded bird
Easily caught, ensnare him, O ye Nymphs,
Ye Oreads chaste, ye dusky Dryades;
And you, ye Earth-winds! you that make at morn
The dew-drops quiver on the spiders' webs!   35
You, O ye wingless Airs! that creep between
The rigid stems of heath and bitten furze,
Within whose scanty shade, at summer-noon,
The mother-sheep hath worn a hollow bed—
Ye, that now cool her fleece with dropless damp,   40
Now pant and murmur with her feeding lamb.
Chase, chase him, all ye Fays, and elfin Gnomes!
With prickles sharper than his darts bemock
His little Godship, making him perforce
Creep through a thorn-bush on yon hedgehog's
    back.   45

This is my hour of triumph! I can now
With my own fancies play the merry fool,
And laugh away worse folly, being free.
Here will I seat myself, beside this old,
Hollow, and weedy oak, which ivy-twine   50
Clothes as with net-work: here will I couch my limbs,

Close by this river, in this silent shade,
As safe and sacred from the step of man
As an invisible world—unheard, unseen,
And listening only to the pebbly brook   55
That murmurs with a dead, yet tinkling sound;
Or to the bees, that in the neighbouring trunk
Make honey-hoards. The breeze, that visits me,
Was never Love's accomplice, never raised
The tendril ringlets from the maiden's brow,   60
And the blue, delicate veins above her cheek;
Ne'er played the wanton—never half disclosed
The maiden's snowy bosom, scattering thence
Eye-poisons for some love-distempered youth,
Who ne'er henceforth may see an aspen-grove   65
Shiver in sunshine, but his feeble heart
Shall flow away like a dissolving thing.

Sweet breeze! thou only, if I guess aright,
Liftest the feathers of the robin's breast,
That swells its little breast, so full of song,   70
Singing above me, on the mountain-ash.
And thou too, desert stream! no pool of thine,
Though clear as lake in latest summer-eve,
Did e'er reflect the stately virgin's robe,
The face, the form divine, the downcast look   75
Contemplative! Behold! her open palm
Presses her cheek and brow! her elbow rests
On the bare branch of half-uprooted tree,
That leans towards its mirror! Who erewhile
Had from her countenance turned, or looked by
        stealth,   80
(For Fear is true-love's cruel nurse), he now
With steadfast gaze and unoffending eye,
Worships the watery idol, dreaming hopes
Delicious to the soul, but fleeting, vain,

E'en as that phantom-world on which he gazed,   85
But not unheeded gazed: for see, ah! see,
The sportive tyrant with her left hand plucks
The heads of tall flowers that behind her grow,
Lychnis, and willow-herb, and fox-glove bells:
And suddenly, as one that toys with time,   90
Scatters them on the pool! Then all the charm
Is broken—all that phantom world so fair
Vanishes, and a thousand circlets spread,
And each mis-shape the other. Stay awhile,
Poor youth, who scarcely dar'st lift up thine eyes!   95
The stream will soon renew its smoothness, soon
The visions will return! And lo! he stays:
And soon the fragments dim of lovely forms
Come trembling back, unite, and now once more
The pool becomes a mirror; and behold   100
Each wildflower on the marge inverted there,
And there the half-uprooted tree—but where,
O where the virgin's snowy arm, that leaned
On its bare branch? He turns, and she is gone!
Homeward she steals through many a woodland
          maze   105
Which he shall seek in vain. Ill-fated youth!
Go, day by day, and waste thy manly prime
In mad love-yearning by the vacant brook,
Till sickly thoughts bewitch thine eyes, and thou
Behold'st her shadow still abiding there,   110
The Naiad of the mirror!
                              Not to thee,
O wild and desert stream! belongs this tale:
Gloomy and dark art thou—the crowded firs
Spire from thy shores, and stretch across thy bed,
Making thee doleful as a cavern-well: 115
Save when the shy king-fishers build their nest
On thy steep banks, no loves hast thou, wild stream!

This be my chosen haunt—emancipate
From Passion's dreams, a freeman, and alone,
I rise and trace its devious course. O lead,   120
Lead me to deeper shades and lonelier glooms.
Lo! stealing through the canopy of firs,
How fair the sunshine spots that mossy rock,
Isle of the river, whose disparted waves
Dart off asunder with an angry sound,   125
How soon to re-unite! And see! they meet,
Each in the other lost and found: and see
Placeless, as spirits, one soft water-sun
Throbbing within them, heart at once and eye!
With its soft neighbourhood of filmy clouds,   130
The stains and shadings of forgotten tears,
Dimness o'erswum with lustre! Such the hour
Of deep enjoyment, following love's brief feuds
And hark, the noise of a near waterfall!
I pass forth into light—I find myself   135
Beneath a weeping birch (most beautiful
Of forest trees, the Lady of the Woods),
Hard by the brink of a tall weedy rock
That overbrows the cataract. How bursts
The landscape on my sight! Two crescent hills   140
Fold in behind each other, and so make
A circular vale, and land-locked, as might seem,
With brook and bridge, and grey stone cottages,
Half hid by rocks and fruit-trees. At my feet,
The whortle-berries are bedewed with spray,   145
Dashed upwards by the furious waterfall.
How solemnly the pendent ivy-mass
Swings in its winnow: All the air is calm.
The smoke from cottage-chimneys, tinged with light,
Rises in columns; from this house alone,   150
Close by the water-fall, the column slants,
And feels its ceaseless breeze. But what is this?

That cottage, with its slanting chimney-smoke,
And close beside its porch a sleeping child,
His dear head pillowed on a sleeping dog—   155
One arm between its fore-legs, and the hand
Holds loosely its small handful of wild-flowers
Unfilletted, and of unequal lengths.
A curious picture, with a master's haste
Sketched on a strip of pinky-silver skin,   1 ᠐
Peeled from the birchen bark! Divinest maid!
Yon bark her canvas, and those purple berries
Her pencil! See, the juice is scarcely dried
On the fine skin! She has been newly here;
And lo! yon patch of heath has been her couch—   ᠐᠐
The pressure still remains! O blesséd couch!
For this may'st thou flower early, and the sun,
Slanting at eve, rest bright, and linger long
Upon thy purple bells! O Isabel!
Daughter of genius! stateliest of our maids!   170
More beautiful than whom Alcaeus wooed,
The Lesbian woman of immortal song!
O child of genius! stately, beautiful,
And full of love to all, save only me,
And not ungentle e'en to me! My heart,   175
Why beats it thus? Through yonder coppice-wood
Needs must the pathway turn, that leads straightway
On to her father's house. She is alone!
The night draws on—such ways are hard to hit—
And fit it is I should restore this sketch,   180
Dropt unawares, no doubt. Why should I yearn
To keep the relique? 'twill but idly feed
The passion that consumes me. Let me haste!
The picture in my hand which she has left;
She cannot blame me that I followed her: 185
And I may be her guide the long wood through.

1802

Inscription for a Fountain
on a Heath

This Sycamore, oft musical with bees,—
Such tents the Patriarchs loved! O long unharmed
May all its agéd boughs o'er-canopy
The small round basin, which this jutting stone
Keeps pure from falling leaves! Long may the Spring, 5
Quietly as a sleeping infant's breath,
Send up cold waters to the traveller
With soft and even pulse! Nor ever cease
Yon tiny cone of sand its soundless dance,
Which at the bottom, like a Fairy's Page, 10
As merry and no taller, dances still,
Nor wrinkles the smooth surface of the Fount.
Here Twilight is and Coolness: here is moss,
A soft seat, and a deep and ample shade.
Thou may'st toil far and find no second tree. 15
Drink, Pilgrim, here; here rest! and if thy heart
Be innocent, here too shalt thou refresh
Thy spirit, listening to some gentle sound,
Or passing gale or hum of murmuring bees!

1802

A Day-Dream

My eyes make pictures, when they are shut:
    I see a fountain, large and fair,
A willow and a ruined hut,
    And thee, and me and Mary there.

O Mary! make thy gentle lap our pillow!   5
Bend o'er us, like a bower, my beautiful green willow!

A wild-rose roofs the ruined shed,
    And that and summer well agree:
And lo! where Mary leans her head,
    Two dear names carved upon the tree!   10
And Mary's tears, they are not tears of sorrow:
Our sister and our friend will both be here to-morrow.

'Twas day! but now few, large, and bright,
    The stars are round the crescent moon!
And now it is a dark warm night,   15
    The balmiest of the month of June!
A glow-worm fall'n, and on the marge remounting
Shines, and its shadow shines, fit stars for our sweet
        fountain.

O ever—ever be thou blest!
    For dearly, Asra! love I thee!   20
This brooding warmth across my breast,
    This depth of tranquil bliss—ah, me!
Fount, tree and shed are gone, I know not whither,
But in one quiet room we three are still together.

The shadows dance upon the wall,   25
    By the still dancing fire-flames made;
And now they slumber, moveless all!
    And now they melt to one deep shade!
But not from me shall this mild darkness steal thee:
I dream thee with mine eyes, and at my heart I feel
        thee!   30

Thine eyelash on my cheek doth play—
    'Tis Mary's hand upon my brow!

But let me check this tender lay
   Which none may hear but she and thou!
Like the still hive at quiet midnight humming,   35
Murmur it to yourselves, ye two beloved women!

                    1802

Answer to a Child's Question

Do you ask what the birds say? The Sparrow, the Dove,
The Linnet and Thrush say, "I love and I love!"
In the winter they're silent—the wind is so strong;
What it says, I don't know, but it sings a loud song.
But green leaves, and blossoms, and sunny warm
    weather,   5
And singing, and loving—all come back together.
But the Lark is so brimful of gladness and love,
The green fields below him, the blue sky above,
That he sings, and he sings; and for ever sings he—
"I love my Love, and my Love loves me!"   10

                    1802

The Pains of Sleep

Ere on my bed my limbs I lay,
It hath not been my use to pray
With moving lips or bended knees;
But silently, by slow degrees,
My spirit I to Love compose,   5
In humble trust mine eye-lids close,
With reverential resignation,
No wish conceived, no thought exprest,
Only a sense of supplication;

A sense o'er all my soul imprest   10
That I am weak, yet not unblest,
Since in me, round me, every where
Eternal Strength and Wisdom are.

But yester-night I prayed aloud
In anguish and in agony,   15
Up-starting from the fiendish crowd
Of shapes and thoughts that tortured me:
A lurid light, a trampling throng,
Sense of intolerable wrong,
And whom I scorned, those only strong!   20
Thirst of revenge, the powerless will
Still baffled, and yet burning still!
Desire with loathing strangely mixed
On wild or hateful objects fixed.
Fantastic passions! maddening brawl!   25
And shame and terror over all!
Deeds to be hid which were not hid,
Which all confused I could not know
Whether I suffered, or I did:
For all seemed guilt, remorse or woe,   30
My own or others' still the same
Life-stifling fear, soul-stifling shame.

So two nights passed: the night's dismay
Saddened and stunned the coming day.
Sleep, the wide blessing, seemed to me   35
Distemper's worst calamity.
The third night, when my own loud scream
Had waked me from the fiendish dream,
O'ercome with sufferings strange and wild,
I wept as I had been a child;   40
And having thus by tears subdued
My anguish to a milder mood,

Such punishments, I said, were due
To natures deepliest stained with sin,—
For aye entempesting anew   45
The unfathomable hell within,
The horror of their deeds to view,
To know and loathe, yet wish and do!
Such griefs with such men well agree,
But wherefore, wherefore fall on me?
To be beloved is all I need,   50
And whom I love, I love indeed.

                                                   1803

Epitaph

Here sleeps at length poor Col. and without screaming,
Who died, as he had always lived, a-dreaming;
Shot dead, while sleeping, by the Gout within,
Alone, and all unknown, at E'nbro' in an Inn.

                                                   1803

The Exchange

We pledged our hearts, my love and I,—
    I in my arms the maiden clasping;
I could not guess the reason why,
    But, oh! I trembled like an aspen.

Her father's love she bade me gain;   5
    I went, but shook like any reed!
I strove to act the man—in vain!
    We had exchanged our hearts indeed.

                                                   1804

Phantom

All look and likeness caught from earth
All accident of kin and birth,
Had pass'd away. There was no trace
Of aught on that illumined face,
Uprais'd beneath the rifted stone   5
But of one spirit all her own;—
She, she herself, and only she,
Shone through her body visibly.

1805

A Sunset

Upon the mountain's edge with light touch resting,
There a brief while the globe of splendour sits
    And seems a creature of the earth; but soon
        More changeful than the Moon,
To wane fantastic his great orb submits,   5
Or cone or mow of fire: till sinking slowly
Even to a star at length he lessens wholly.

Abrupt, as Spirits vanish, he is sunk!
A soul-like breeze possesses all the wood.
    The boughs, the sprays have stood   10
As motionless as stands the ancient trunk!
But every leaf through all the forest flutters,
And deep the cavern of the fountain mutters.

1805

What Is Life?

Resembles life what once was deem'd of light,
Too ample in itself for human sight?
An absolute self—an element ungrounded—
All that we see, all colours of all shade
    By encroach of darkness made?—   5
Is very life by consciousness unbounded?
And all the thoughts, pains, joys of mortal breath,
A war-embrace of wrestling life and death?

1805

The Blossoming of the Solitary Date-Tree

A LAMENT

1

Beneath the blaze of a tropical sun the mountain peaks are the Thrones of Frost, through the absence of objects to reflect the rays. "What no one with us shares, seems scarce our own." The presence of a ONE,

    The best belov'd, who loveth me the best,

is for the heart, what the supporting air from within is for the hollow globe with its suspended car. Deprive it of this, and all without, that would have buoyed it aloft even to the seat of the gods, becomes a burthen and crushes it into flatness.

2

The finer the sense for the beautiful and the lovely, and the fairer and lovelier the object presented to the sense; the more exquisite the individual's capacity of joy, and the more ample his means and opportunities of enjoyment, the more heavily will he feel the ache of solitariness, the more unsubstantial becomes the feast spread around him. What matters it, whether in fact the viands and the ministering graces are shadowy or real, to him who has not hand to grasp nor arms to embrace them?

3

Imagination; honourable aims;
Free commune with the choir that cannot die;
Science and song; delight in little things,
The buoyant child surviving in the man;
Fields, forests, ancient mountains, ocean, sky,   5
With all their voices—O dare I accuse
My earthly lot as guilty of my spleen,
Or call my destiny niggard! O no! no!
It is her largeness, and her overflow,
Which being incomplete, disquieteth me so!   10

4

For never touch of gladness stirs my heart,
But tim'rously beginning to rejoice
Like a blind Arab, that from sleep doth start
In lonesome tent, I listen for thy voice.
Belovéd! 'tis not thine; thou art not there!   15
Then melts the bubble into idle air,
And wishing without hope I restlessly despair.

5

The mother with anticipated glee
Smiles o'er the child, that, standing by her chair
And flatt'ning its round cheek upon her knee,   20
Looks up, and doth its rosy lips prepare
To mock the coming sounds. At that sweet sight
She hears her own voice with a new delight;
And if the babe perchance should lisp the notes aright,

6

Then is she tenfold gladder than before!   25
But should disease or chance the darling take,
What then avail those songs, which sweet of yore
Were only sweet for their sweet echo's sake?
Dear maid! no prattler at a mother's knee
Was e'er so dearly prized as I prize thee: 30
Why was I made for Love and Love denied to me?

1805

Metrical Feet

LESSON FOR A BOY

Trōchĕe trīps frŏm lōng tŏ shōrt;
From long to long in solemn sort
Slōw Spōndēe stālks; strŏng fōot! yet ill able
Ēvĕr tŏ cōme ŭp wĭth Dāctўl trĭsȳllăblĕ.
Īāmbĭcs mārch frŏm shŏrt tŏ lōng;—
Wĭth ă lēap ănd ă bōund thĕ swĭft Ānăpǽests thrōng;
One syllable long, with one short at each side,
Ămphĭbrăchўs hāstes wĭth ă stātelў stride;—
Fīrst ănd lāst bēĭng lōng, mĭddlĕ shōrt, Ămphĭmācer
Strīkes hĭs thūndērĭng hōofs like ă prōud hĭgh-brĕd
        Rācer.   10

If Derwent be innocent, steady, and wise,
And delight in the things of earth, water, and skies;
Tender warmth at his heart, with these metres to show
     it,
With sound sense in his brains, may make Derwent a
     poet,—
May crown him with fame, and must win him the
     love   15
Of his father on earth and his Father above.
     My dear, dear child!
Could you stand upon Skiddaw, you would not from its
     whole ridge
See a man who so loves you as your fond S. T.
     COLERIDGE.

                                1806

To William Wordsworth

COMPOSED ON THE NIGHT AFTER HIS RECITATION OF A POEM ON THE GROWTH OF AN INDIVIDUAL MIND

Friend of the wise! and Teacher of the Good!
Into my heart have I received that Lay
More than historic, that prophetic Lay
Wherein (high theme by thee first sung aright)
Of the foundations and the building up   5
Of a Human Spirit thou hast dared to tell
What may be told, to the understanding mind
Revealable; and what within the mind
By vital breathings secret as the soul
Of vernal growth, oft quickens in the heart   10
Thoughts all too deep for words!—

Theme hard as high!

Of smiles spontaneous, and mysterious fears
(The first-born they of Reason and twin-birth),
Of tides obedient to external force,
And currents self-determined, as might seem,   15
Or by some inner Power; of moments awful,
Now in thy inner life, and now abroad,
When power streamed from thee, and thy soul received
The light reflected, as a light bestowed—
Of fancies fair, and milder hours of youth,   20
Hyblean murmurs of poetic thought
Industrious in its joy, in vales and glens
Native or outland, lakes and famous hills!
Or on the lonely high-road, when the stars
Were rising; or by secret mountain-streams,   25
The guides and the companions of thy way!

Of more than Fancy, of the Social Sense
Distending wide, and man beloved as man,
Where France in all her towns lay vibrating
Like some becalméd bark beneath the burst   30
Of Heaven's immediate thunder, when no cloud
Is visible, or shadow on the main.
For thou wert there, thine own brows garlanded,
Amid the tremor of a realm aglow,
Amid a mighty nation jubilant,   35
When from the general heart of human kind
Hope sprang forth like a full-born Deity!
——Of that dear Hope afflicted and struck down,
So summoned homeward, thenceforth calm and sure
From the dread watch-tower of man's absolute self,   40
With light unwaning on her eyes, to look
Far on—herself a glory to behold,
The Angel of the vision! Then (last strain)

Of Duty, chosen Laws controlling choice,
Action and joy!—An Orphic song indeed,   45
A song divine of high and passionate thoughts
To their own music chaunted!

      O great Bard!
Ere yet that last strain dying awed the air,
With stedfast eye I viewed thee in the choir
Of ever-enduring men. The truly great   50
Have all one age, and from one visible space
Shed influence! They, both in power and act,
Are permanent, and Time is not with them,
Save as it worketh for them, they in it.
Nor less a sacred Roll, than those of old,   55
And to be placed, as they, with gradual fame
Among the archives of mankind, thy work
Makes audible a linkéd lay of Truth,
Of Truth profound a sweet continuous lay,
Not learnt, but native, her own natural notes!   60
Ah! as I listened with a heart forlorn,
The pulses of my being beat anew:
And even as Life returns upon the drowned,
Life's joy rekindling roused a throng of pains—
Keen pangs of Love, awakening as a babe   65
Turbulent, with an outcry in the heart;
And fears self-willed, that shunned the eye of Hope;
And Hope that scarce would know itself from Fear;
Sense of past Youth, and Manhood come in vain,
And Genius given, and knowledge won in vain;   70
And all which I had culled in wood-walks wild,
And all which patient toil had reared, and all,
Commune with thee had opened out—but flowers
Strewed on my corse, and borne upon my bier
In the same coffin, for the self-same grave!   75

That way no more! and ill beseems it me,
Who came a welcomer in herald's guise,
Singing of Glory, and Futurity,
To wander back on such unhealthful road,
Plucking the poisons of self-harm! And ill   80
Such intertwine beseems triumphal wreaths
Strew'd before thy advancing!

                    Nor do thou,
Sage Bard! impair the memory of that hour
Of thy communion with my nobler mind
By pity or grief, already felt too long!   85
Nor let my words import more blame than needs.
The tumult rose and ceased: for Peace is nigh
Where Wisdom's voice has found a listening heart.
Amid the howl of more than wintry storms,
The Halcyon hears the voice of vernal hours   90
Already on the wing.

                 Eve following eve,
Dear tranquil time, when the sweet sense of Home
Is sweetest! moments for their own sake hailed
And more desired, more precious, for thy song,
In silence listening, like a devout child,   95
My soul lay passive, by thy various strain
Driven as in surges now beneath the stars,
With momentary stars of my own birth,
Fair constellated foam, still darting off
Into the darkness; now a tranquil sea,   100
Outspread and bright, yet swelling to the moon.

And when—O Friend! my comforter and guide!
Strong in thyself, and powerful to give strength!—
Thy long sustainéd Song finally closed,
And thy deep voice had ceased—yet thou thyself   105

Wert still before my eyes, and round us both
That happy vision of belovéd faces—
Scarce conscious, and yet conscious of its close
I sate, my being blended in one thought
(Thought was it? or aspiration? or resolve?)   110
Absorbed, yet hanging still upon the sound—
And when I rose, I found myself in prayer.

January 1807

An Angel Visitant

Within these circling hollies woodbine-clad—
Beneath this small blue roof of vernal sky—
How warm, how still! Tho' tears should dim mine eye,
Yet will my heart for days continue glad,
For here, my love, thou art, and here am I!   5

1801(?)

Recollections of Love

I

How warm this woodland wild Recess!
   Love surely hath been breathing here;
   And this sweet bed of heath, my dear!
Swells up, then sinks with faint caress,
   As if to have you yet more near.   5

II

Eight springs have flown, since last I lay
   On sea-ward Quantock's heathy hills,
   Where quiet sounds from hidden rills
Float here and there, like things astray,
   And high o'er head the sky-lark shrills.   10

III

No voice as yet had made the air
  Be music with your name; yet why
  That asking look? that yearning sigh?
That sense of promise every where?
  Belovéd! flew your spirit by?   15

IV

As when a mother doth explore
  The rose-mark on her long-lost child,
  I met, I loved you, maiden mild!
As whom I long had loved before—
  So deeply had I been, beguiled.   20

V

You stood before me like a thought,
  A dream remembered in a dream.
  But when those meek eyes first did seem
To tell me, Love within you wrought—
  O Greta, dear domestic stream!   25

VI

Has not, since then, Love's prompture deep,
  Has not Love's whisper evermore
  Been ceaseless, as thy gentle roar?
Sole voice, when other voices sleep,
  Dear under-song in clamor's hour.   30
                                                   1807

[Its Own Delight]

And in Life's noisiest hour
There whispers still the ceaseless love of thee,
The heart's self-solace ⎱ and soliloquy.
          commune ⎰

You mould my Hopes you fashion me within:
And to the leading love-throb in the heart,
Through all my being, through my pulses beat;
You lie in all my many thoughts like Light,
Like the fair light of Dawn, or summer Eve,
On rippling stream, or cloud-reflecting lake;
And looking to the Heaven that bends above you,
How oft! I bless the lot that made me love you.
And my heart mantles in its own delight.

                                 1807

To Two Sisters

[MARY MORGAN AND CHARLOTTE BRENT]

A WANDERER'S FAREWELL

To know, to esteem, to love,—and then to part—
Makes up life's tale to many a feeling heart;
Alas for some abiding-place of love,
O'er which my spirit, like the mother dove,
Might brood with warming wings!
                         O fair! O kind! 5
Sisters in blood, yet each with each intwined

More close by sisterhood of heart and mind!
Me disinherited in form and face
By nature, and mishap of outward grace;
Who, soul and body, through one guiltless fault   10
Waste daily with the poison of sad thought,
Me did you soothe, when solace hoped I none!
And as on unthaw'd ice the winter sun,
Though stern the frost, though brief the genial day,
You bless my heart with many a cheerful ray;   15
For gratitude suspends the heart's despair,
Reflecting bright though cold your image there.
Nay more! its music by some sweeter strain
Makes us live o'er our happiest hours again,
Hope re-appearing dim in memory's guise—   20
Even thus did you call up before mine eyes
Two dear, dear Sisters, prized all price above,
Sisters, like you, with more than sister's love;
So like you *they*, and so in *you* were seen
Their relative statures, tempers, looks, and mien,   25
That oft, dear ladies! you have been to me
At once a vision and reality.
Sight seem'd a sort of memory, and amaze
Mingled a trouble with affection's gaze.

Oft to my eager soul I whisper blame,   30
A Stranger bid it feel the Stranger's shame—
My eager soul, impatient of the name,
No strangeness owns, no Stranger's form descries:
The chidden heart spreads trembling on the eyes.
First-seen I gazed, as I would look you thro'!   35
My best-beloved regain'd their youth in you,—
And still I ask, though now familiar grown,
Are you for *their* sakes dear, or for your own?
O doubly dear! may Quiet with you dwell!

In Grief I love you, yet I love you well! 40
Hope long is dead to me! an orphan's tear
Love wept despairing o'er his nurse's bier.
Yet still she flutters o'er her grave's green slope:
For Love's despair is but the ghost of Hope!

Sweet Sisters! were you placed around one hearth 45
With those, your other selves in shape and worth,
Far rather would I sit in solitude,
Fond recollections all my fond heart's food,
And dream of *you*, sweet Sisters! (ah! not mine!)
And only *dream* of you (ah! dream and pine!) 50
Than boast the presence and partake the pride,
And shine in the eye, of all the world beside.

1807

Psyche

The butterfly the ancient Grecians made
The soul's fair emblem, and its only name—
But of the soul, escaped the slavish trade
Of mortal life!—For in this earthly frame
Ours is the reptile's lot, much toil, much blame, 5
Manifold motions making little speed,
And to deform and kill the things whereon we feed.

1808

A Tombless Epitaph

'Tis true, Idoloclastes Satyrane!
(So call him, for so mingling blame with praise,
And smiles with anxious looks, his earliest friends,

Masking his birth-name, wont to character
His wild-wood fancy and impetuous zeal,)   5
'Tis true that, passionate for ancient truths,
And honouring with religious love the Great
Of elder times, he hated to excess,
With an unquiet and intolerant scorn,
The hollow Puppets of a hollow Age,   10
Ever idolatrous, and changing ever
Its worthless Idols! Learning, Power, and Time,
(Too much of all) thus wasting in vain war
Of fervid colloquy. Sickness, 'tis true,
Whole years of weary days, besieged him close,   15
Even to the gates and inlets of his life!
But it is true, no less, that strenuous, firm,
And with a natural gladness, he maintained
The citadel unconquered, and in joy
Was strong to follow the delightful Muse.   20
For not a hidden path, that to the shades
Of the beloved Parnassian forest leads,
Lurked undiscovered by him; not a rill
There issues from the fount of Hippocrene,
But he had traced it upward to its source,   25
Through open glade, dark glen, and secret dell,
Knew the gay wild flowers on its banks, and culled
Its med'cinable herbs. Yea, oft alone,
Piercing the long-neglected holy cave,
The haunt obscure of old Philosophy,   30
He bade with lifted torch its starry walls
Sparkle, as erst they sparkled to the flame
Of odorous lamps tended by Saint and Sage.
O framed for calmer times and nobler hearts!
O studious Poet, eloquent for truth!   35
Philosopher! contemning wealth and death,
Yet docile, childlike, full of Life and Love!
Here, rather than on monumental stone,

This record of thy worth thy Friend inscribes,
Thoughtful, with quiet tears upon his cheek.   40

1809(?)

For a Market-Clock

(IMPROMPTU)

What now, O Man! thou dost or mean'st to do
Will help to give thee peace, or make thee rue,
When hovering o'er the Dot this hand shall tell
The moment that secures thee Heaven or Hell!

1809

The Visionary Hope

Sad lot, to have no Hope! Though lowly kneeling
He fain would frame a prayer within his breast,
Would fain entreat for some sweet breath of healing,
That his sick body might have ease and rest;
He strove in vain! the dull sighs from his chest   5
Against his will the stifling load revealing,
Though Nature forced; though like some captive guest,
Some royal prisoner at his conqueror's feast,
An alien's restless mood but half concealing,
The sternness on his gentle brow confessed,   10
Sickness within and miserable feeling:
Though obscure pangs made curses of his dreams,
And dreaded sleep, each night repelled in vain,
Each night was scattered by its own loud screams:
Yet never could his heart command, though fain,   15
One deep full wish to be no more in pain.

That Hope, which was his inward bliss and boast,
Which waned and died, yet ever near him stood,
Though changed in nature, wander where he would—
For Love's Despair is but Hope's pining Ghost!   20
For this one hope he makes his hourly moan,
He wishes and can wish for this alone!
Pierced, as with light from Heaven, before its gleams
(So the love-stricken visionary deems)
Disease would vanish, like a summer shower,   25
Whose dews fling sunshine from the noon-tide bower!
Or let it stay! yet this one Hope should give
Such strength that he would bless his pains and live.

                                        1810(?)

Time, Real and Imaginary

AN ALLEGORY

On the wide level of a mountain's head,
(I knew not where, but 'twas some faery place)
Their pinions, ostrich-like, for sails out-spread,
Two lovely children run an endless race,
          A sister and a brother!   5
          This far outstripp'd the other;
     Yet ever runs she with reverted face,
     And looks and listens for the boy behind:
          For he, alas! is blind!
O'er rough and smooth with even step he passed,   10
And knows not whether he be first or last.

                                        1812(?)

An Invocation

FROM *Remorse*
[*Act III, scene i, lines 69–82.*]

Hear, sweet Spirit, hear the spell,
Lest a blacker charm compel!
So shall the midnight breezes swell
With thy deep long-lingering knell.

And at evening evermore,   5
In a chapel on the shore,
Shall the chaunter, sad and saintly,
Yellow tapers burning faintly,
Doleful masses chaunt for thee,
    Miserere Domine!   10

Hush! the cadence dies away
    On the quiet moonlight sea:
The boatmen rest their oars and say,
    Miserere Domine!

1812

Human Life

ON THE DENIAL OF IMMORTALITY

If dead, we cease to be; if total gloom
    Swallow up life's brief flash for aye, we fare
As summer-gusts, of sudden birth and doom,
    Whose sound and motion not alone declare,
But are their whole of being! If the breath   5

Be Life itself, and not its task and tent,
If even a soul like Milton's can know death;
    O Man! thou vessel purposeless, unmeant,
Yet drone-hive strange of phantom purposes!
    Surplus of Nature's dread activity,   10
Which, as she gazed on some nigh-finished vase,
Retreating slow, with meditative pause,
    She formed with restless hands unconsciously.
Blank accident! nothing's anomaly!
    If rootless thus, thus substanceless thy state,   15
Go, weigh thy dreams, and be thy hopes, thy fears,
The counter-weights!—Thy laughter and thy tears
    Mean but themselves, each fittest to create
And to repay the other! Why rejoices
    Thy heart with hollow joy for hollow good?   20
Why cowl thy face beneath the mourner's hood?
Why waste thy sighs, and thy lamenting voices,
    Image of Image, Ghost of Ghostly Elf,
That such a thing as thou feel'st warm or cold?
Yet what and whence thy gain, if thou withhold   25
    These costless shadows of thy shadowy self?
Be sad! be glad! be neither! seek, or shun!
Thou hast no reason why! Thou canst have none;
Thy being's being is contradiction.

                                                    1815(?)

Song

FROM *Zapolya*

A sunny shaft did I behold,
    From sky to earth it slanted:
And poised therein a bird so bold—
    Sweet bird, thou wert enchanted!

He sank, he rose, he twinkled, he trolled   5
  Within that shaft of sunny mist;
His eyes of fire, his beak of gold,
  All else of amethyst!

And thus he sang: "Adieu! adieu!
Love's dreams prove seldom true.   10
The blossoms they make no delay:
The sparkling dew-drops will not stay.
  Sweet month of May,
    We must away;
      Far, far away!   15
        To-day! to-day!"

                                                   1815

Hunting Song

FROM *Zapolya*

Up, up! ye dames, and lasses gay!
To the meadows trip away.
'Tis you must tend the flocks this morn,
And scare the small birds from the corn.
  Not a soul at home may stay: 5
    For the shepherds must go
      With lance and bow
  To hunt the wolf in the woods to-day.

Leave the hearth and leave the house
To the cricket and the mouse: 10
Find grannam out a sunny seat,
With babe and lambkin at her feet.
  Not a soul at home may stay:

For the shepherds must go
With lance and bow   15
To hunt the wolf in the woods to-day.

1815

To Nature

It may indeed be phantasy, when I
  Essay to draw from all created things
  Deep, heartfelt, inward joy that closely clings;
And trace in leaves and flowers that round me lie
Lessons of love and earnest piety.   5
  So let it be; and if the wide world rings
  In mock of this belief, it brings
Nor fear, nor grief, nor vain perplexity.
So will I build my altar in the fields,
  And the blue sky my fretted dome shall be,   10
And the sweet fragrance that the wild flower yields
  Shall be the incense I will yield to Thee,
Thee only God! and thou shalt not despise
Even me, the priest of this poor sacrifice.

1820(?)

Fragment

The body,
Eternal Shadow of the finite Soul,
The Soul's self-symbol, its image of itself.
Its own yet not itself.

Limbo

.   .   .   .

The sole true Something—This! In Limbo's Den
It frightens Ghosts, as here Ghosts frighten men.
Thence cross'd unseiz'd—and shall some fated hour
Be pulveris'd by Demogorgon's power,
And given as poison to annihilate souls—   5
Even now it shrinks them—they shrink in as Moles
(Nature's mute monks, live mandrakes of the ground)
Creep back from Light—then listen for its sound;—
See but to dread, and dread they know not why—
The natural alien of their negative eye.   10

'Tis a strange place, this Limbo!—not a Place,
Yet name it so;—where Time and weary Space
Fettered from flight, with night-mare sense of fleeing,
Strive for their last crepuscular half-being;—
Lank Space, and scytheless Time with branny hands   15
Barren and soundless as the measuring sands,
Not mark'd by flit of Shades,—unmeaning they
As moonlight on the dial of the day!
But that is lovely—looks like Human Time,
An Old Man with a steady look sublime,   20
That stops his earthly task to watch the skies;
But he is blind—a Statue hath such eyes;—
Yet having moonward turn'd his face by chance,
Gazes the orb with moon-like countenance,
With scant white hairs, with foretop bald and high, 25
He gazes still,—his eyeless face all eye;—
As 'twere an organ full of silent sight,
His whole face seemeth to rejoice in light!
Lip touching lip, all moveless, bust and limb—

He seems to gaze at that which seems to gaze on
    him!   30
  No such sweet sights doth Limbo den immure,
Wall'd round, and made a spirit-jail secure,
By the mere horror of blank Naught-at-all,
Whose circumambience doth these ghosts enthral.
A lurid thought is growthless, dull Privation,   35
Yet that is but a Purgatory curse;
Hell knows a fear far worse,
A fear—a future state;—'tis positive Negation!

                                    1817

Ne Plus Ultra

        Sole Positive of Night!
        Antipathist of Light!
Fate's only essence! primal scorpion rod—
The one permitted opposite of God!—
Condenséd blackness and abysmal storm   5
      Compacted to one sceptre
      Arms the Grasp enorm—
        The Intercepter—
The Substance that still casts the shadow Death!—
      The Dragon foul and fell—   10
      The unrevealable,
And hidden one, whose breath
Gives wind and fuel to the fires of Hell!
      Ah! sole despair
      Of both th' eternities in Heaven!   15
Sole interdict of all-bedewing prayer,
      The all-compassionate!
      Save to the Lampads Seven
Reveal'd to none of all th' Angelic State,

Save to the Lampads Seven,   20
That watch the throne of Heaven!

1826(?)

The Knight's Tomb

Where is the grave of Sir Arthur O'Kellyn?
Where may the grave of that good man be?—
By the side of a spring, on the breast of Helvellyn,
Under the twigs of a young birch tree!
The oak that in summer was sweet to hear,   5
And rustled its leaves in the fall of the year,
And whistled and roared in the winter alone,
Is gone,—and the birch in its stead is grown.—
The Knight's bones are dust,
And his good sword rust;—   10
His soul is with the saints, I trust.

1817(?)

On Donne's Poetry

With Donne, whose muse on dromedary trots,
Wreathe iron pokers into true-love knots;
Rhyme's sturdy cripple, fancy's maze and clue,
Wit's forge and fire-blast, meaning's press and screw.

1818(?)

Youth and Age

Verse, a breeze mid blossoms straying,
Where Hope clung feeding, like a bee—

Both were mine! Life went a-maying
    With Nature, Hope, and Poesy,
        When I was young!   5

When I was young?—Ah, woful When!
Ah! for the change 'twixt Now and Then!
This breathing house not built with hands,
This body that does me grievous wrong,
O'er aery cliffs and glittering sands,   10
How lightly then it flashed along:—
Like those trim skiffs, unknown of yore,
On winding lakes and rivers wide,
That ask no aid of sail or oar,
That fear no spite of wind or tide!   15
Nought cared this body for wind or weather
When Youth and I lived in't together.

Flowers are lovely; Love is flower-like;
Friendship is a sheltering tree;
O! the joys, that came down shower-like,   20
Of Friendship, Love, and Liberty,
        Ere I was old!

Ere I was old? Ah woful Ere,
Which tells me, Youth's no longer here!
O Youth! for years so many and sweet,   25
'Tis known, that Thou and I were one,
I'll think it but a fond conceit—
It cannot be that Thou art gone!
Thy vesper-bell hath not yet toll'd:—
And thou wert aye a masker bold!   30
What strange disguise hast now put on,
To make believe, that thou art gone?
I see these locks in silvery slips,
This drooping gait, this altered size:

But Spring-tide blossoms on thy lips,   35
And tears take sunshine from thine eyes!
Life is but thought; so think I will
That Youth and I are house-mates still.

Dew-drops are the gems of morning,
But the tears of mournful eve!   40
Where no hope is, life's a warning
That only serves to make us grieve,
                        When we are old:

That only serves to make us grieve
With oft and tedious taking-leave,   45
Like some poor nigh-related guest,
That may not rudely be dismist;
Yet hath outstay'd his welcome while,
And tells the jest without the smile.

                                            1823–1832

First Advent of Love

O fair is Love's first hope to gentle mind!
As Eve's first star thro' fleecy cloudlet peeping;
And sweeter than the gentle south-west wind.
O'er willowy meads, and shadow'd waters creeping,
And Ceres' golden fields;—the sultry hind   5
Meets it with brow uplift, and stays his reaping.

                                            1824(?)

Work Without Hope

LINES COMPOSED 21ST FEBRUARY 1825

All Nature seems at work. Slugs leave their lair—
The bees are stirring—birds are on the wing—

And Winter slumbering in the open air,
Wears on his smiling face a dream of Spring!
And I the while, the sole unbusy thing,   5
Nor honey make, nor pair, nor build, nor sing.

Yet well I ken the banks where amaranths blow,
Have traced the fount whence streams of nectar flow.
Bloom, O ye amaranths! bloom for whom ye may,
For me ye bloom not! Glide, rich streams, away!   10
With lips unbrightened, wreathless brow, I stroll:
And would you learn the spells that drowse my soul?
Work without Hope draws nectar in a sieve,
And Hope without an object cannot live.

                                                1825

Song

Though veiled in spires of myrtle-wreath,
Love is a sword which cuts its sheath,
And through the clefts itself has made,
We spy the flashes of the blade!
But through the clefts itself has made   5
We likewise see Love's flashing blade,
By rust consumed, or snapt in twain;
And only hilt and stump remain.

                                            1825(?)

A Character

A bird, who for his other sins
Had liv'd amongst the Jacobins;
Though like a kitten amid rats,
Or callow tit in nest of bats,

He much abhorr'd all democrats;　　　　　　5
Yet nathless stood in ill report
Of wishing ill to Church and Court,
Tho' he'd nor claw, nor tooth, nor sting,
And learnt to pipe God save the King;
Tho' each day did new feathers bring,　　　10
All swore he had a leathern wing;
Nor polish'd wing, nor feather'd tail,
Nor down-clad thigh would aught avail;
And tho'—his tongue devoid of gall—
He civilly assur'd them all:—　　　　　　15
"A bird am I of Phoebus' breed,
And on the sunflower cling and feed;
My name, good Sirs, is Thomas Tit!"
The bats would hail him Brother Cit,
Or, at the furthest, cousin-german.　　　　20
At length the matter to determine,
He publicly denounced the vermin;
He spared the mouse, he praised the owl;
But bats were neither flesh nor fowl.
Blood-sucker, vampire, harpy, goul,　　　25
Came in full clatter from his throat,
Till his old nest-mates chang'd their note
To hireling, traitor, and turncoat,—
A base apostate who had sold
His very teeth and claws for gold;—　　　30
And then his feathers!—sharp the jest—
No doubt he feather'd well his nest!
　　"A Tit indeed! aye, tit for tat—
With place and title, brother Bat,
We soon shall see how well he'll play　　　35
Count Goldfinch, or Sir Joseph Jay!"
　　Alas, poor Bird! and ill-bestarr'd—
Or rather let us say, poor Bard!
And henceforth quit the allegoric,

With metaphor and simile,   40
For simple facts and style historic:—
Alas, poor Bard! no gold had he;
Behind another's team he stept,
And plough'd and sow'd, while others reapt;
The work was his, but theirs the glory,   45
Sic vos non vobis, his whole story.
Besides, whate'er he wrote or said
Came from his heart as well as head;
And though he never left in lurch
His king, his country, or his church,   50
'Twas but to humour his own cynical
Contempt of doctrines Jacobinical;
To his own conscience only hearty,
'Twas but by chance he serv'd the party;—
The self-same things had said and writ,   55
Had Pitt been Fox, and Fox been Pitt;
Content his own applause to win,
Would never dash thro' thick and thin,
And he can make, so say the wise,
No claim who makes no sacrifice;—   60
And bard still less:—what claim had he,
Who swore it vex'd his soul to see
So grand a cause, so proud a realm,
With Goose and Goody at the helm;
Who long ago had fall'n asunder   65
But for their rivals' baser blunder,
The coward whine and Frenchified
Slaver and slang of the other side?—

Thus, his own whim his only bribe,
Our Bard pursued his old A. B. C.   70
Contented if he could subscribe
In fullest sense his name ''Εστησε;
('Tis Punic Greek for "he hath stood!")

Whate'er the men, the cause was good;
And therefore with a right good will,   75
Poor fool, he fights their battles still.
Tush! squeak'd the Bats;—a mere bravado
To whitewash that base renegado;
'Tis plain unless you're blind or mad,
His conscience for the bays he barters;—   80
And true it is—as true as sad—
These circlets of green baize he had—
But then, alas! they were his garters!
    Ah! silly Bard, unfed, untended,
His lamp but glimmer'd in its socket;   85
He lived unhonour'd and unfriended
With scarce a penny in his pocket;—
Nay—tho' he hid it from the many—
With scarce a pocket for his penny!

                                                             1825

Constancy to an Ideal Object

Since all that beat about in Nature's range,
Or veer or vanish; why should'st thou remain
The only constant in a world of change,
O yearning Thought! that liv'st but in the brain?
Call to the Hours, that in the distance play,   5
The faery people of the future day——
Fond Thought! not one of all that shining swarm
Will breathe on thee with life-enkindling breath,
Till when, like strangers shelt'ring from a storm,
Hope and Despair meet in the porch of Death!   10
Yet still thou haunt'st me; and though well I see,
She is not thou, and only thou art she,
Still, still as though some dear embodied Good,
Some living Love before my eyes there stood

With answering look a ready ear to lend,   15
I mourn to thee and say—"Ah! loveliest friend!
That this the meed of all my toils might be,
To have a home, an English home, and thee!"
Vain repetition! Home and Thou are one.
The peacefull'st cot, the moon shall shine upon,   20
Lulled by the thrush and wakened by the lark,
Without thee were but a becalméd bark,
Whose Helmsman on an ocean waste and wide
Sits mute and pale his mouldering helm beside.

And art thou nothing? Such thou art, as when   25
The woodman winding westward up the glen
At wintry dawn, where o'er the sheep-track's maze
The viewless snow-mist weaves a glist'ning haze,
Sees full before him, gliding without tread,
An image with a glory round its head;   30
The enamoured rustic worships its fair hues,
Nor knows he makes the shadow, he pursues!

                                        1826(?)

Phantom or Fact

A DIALOGUE IN VERSE

AUTHOR

A lovely form there sate beside my bed,
And such a feeding calm its presence shed,
A tender love so pure from earthly leaven,
That I unnethe the fancy might control,
'Twas my own spirit newly come from heaven,   5
Wooing its gentle way into my soul!
But ah! the change—It had not stirr'd, and yet—
Alas! that change how fain would I forget!

That shrinking back, like one that had mistook!
That weary, wandering, disavowing look!   10
'Twas all another, feature, look, and frame,
And still, methought, I knew, it was the same!

FRIEND

This riddling tale, to what does it belong?
Is't history? vision? or an idle song?
Or rather say at once, within what space   15
Of time this wild disastrous change took place?

AUTHOR

Call it a moment's work (and such it seems)
This tale's a fragment from the life of dreams;
But say, that years matur'd the silent strife,
And 'tis a record from the dream of life.   20
                                             1830(?

Reason

[*"Finally, what is Reason? You have often asked me: and
this is my answer":*—]

Whene'er the mist, that stands 'twixt God and thee,
Defecates to a pure transparency,
That intercepts no light and adds no stain—
There Reason is, and then begins her reign!

But alas!   5
        ——"tu stesso, ti fai grosso
    Col falso immaginar, sì che non vedi
    Ciò che vedresti, se l'avessi scosso."
                            Dante, *Paradiso*, Canto i.
                                            1830

Self-Knowledge

—*E coelo descendit* γνῶθι σεαυτόν.—Juvenal, xi, 27.

Γνῶθι σεαυτόν!—and is this the prime
And heaven-sprung adage of the olden time!—
Say, canst thou make thyself?—Learn first that trade;—
Haply thou mayst know what thyself had made.
What hast thou, Man, that thou dar'st call thine
    own?—   5
What is there in thee, Man, that can be known?—
Dark fluxion, all unfixable by thought,
A phantom dim of past and future wrought,
Vain sister of the worm,—life, death, soul, clod—
Ignore thyself, and strive to know thy God!   10
                            1832

Epitaph

Stop, Christian passer-by!—Stop, child of God,
And read with gentle breast. Beneath this sod
A poet lies, or that which once seem'd he.
O, lift one thought in prayer for S. T. C.;
That he who many a year with toil of breath   5
Found death in life, may here find life in death!
Mercy for praise—to be forgiven for fame
He ask'd, and hoped, through Christ. Do thou the same!
                        9th November, 1833

LETTERS

EDITOR'S NOTE

The letters are taken from two sources: *Letters of Samuel Taylor Coleridge,* edited by Ernest Hartley Coleridge (London: Heinemann, 1895) and *Unpublished Letters of Samuel Taylor Coleridge,* edited by Earl Leslie Griggs (New Haven: Yale University Press, 1933). They are arranged in chronological order, except for the autobiographical letters to Thomas Poole, which are grouped at the beginning of the section because they tell a continuous story of Coleridge's early years. In order to identify the source without unduly disturbing the reader, letters from the E. H. Coleridge volume are marked (L) and those from the Griggs volume (UL) after the name of the addressee.

TO THOMAS POOLE (L)

Monday, February, 1797.

My dear Poole,

I could inform the dullest author how he might write an interesting book. Let him relate the events of his own life with honesty, not disguising the feelings that accompanied them. I never yet read even a Methodist's Experience in the "Gospel Magazine" without receiving instruction and amusement; and I should almost despair of that man who could peruse the Life of John Woolman without an amelioration of heart. As to my Life, it has all the charms of variety,—high life and low life,

217

vices and virtues, great folly and some wisdom. However, what I am depends on what I have been; and you, *my best Friend!* have a right to the narration. To me the task will be a useful one. It will renew and deepen my reflections on the past; and it will perhaps make you behold with no unforgiving or impatient eye those weaknesses and defects in my character, which so many untoward circumstances have concurred to plant there. . . .

Sunday, March, 1797.

. . . My brother George is a man of reflective mind and elegant genius. He possesses learning in a greater degree than any of the family, excepting myself. His manners are grave and hued over with a tender sadness. In his moral character he approaches every way nearer to perfection than any man I ever yet knew; indeed, he is worth the whole family in a lump. . . . The tenth and last child was S. T. Coleridge, the subject of these epistles, born (as I told you in my last) October 20,[1] 1772. . . .

From October 20, 1773, to October 20, 1774. In this year I was carelessly left by my nurse, ran to the fire, and pulled out a live coal—burnt myself dreadfully. While my hand was being dressed by a Mr. Young, I spoke for the first time (so my mother informs me) and said, "nasty Doctor Young!" The snatching at fire, and the circumstance of my first words expressing hatred to professional men—are they at all *ominous?* This year I went to school.

From October 20, 1774, to October 20, 1775. I was inoculated; which I mention because I distinctly remember it, and that my eyes were bound; at which I manifested so much obstinate indignation, that at last they

[1] A mistake for October 21st.—*E. H. Coleridge*

removed the bandage, and unaffrighted I looked at the lancet, and suffered the scratch. At the close of the year I could read a chapter in the Bible.

Here I shall end, because the remaining years of my life *all* assisted to form *my particular mind;*—the three first years had nothing in them that seems to relate to it.

October 9, 1797.

My dearest Poole,

From March to October—a long silence! But [as] it is possible that I may have been preparing materials for future letters, the time cannot be considered as altogether subtracted from you.

From October, 1775, to October, 1778. These three years I continued at the Reading School, because I was too little to be trusted among my father's schoolboys. After breakfast I had a halfpenny given me, with which I bought three cakes at the baker's close by the school of my old mistress; and these were my dinner on every day except Saturday and Sunday, when I used to dine at home, and wallowed in a beef and pudding dinner. I am remarkably fond of beans and bacon; and this fondness I attribute to my father having given me a penny for having eat a large quantity of beans on Saturday. For the other boys did not like them, and as it was an economic food, my father thought that my attachment and penchant for it ought to be encouraged. My father was very fond of me, and I was my mother's darling: in consequence I was very miserable. For Molly, who had nursed my brother Francis, and was immoderately fond of him, hated me because my mother took more notice of me than of Frank, and Frank hated me because my mother gave me now and then a bit of cake, when he had none,—quite forgetting that for one bit of

cake which I had and he had not, he had twenty sops
in the pan, and pieces of bread and butter with sugar on
them from Molly, from whom I received only thumps
and ill names.

So I became fretful and timorous, and a tell-tale; and
the schoolboys drove me from play, and were always
tormenting me, and hence I took no pleasure in boyish
sports, but read incessantly. My father's sister kept an
everything shop at Crediton, and there I read through
all the gilt-covered little books that could be had at that
time, and likewise all the uncovered tales of Tom Hicka-
thrift, Jack the Giant-killer, etc., etc., etc., etc. And I
used to lie by the wall and *mope,* and my spirits used to
come upon me suddenly; and in a flood of them I was
accustomed to race up and down the churchyard, and
act over all I had been reading, on the docks, the nettles,
and the rank grass. At six years old I remember to have
read Belisarius, Robinson Crusoe, and Philip Quarles;
and then I found the Arabian Nights' Entertainments,
one tale of which (the tale of a man who was compelled
to seek for a pure virgin) made so deep an impression
on me (I had read it in the evening while my mother
was mending stockings), that I was haunted by spec-
tres, whenever I was in the dark: and I distinctly re-
member the anxious and fearful eagerness with which
I used to watch the window in which the books lay, and
whenever the sun lay upon them, I would seize it, carry
it by the wall, and bask and read. My father found out
the effect which these books had produced, and burnt
them.

So I became a *dreamer,* and acquired an indisposition
to all bodily activity; and I was fretful, and inordinately
passionate, and as I could not play at anything, and was
slothful, I was despised and hated by the boys; and be-

cause I could read and spell and had, I may truly say, a memory and understanding forced into almost an unnatural ripeness, I was flattered and wondered at by all the old women. And so I became very vain, and despised most of the boys that were at all near my own age, and before I was eight years old I was a *character*. Sensibility, imagination, vanity, sloth, and feelings of deep and bitter contempt for all who traversed the orbit of my understanding, were even then prominent and manifest.

From October, 1778, to 1779. That which I began to be from three to six I continued from six to nine. In this year [1778] I was admitted into the Grammar School, and soon outstripped all of my age. I had a dangerous putrid fever this year. My brother George lay ill of the same fever in the next room. My poor brother Francis, I remember, stole up in spite of orders to the contrary, and sat by my bedside and read Pope's Homer to me. Frank had a violent love of beating me; but whenever that was superseded by any humour or circumstances, he was always very fond of me, and used to regard me with a strange mixture of admiration and contempt. Strange it was not, for he hated books, and loved climbing, fighting, playing and robbing orchards, to distraction.

My mother relates a story of me, which I repeat here, because it must be regarded as my first piece of wit. During my fever, I asked why Lady Northcote (our neighbour) did not come and see me. My mother said she was afraid of catching the fever. I was piqued, and answered, "Ah, Mamma! the four Angels round my bed an't afraid of catching it!" I suppose you know the prayer:—

> Matthew! Mark! Luke and John!
> God bless the bed which I lie on.

Four angels round me spread,
Two at my foot, and two at my head.

This prayer I said nightly, and most firmly believed the truth of it. Frequently have I (half-awake and half-asleep, my body diseased and fevered by my imagination), seen armies of ugly things bursting in upon me, and these four angels keeping them off. In my next I shall carry on my life to my father's death.

God bless you, my dear Poole, and your affectionate
                                     S. T. Coleridge.

                                     October 16, 1797.
Dear Poole,
From October, 1779, to October, 1781. I had asked my mother one evening to cut my cheese entire, so that I might toast it. This was no easy matter, it being a *crumbly* cheese. My mother, however, did it. I went into the garden for something or other, and in the mean time my brother Frank *minced* my cheese "to disappoint the favorite." I returned, saw the exploit, and in an agony of passion flew at Frank. He pretended to have been seriously hurt by my blow, flung himself on the ground, and there lay with outstretched limbs. I hung over him moaning, and in a great fright; he leaped up, and with a horse-laugh gave me a severe blow in the face. I seized a knife, and was running at him, when my mother came in and took me by the arm. I expected a flogging, and struggling from her I ran away to a hill at the bottom of which the Otter flows, about one mile from Ottery. There I stayed; my rage died away, but my obstinacy vanquished my fears, and taking out a little shilling book which had, at the end, morning and evening prayers, I very devoutly repeated them—thinking at the *same time* with inward and gloomy satisfaction how miserable my mother must be! I distinctly remember my feelings

when I saw a Mr. Vaughan pass over the bridge, at
about a furlong's distance, and how I watched the calves
in the fields[1] beyond the river. It grew dark and I fell
asleep. It was towards the latter end of October, and it
proved a dreadful stormy night. I felt the cold in my
sleep, and dreamt that I was pulling the blanket over
me, and actually pulled over me a dry thorn bush which
lay on the hill. In my sleep I had rolled from the top of
the hill to within three yards of the river, which flowed
by the unfenced edge at the bottom. I awoke several
times, and finding myself wet and stiff and cold, closed
my eyes again that I might forget it.

In the mean time my mother waited about half an
hour, expecting my return when the *sulks* had evapo-
rated. I not returning, she sent into the churchyard and
round the town. Not found! Several men and all the
boys were sent to ramble about and seek me. In vain!
My mother was almost distracted; and at ten o'clock at
night I was *cried* by the crier in Ottery, and in two vil-
lages near it, with a reward offered for me. No one went
to bed; indeed, I believe half the town were up all the
night. To return to myself. About five in the morning,
or a little after, I was broad awake, and attempted to
get up and walk; but I could not move. I saw the shep-
herds and workmen at a distance, and cried, but so
faintly that it was impossible to hear me thirty yards
off. And there I might have lain and died; for I was now
almost given over, the ponds and even the river, near

[1] Compare a MS. note dated July 19, 1863. "Intensely hot
day, left off a waistcoat, and for yarn wore silk stockings.
Before nine o'clock had unpleasant chillness, heard a noise
which I thought Derwent's in sleep; listened and found it
was a calf bellowing. Instantly came on my mind that night
I slept out at Ottery, and the calf in the field across the river
whose lowing so deeply impressed me. Chill and child and
calf lowing."—*E. H. Coleridge*

where I was lying, having been dragged. But by good
luck, Sir Stafford Northcote, who had been out all night,
resolved to make one other trial, and came so near that
he heard me crying. He carried me in his arms for near
a quarter of a mile, when we met my father and Sir
Stafford's servants. I remember and never shall forget
my father's face as he looked upon me while I lay in the
servant's arms—so calm, and the tears stealing down his
face; for I was the child of his old age. My mother, as
you may suppose, was outrageous with joy. [Meantime]
in rushed a *young lady*, crying out, "I hope you'll whip
him, Mrs. Coleridge!" This woman still lives in Ottery;
and neither philosophy or religion have been able to
conquer the antipathy which I *feel* towards her when-
ever I see her. I was put to bed and recovered in a day
or so, but I was certainly injured. For I was weakly and
subject to the ague for many years after.

My father (who had so little of parental ambition in
him, that he had destined his children to be blacksmiths,
etc., and had accomplished his intention but for my
mother's pride and spirit of aggrandizing her family)—
my father had, however, resolved that I should be a
parson. I read every book that came in my way without
distinction; and my father was fond of me, and used to
take me on his knee and hold long conversations with
me. I remember that at eight years old I walked with
him one winter evening from a farmer's house, a mile
from Ottery, and he told me the names of the stars and
how Jupiter was a thousand times larger than our world,
and that the other twinkling stars were suns that had
worlds rolling round them; and when I came home he
shewed me how they rolled round. I heard him with a
profound delight and admiration: but without the least
mixture of wonder or incredulity. For from my early

reading of fairy tales and genii, etc., etc., my mind had
been habituated *to the Vast,* and I never regarded *my
senses* in any way as the criteria of my belief. I regulated
all my creeds by my conceptions, not by my *sight,* even
at that age. Should children be permitted to read ro-
mances, and relations of giants and magicians and genii?
I know all that has been said against it; but I have
formed my faith in the affirmative. I know no other way
of giving the mind a love of the Great and the Whole.
Those who have been led to the same truths step by
step, through the constant testimony of their senses,
seem to me to want a sense which I possess. They con-
template nothing but *parts,* and all *parts* are necessarily
little. And the universe to them is but a mass of *little
things.* It is true, that the mind *may* become credulous
and prone to superstition by the former method; but are
not the experimentalists credulous even to madness in
believing any absurdity, rather than believe the grandest
truths, if they have not the testimony of their own senses
in their favour? I have known some who have been *ra-
tionally* educated, as it is styled. They were marked by
a microscopic acuteness, but when they looked at great
things, all became a blank and they saw nothing, and
denied (very illogically) that anything could be seen,
and uniformly put the negation of a power for the pos-
session of a power, and called the want of imagination
judgment and the never being moved to rapture phi-
losophy!

Towards the latter end of September, 1781, my father
went to Plymouth with my brother Francis, who was to
go as midshipman under Admiral Graves, who was a
friend of my father's. My father settled my brother, and
returned October 4, 1781. He arrived at Exeter about
six o'clock, and was pressed to take a bed there at the

Harts', but he refused, and, to avoid their entreaties, he told them, that he had never been superstitious, but that the night before he had had a dream which had made a deep impression. He dreamt that Death had appeared to him as he is commonly painted, and touched him with his dart. Well, he returned home, and all his family, I excepted, were up. He told my mother his dream; but he was in high health and good spirits, and there was a bowl of punch made, and my father gave a long and particular account of his travel, and that he had placed Frank under a religious captain, etc. At length he went to bed, very well and in high spirits. A short time after he had lain down he complained of a pain in his bowels. My mother got him some peppermint water, and, after a pause, he said, "I am much better now, my dear!" and lay down again. In a minute my mother heard a noise in his throat, and spoke to him, but he did not answer; and she spoke repeatedly in vain. Her *shriek* awaked me, and I said, "Papa is dead!" I did not know of my father's return, but I knew that he was expected. How I came to think of his death I cannot tell; but so it was. Dead he was. Some said it was the gout in the heart;—probably it was a fit of apoplexy. He was an Israelite without guile, simple, generous, and taking some Scripture texts in their literal sense, he was conscientiously indifferent to the good and the evil of this world.

God love you and

S. T. Coleridge.

February 19, 1798.

From October, 1781, to October, 1782.

After the death of my father, we of course changed houses, and I remained with my mother till the spring of 1782, and was a day-scholar to Parson Warren, my father's successor. He was not very deep, I believe; and I used to delight my mother by relating little instances of his deficiency in grammar knowledge,—every detraction from his merits seemed an oblation to the memory of my father, especially as Parson Warren did certainly *pulpitize* much better. Somewhere I think about April, 1782, Judge Buller, who had been educated by my father, sent for me, having procured a Christ's Hospital Presentation. I accordingly went to London, and was received by my mother's brother, Mr. Bowdon, a tobacconist and (at the same time) clerk to an underwriter. . . . My uncle was very proud of me, and used to carry me from coffee-house to coffee-house and tavern to tavern, where I drank and talked and disputed, as if I had been a man. Nothing was more common than for a large party to exclaim in my hearing that I was a *prodigy*, etc., etc., etc., so that while I remained at my uncle's I was most completely spoiled and pampered, both mind and body.

At length the time came, and I donned the *blue* coat and yellow stockings and was sent down into Hertford, a town twenty miles from London, where there are about three hundred of the younger Blue-Coat boys. At Hertford I was very happy, on the whole, for I had plenty to eat and drink, and pudding and vegetables almost every day. I stayed there six weeks, and then was drafted up to the great school at London, where I arrived in September, 1782. . . .

TO GEORGE COLERIDGE (UL)

On December 2, 1793, pressed by his college debts and scarce knowing what to do, Coleridge enlisted under the name of Silas Tomkyn Comberbacke in the 15th or King's

Regiment of Light Dragoons. On learning of his plight, his
family immediately took steps to procure his release, and he
was discharged on April 7, 1794.

Sunday night, Feb. 23, 1794.

. . . Sweet in the sight of God and celestial Spirits
are the tears of Penitance—the pearls of heaven—the
wine of Angels! Such has been the language of Divines,
but Divines have exaggerated. Repentance may bestow
that tranquillity, which will enable man to pursue a
course of undeviating harmlessness, but it cannot restore
to the mind that inward sense of Dignity, which is the
Parent of every kindling energy! I am not what I was:—
Disgust—I feel, as if I had jaundiced all my Faculties.

I laugh almost like an insane person when I cast my
eye backward on the prospect of my past two years.
What a gloomy *Huddle* of eccentric actions, and dim-
discovered motives! To real happiness I bade adieu from
the moment, I received my first "Tutors' Bill"; since
that time, since that period my mind has been irradiated
by Bursts only of sunshine, at all other times gloomy
with clouds, or turbulent with tempests. Instead of man-
fully disclosing the disease, I concealed it with a shame-
ful cowardice of sensibility, till it cankered my very
Heart. I became a proverb to the University for Idle-
ness. The time, which I should have bestowed on the
academic studies, I employed in dreaming out wild
schemes of impossible extrication. It had been better for
me, if my Imagination had been less vivid. I could not
with such facility have shoved aside Reflection! How
many and how many hours have I stolen from the bitter-
ness of Truth in these soul-enervating Reveries—in
building magnificent edifices of Happiness on some
fleeting shadow of Reality! My affairs became more and
more involved. I fled to Debauchery; fled pure silent
and solitary Anguish to all the uproar of senseless mirth.

Having, or imagining that I had, no *stock* of Happiness to which I could look forward, I seized the empty gratifications of the moment, and snatched at the Foam, as the wave passed by me. I feel a painful blush on my cheek, while I write it, but even for the Un. Scholarship, for which I affected to have read so severely, I did not read three days uninterruptedly—for the whole six weeks, that preceded the examination, I was almost constantly intoxicated! My Brother! you shudder as you read.

When the state of my affairs became known to you and by your exertions and my Brothers' generous Confidence a fair Road seemed open to extrication, Almighty God! what a sequel! I loitered away more money on the road, and in town than it was possible for me to justify to my Conscience; and when I returned to Cambridge a multitude of petty embarrassments buzzed round me, like a nest of Hornets, Embarrassments, which in my wild carelessness I had forgotten, and many of which I had contracted almost without knowing it. So small a sum remained, that I could not mock my Tutor with it. My agitations were delirium— I formed a Party, dashed to London at eleven o'clock at night, and for three days lived in all the tempest of Pleasure—resolved on my return—but I will not shock your religious feelings. I again returned to Cambridge—staid a *week*—such a week! Where Vice has not annihilated sensibility, there is little need of a Hell! On Sunday night I packed up a few things, went off in the mail, staid about a week in a strange way, still looking forward with a kind of recklessness to the *dernier ressort* of misery—an accident of a very singular kind prevented me, and led me to adopt my present situation—where what I have suffered—but enough, may he, who in mercy dispenseth anguish be gracious to me. . . .

S. T. Coleridge.

TO ROBERT SOUTHEY (L)

Gloucester, Sunday morning, July 6, 1794.

S. T. Coleridge to R. Southey, Health and Republicanism to be! When you write, direct to me, "To be kept at the Post Office, Wrexham, Denbighshire, N. Wales." I mention this circumstance *now*, lest carried away by a flood of confluent ideas I should forget it. You are averse to gratitudinarian flourishes, else would I talk about hospitality, attentions, etc. However, as I must not thank you, I will thank my stars. Verily, Southey, I like not Oxford nor the inhabitants of it. I would say, thou art a nightingale among owls, but thou art so songless and heavy towards night that I will rather liken thee to the matin lark. Thy *nest* is in a blighted cornfield, where the sleepy poppy nods its red-cowled head, and the weak-eyed mole plies his dark work; but thy soaring is even unto heaven. Or let me add (for my appetite for similes is truly canine at this moment) that as the Italian nobles their new-fashioned doors, so thou dost make the adamantine gate of democracy turn on its golden hinges to most sweet music. Our journeying has been intolerably fatiguing from the heat and whiteness of the roads, and the *unhedged* country presents nothing but *stone* fences, dreary to the eye and scorching to the touch. But we shall soon be in Wales.

Gloucester is a nothing-to-be-said-about town. The women have almost all of them sharp noses.

•   •   •   •   •   •   •   •   •

It is *wrong*, Southey! for a little girl with a half-famished sickly baby in her arms to put her head in at the window of an inn—"Pray give me a bit of bread and meat!" from a party dining on lamb, green peas, and

salad. Why? Because it is *impertinent* and *obtrusive!* "I
am a gentleman! and wherefore the clamorous voice of
woe intrude upon mine ear?" My companion is a man
of cultivated, though not vigorous understanding; his
feelings are all on the side of humanity; yet such are
the unfeeling remarks, which the lingering remains of
aristocracy occasionally prompt. When the pure system
of pantisocracy shall have *aspheterized*—from ἀ, non,
and σφέτερος, proprius (we really *wanted* such a word),
instead of travelling along the circuitous, dusty, beaten
highroad of diction, you thus cut across the soft, green,
pathless field of novelty! Similes for ever! Hurrah! I
have bought a little blank book, and portable ink horn;
[and] as I journey onward, I ever and anon pluck the
wild flowers of poesy, "inhale their odours awhile," then
throw them away and think no more of them. I will not
do so! Two lines of mine:—

> And o'er the sky's unclouded blue
> The sultry heat *suffus'd* a *brassy* hue.

The cockatrice is a foul dragon with a *crown* on its head.
The Eastern nations believe it to be hatched by a viper
on a cock's egg. Southey, dost thou not see wisdom in
her *Coan* vest of allegory? The cockatrice is emblematic
of monarchy, a *monster* generated by *ingratitude* or *ab-
surdity*. When serpents *sting*, the only remedy is to kill
the *serpent*, and *besmear* the *wound* with the *fat*. Would
you desire better sympathy?

Description of heat from a poem I am manufacturing,
the title: "Perspiration. A Travelling Eclogue."

> The dust flies smothering, as on clatt'ring wheel
> Loath'd aristocracy careers along;
> The distant track quick vibrates to the eye,
> And white and dazzling undulates with heat,
> Where scorching to the unwary travellers' touch,

The stone fence flings its narrow slip of shade;
Or, where the worn sides of the chalky road
Yield their scant excavations (sultry grots!),
Emblem of languid patience, we behold
The fleecy files faint-ruminating lie.

Farewell, sturdy Republican! Write me concerning
Burnett and thyself, and concerning etc., etc. My next
shall be a more sober and chastened epistle; but, you
see, I was in the humour for metaphors, and, to tell thee
the truth, I have so often serious reasons to quarrel with
my inclination, that I do not choose to contradict it for
trifles. To Lovell, fraternity and civic remembrances!
Hucks' compliments.

Wrexham, Sunday, July 15, 1794.
Your letter, Southey! made me melancholy. Man is a
bundle of habits, but of all habits the habit of despond-
ence is the most pernicious to virtue and happiness. I
once shipwrecked my frail bark on that rock; a friendly
plank was vouchsafed me. Be you wise by my experi-
ence, and receive unhurt the flower, which I have
climbed precipices to pluck. Consider the high advan-
tages which you possess in so eminent a degree—health,
strength of mind, and confirmed habits of strict morality.
Beyond all doubt, by the creative powers of your gen-
ius, you might supply whatever the stern simplicity of
republican wants could require. Is there no possibility
of procuring the office of clerk in a compting-house? A
month's application would qualify you for it. For God's
sake, Southey! enter not into the church. Concerning
Allen I say little, but I feel anguish at times. This ear-
nestness of remonstrance! I will not offend you by asking
your pardon for it. The following is a *fact*. A friend of
Hucks' after long struggles between principle and *inter-*

est, as it is improperly called, accepted a place under government. He took the oaths, shuddered, went home and threw himself in an agony out of a two-pair of stairs window! These dreams of despair are most soothing to the imagination. I well know it. We shroud ourselves in the mantle of distress, and tell our poor hearts, "This is *happiness!*" There is a dignity in all these solitary emotions that flatters the pride of our nature. Enough of sermonizing. . . .

Monday, 11 o'clock. Well, praised be God! here I am. Videlicet, Ruthin, sixteen miles from Wrexham. At Wrexham Church I glanced upon the face of a Miss E. Evans, a young lady with [whom] I had been in habits of fraternal correspondence. She turned excessively pale; she thought it my ghost, I suppose. I retreated with all possible speed to our inn. There, as I was standing at the window, passed by Eliza Evans, and with her to my utter surprise her sister, Mary Evans, *quam efflictim et perdite amabam.* I apprehend she is come from London on a visit to her grandmother, with whom Eliza lives. I turned sick, and all but fainted away! The two sisters, as H. informs me, passed by the window anxiously several times afterwards; but I had retired.

> *Vivit, sed mihi non vivit—nova forte marita,*
> *Ah dolor! alterius carâ a cervice pependit.*
> *Vos, malefida valete accensæ insomnia mentis,*
> *Littora amata valete! Vale, ah! formosa Maria!*

My fortitude would not have supported me, had I *recognized* her—I mean *appeared* to do it! I neither ate nor slept yesterday. But love is a local anguish; I am sixteen miles distant, and am not half so miserable. I must endeavour to forget it amid the terrible graces of the wild wood scenery that surround me. I never durst even in a whisper avow my passion, though I knew she loved me. Where were my fortunes? and why should I make her miserable! Almighty God bless her! Her image is in the sanctuary of my heart, and never can it be torn away but with the strings that grapple it to life. Southey! there are few men of whose delicacy I think so highly as to have written all this. I am glad I have so deemed of you. We are soothed by communications.

10 o'clock, Thursday morning,
September 18, 1794.

Well, my dear Southey! I am at last arrived at Jesus. My God! how tumultuous are the movements of my heart. Since I quitted this room what and how important events have been evolved! America! Southey! Miss Fricker! Yes, Southey, you are right. Even Love is the creature of strong motive. I certainly love her. I *think* of her incessantly and with unspeakable tenderness,— with that inward melting away of soul that symptomatizes it.

Pantisocracy! Oh, I shall have such a scheme of it! My head, my heart, are all alive. I have drawn up my arguments in battle array. . . .

October 21, 1794.

To you alone, Southey, I write the first part of this letter. To yourself confine it.

"Is this handwriting altogether erased from your memory? To whom am I addressing myself? For whom am I now violating the rules of female delicacy? Is it for the same Coleridge, whom I once regarded as a sister her best-beloved Brother? Or for one who will *ridicule* that advice from me, which he has *rejected* as offered by his family? I will hazard the attempt. I have no right nor do I feel myself inclined to reproach you for the

Past. God forbid! You have already suffered too much
from self-accusation. But I conjure you, Coleridge, ear-
nestly and solemnly conjure you to consider long and
deeply, before you enter into any rash schemes. There
is an Eagerness in your Nature, which is ever hurrying
you in the sad Extreme. I have heard that you mean
to leave England, and on a Plan so absurd and extrava-
gant that were I for a moment to imagine it *true,* I
should be obliged to listen with a more patient Ear to
suggestions, which I have rejected a thousand times with
scorn and anger. Yes! whatever Pain I might suffer, I
should be forced to exclaim, 'O what a noble mind is
here *o'erthrown,* Blasted with ecstacy.' You have a coun-
try, does it demand nothing of you? You have doting
Friends! Will you break their Hearts! There is a God—
Coleridge! Though I have been told (*indeed* I do not
believe it) that you doubt of his existence and disbelieve
a hereafter. No! you have too much sensibility to be an
Infidel. You know I never was rigid in my opinions con-
cerning Religion—and have always thought *Faith* to be
only Reason applied to a particular subject. In short,
I am the same Being as when you used to say, 'We
thought in all things alike.' I often reflect on the happy
hours we spent together and regret the Loss of your
Society. I cannot easily forget those whom I once loved
—nor can I easily form new Friendships. I find women
in general vain—all of the same Trifle, and therefore
little and envious, and (I am afraid) without sincerity;
and of the other sex those who are offered and held up
to my esteem are very prudent, and very worldly. If you
value my peace of mind, you must *on no account* an-
swer this letter, or take the least notice of it. I *would*
not for the world *any part* of my Family should suspect
that I have written to you. My mind is sadly tempered
by being perpetually obliged to resist the solicitations of

those whom I love. I need not explain myself. Farewell, Coleridge! I shall always feel that I have been your *Sister*."

No name was signed,—it was from Mary Evans. I received it about three weeks ago. I loved her, Southey, almost to madness. Her image was never absent from me for three years, for *more* than three years. My resolution has not faltered, but I want a comforter. I have done nothing, I have gone into company, I was constantly at the theatre here till they left us, I endeavoured to be perpetually with Miss Brunton, I even hoped that her exquisite beauty and uncommon accomplishments might have cured one passion by another. The latter I could easily have dissipated in her absence, and so have restored my affections to her whom I do not love, but whom by every tie of reason and honour I ought to love. I am resolved, but wretched! But time shall do much. You will easily believe that with such feelings I should have found it no easy task to write to ——. I should have detested myself, if after my first letter I had written coldly—how could I write *as warmly?* I was vexed too and alarmed by your letter concerning Mr. and Mrs. Roberts, Shad, and little Sally. I was wrong, very wrong, in the affair of Shad, and have given you reason to suppose that I should assent to the innovation. I will most assuredly go with you to America, on this plan, but remember, Southey, this is *not our plan*, nor can I defend it. "Shad's children will be educated as ours, and the education we shall give them will be such as to render them incapable of blushing at the want of it in their parents"—*Perhaps!* With this one word would every Lilliputian reasoner demolish the system. Wherever men *can* be vicious, some *will* be. The leading idea of pantisocracy is to make men *necessarily* virtuous by removing all motives to evil—all possible temptation. "Let them dine with us and be treated with as much equality as they would wish, but perform that part of labour for which their education has fitted them." *Southey* should not have written this sentence. My friend, my noble and high-souled friend should have said to his dependents, "Be my slaves, and ye shall be my equals;" to his wife and sister, "Resign the *name* of Ladyship and ye shall retain the *thing.*" Again. Is every family to possess one of these unequal equals, these Helot Egalités? Or are the few you have mentioned, "with more toil than the peasantry of England undergo," to do for all of us "that part of labour which their education has fitted them for"? If your remarks on the other side are just, the inference is that the scheme of pantisocracy is impracticable, but I hope and believe that it is not a *necessary* inference. . . . If Mrs. S. and Mrs. F. go with us, they can at least prepare the food of simplicity for us. Let the married women do only what is absolutely convenient and customary for pregnant women or nurses. Let the husband do all the rest, and what will that all be? Washing with a machine and cleaning the house. One hour's addition to our daily labor, and *pantisocracy* in its most perfect sense is practicable. That the greater part of our female companions should have the task of maternal exertion at the same time is very *improbable;* but, though it were to happen, an infant is almost always sleeping, and during its slumbers the mother may in the same room perform the little offices of ironing clothes or making shirts. But the hearts of the women are not *all* with us. I do believe that Edith and Sarah are exceptions, but do even they know the bill of fare for the day, every duty that will be incumbent upon them?

All necessary knowledge in the branch of ethics is comprised in the word justice: that the good of the whole is the good of each individual, that, of course, it is each individual's *duty* to be just, *because* it is his *interest*. To perceive this and to assent to it as an abstract proposition is easy, but it requires the most wakeful attentions of the most reflective mind in all moments to bring it into practice. It is not enough that we have once swallowed it. The *heart* should have *fed* upon the *truth*, as insects on a leaf, till it be tinged with the colour, and show its food in every the minutest fibre. In the book of pantisocracy I hope to have comprised all that is good in Godwin, of whom and of whose book I will write more fully in my next letter (I think not so highly of him as you do, and I have read him with the greatest attention). This will be an advantage to the *minds* of our women.

What have been your feelings concerning the War with America, which is now inevitable? To go from Hamburg will not only be a heavy additional expense, but dangerous and uncertain, as nations at war are in the habit of examining neutral vessels to prevent the importation of arms and seize subjects of the hostile governments. It is said that one cause of the ministers having been so cool on the business is that it will prevent emigration, which it seems would be treasonable to a hostile country. Tell me all you think on these subjects. What think you of the difference in the prices of land as stated by Cowper from those given by the American agents? By all means read, ponder on Cowper, and when I hear your thoughts I will give you the result of my own.

> Thou bleedest, my poor Heart! and thy distress
> Doth Reason ponder with an anguished smile,
> Probing thy sore wound sternly, tho' the while
> Her eye be swollen and dim with heaviness.
> Why didst thou *listen* to Hope's whisper bland?
> Or, listening, why forget its healing tale,

When Jealousy with feverish fancies pale
Jarr'd thy fine fibres with a maniac's hand?
Faint was that Hope, and rayless. Yet 'twas fair
And sooth'd with many a dream the hour of rest:
Thou should'st have loved it most, when most opprest,
And nursed it with an agony of care,
E'en as a mother her sweet infant heir
That pale and sickly droops upon her breast!

When a man is unhappy he writes damned bad poetry,
I find. . . .

Till I dated this letter I never recollected that yester-
day was my birthday—twenty-two years old.

I have heard from my brothers—from him particu-
larly who has been friend, brother, father. 'Twas all
remonstrance and anguish, and suggestions that I am
deranged! Let me receive from you a letter of consola-
tion; for, believe me, I am completely wretched.

Yours most affectionately,
S. T. Coleridge

TO THE REVEREND F. WRANGHAM (UL)

October 24, 1794.

. . . My head throbs so violently and my Spirits are
so low, that I shall just add a Sonnet and conclude—It
was occasioned by a letter, which I lately received from
a young Lady, whom for five years I loved—almost to
madness, dissuasive from my American Scheme—but
where Justice leads, I will follow—though the Path be
through thorns and roughness—The Scotts desire their
Compliments. *Compliments!* Cold aristocratic Inanities!
I abjure their Nothingness. If there be any whom I
deem worthy of remembrance—I am their Brother. I
call even my Cat Sister in the Fraternity of universal

Nature. Owls I respect and Jack Asses I love: for Alder-
men and Hogs, Bishops and Royston Crows I have not
particular partiality—they are my Cousins however, at
least by Courtesy. But Kings, Wolves, Tygers, Generals,
Ministers, and Hyaenas, I renounce them all—or if they
must be my kinsmen, it shall be in the 50th Remove—
May the Almighty Pantisocratizer of Souls pantisocratize
the Earth, and bless you and

S. T. Coleridge!

TO MARY EVANS (L)

December 24, 1794.
I have this moment received your letter, Mary Evans.
Its firmness does honour to your understanding, its
gentleness to your humanity. You condescend to ac-
cuse yourself—most unjustly! You have been altogether
blameless. In my wildest day-dream of vanity, I never
supposed that you entertained for me any other than
a common friendship.

To love you, habit has made unalterable. This pas-
sion, however, divested as it now is of all shadow of
hope, will lose its disquieting power. Far distant from
you I shall journey through the vale of men in calmness.
He cannot long be wretched, who dares be actively vir-
tuous.

I have burnt your letters—forget mine; and that I
have pained you, forgive me!

May God infinitely love you!

S. T. Coleridge.

TO ROBERT SOUTHEY (L)

December, 1794.

I am calm, dear Southey! as an autumnal day, when
the sky is covered with gray moveless clouds. To *love
her,* habit has made unalterable. I had placed her in the
sanctuary of my heart, nor can she be torn from thence
but with the strings that grapple it to life. This passion,
however, divested as it now is of all shadow of hope,
seems to lose its disquieting power. Far distant, and
never more to behold or hear of her, I shall sojourn in
the vale of men, sad and in loneliness, yet not unhappy.
He cannot be long wretched who dares be actively vir-
tuous. . . .

To lose her! I can rise above that selfish pang. But
to marry another. O Southey! bear with my weakness.
Love makes all things pure and heavenly like itself,—
but to marry a woman whom I do not *love,* to degrade
her whom I call my wife by making her the instrument
of low desire, and on the removal of a desultory appetite
to be perhaps not displeased with her absence! Enough!
These refinements are the wildering fires that lead me
into vice. Mark you, Southey! *I will do my duty.* . . .

TO GEORGE DYER (UL)

[1795.]

No. 25 College Street, Bristol.

My dear Sir

Intending to return from day to day I postponed
writing to you—I will however delay it no longer. I am
anxious and perturbed beyond measure concerning my
proposed expedition to Scotland—I will pour out my
heart before you as water. In the Autumn of last year,

you know, we formed our American Plan and with pre-
cipitance that did credit to our hearts rather than heads,
fixed on the coming April as the time of our embarka-
tion. *This* following circumstances have rendered im-
practicable—but there are other engagements not so
dissoluble. In expectation of emigrating on the Pan-
tisocratic Plan I payed my addresses to a young Lady,
whom "οὔτ' αἰνεῖν ἐστι κακοῖσι θέμις!" Independently
of the Love and Esteem which her Person, and polished
understanding may be supposed to have inspired into a
young Man, I consider myself as under particular Ties
of Gratitude to her—since in confidence of my Affection
she had rejected the Addresses of two Men, one of them
of large Fortune—and by her perseverant Attachment
to me disobliged her Relations in a very uncomfortable
Degree. Perpetually obliged to resist the entreaties and
to endure the reproachful admonitions of her Uncle etc.,
she vainly endeavors to conceal from me how heavy her
heart is with anxiety, how disquieted by Suspense— To
leave her for two or three years would, I fear, be sacrific-
ing her health and happiness— In short, why should I
write circuitously to you? So commanding are the re-
quests of her Relations, that a short Time must decide
whether she marries me whom she loves with an affec-
tion to the ardor of which my Deserts bear no proportion
—or a man whom she strongly dislikes, in spite of his
fortune and solicitous attentions to her. These peculiar
circumstances she had with her usual Delicacy con-
cealed from me till my arrival at Bristol. . . .

Since I have been in Bristol I have endeavored to dis-
seminate Truth by three political Lectures—I believe, I
shall give a fourth— But the opposition of the Aristocrats
is so furious and determined, that I begin to fear, that
the Good I do is not proportionate to the Evil I occa-
sion— Mobs and Mayors, Blockheads and Brickbats,

Placards and Press gangs have leagued in horrible Con-
spiracy against me— The Democrats are as sturdy in
the support of me—but their number is comparatively
small. Two or three uncouth and untrained Automata
have threatened my Life—and in the last Lecture the
Genus infimum were scarcely restrained from attacking
the house in which the "damn'd Jacobin was jawing
away."

The first Lecture I was *obliged* to publish, it having
been confidently asserted that there was Treason in it.
Written at one sitting between the hours of twelve at
night and the Breakfast Time of the day, on which it
was delivered, believe me that no literary Vanity
prompted me to the printing of it— The reasons which
compelled me to publish it forbad me to correct it. . . .

TO THOMAS POOLE (L)

Wednesday evening, October 7, 1795.
My dear Sir,
God bless you; or rather, God be praised for that he
has blessed you!

On Sunday morning I was *married* at St. Mary's Red-
cliff, poor Chatterton's church! The thought gave a
tinge of melancholy to the solemn joy which I felt,
united to the woman whom I love best of all created
beings. We are settled, nay, quite domesticated, at
Clevedon, our comfortable cot!

Mrs. Coleridge! I like to write the name. Well, as I
was saying, Mrs. Coleridge desires her affectionate re-
gards to you. I talked of you on my wedding night. God
bless you! I hope that some ten years hence you will
believe and know of my affection towards you what I
will not now profess.

The prospect around is perhaps more *various* than any

in the kingdom. Mine eye gluttonizes the sea, the distant islands, the opposite coast! I shall assuredly write rhymes, let the nine Muses prevent it if they can. . . .

. . . My respectful and grateful remembrance to your mother, and believe me, dear Poole, your affectionate and mindful *friend,* shall I so soon dare to say? Believe me, my heart prompts it.

S. T. Coleridge.

TO ROBERT SOUTHEY (L)

Friday morning, November 13, 1795.

Southey, I *have* lost friends—friends who still cherish for me sentiments of high esteem and unextinguished tenderness. For the sum total of my misbehaviour, the Alpha and Omega of their accusations, is epistolary neglect. I never speak of them without affection, I never think of them without reverence. Not "to this catalogue," Southey, have I *"added your* name." You are *lost* to *me,* because you are lost to Virtue. As this will probably be the last time I shall have occasion to address you, I will begin at the beginning and regularly retrace your conduct and my own. In the month of June, 1794, I first became acquainted with your person and character. Before I quitted Oxford, we had struck out the leading features of a pantisocracy. While on my journey through Wales you invited me to Bristol with the full hopes of realising it. During my abode at Bristol the plan was matured, and I returned to Cambridge hot in the anticipation of that happy season when we should remove the *selfish* principle from ourselves, and prevent it in our children, by an abolition of property; or, in whatever respects this might be impracticable, by such similarity of property as would amount to a *moral* sameness, and answer all the purposes of *abolition.* Nor were you less zealous, and thought and expressed your opinion, that if any man embraced our system he must comparatively disregard "his father and mother and wife and children and brethren and sisters, yea, and his own life also, or he could not be our disciple." . . .

Previously to my departure from Jesus College, and during my melancholy detention in London, what convulsive struggles of feeling I underwent, and what sacrifices I made, you know. The liberal proposal from my family affected me no further than as it pained me to wound a revered brother by the positive and immediate refusal which duty compelled me to return. But there was a—I need not be particular; you remember what a fetter I burst, and that it snapt as if it had been a sinew of my heart. However, I returned to Bristol, and my addresses to Sara, which I at first paid from principle, not feeling, from feeling and from principle I renewed; and I met a reward more than proportionate to the greatness of the effort. I love and I am beloved, and I am happy!

Your letter to Lovell (two or three days after my arrival at Bristol), in answer to some objections of mine to the Welsh scheme, was the first thing that alarmed me. Instead of "It is our duty," "Such and such are the reasons," it was "I and I" and "will and will,"—sentences of gloomy and self-centering resolve. . . .

We commenced lecturing. Shortly after, you began to recede in your conversation from those broad principles in which pantisocracy originated. I opposed you with vehemence, for I well knew that no notion of morality or its motives could be without consequences. And once (it was just before we went to bed) you confessed to me that you had acted wrong. But you relapsed; your manner became cold and gloomy, and pleaded with increased pertinacity for the wisdom of making Self an undiverging Center. At Mr. Jardine's your language was *strong indeed*. Recollect it. You had left the table, and we were standing at the window. Then darted into my mind the dread that you were meditating a separation. At *Chepstow* your conduct renewed my suspicion, and I was greatly agitated, even to many tears. But in Peirce-field Walks you assured me that my suspicions were altogether unfounded, that our differences were merely speculative, and that you would certainly go into Wales. I was glad and satisfied. For my heart was never bent from you but by violent strength, and heaven knows how it leapt back to esteem and love you. But alas! a short time passed ere your departure from our first principles became too flagrant. Remember when we went to Ashton on the strawberry party. Your conversation with George Burnett on the day following he detailed to me. It scorched my throat. Your private resources were to remain your individual property, and everything to be separate except a farm of five or six acres. In short, we were to commence partners in a petty farming trade. This was the mouse of which the mountain Pantisocracy was at last safely delivered. I received the account with indignation and loathings of unutterable contempt. . . .

TO JOHN THELWALL (L)

Wednesday, June 22, 1796.

. . . To the last sentence in your letter I subscribe fully and with all my inmost affections. "He who thinks and *feels* will be virtuous; and he who is absorbed in self will be vicious, whatever may be his speculative opinions." Believe me, Thelwall, it is not his atheism that has prejudiced me against Godwin, but Godwin who has, perhaps, *prejudiced* me against atheism. Let me see you—I already know a deist, and Calvinists, and Moravians whom I love and reverence—and I shall leap forwards to realise my *principles* by *feeling* love and honour for an atheist. By the bye, are you an atheist? For I was told that Hutton was an atheist, and procured his three massy quartos of the principle of knowledge in the hopes of finding some arguments in favor of atheism, but lo! I discovered him to be a profoundly pious deist, —"independent of fortune, satisfied with himself, pleased with his species, confident in his Creator."

God bless you, my dear Thelwall! Believe me with high esteem and *anticipated* tenderness,

Yours sincerely,

S. T. Coleridge.

P.S. We have a hundred lovely scenes about Bristol, which would make you exclaim, O admirable *Nature!* and me, O Gracious *God!*

TO THOMAS POOLE (L)

Saturday night, November 5, 1796.

Thanks, my heart's warm thanks to you, my beloved friend, for your tender letter! Indeed, I did not deserve so kind a one; but by this time you have received my last.

To live in a beautiful country, and to enure myself as much as possible to the labour of the field, have been for this year past my dream of the day, my sigh at midnight. But to enjoy these blessings *near* you, to see you daily, to tell you all my thoughts in their first birth, and to hear yours, to be mingling identities with you as it were,—the vision-wearing fancy has indeed often pictured such things, but hope never dared whisper a promise. Disappointment! Disappointment! dash not from my trembling hand the bowl which almost touches my lips. Envy me not this immortal draught, and I will forgive thee all thy persecutions. Forgive thee! Impious! *I will bless thee*, black-vested minister of optimism, stern pioneer of happiness! Thou hast been *"the cloud"* before me from the day that I left the flesh-pots of Egypt, and was led through the way of a wilderness— the cloud that hast been guiding me to a land flowing with milk and honey—the milk of innocence, the honey of friendship!

I wanted such a letter as yours, for I am very unwell. On Wednesday night I was seized with an intolerable pain from my right temple to the tip of my right shoulder, including my right eye, cheek, and jaw, and that side of the throat. I was nearly frantic, and ran about the house naked, endeavouring by every means to excite sensations in different parts of my body, and so to weaken the enemy by creating division. It continued from one in the morning till half past five, and left me pale and fainting. It came on fitfully, but not so violently, several times on Thursday, and began severer threats towards night; but I took between sixty and seventy drops of laudanum, and *sopped* the Cerberus, just as his mouth began to open. On Friday it only *niggled*, as if the chief had departed from a conquered place, and merely left a small garrison behind, or as if he had evacuated the Corsica, and a few straggling pains only remained. But *this morning* he returned in full force, and his name is Legion. Giant-fiend of a hundred hands, with a shower of arrowy death-pangs he transpierced me, and then he became a wolf, and lay a-gnawing at my bones! I am not mad, most noble

Festus, but in sober sadness I have suffered this day
more bodily pain than I had before a conception of. My
right cheek has certainly been placed with admirable
exactness under the focus of some invisible burning-
glass, which concentrated all the rays of a Tartarean
sun. My medical attendant decides it to be altogether
nervous, and that it originates either in severe applica-
tion, or excessive anxiety. My beloved Poole! in exces-
sive anxiety, I believe it might originate. I have a blister
under my right ear, and I take twenty-five drops of
laudanum every five hours, the ease and *spirits* gained
by which have enabled me to write you this flighty but
not exaggerated account. With a gloomy wantonness of
imagination I had been coquetting with the hideous *pos-
sibles* of disappointment. I drank fears like wormwood,
yea, made myself drunken with bitterness; for my ever-
shaping and distrustful mind still mingled gall-drops,
till out of the cup of hope I almost *poisoned* myself
with despair. . . .

I am anxious beyond measure to be in the country as
soon as possible. I would it were possible to get a tem-
porary residence till Adscombe is ready for us. I would
that it could be that we could have three rooms in Bill
Poole's large house for the winter. Will you try to look
out for a fit servant for us—simple of heart, physiog-
nomically handsome, and scientific in vaccimulgence?
That last word is a new one, but soft in sound and full
of expression. Vaccimulgence! I am pleased with the
word. Write to me all things about yourself. Where I
cannot advise I can condole and communicate, which
doubles joy, halves sorrow.

Tell me whether you think it at all possible to make
any terms with William Poole. You know I would not
wish to touch with the edge of the nail of my great toe

the line which should be but half a barley-corn out of the niche of the most trembling delicacy. I will write Cruikshank to-morrow, if God permit me.

God bless and protect you, friend, brother, beloved!
S. T. Coleridge.

Sara's best love, and Lloyd's. David Hartley is well, saving that he is sometimes inspired by the god Æolus, and like Isaiah, "his bowels sound like an harp." My filial love to your dear mother. Love to Ward. Little Tommy, I often think of thee.

Monday night, November 7, 1796.
My dearest Poole,
I wrote you on Saturday night under the immediate inspiration of laudanum, and wrote you a flighty letter, but yet one most accurately descriptive both of facts and feelings. Since then my pains have been lessening, and the greater part of this day I have enjoyed perfect ease, only I am totally inappetent of food, and languid, even to an inward perishing. . . .

TO JOHN THELWALL (L)

Saturday, November 19 [1796]
Oxford Street, Bristol.
. . . Your portrait of yourself interested me. As to me, my face, unless when animated by immediate eloquence, expresses great sloth, and great, indeed, almost idiotic good-nature. 'Tis a mere carcass of a face,[1] fat,

[1] The "Reminiscences of an Octogenarian" (The Rev. Leapidge Smith), contributed to the *Leisure Hour*, convey a different impression: "In person he was a tall, dark, handsome young man, with long, black, flowing hair; eyes not merely

flabby, and expressive chiefly of inexpression. Yet I am told that my eyes, eyebrows, and forehead are physiognomically good; but of this the deponent knoweth not. As to my shape, 't is a good shape enough if measured, but my gait is awkward, and the walk of the whole man indicates *indolence capable of energies.* I am, and ever have been, a great reader, and have read almost everything—a library cormorant. I am *deep* in all out of the way books, whether of the monkish times, or of the puritanical era. I have read and digested most of the historical writers; but I do not *like* history. Metaphysics and poetry and "facts of mind," that is, accounts of all the strange phantasms that ever possessed "your philosophy"; dreamers, from Thoth the Egyptian to Taylor the English pagan, are my darling studies. In short, I seldom read except to amuse myself, and I am almost always reading. Of useful knowledge, I am a so-so chemist, and I love chemistry. All else is *blank;* but I *will* be (please God) an horticulturalist and a farmer. I compose very little, and I absolutely hate composition, and such is my dislike that even a sense of duty is sometimes too weak to overpower it.

I cannot breathe through my nose, so my mouth, with sensual thick lips, is almost always open. In conversation I am impassioned, and oppose what I deem error with an eagerness which is often mistaken for personal asperity; but I am ever so swallowed up in the *thing* that I perfectly forget my *opponent.* Such am I. . . .

---

dark, but black, and keenly penetrating; a fine forehead, a deep-toned, harmonious voice; a manner never to be forgotten, full of life, vivacity, and kindness; dignified in person and, added to all these, exhibiting the elements of his future greatness." *Leisure Hour,* 1870, p. 651.—*E. H. Coleridge*

December 17, 1796.

. . . "Poetry to have its highest relish must be impassioned." True. But, firstly, poetry ought not always to have its *highest* relish; and, secondly, judging of the cause from its effect, poetry, though treating on lofty and abstract truths, ought to be deemed *impassioned* by him who reads it with impassioned feelings. Now Collins's "Ode on the Poetical Character,"—that part of it, I should say, beginning with "The band (as faery legends say) Was wove on that creating day,"—has inspired and whirled *me* along with greater agitation of enthusiasm than any the most *impassioned* scene in Schiller or Shakespeare, using "impassioned" in its confined sense, for writing in which the human passions of pity, fear, anger, revenge, jealousy, or love are brought into view with their workings. Yet I consider the latter poetry as more valuable, because it gives *more general* pleasure, and I judge of all things by their utility. I feel strongly and I think strongly, but I seldom feel without thinking or think without feeling. Hence, though my poetry has in general a hue of tenderness or passion over it, yet it seldom exhibits unmixed and simple tenderness or passion. My philosophical opinions are blended with or deduced from my feelings, and this, I think, peculiarises my style of writing, and, like everything else, it is sometimes a beauty and sometimes a fault. But do not let us introduce an Act of Uniformity against Poets. I have room enough in *my* brain to admire, aye, and almost equally, the *head* and fancy of Akenside, and the heart and fancy of Bowles, the solemn lordliness of Milton, and the divine chit-chat of Cowper. And whatever a man's excellence is, that will be likewise his fault. . . .

As to your Poems which you informed me in the ac-

companying letter that you had sent in the same parcel
with the pamphlets, whether or no your verses had more
than their *proper number of feet* I cannot say; but cer-
tain it is, that somehow or other they *marched off.* No
"Poems by John Thelwall" could I find. . . .

My dear Thelwall! "It is the principal felicity of life
and the chief glory of manhood to speak out fully on all
subjects." I will avail myself of it. I will express *all* my
feelings, but will previously take care to make my feel-
ings benevolent. Contempt is hatred without fear; an-
ger, hatred accompanied with apprehension. But because
hatred is always evil, contempt must be always evil, and
a good man ought to speak *contemptuously* of nothing.
I am sure a wise man will not of opinions which have
been held by men, in *other* respects at least, confessed
of more powerful intellect than himself. 'Tis an assump-
tion of *infallibility;* for if a man were wakefully mindful
that what he now thinks foolish he may himself here-
after think wise, it is not in nature that he should *despise*
those who now believe what it is possible he may him-
self hereafter believe; and if he deny the possibility he
must *on that point* deem himself infallible and immu-
table. . . .

December 31, 1796.
. . . The passage in your letter respecting your
mother affected me greatly. Well, true or false, heaven
is a less gloomy idea than annihilation. Dr. Beddoes and
Dr. Darwin think that *Life* is utterly inexplicable, writ-
ing as materialists. You, I understand, have adopted the
idea that it is the result of organised matter acted on by
external stimuli. As likely as any other system, but you
assume the thing to be proved. The "capability of being
stimulated into sensation" . . . is my definition of *ani-*

mal life. Monro believes in a plastic, immaterial nature, all-pervading.

> And what if all of animated nature
> Be but organic harps diversely framed,
> That tremble into thought, as o'er them sweeps
> Plastic and vast, etc.

(By the bye, that is the favourite of *my* poems; do you like it?) Hunter says that the *blood* is the life, which is saying nothing at all; for, if the blood were *life,* it could never be otherwise than life, and to say it is *alive* is saying nothing; and Ferriar believes in a *soul,* like an orthodox churchman. So much for physicians and surgeons! Now as to the metaphysicians. Plato says it is *harmony.* He might as well have said a fiddlestick's end; but I love Plato, his dear, *gorgeous* nonsense; and I, *though last not least, I* do not know what to think about it. On the whole, I have rather made up my mind that I am a mere *apparition,* a naked spirit, and that life is, I myself I; which is a mighty clear account of it. Now I have written all this, not to express my ignorance (that is an accidental effect, not the final cause), but to shew you that I want to see your essay on "Animal Vitality," of which Bowles the surgeon spoke in high terms. Yet *he* believes in a *body* and a *soul.* . . . In your next letter tell me what you think of the *scattered* poems I sent you. Send me any poems, and I will be minute in criticism. For, O Thelwall, even a long-winded abuse is more consolatory to an *author's* feelings than a short-breathed, asthma-lunged panegyric. Joking apart, I would to God we could sit by a fireside and joke *vivâ voce,* face to face—Stella and Sara, Jack Thelwall and I. . . .

July, 1797.

. . . I am as much a Pangloss as ever, only less con-
temptuous than I used to be, when I argue how unwise
it is to feel contempt for anything.

I had been on a visit to Wordsworth's at Racedown,
near Crewkerne, and I brought him and his sister back
with me, and here I have *settled them.* By a combina-
tion of curious circumstances a gentleman's seat, with
a park and woods, elegantly and completely furnished,
with nine lodging rooms, three parlours, and a hall, in
the most beautiful and romantic situation by the seaside,
four miles from Stowey,—this we have got for Words-
worth at the *rent of twenty-three pounds a year, taxes
included!* The park and woods are *his* for all purposes
he wants them, and the large gardens are altogether and
entirely his. Wordworth is a very great man, the only
man to whom *at all times* and *in all modes of excellence*
I feel myself inferior, the only one, I mean, whom *I have
yet met with,* for the London *literati* appear to me to be
very much like little potatoes, that is, *no great things,* a
compost of nullity and dullity.

Charles Lamb has been with me for a week. He left
me Friday morning. The second day after Wordsworth
came to me, dear Sara accidentally emptied a skillet of
boiling milk on my foot, which confined me during the
whole time of C. Lamb's stay and still prevents me from
all *walks* longer than a furlong. While Wordsworth, his
sister, and Charles Lamb were out one evening, sitting
in the arbour of T. Poole's garden, which communicates
with mine I wrote these lines, with which I am pleased
["This Lime-Tree Bower My Prison"]. . . .

TO JOHN THELWALL (L)

Saturday morning [October 16], 1797.
My dear Thelwall,

I have just received your letter, having been absent a day or two, and have already, before I write to you, written to Dr. Beddoes. I would to Heaven it were in my power to serve you; but alas! I have neither money or influence, and I suppose that at last I must become a Unitarian minister, as a less evil than starvation. For I get nothing by literature. . . . You have my wishes and, what is very liberal in me for such an atheist reprobate, my prayers. I can *at times* feel strongly the beauties you describe, in themselves and for themselves; but more frequently *all things* appear *little,* all the knowledge that can be acquired child's play; the universe itself! what but an immense heap of *little* things? I can contemplate nothing but *parts,* and parts are all *little!* My mind feels as if it ached to behold and know something *great,* something *one* and *indivisible.* And it is only in the faith of that that rocks or waterfalls, mountains or caverns, give me the sense of sublimity or majesty! But in this faith *all things* counterfeit infinity. . . .

It is but seldom that I raise and spiritualize my intellect to this height; and at other times I adopt the Brahmin creed, and say, "It is better to sit than to stand, it is better to lie than to sit, it is better to sleep than to wake, but Death is the best of all!" I should much wish, like the Indian Vishnu, to float about along an infinite ocean cradled in the flower of the Lotus, and wake once in a million years for a few minutes just to know that I was going to sleep a million years more. . . .

TO THOMAS POOLE (UL)

Saturday Morning
[Poole's endorsement—Jan. 27, 1798.]

My dearest Poole

I thank you, heart-wise, for the Joy you have in my Joy—I received a very affectionate letter from Thomas Wedgewood last night—and answered it immediately. He desires me to meet him at Cote House—I shall therefore leave this place on Monday morning—and shall, God willing, breakfast with him on Tuesday morning— on which day I will write you—The people here absolutely *consume* me—the Clergymen of the Church are eminently courteous, and some of them come and hear me. If I had stayed, I have reason to think that I should have doubled the congregation almost immediately. With two sermons to meditate in each week, with many letters to write, with invitations for dinner, tea, and supper in each day, and people calling in, and I forced to return morning calls, every morning, you will not be surprized, tho' you will be vexed to hear, that I have written nothing for the Morning Post—but I shall write immediately to the Editor.

I long to be at home with you, and to settle and persevere in, some mode of repaying the Wedgewoods thro' the medium of Mankind—I wish to be at home with you indeed, indeed—My joy is only in the bud here—I am like that Tree, which fronts me—The Sun shines bright and warm, as if it were summer—but it is not summer— and so it shines on leafless boughs. The beings who know how to sympathize with me are my foliage.

My filial love to your dear Mother and believe me, my best dear friend!

ever, ever most affectionately your's,
S. T. Coleridge.

P.S. My love to Ward, the Coryphaeus of Transcribers and Rescribers! ! when the Evil times come, I will use my Interest to save him from the Proscribers. That joke is like the last drop of greasy water wrung out of an afternoon dishclout—it came with difficulty and might as well have stayed behind.

TO GEORGE COLERIDGE (L)

April, 1798.

My Dear Brother,

An illness, which confined me to my bed, prevented me from returning an immediate answer to your kind and interesting letter. My indisposition originated in the stump of a tooth over which some matter had formed; this affected my eye, my eye my stomach, my stomach my head, and the consequence was a general fever, and the sum of pain was considerably increased by the vain attempts of our surgeon to extract the offending member. Laudanum gave me repose, not sleep; but you, I believe, know how divine that repose is, what a spot of enchantment, a green spot of fountain and flowers and trees in the very heart of a waste of sands! God be praised, the matter has been absorbed; and I am now recovering apace, and enjoy that newness of sensation from the fields, the air, and the sun which makes convalescence almost repay one for disease. . . .

I am prepared to suffer without discontent the consequences of my follies and mistakes; and unable to conceive how that which I am of Good could have been without that which I have been of evil, it is withheld from me to regret anything. I therefore consent to be deemed a Democrat and a Seditionist. A man's character follows him long after he has ceased to deserve it;

but I have snapped my squeaking baby-trumpet of sedi-
tion, and the fragments lie scattered in the lumber-room
of penitence. I wish to be a good man and a Christian,
but I am no Whig, no Reformist, no Republican, and
because of the multitude of fiery and undisciplined spir-
its that lie in wait against the public quiet under these
titles, because of them I chiefly accuse the present min-
isters, to whose folly I attribute, in a great measure, their
increased and increasing numbers. You think differently,
and if I were called upon by you to prove my assertions,
although I imagine I could make them appear plausible,
yet I should feel the insufficiency of my data. The Min-
isters may have had in their possession facts which alter
the whole state of the argument, and make my syllo-
gisms fall as flat as a baby's card-house. And feeling
this, my brother! I have for some time past withdrawn
myself totally from the consideration of *immediate
causes*, which are infinitely complex and uncertain, to
muse on fundamental and general causes the "causæ
causarum." I devote myself to such works as encroach
not on the anti-social passions—in poetry, to elevate the
imagination and set the affections in right tune by the
beauty of the inanimate impregnated as with a living
soul by the presence of life—in prose to the seeking
with patience and a slow, very slow mind, "Quid sumus,
et quidnam victuri gignimus,"—what our faculties are
and what they are capable of becoming. I love fields and
woods and mountains with almost a visionary fondness.
And because I have found benevolence and quietness
growing within me as that fondness has increased, there-
fore I should wish to be the means of implanting it in
others, and to destroy the bad passions not by combat-
ing them but by keeping them in inaction. . . .

With regard to myself, it is my habit, on whatever
subject I think, to endeavour to discover all the good

that has resulted from it, that does result, or that can result. To this I bind down my mind, and after long meditation in this tract slowly and gradually make up my opinions on the quantity and nature of the evil. I consider this as the most important rule for the regulation of the intellect and the affections, as the only means of preventing the passions from turning reason into a hired advocate. . . .

TO WILLIAM GODWIN (UL)

T. Poole's, Nether Stowey, Bridgewater.
Wednesday, May 21, 1800.

. . . I left Wordsworth on the 4th of this month. If I cannot procure a suitable house at Stowey I return to Cumberland and settle at Keswick, in a house of such a prospect, that if according to you and Hume, impressions and ideas *constitute* our being, I shall have a tendency to become a god, so sublime and beautiful will be the series of my visual existence. But whether I continue here or migrate thither, I shall be in a beautiful country, and have house-room and heart-room for you, and you must come and write your next work at my house. . . . My poor Lamb! How cruelly afflictions crowd upon him! I am glad that you think of him as I think; he has an affectionate heart, a mind *sui generis;* his taste acts so as to appear like the unmechanic simplicity of an instinct—in brief he is worth an hundred men of *mere* talents. Conversation with the latter tribe is like the use of leaden bells—one warms by exercise—Lamb every now and then *irradiates,* and the beam, though single and fine as a hair, is yet rich with colours, and I both see and feel it. . . .

TO SIR HUMPHRY DAVY (UL)

Greta Hall, Keswick, Cumberland,
Friday Evening, July 25, 1800.

My dear Davy

Work hard, and if Success do not dance up like the bubbles in the Salt (with the Spirit Lamp under it) may the Devil and his Dame take success! Sdeath, my dear fellow! from the Window before me there is a great *Camp* of Mountains—Giants seem to have pitch'd their tents there—Each mountain is a Giant's tent—and how the light streams from them—and the shadows that travel upon them! Davy! I *ake* for you to be with us.

W. Wordsworth is such a lazy fellow that I bemire myself by making promises for him—the moment, I received your letter, I wrote to him. . . . I trust however that I have invoked the sleeping Bard with a spell so potent, that he will awake and deliver up that Sword of Argantyr, which is to rive the Enchanter *Gaudy-verse* from his Crown to his Fork. . . .

We drank tea the night before I left Grasmere, on the Island in that lovely lake, our kettle swung over the fire hanging from the branch of a Fir-tree, and I lay and saw the woods and mountains, and lake all trembling, and as it were *idealized* thro' the subtle smoke which rose up from the clear red embers of the fir-apples, which we had collected; afterwards, we made a glorious Bonfire on the margin, by some elder bushes, whose twigs heaved and sobbed in the uprushing column of smoke —and the Image of the Bonfire, and of us that danced round it—ruddy laughing faces in the twilight—the Image of this in a Lake smooth as that sea, to whose waves the Son of God had said, *Peace!* May God and all his Sons, love you as I do—

S. T. Coleridge.

Sara desires her kind remembrances—Hartley is a spirit
that dances on an aspen leaf—the air that yonder sal-
low-faced and yawning Tourist is breathing, is to my
Babe a perpetual Nitrous Oxide. Never was more joyous
creature born. Pain with him is so wholly trans-substan-
tiated by the Joys that had rolled on before, and rushed
in after, that oftentimes 5 minutes after his mother had
whipt him, he has gone up and asked her to whip him
again.

TO WILLIAM GODWIN (UL)

Monday, Sep. 22, 1800.

. . . Your tragedy to be exhibited at Christmas! I
have indeed merely read your letter, so it is not strange
that my heart still continues beating out of time. Indeed,
indeed, Godwin, such a stream of hope and fear rushed
in on me, when I read the sentence, as you would not
permit yourself to feel. If there be anything yet un-
dreamed of in our philosophy; if it be, or if it be pos-
sible, that thought can impel Thought out of the visual
limit of a man's own skull and heart; if the clusters of
ideas, which contribute our identity, do ever connect
and unite with a greater whole; if feelings could ever
propagate themselves without the servile ministrations
of undulating air or reflected light—I seem to feel within
myself a strength and a power of desire that might start
a modifying, commanding impulse on a whole theatre.
What does all this mean? Alas! that sober sense should
know no other to construe all this, except by the tame
phrase, I wish you success . . . . [sic]

Your feelings respecting Baptism are, I suppose, much
like mine! At times I dwell on man with such reverence,
resolve all his follies and superstitions into such grand

primary laws of intellect, and in such wise so contemplate them as ever-varying incarnations of the Eternal Life—that the Llama's dung-pellet, or the cow-tail which the dying Brahmin clutches convulsively become sanctified and sublime by the feelings which cluster round them. In that mood I exclaim, my boys shall be christened! But then another fit of moody philosophy attacks me. I look at my doted-on Hartley—he moves, he lives, he finds impulses from within and from without, he is the darling of the sun and of the breeze. Nature seems to bless him as a thing of her own. He looks at the clouds, the mountains, the living beings of the earth, and vaults and jubilates! Solemn looks and solemn words have been hitherto connected in his mind with great and magnificent objects only: with lightning, with thunder, with the waterfall blazing in the sunset. Then I say, shall I suffer him to see grave countenances and hear grave accents, while his face is sprinkled? Shall I be grave myself and tell a lie to him? Or shall I laugh, and teach him to insult the feelings of his fellowmen? Besides, are we not all in this present hour fainting beneath the duty of Hope? From such thoughts I stand up, and vow a book of severe analysis, in which I will tell *all* I believe to be truth in the nakedest language in which it can be told.

My wife is now quite comfortable. Surely you might come and spend the very next four weeks, not without advantage to both of us. The very glory of the place is coming on. The local Genius is just arranging himself in his attributes. But above all, I press it, because my mind has been busied with speculations that are closely connected with those pursuits which have hitherto constituted your ability and importance; and ardently as I wish you success on the stage, I yet cannot frame myself to the thought that you should cease to appear as a *bold*

moral thinker. I wish you to write a book on the power
of the words, and the processes by which the human
feelings form affinities with them. In short, I wish you
to philosophize Horne Tooke's system, and to solve the
great questions, whether there be reason to hold that an
action bearing all the semblance of predesigning con-
sciousness may yet be simply organic, and whether a
series of such actions are possible? And close on the
heels of this question would follow, Is Logic the *Essence*
of thinking? In other words Is *Thinking* impossible with-
out arbitrary signs? And how far is the word "arbitrary"
a misnomer? Are not words, etc., parts and germinations
of the plant? And what is the law of their growth? In
something of this sort I would endeavour to destroy the
old antithesis of Words and Things; elevating, as it
were, Words into Things and living things too. All the
nonsense of vibrating etc., you would of course dismiss.
If what I have written appear nonsense to you, or com-
monplace thoughts in a harlequinade of *Outré* expres-
sions, suspend your judgment till we see each other.

TO SIR HUMPHRY DAVY (L)

Thursday night, October 9, 1800.

My dear Davy,

I was right glad, glad with a *stagger* of the heart, to
see your writing again. Many a moment have I had all
my France and England curiosity suspended and lost,
looking in the advertisement front column of the "Morn-
ing Post Gazeteer" for *Mr. Davy's Galvanic habitudes of
charcoal.*—Upon my soul I believe there is not a letter
in those words round which a world of imagery does
not circumvolve; your room, the garden, the cold bath,
the moonlight rocks, Barristed, Moore, and simple-look-
ing Frere, and dreams of wonderful things attached to

your name,—and Skiddaw, and Glaramara, and Eagle
Crag, and you, and Wordsworth, and me, on the top of
them! I pray you do write to me immediately, and tell
me what you mean by the possibility of your assuming
a new occupation. Have you been successful to the ex-
tent of your expectations in your late chemical inquiries?

As to myself, I am doing little worthy the relation. I
write for Stuart in the "Morning Post," and I am com-
pelled by the god Pecunia—which was one name of
the supreme Jupiter—to give a volume of letters from
Germany, which will be a decent *lounge* book, and not
an atom more. The "Christabel" was running up to
1,300 lines,[1] and was so much admired by Wordsworth,
that he thought it indelicate to print two volumes with
his name, in which so much of another man's was in-
cluded; and, which was of more consequence, the poem
was in direct opposition to the very purpose for which
the lyrical ballads were published, viz., an experiment to
see how far those passions which alone give any value
to extraordinary incidents were capable of interesting,
in and for themselves, in the incidents of common life.
We mean to publish the "Christabel," therefore, with a
long blank-verse poem of Wordsworth's, entitled "The
Pedlar," [2] I assure you I think very differently of "Chris-
tabel." I would rather have written "Ruth," and "Na-
ture's Lady," than a million such poems. But why do
I calumniate my own spirit by saying "I would rather"?
God knows it is as delightful to me that they *are* written.

[1] It is impossible to explain this statement, which was re-
peated in a letter to Josiah Wedgewood, dated November 1,
1800. The printed "Christabel," even including the conclu-
sion to Part II, makes only 677 lines, and the discarded por-
tion, if it ever existed, has never come to light. See Mr. Dykes
Campbell's valuable and exhaustive note on "Christabel," *Po-
etical Works*, pp. 601–607.—*E. H. Coleridge*

[2] A former title of *The Excursion.*—*E. H. Coleridge*

I *know* that at present, and I *hope* that it *will be so;* my mind has *disciplined* itself into a willing exertion of its powers, without any reference to their comparative value. . . .

The works which I gird myself up to attack as soon as money concerns will permit me are the Life of Lessing, and the Essay on Poetry. The latter is still more at my heart than the former: its title would be an essay on the elements of poetry,—it would be in reality a disguised system of morals and politics. When you write,— and do write soon,—tell me how I can get your essay on the nitrous oxide. . . .

My wife and children are well; the baby was dying some weeks ago, so the good people would have it baptized; his name is Derwent Coleridge, so called from the river, for, fronting our house, the Greta runs into the Derwent. Had it been a girl the name should have been Greta. By the bye, Greta, or rather Grieta, is exactly the Cocytus of the Greeks. The word, literally rendered in modern English, is "the loud lamenter;" to griet in the Cambrian dialect, signifying to roar aloud for grief or pain, and it does *roar* with a vengeance! I will say nothing about spring—a thirsty man tries to think of anything but the stream when he knows it to be ten miles off! God bless you!

TO THOMAS POOLE (UL)

[Postmark, Oct. 14, 1800.]

For the last fortnight, my dear Poole, I have been *about* to write you—but jolts and ruts, and flings have constantly unhoused my Resolves. The truth is, the endeavor to finish Christabel, (which has swelled into a Poem of 1400 lines)[1] for the second Volume of the

---

[1] See note, page 265.

Lyrical Ballads threw my business terribly back—and now I am sweating for it—Dunning letters etc. etc.—all the hell of an Author. I wish, I had been a Tanner. However to come to business—The essays have been published in the *Morning Post,* and have to use the cant phrase, made great sensation. . . .

TO SIR HUMPHRY DAVY (L)

Greta Hall, Tuesday night, December 2, 1800.
My dear Davy,

By an accident I did not receive your letter till this evening. I would that you had added to the account of your indisposition the probable causes of it. It has left me anxious whether or no you have not exposed yourself to unwholesome influences in your chemical pursuits. There are *few* beings both of hope and performance, but few who combine the "are" and the "will be." For God's sake, therefore, my dear fellow, do not rip open the bird that lays the golden eggs. . . . Did Carlisle ever communicate to you, or has he in any way published his facts concerning *pain* which he mentioned when we were with him? It is a subject which *exceedingly interests* me. I want to read something by somebody expressly on *pain,* if only to give an *arrangement* to my own thoughts, though if it were well treated I have little doubt it would revolutionize them. For the last month I have been trembling on through sands and swamps of evil and bodily grievance. My eyes have been inflamed to a degree that rendered reading and writing scarcely possible; and, strange as it seems, the act of metre composition, as I lay in bed, perceptibly affected them, and my voluntary ideas were every minute passing, more or less transformed into vivid spectra. I had leeches repeatedly applied to my temples, and a blister behind my ear—and my eyes are now my own, but in the place where the blister was, six small but excruciating boils have appeared, and harass me almost beyond endurance. In the mean time my darling Hartley has been taken with a stomach illness, which has ended in the yellow jaundice; and this greatly alarms me. So much for the doleful! Amid all these changes, and humiliations, and fears, the sense of the Eternal abides in me, and preserves unsubdued my cheerful faith, that all I endure is full of blessings!

At times, indeed, I would fain be somewhat of a more tangible utility than I am; but so I suppose it is with all of us—one while cheerful, stirring, feeling in resistance nothing but a joy and a stimulus; another while drowsy, self-distrusting, prone to rest, loathing our own self-promises, withering our own hopes—our hopes, the vitality and cohesion of our being! . . .

There is a deep blue cloud over the heavens; the lake, and the vale, and the mountains are all in darkness; only the *summits* of all the mountains in long ridges, covered with snow, are bright to a dazzling excess. A glorious scene! Hartley was in my arms the other evening, looking at the sky; he saw the moon glide into a large cloud. Shortly after, at another part of the cloud, several stars sailed in. Says he, "Pretty creatures! they are going in to see after their mother moon." . . .

TO THOMAS POOLE (L)

Greta Hall, Keswick, Saturday night,
December 5, 1800.

My dearest Friend,

I have been prevented from answering your last letter entirely by the state of my eyes, and my wish to

write more fully to you than their weakness would per-
mit. For the last month and more I have indeed been a
very crazy machine. . . . You will scarcely exact a very
severe account of what a man has been doing who has
been obliged for days and days together to keep his bed.
Yet I have not been altogether idle, having in my own
conceit gained great light into several parts of the hu-
man mind which have hitherto remained either wholly
unexplained or most falsely explained. To one resolu-
tion I am wholly made up, to wit, that as soon as I am
a freeman in the world of money I will never write a
line for the express purpose of money (but only as
believing it good and useful, in some way or other).
Although I am certain that I have been greatly improv-
ing both in knowledge and power in these last twelve
months, yet still at times it presses upon me with a pain-
ful weight that I have not evidenced a more tangible
utility. I have too much trifled with my reputation. You
have conversed much with Davy; he is delighted with
you. What do you think of him? Is he not a great man,
think you? . . . If I cannot come, I will write you a
very, very long letter, containing the most important of
the many thoughts and feelings which I want to com-
municate to you, but hope to do it face to face. . . .

Believe me to be what I have been ever, and am,
attached to you *one* degree more at least than to any
other living man.

TO SIR HUMPHRY DAVY (L)

February 3, 1801.

My dear Davy,

I can scarcely reconcile it to my conscience to make
you pay postage for another letter. Oh, what a fine un-

veiling of modern politics it would be if there were pub-
lished a minute detail of all the sums received by gov-
ernment from the post establishment, and of all the
outlets in which the sums so received flowed out again!
and, on the other hand, all the domestic affections which
had been stifled, all the intellectual progress that would
have been, but is not, on account of the heavy tax, etc.,
etc. The letters of a nation ought to be paid for as
an article of national expense. Well! but I did not take
up this paper to flourish away in splenetic politics. A
gentleman resident here, his name Calvert, an idle,
good-hearted, and ingenious man, has a great desire to
commence fellow-student with me and Wordsworth in
chemistry. He is an intimate friend of Wordsworth's,
and he has proposed to W. to take a house which he
(Calvert) has nearly built, called Windy Brow, in a
delicious situation, scarce half a mile from Greta Hall,
the residence of S. T. Coleridge, Esq., and so for him
(Calvert) to live with them, that is, Wordsworth and his
sister. In this case he means to build a little laboratory,
etc. . . . This opportunity is exceedingly precious to
me, as on my own account I could not afford the least
additional expense, having been already, by long and
successive illnesses, thrown behindhand so much that
for the next four or five months I fear, let me work as
hard as I can, I shall not be able to do what my heart
within me *burns* to do, that is, to *concentre* my free
mind to the affinities of the feelings with words and
ideas under the title of "Concerning Poetry, and the
nature of the Pleasures derived from it." I have faith
that I do understand the subject, and I am sure that if I
write what I ought to do on it, the work would super-
sede all the books of metaphysics, and all the books of
morals too. To whom shall a young man utter *his pride,*
if not to a young man whom he loves? . . .

I have been *thinking* vigorously during my illness, so that I cannot say that my long, long wakeful nights have been all lost to me. The subject of my meditations has been the relations of thoughts to things; in the language of Hume, of ideas to impressions. I may be truly described in the words of Descartes: I have been "res cogitans id est, dubitans, affirmans, negans, pauca intelligens, multa ignorans, volens, nolens, imaginans etiam, et sentiens." I please myself with believing that you will receive no small pleasure from the result of these broodings, although I expect in you (in some points) a determined opponent, but I say of my mind in this respect: "Manet imperterritus ille hostem magnanimum opperiens, et mole suâ stat." Every poor fellow has his proud hour sometimes, and this I suppose is mine. . . .

TO THOMAS POOLE (L)

Monday, March 16, 1801.

My dear Friend,

The interval since my last letter has been filled up by me in the most intense study. If I do not greatly delude myself, I have not only *completely extricated the notions of time and space,* but have overthrown the doctrine of association, as taught by Hartley, and with it all the irreligious metaphysics of modern infidels—especially the doctrine of necessity. This I have *done;* but I trust that I am about to do more—namely, that I shall be able to evolve all the five senses, that is, to deduce them from one sense, and to state their growth and the causes of their difference, and in this evolement to solve the process of life and consciousness. *I write this to you only, and I pray you, mention what I have written to no one.* At Wordsworth's advice, or rather fervent entreaty, I have intermitted the pursuit. The intensity of thought, and the number of minute experiments with light and figure, have made me so nervous and feverish that I cannot sleep as long as I ought and have been used to do; and the sleep which I have is made up of ideas so connected, and so little different from the operations of reason, that it does not afford me the due refreshment. I shall therefore take a week's respite, and make "Christabel" ready for the press; which I shall publish by itself, in order to get rid of all my engagements with Longman. . . . I shall propose to Longman to accept instead of these Travels a work on the originality and merits of Locke, Hobbes, and Hume, which work I mean as a *pioneer* to my greater work, and as exhibiting a proof that I have not formed opinions without an attentive perusal of the works of my predecessors, from Aristotle to Kant.

I am confident that I can prove that the reputation of these three men has been wholly unmerited, and I have in what I have already written traced the whole history of the causes that effected this reputation entirely to Wordsworth's satisfaction. . . .

Monday, March 23, 1801.

My dear Friend,

I received your kind letter of the 14th. I was agreeably disappointed in finding that you had been interested in the letter respecting Locke. Those which follow are abundantly more entertaining and important; but I have no one to transcribe them. Nay, three letters are written which have not been sent to Mr. Wedgwood, because I have no one to transcribe them for me, and I do not wish to be without copies. Of that letter which you have I have no copy. It is somewhat unpleasant to me that Mr. Wedgwood has never answered my letter requesting his opinion of the utility of such a work, nor

acknowledged the receipt of the long letter containing
the evidences that the whole of Locke's system, as far
as it was a system, and with the exclusion of those parts
only which have been given up *as absurdities* by his
warmest admirers, preëxisted in the writings of Des-
cartes, in a far more pure, elegant, and delightful form.
Be not afraid that I shall join the party of the *Little-ists*.
I believe that I shall delight you by the detection of their
artifices. *Now Mr. Locke was the founder of this sect,
himself a perfect Little-ist.*

My opinion is thus: that deep thinking is attainable
only by a man of deep feeling, and that all truth is a
species of revelation. The more I understand of Sir
Isaac Newton's works, the more boldly I dare utter to
my own mind, and therefore to *you,* that I believe the
souls of five hundred Sir Isaac Newtons would go to
the making up of a Shakespeare or a Milton. But if it
please the Almighty to grant me health, hope, and a
steady mind (always the three clauses of my hourly
prayers), before my thirtieth year I will thoroughly un-
derstand the whole of Newton's works. At present I
must content myself with endeavouring to make myself
entire master of his easier work, that on Optics. I am
exceedingly delighted with the beauty and neatness of
his experiments, and with the accuracy of his *immedi-
ate* deductions from them; but the opinions founded on
these deductions, and indeed his whole theory is, I am
persuaded, so exceedingly superficial as without im-
propriety to be deemed false. Newton was a mere mate-
rialist. *Mind,* in his system, is always *passive,*—a lazy
Looker-on on an external world. If the mind be not *pas-
sive,* if it be indeed made in God's Image, and that, too,
in the sublimest sense, the *Image of the Creator,* there
is ground for suspicion that any system built on the
passiveness of the mind must be false, as a system. I

need not observe, my dear friend, how unutterably silly
and contemptible these opinions would be if written to
any but to another self. I assure you, solemnly assure
you, that you and Wordsworth are the only men on
earth to whom I would have uttered a word on this
subject.

It is a rule, by which I hope to direct all my literary
efforts, to let my opinions and my proofs go together. It
is *insolent* to *differ* from the public *opinion* in *opinion*,
if it be only *opinion*. It is sticking up little *i by itself*, *i*
against the whole alphabet. But one *word* with *meaning*
in it is worth the whole alphabet together. Such is a
sound argument, an incontrovertible fact.

Oh, for a Lodge in a land where human life was an
end to which labour was only a means, instead of being,
as it is here, a mere means of carrying on labour. I am
oppressed at times with a true heart-gnawing melan-
choly when I contemplate the state of my poor op-
pressed country. God knows, it is as much as I can do
to put meat and bread on my own table, and hourly
some poor starving wretch comes to my door to put in
his claim for part of it. It fills me with indignation to
hear the *croaking* account which the English emigrants
send home of America. "The society so bad, the manners
so vulgar, the servants so insolent!" Why, then, do they
not seek out one another and make a society? It is arrant
ingratitude to talk so of a land in which there is no
poverty but as a consequence of absolute idleness; and
to talk of it, too, with abuse comparatively with Eng-
land, with a place where the laborious poor are dying
with grass in their bellies. It is idle to talk of the seasons,
as if that country must not needs be miserably governed
in which an unfavourable season introduces a famine.
No! no! dear Poole, it is our pestilent commerce, our

unnatural crowding together of men in cities, and our government by rich men, that are bringing about the manifestations of offended Deity. I am assured that such is the depravity of the public mind, that no literary man can find bread in England except by misemploying and debasing his talents; that nothing of real excellence would be either felt or understood. The annuity which I hold, *perhaps by a very precarious tenure,* will shortly from the decreasing value of money become less than one half what it was when first allowed to me. If I were allowed to retain it, I would go and settle near Priestley, in America. I shall, no doubt, get a certain price for the two or three works which I shall next publish, but I foresee they will not sell. The booksellers, finding this, will treat me as an unsuccessful author, that is, they will employ me only as an anonymous translator at a guinea a sheet. I have no doubt that I could make £500 a year if I liked. But then I must forego all desire of truth and excellence. I say I would go to America if Wordsworth would go with me, and we could persuade two or three farmers of this country, who are exceedingly attached to us, to accompany us. I would go, if the difficulty of procuring sustenance in this country remain in the state and degree in which it is at present; not on any romantic scheme, but merely because society has become a matter of great indifference to me. I grow daily more and more attached to solitude; but it is a matter of the utmost importance to be removed from seeing and suffering want.

God love you, my dear friend.

S. T. Coleridge.

TO WILLIAM GODWIN (UL)

Greta Hall, Keswick,
Wednesday, March 25, 1801.

Dear Godwin,

I fear your tragedy will find me in a very unfit state
of mind to sit in judgment on it. I have been during the
last three months undergoing a process of intellectual
exsiccation. During my long illness I had compelled into
hours of delight many a sleepless painful hour of dark-
ness by chasing down metaphysical game, and since
then I have continued the hunt, till I found myself, un-
aware, at the root of pure mathematics, and up that tall
smooth tree, whose few poor branches are all at the very
summit, am I climbing by pure adhesive strength of
arms and thighs, still slipping down, still renewing my
ascent. You would not know me! All sounds of similitude
keep at such a distance from each other in my mind,
that I have forgotten how to make a rhyme. I look at
the mountains (that visible God Almighty that looks in
at all my windows)—I look at the mountains only for
the curves of their outlines; the stars, as I behold them,
form themselves into triangles; and my hands are
scarred with scratches from a cat, whose back I was
rubbing in the dark in order to see whether the sparks
from it were refrangible by a prism. The Poet is dead
in me; my imagination (or rather the Somewhat that
had been imaginative) lies like a cold snuff on the circu-
lar rim of a brass candle-stick, without even a stink of
tallow to remind you that it was once clothed and
mitred with flame. That is past by! I was once a volume
of gold leaf, rising and riding on every breath of Fancy,
but I have beaten myself back into weight and density,
and now I sink in quicksilver and remain squat and

square on the earth amid the hurricane that makes oaks and straws join in one dance, fifty yards high in the element. . . .

Have you seen the second volume of the *Lyrical Ballads,* and the preface prefixed to the first? I should judge of a man's heart and intellect precisely according to the degree and intensity of the admiration with which he read these poems. Perhaps, instead of heart I should have said Taste; but, when I think of *The Brothers*, of *Ruth*, and of *Michael*, I recur to the expression and am enforced to say heart. If I die, and the booksellers will give you anything for my life, be sure to say, "Wordsworth descended on him like the Γνῶθι σεαυτόν from Heaven; by showing to him what true poetry was, he made him know that he himself was no Poet."

In your next letter you will, perhaps, give me some hints respecting your prose plans.

God bless you, and

S. T. Coleridge.

TO ROBERT SOUTHEY (L)

Durham, Saturday, July 25, 1801.

. . . Now you will think what follows a lie, and it is not. I asked a stupid haughty fool, who is the Librarian of the Dean and Chapter's Library in this city, if it had Leibnitz. He answered, "We have no Museum in this Library for natural curiosities; but there is a Mathematical Instrument setter in the town, who shews such animalcula through a glass of great magnifying powers." Heaven and earth! he understood the word *"live nits."* Well, I return early to-morrow to Middleham; to a quiet good family that love me dearly—a young farmer and his sister, and he makes very droll verses in the northern dialects, and in the metre of Burns, and is a great humourist, and the woman is so very good a woman that I have seldom indeed seen the like of her.

Scarborough, August 1, 1801.

My dear Southey,

On my return from Durham (I foolishly walked back), I was taken ill, and my left knee swelled "pregnant with agony," as Mr. Dodsley says in one of his poems. Dr. Fenwick has earnestly persuaded me to try horse-exercise and warm sea-bathing, and I took the opportunity of riding with Sara Hutchinson to her brother Tom, who lives near the place, where I can ride to and fro, and bathe with no other expense there than that of the bath. The fit comes on me either at nine at night, or two in the morning. In the former case it continues nine hours, in the latter five. I am often literally *sick* with pain. In the daytime, however, I am well, surprisingly so indeed, considering how very little sleep I am able to snatch. . . .

All I ever wish of you with regard to wintering at Keswick is to stay with me till you find the climate injurious. When I read that cheerful sentence, "We will climb Skiddaw this year and scale Etna the next," with a right piteous and humorous smile did I ogle my poor knee, which at this present moment is larger than the thickest part of my thigh.

A little Quaker girl (the daughter of the great Quaker mathematician Slee, a friend of anti-negro-trade Clarkson, who has a house at the foot of Ulleswater, which Slee Wordsworth dined with, a pretty parenthesis!), this little girl, four years old, happened after a very hearty meal to *eructate*, while Wordsworth was there. Her mother *looked* at her, and the little creature immediately and *formally* observed: "Yan belks when yan's fu, and when yan's empty." That is, "One belches when one's

full and when one's empty." Since that time this is a
favourite piece of slang at Grasmere and Greta Hall,
whenever we talk of poor Joey, George Dyer, and other
perseverants in the noble trade of scribbleism. . . .

TO WILLIAM SOTHEBY (L)

Greta Hall, Keswick, Tuesday, July 13, 1802.

. . . After I had left you on the road between Amble-
side and Grasmere, I was dejected by the apprehension
that I had been unpardonably loquacious, and had op-
pressed you, and still more Mrs. Sotheby, with my many
words so impetuously uttered! But in simple truth, you
were yourselves, in part, the innocent causes of it. For
the meeting with you, the manner of the meeting, your
kind attentions to me, the deep and healthful delight
which every impressive and beautiful object seemed to
pour out upon you; kindred opinions, kindred pursuits,
kindred feelings in persons whose habits, and, as it were,
walk of life, have been so different from my own,—
these and more than these, which I would but cannot
say, all flowed in upon me with unusually strong im-
pulses of pleasure,—and pleasure in a body and soul
such as I happen to possess "intoxicates more than
strong wine." However, *I promise to be a much more
subdued creature when you next meet me*, for I had but
just recovered from a state of extreme dejection, brought
on in part by ill health, partly by other circumstances;
and solitude and solitary musings do of themselves im-
pregnate our thoughts, perhaps, with more life and sen-
sation than will leave the balance quite even. But you,
my dear sir! looked at a brother poet with a brother's
eyes. Oh that you were now in my study and saw, what
is now before the window at which I am writing,—that
rich mulberry-purple which a floating cloud has thrown

on the lake, and that quiet boat making its way through
it to the shore! . . .

The latter part of your letter made me truly happy.
Uriel himself should not be half as welcome; and indeed
he, I must admit, was never any great favourite of mine.
I always thought him a bantling of zoneless Italian
muses, which Milton heard cry at the door of his imag-
ination and took in out of charity. . . .

Keswick, July 19, 1802.

. . . I wished to force myself out of metaphysical
trains of thought, which, when I wished to write a
poem, beat up game of far other kind. Instead of a covey
of poetic partridges with whirring wings of music, or
wild ducks *shaping* their rapid flight in forms always
regular (a still better image of verse), up come a meta-
physical bustard, urging its slow, heavy, laborious,
earth-skimming flight over dreary and level wastes. To
have done with poetical prose (which is a very vile
Olio), sickness and some other and worse afflictions first
forced me into downright metaphysics. For I believe
that by nature I have more of the poet in me. . . .

Greta Hall, Keswick, September 10, 1802.

. . . Bowles's stanzas on "Navigation" are among the
best in that second volume, but the whole volume is
wofully inferior to its predecessor. There reigns through
all the blank verse poems such a perpetual trick of
moralizing everything, which is very well, occasionally,
but never to see or describe any interesting appearance
in nature without connecting it, by dim analogies, with
the moral world proves faintness of impression. Nature
has her proper interest, and he will know what it is who
believes and feels that everything has a life of its own,

and that we are all *One Life.* A poet's heart and intellect should be *combined,* intimately combined and unified with the great appearances of nature, and not merely held in solution and loose mixture with them, in the shape of formal similes. I do not mean to exclude these formal similes; there are moods of mind in which they are natural, pleasing moods of mind, and such as a poet will often have, and sometimes express; but they are not his highest and most appropriate moods. . . .

. . . It has struck me with great force lately that the Psalms afford a most complete answer to those who state the Jehovah of the Jews, as a personal and national God, and the Jews as differing from the Greeks only in calling the minor Gods Cherubim and Seraphim, and confining the word "God" only to their Jupiter. It must occur to every reader that the Greeks in their religious poems address always the Numina Loci, the Genii, the Dryads, the Naiads, etc., etc. All natural objects were *dead,* mere hollow statues, but there was a Godkin or Goddessling *included* in each. In the Hebrew poetry you find nothing of this poor stuff, as poor in genuine imagination as it is mean in intellect. At best, it is but fancy, or the aggregating faculty of the mind, not imagination or the *modifying* and coadunating faculty. This the Hebrew poets appear to me to have possessed beyond all others, and next to them the English. In the Hebrew poets each thing has a life of its own, and yet they are all our life. In God they move and live and *have* their being; not *had,* as the cold system of Newtonian Theology represents, but *have.* Great pleasure indeed, my dear sir, did I receive from the latter part of your letter. If there be any two subjects which have in the very depths of my nature interested me, it has been the Hebrew and Christian Theology, and the The-

ology of Plato. Last winter I read the Parmenides and
the Timæus with great care, and oh, that you were here
—even in this howling rainstorm that dashes itself
against my windows—on the other side of my blazing
fire, in that great armchair there! I guess we should en-
croach on the morning ere we parted. How little the
commentators of Milton have availed themselves of the
writings of Plato, Milton's darling! But alas, commenta-
tors only hunt out verbal parallelisms—*numen abest.*
I was much impressed with this in all the many notes
on that beautiful passage in "Comus" from l. 629 to
641. All the puzzle is to find out what plant Hæmony
is; which they discover to be the English spleenwort,
and decked out as a mere play and licence of poetic
fancy with all the strange properties suited to the pur-
pose of the drama. They thought little of Milton's pla-
tonizing spirit, who wrote nothing without an interior
meaning. "Where more is meant than meets the ear,"
is true of himself beyond all writers. He was so great a
man that he seems to have considered fiction as profane
unless where it is consecrated by being emblematic of
some truth. What an unthinking and ignorant man we
must have supposed Milton to be, if, without any hid-
den meaning, he had described it as growing in such
abundance that the dull swain treads on it daily, and
yet as never *flowering.* Such blunders Milton of all
others was least likely to commit. Do look at the pas-
sage. Apply it as an allegory of Christianity, or, to speak
more precisely, of the Redemption by the Cross, every
syllable is full of light! *"A small unsightly root."*—"To
the Greeks folly, to the Jews a stumbling-block"—*"The
leaf was darkish and had prickles on it"*—"If in this life
only we have hope, we are of all men the most miser-
able," and a score of other texts. *"But in another coun-
try, as he said, Bore a bright golden flower"*—"The

exceeding weight of glory prepared for us hereafter"—
*"But not in this soil; Unknown and like esteemed and
the dull swain Treads on it daily with his clouted shoon"*
—The promises of Redemption offered daily and hourly,
and to all, but accepted scarcely by any—*"He called it
Hæmony."* Now what is Hæmony? αἷμα οἶνος, Blood-
wine. "And he took the wine and blessed it and said,
'This is my blood,' "—the great symbol of the Death
on the Cross. There is a general ridicule cast on all
allegorising of poets. Read Milton's prose works, and
observe whether he was one of those who joined in this
ridicule. . . .

Greta Hall, Keswick
Tuesday, September 27, 1802.

My dear Sir,

The river is full, and Lodore is full, and silver-fillets
come out of clouds and glitter in every ravine of all the
mountains; and the hail lies like snow, upon their tops,
and the impetuous gusts from Borrowdale snatch the
water up high, and continually at the bottom of the lake
it is not distinguishable from snow slanting before the
wind—and under this seeming snowdrift the sunshine
gleams, and over all the nether half of the Lake it is
bright and *dazzles*, a cauldron of melted silver boiling!
It is in very truth a sunny, misty, cloudy, dazzling,
howling, omniform day, and I have been looking at as
pretty a sight as a father's eyes could well see—Hartley
and little Derwent running in the green where the gusts
blow most madly, both with their hair floating and toss-
ing, a miniature of the agitated trees, below which they
were playing, inebriate both with the pleasure—Hartley
whirling round for joy, Derwent eddying, half-willingly,
half by the force of the gust,—driven backward, strug-
gling forward, and shouting his little hymn of joy. . . .

TO TOM WEDGWOOD (UL)

Greta Hall, Keswick
October 20, 1802.

My dear Sir

This is my Birthday, my thirtieth. It will not appear wonderful to you therefore, when I tell you that before the arrival of your Letter I had been thinking with a great weight of different feelings concerning you and your dear Brother. For I have good reason to believe, that I should not now have been alive, if in addition to other miseries I had had immediate poverty pressing upon me. I will never again remain silent so long. It has not been altogether Indolence or my habits of Procrastination which have kept me from writing, but an eager wish, I may truly say, a Thirst of Spirit, to have something honorable to tell you of myself— At present I must be content to tell you something cheerful. My Health is very much better. I am stronger in every respect: and am not injured by study or the act of sitting at my writing Desk. But my eyes suffer if at any time I have been intemperate in the use of Candle-light. This account supposes another, namely, that my mind is calm and more at ease. My dear Sir! when I was last with you at Stowey, my heart was often full, and I could scarcely keep from communicating to you the tale of my distresses. But how could I add to your depression, when you were low? Or how interrupt, or cast a shade on your good spirits, that were so rare and so precious to you? After my return to Keswick, I was, if possible, more miserable than before. Scarce a day passed without such a scene of discord between me and Mrs. Coleridge, as quite incapacitated me for any worthy exertion of my faculties by degrading me in my own estimation.

I found my temper impaired, and daily more so; the good and pleasurable thoughts, which had been the support of my moral character, departed from my solitude. I determined to go abroad—but alas! the less I loved my wife, the more dear and necessary did my children seem to me. I found no comfort except in the driest speculations—In the Ode to Dejection, which you were pleased with, these lines in the original followed the line—My shaping spirit of Imagination—

> For not to think of what I needs must feel,
> But to be still and patient, all I can,
> And haply by abstruse Research to steal
> From my own Nature all the natural man—
> This was my sole resource, my only plan,
> And that which suits a part infects the whole
> And now is almost grown the Temper of my Soul.

I give you these lines for the Truth and not for the Poetry. However about two months ago after a violent quarrel I was taken suddenly ill with spasms in my stomach—I expected to die—Mrs. C. was, of course, shocked and frightened beyond measure—and two days after, I being still very weak and pale as death, she threw herself upon me, and made a solemn promise of amendment—and she has kept her promise beyond any hope, I could have flattered myself with: and I have reason to believe, that two months of tranquillity, and the sight of my now not colourless and cheerful countenance, have really made her feel as a Wife ought to feel. If any woman wanted an exact and copious Recipe, "How to make a Husband compleatly miserable," I could her furnish with one—with a Probatum est, tacked to it. Ill-tempered Speeches sent after me when I went out of the House, ill-tempered Speeches on my return, my friends received with freezing looks, the

least opposition or contradiction occasioning screams of
passion, and the sentiments which I held most base,
ostentatiously avowed—all this added to the utter nega-
tion of all, which a Husband expects from a Wife—
especially, living in retirement—and the consciousness
that I was myself growing a worse man. O dear Sir! no
one can tell what I have suffered. I can say with strict
truth, that the happiest half-hours, I have had, were
when all of a sudden, as I have been sitting in my Study
I have burst into tears. . . .

S. T. Coleridge.

TO MRS. S. T. COLERIDGE (UL)

Crescelly,
Thursday Morning, 7 o'clock,
Dec. 16, 1802.

My dear Love

I write with trembling—at what time or in what state
my letter may find you, how can I tell? Small need is
there for saying, how anxious I am, how full of terrors
and prayers! I trust in God, that this letter which I write
with a palpitating heart, you will read with a chearful
one—the new baby at your breast—O may God Al-
mighty preserve you!

We leave this place in less than an hour. Our route
lies thro'. . . .

TO ROBERT SOUTHEY (UL)

Monday Evening, August 1, 1803.

My dear old friend

On whatever plan you determine I will be your faith-
ful servant and fellow-errant. If you were with me and

health were not far away, I could now rely on myself, but my health is a very weighty, perhaps insuperable objection. Else the sense of responsibility to my own mind is growing deeper and deeper with me from many causes, chiefly, from the knowledge that I am not of no significance, relatively to, comparatively with other men, my contemporaries. I was thought *vain*—if there be no better word to express what I was, so let it be; but if Cottle be *vain*, Dyer vain, J. Jennings be *vain*, the word is a vague one. It was in me, the heat, bustle and overflowing of a mind, too vehemently pushed on from within to be regardful of the objects upon which it was moving; an instinct to have my power proved to me by transient evidences, arising from an inward feeling of weakness, both the one and the other working in me unconsciously; above all a faulty delight in the being beloved without having examined my heart, whether if beloved, I had anything to give in return beyond general kindness, and general sympathy, both indeed unusually warm, but which being still *general*, were not a return in kind, for that which I was unconsciously desiring to inspire. All this added together might possibly have been a somewhat far worse than vanity, but it would still have been different from it; far worse if it had not existed in a nature where better things were indigenous— A sense of weakness, a haunting sense that I was an herbaceous plant, as large as a large tree, with a trunk of the same girth, and branches as large and shadowing, but with pith within the trunk, not heart of wood—that I had power not strength, an involuntary impostor, that I had no real Genius, no real depth. This on my honor is as fair a statement of my habitual haunting, as I could give before the tribunal of Heaven. How it arose in me, I have but lately discovered; still it works within me, but only as a disease, the cause and meaning of which I know. The whole History of this feeling would form a curious page in a *nosologia spiritualis*. . . .

Sunday, Aug. 14, 1803.

Your letter affected me very deeply. I did not feel it so much the two first days, as I have since done. I have been very ill, and in serious dread of a paralytic stroke in my whole left side. Of my disease there now remains no shade of doubt—it is a compleat and almost heartless case of atonic Gout. If you would look at the article "Medicine" in the Encycl. Brit: Vol. XI. Part I. No 213, p. 181, and the first 5 paragraphs of the second column you will read almost the very words, in which before I had seen this article I had described my case to Wordsworth. The only non-agreement is—"an imaginary aggravation of the slightest feelings, and an apprehension of danger from them." The first sentence is unphilosophically expressed—there is a state of mind, wholly unnoticed, as far as I know, by any physical or metaphysical writer hitherto, and yet which is necessary to the explanation of some of the most important phenomena of sleep and disease—it is a transmutation of the *succession* of time into the *juxtaposition* of space, by which the smallest impulses quickly and regularly recurrent *aggregate* themselves and attain a kind of visual magnitude with a correspondent intensity of general feeling. The simplest illustration would be the *circle* of Fire made by whirling round a live coal—only here the mind is passion. Suppose the same effect produced ab intra, and you have a clue to the whole mystery of frightful dreams and hypochondriacal delusions (I merely hint this, but I could detail the whole process complex as it is). Instead

of an imaginary aggravation etc., it would be better to
say "an *aggregation* of slight feelings by the force of a
decidedly retentive imagination." As to the *apprehension
of danger*—it would belong to my disease if it could
belong to me. But Sloth, carelessness, resignation in all
things that have reference to mortal life is not merely
in me, it is me. (Spite of grammar *i.e.* Lowth's, for I
affirm that in such instances "it is *me*" is genuine Eng-
lish and philosophical grammar). . . .

TO TOM WEDGWOOD (UL)

Greta Hall, Keswick,
September 16, Friday [1803.]

My dear Wedgewood

I reached home on yesterday noon, and it was not a
Post Day. William Hazlitt is a thinking, observant, origi-
nal man, of great power as a Painter of Character Por-
traits, and far more in the manner of the old Painters,
than any living Artist, but the objects must be *before*
him; he has no imaginative memory. So much for his
Intellectuals. His manners are to 99 in 100 singularly
repulsive—: brow-hanging, shoe-contemplative, *strange*.
Sharp seemed to like him; but Sharp saw him only for
half an hour, and that walking—he is, I verily believe,
kindly-natured—is very fond of, attentive to, and patient
with, children; but he is jealous, gloomy, and of an irrita-
ble Pride—and addicted to women, as objects of sexual
Indulgence. With all this, there is much good in him—
he is disinterested, an enthusiastic lover of the great men,
who have been before us—he says things that are his
own in a way of his own—and tho' from habitual Shy-
ness and the outside and bearskin at least of misan-
thropy, (he is strangely confused and dark in his conver-
sation and delivers himself of almost all his conceptions

with a Forceps, yet he says more than any man, I ever knew, yourself only excepted, that is his own in a way of his own) and oftentimes when he has warmed his mind, and the synovial juice has come out and spread over his joints, he will gallop for half an hour together with real Eloquence. He sends well-headed and well-feathered Thoughts straight forwards to the mark with a Twang of the Bow-string. If you could recommend him, as a Portrait-painter, I should be glad. To be your Companion he is, in my opinion, utterly unfit. His own Health is fitful. I have written, as I ought to do, to you most freely imo ex corde; you know me, both head and heart, and will make what deductions, your reason will dictate to you. I can think of no other person. What wonder? For the last years I have been shy of all mere acquaintances—

To live belov'd is all, I need,
And when I love, I love indeed.

I never had any ambition; and now, I trust, I have almost as little Vanity.

For 5 months past my mind has been strangely shut up. I have taken the paper with the intention to write to you many times; but it has been all one blank Feeling, one blank idealess Feeling. I had nothing to say, I could say nothing. How dearly I love you, my very Dreams make known to me. I will not trouble you with the gloomy Tale of my Health. While I am awake, by patience, employment, effort of mind, and walking I can keep the fiend at Arm's length; but the Night is my Hell, Sleep my tormenting Angel. Three nights out of four I fall asleep, struggling to lie awake—and my frequent Night-screams have almost made me a nuisance in my own House. Dreams with me are no Shadows, but the very Substances and foot-thick Calamities of my Life. Beddoes, who has been to me ever a very kind man, suspects that my stomach "brews vinegar." . . . I myself fully believe it to be either atonic, hypochondriacal Gout, or a scrophulous affection of the mesenteric Glands. In the hope of drawing the Gout, if Gout it should be, into my feet, I walked, previously to my getting into the Coach at Perth, 263 miles in eight Days, with no unpleasant fatigue: and if I could do you any service by coming to town, and there were no Coaches, I would undertake to be with you, on foot, in 7 days. I must have strength somewhere; my head is indefatigably strong; my limbs too are strong; but acid or not acid, Gout or Scrofula, something there is [in] my stomach or Guts that transubstantiates my Bread and Wine into the Body and Blood of the Devil—Meat and Drink I should say—for I eat but little bread, and take nothing, in any form, spiritual or narcotic, stronger than Table Beer. . . .

To diversify this dusky letter I will write as a Postscript an Epitaph, which I composed in my sleep for myself, while dreaming that I was dying. To the best of my recollection I have not altered a word. Your's dear Wedgewood, and of all, that are dear to you at Gunville, gratefully and most affectionately,

S. T. Coleridge.

Epitaph.

Here sleeps at length poor Col. and without Screaming,
Who died, as he had always liv'd, a dreaming:
Shot dead, while sleeping, by the Gout within,
Alone, and all unknown, at E'nbro' in an Inn.

It was on Tuesday Night last at the Black Bull, Edinburgh.

Greta Hall, Keswick,
Sunday Evening, Oct. 2, 1803.

My dear Brother

I have this moment received yours of Sept. 28th. It is,
indeed, very long since I have written to you—the sole
reason has been that I had nothing to communicate that
was not of a depressing nature; and I am sick to the very
soul of speaking or writing concerning my bodily miseries. . . . While I am awake and retain possession of my
will and reason I can contrive to keep the Fiend at arm's
length. [With] sleep [are] thrown wide open all the
gates of the beleaguered city and such a host of Horrors
rush in that three nights out of four, I fall asleep struggling to lie awake, and start up and bless my own loud
screams that have awakened me. . . . I have sometimes
derived a comfort from the notion, that possibly these
horrid Dreams with all their mockery of Crimes and
Remorse and Shame and terror might have been sent
upon me to arouse me out of that proud and stoical
apathy, into which I had fallen—it was resignation, for
I was not an atheist; but it was resignation without religion, because it was without struggle, without difficulty,
because it originated in the Understanding, and a stealing . . . contempt, not in the affections. But amid all
my . . .[1] I have been a serene, perhaps too serene a
student—I have [written] much and prepared materials
for more—and yet I trust [that I do not] deceive myself
when I say that I could leave all . . . without a pang. I
have not read on an average less than 8 hours a day for
the last three years—but all is vanity. I feel it more and
more; all is vanity that does not lead to quietness and

[1] MS. mutilated.—*E. L. Griggs.*

unity of heart, and to the silent awful idealess watching of that living spirit, and of that Life within us, which is the motion of that spirit—that Life which passeth all understanding. Before I finish, let me say that there is yet one other cause of my silence. Your last letter on Faith and Reason had affected me very deeply. I was sure that we agreed in the depth and bottom of our meanings, and yet I thought that you had expressed yourself inaccurately, and began to reflect and make notes on the fine boundaries of Faith and Reason—till I found that I should have written a treatise instead of a letter. . . .

TO THOMAS CLARKSON (UL)

Bury, St. Edmunds,
Oct. 13, 1806.

My dear Sir:

You have proposed to me questions not more awful than difficult of Solution. What metaphysically the Spirit of God *is?* What the Soul? What the difference between the Reason, and the Understanding (νοῦς καὶ ἐπιστήμη, Vernunft, und Verstand) and how metaphysically we may explain St. Paul's assertion, that the Spirit of God bears witness to the Spirit of man? In the first place I must reduce the two first questions to the *form* of the 3rd and fourth. What the Spirit of God *is,* and what the Soul *is,* I dare not suppose myself capable of *conceiving:* according to my religious and philosophical creed they are *known* by those, to whom they are revealed, even (tho' in a higher and deeper degree) as color (blue for instance); or motion; or the difference between the Spirals of the Hop-plant and the Scarlet Bean. *Datur,* non intelligitur. They can only be explained by images, that themselves require the same explanation, as in the latter

Instance, that the one turns to the right, the other to the Left, the one is with, the other against the Sun, i.e. by relative and dependent, not positive and fundamental, notions. The only reasonable form of question appears to me to be, under what connection of ideas we may conceive and express ourselves concerning them, as that there shall be no inconsistency to be detected in our definitions, and no falsehood felt during their enunciation, which might war with our internal sense of their actuality. And in this sense these definitions are not without their use—they remove the stumbling-block out of the way of honest Infidels, that we are either Enthusiasts or Fanatics, that is, that our faith is built wholly either on blind bodily feelings arising in ourselves or caught contagiously by sympathy with the agitation of a superstitious crowd around the Fanes. (*Fanatics*) And further, Seraphs and purified Spirits may burn unextinguishably in the pure elementary fire of direct knowledge, which has it's life and all the conditions of it's power in itself—but our Faith resembles sublunary Fire, that needs the Fuel of congruous, tho' perhaps perishable, notions to call it into actuality, and maintain it in clearness and the flame that rises heaven-ward, thus raising and glorifying the thick Vapor of our earthly Being. This premised, I venture—(most unfeignedly not without trembling and religious awe—) to proceed in an attempt to answer your first question: First then 1— What is the difference or distinction between THING and THOUGHT? (or between those experiences of our nature, which in the unphilosophical jargon of Mr. Hume and his Followers, in *opposition* say rather, in direct contrariety, to the original and natural sense of the words, it is now fashionable to misname, IMPRESSIONS and IDEAS—) In other words, what do we mean by Reality?—I answer—that there exist a class of notices which have all

a ratio of vividness each with the other, so that tho' the
one may be more vivid than the other, yet in the same
and ordinary course of our nature, they are all alike
contra-distinguishable to another class of notices, which
are felt and conceived as dependent on the former, and
to be to them the same sort as a stamp on paper, is to a
seal sharp-cut in hand stone. The first class we call *Things*
and *Realities;* and find in them—not indeed absolutely,
but in a sense which we all *understand*—(and I am not
now disputing with a quibbler in mock-logic, but ad-
dressing myself to a Reasoner, who *seeks* to understand,
and looks into himself for a sense, which my words may
excite in him, not *to* my words for a sense, which they
must against his own will *force* on him) we find, I say,
in this first class a *permanancy,* and *expectability* so
great, as to be capable of being contra-distinguished
both by these, and by their *vividness* to the second class,
that is our Thoughts, which therefore as appearing pos-
terior and faint we deem the Images and imperfect
Shadows of the former. Language seems to mark this
process of our minds. Res—Reor. So Thought is the
participle of the Past: *Thing,* derived from the Participle
present, or actuality in full and immediate action. Con-
sequently, all *our* Thoughts are in the language of the
old Logicians *inadequate:* i.e. no *thought,* which I have,
of any *thing* comprizes the whole of that Thing. I have
a distinct Thought of a Rose-Tree; but what countless
properties and goings-on of that plant are there, not in-
cluded in my *Thought* of it? But the Thoughts of God,
in the strict nomenclature of Plato, are all *Ideas,* arche-
typal, and anterior to all but himself alone: therefore
consummately *adequate:* and therefore according to our
common habits of conception and expression, incompara-
bly more *real* than all things besides, and which do all
depend on and proceed from them in some sort perhaps

as our Thoughts from those *Things;* but in a more philo-
sophical language we dare with less hesitation to say,
that they are more intensely *actual;* inasmuch as the
human understanding never took an higher or more hon-
orable flight, than when it defined the Deity to be—
Actus purissimus sine potentialitate: and Eternity, the
incommunicable attribute, and may we not say, the Syn-
onime of God, to be the simultaneous possession of all
equally. These considerations, my dear Sir! appear to me
absolutely necessary, as pioneers, to cut a way thro' to
the direct solution of your first Question—What is (i.e.
What can we without detectable incongruity conceive
of) the Spirit of God? Answer—God's Thoughts are all
consummately adequate Ideas, which are all incompara-
bly more *real* than what we call *Things.* God is the sole
self-comprehending Being, i.e. he has an Idea of himself,
and that Idea is consummately adequate, and superla-
tively real—or as great men have said in the throes and
strivings of deep and holy meditation, not only substan-
tial or essential, but super-substantial, super-essential.
This Idea therefore from all eternity co-existing with,
and yet filiated, by the absolute Being (for as *our* purest
Thoughts are *conceived,* so are God's not first conceived,
but *begotten:* and thence is he verily and eminently *the
Father*) is the same, as the Father in all things, but the
impossible one, of self-origination. He is the substantial
Image of God, in whom the Father beholds well-pleased
his whole Being—and being substantial (ὁμοούσιος) he
of divine and permanent will, and a necessity which is
the absolute opposite of compulsion, as delightedly and
with as intense *Love* contemplates the Father in the
Father, and the Father in himself, and himself in the
Father. But all the actions of the Deity are intensely real
or substantial; therefore the action of Love, by which
the Father contemplates the Son, and the Son the Father,

is equally real with the Father and the Son; and pro-
ceeds co-eternally both from the Father and the Son—
and neither of these three *can* be conceived *apart,* nor
confusedly—so that the Idea of God involves that of a
Tri-unity; and as that Unity or Indivisibility is the inter-
est, and the Archetype, yea, the very substance and ele-
ment of all other Unity and Union, so is that Distinction
the most manifest, and indestructible of all distinctions
—and Being, Intellect, and Action, which in their abso-
luteness are the Father, the Word, and the Spirit will
and must for ever be and remain the "genera general-
issima" of all knowledge. Unitarianism in it's immediate
intelligential (the Spirit of Love forbid, that I should
say or think, in it's intentional and actual) consequences,
is Atheism or Spinozism—God becomes a mere power
in darkness, even as Gravitation, and instead of a Moral
Religion of practical Influence we shall have only a phys-
ical Theory to gratify ideal curiosity—no Sun, no Light
with vivifying Warmth, but a cold and dull moonshine, or
rather star-light which shews itself but shews nothing else
—Hence too, the Heresy of the Greek Church in affirm-
ing, that the Holy Spirit proceeds only from the Father,
renders the thrice sacred doctrine of the Tri-unity not
only above, but against, Reason. Hence too, the doctrine
of the Creation assumes it's intelligibility—for the Deity
in all it's three distinctions being absolutely perfect, nei-
ther susceptible of additions—or diminution, the Father
in his Son as the Image of himself surveying the Possibil-
ity of all things possible, and with that Love, which is the
Spirit of holy Action (τὸ ἅγιον πνεῦμα as the air + mo-
tion = a wind) exerted that Love *in* that Intelligence,
and that Intelligence *with* that Love (as nothing new
could be effected on the divine Nature, in it's whole
Self) therefore in giving to all possible things contem-
plated in and thro' the Son that degree of Reality, of

which it's Nature was susceptible. And this leads directly to your Second Question, namely—

2. What is (that is, what can we congruously conceive of) the Soul?—

As the Father by and for the Word, and with and thro' the Holy Spirit has given to all possible existences all susceptible perfection, it is in the highest degree probable that all things, susceptible of Progression, are progressive; and as Intelligence involves the notion of *order,* it follows necessarily, that as we can have no notion of desirable Progression (i.e. desirable for the Progressor, as well as for all others) but what supposes a growth of consciousness—or the image of that incommunicable attribute of self-comprehension, to which all creatures make approaches such as the Geometricians figure to us in the demonstration of Asymptotes. Now from those Possibilities, which exist only in the consciousness of others (and hence the absolutely inanimate is called by the Platonists, τά μὴ ὄντα) to the highest consciousness short of Deity there must subsist infinite orderly degrees —1. those who exist to themselves only in *moments,* and whose consciousness exists in higher minds. 2. those who are conscious of consciousness, but not only of their whole consciousness, but who do not make that consciousness of a continuousness an object of secondary consciousness—i.e. who are not endued with reflex Faculties. 3. Those who tho' not conscious of the whole, of their continuousness, are yet both conscious of *a* continuousness—and make that the object of a reflex consciousness—and of this third Class the Species are infinite; and the first or lowest, as far as we know, is Man, or the human Soul. For Reflexion seems the first approach to, and shadow of, the divine Permanency; the first effect of divine working in us to find the Past and Future with the Present, and thereby to let in upon us some faint glimmering of that State in which Past, Present, and Future are co-adunated in the adorable I AM. But this state and growth of reflex consciousness (my Time will not permit me to supply all the Links; but by a short meditation you will convince yourself) is not conceivable without the action of kindred souls on each other, i.e. the modification of each by each, and of each by the whole. A male and female Tyger is neither more or less whether you suppose them existing in their appropriate wilderness, or whether you suppose a thousand Pairs. But man is truly altered by the co-existence of other men; his faculties cannot be developed in himself alone, and only by himself. Therefore the human race not by a bold metaphor, but in a sublime reality, approach to and might become, one body whose Head is Christ (the Logos). Hence with a certain degree of satisfaction to my own mind I can define the human Soul to be that class of Being, as far as we are permitted to know, the first and lowest of that class, which is endued with a reflex consciousness of it's own continuousness, and the great end and purpose of all it's energies and sufferings is the growth of that reflex consciousness: that class of Being too, in which the Individual is capable of being itself contemplated as a Species of itself, namely, by it's conscious continuousness moving on in an unbroken Line, while at the same time the whole Species is capable of being regarded as one Individual. Now as the very idea of consciousness implies a recollection of the last Links, and the growth of it an extension of that retrospect, Immortality—or the recollection after the Sleep and Change (probably and by strict analogy the growth) of Death (for growth of body and the conditional causes of intellectual growth are found all to take place during Sleep, and Sleep is the Term repeatedly and as it were fondly used by the inspired Writers as the Exponent of Death, and without it the aweful, and undoubtedly taught, Doctrine of the Resurrection has no possible meaning)—the very idea of such a consciousness, permit me to repeat, implies a recollection after the Sleep of Death of all material circumstances that were at least immediately previous to it. A spacious field here opens itself for moral reflection, both for Faith, and for Consolation, when we consider the growth of consciousness (and of what kind our's is, our *conscience* sufficiently reveals to us: for of what use or meaning could *Conscience* be to a Being, who in any state of it's Existence should become to itself utterly lost, and entirely new?) as the end of our earthly Being—when we reflect too, how habits of Vice of all kinds tend to retard the growth, and how all our sufferings tend to extend and open it out, and how all our Virtues and virtuous and loving affections tend to bind it, and as it were to inclose the fleeting Retrospect as within a wall!—And again, what sublime motives to self-respect with humble Hope does not the Idea give, that each Soul is a Species in itself; and what Impulses to more than brotherly Love of our fellow-creatures, the Idea that all men form as it were, one Soul!—

Your third Question admits—in consequence of the preceding—of a briefer and more immediate Answer. What is the difference between the Reason, and the Understanding? I would reply, that that Faculty of the Soul which apprehends and retains the mere notices of Experience, as for instance that such an object has a triangular figure, that it is of such or such a magnitude, and of such and such a color, and consistency, with the anticipation of meeting the same under the same circumstances, in other words, all the mere φαινόμενα of our nature, we may call the Understanding. But all such notices, as are characterized by *Universality* and *Neces-*

sity, as that every Triangle *must* in all places and at all times have it's two sides greater than it's third—and which are evidently not the effect of any Experience, but the condition of all Experience—that indeed without which Experience itself would be inconceivable, we may call Reason—and this class of knowledge was called by the Ancients Νοούμενα in distinction from the former, or Φαινόμενα. Reason is therefore most eminently the Revelation of an immortal soul, and it's best Synonime—it is the forma formans, which contains in itself the law of it's own conceptions. Nay it is highly probable, that the contemplation of essential Form as remaining the same thro' all varities of color and magnitude and development, as in the acorn even as in the Oak, first gave to the mind the ideas, by which it explained to itself those notices of it's Immortality revealed to it by it's conscience.

Your fourth Question appears to me to receive a full answer from the preceding Data. For if God with the Spirit of God created the Soul of Man as far as it was possible according to his own Likeness, and if he be an omnipresent Influence, it necessarily follows, that his action on the Soul of Man must awake in it a conscious-[ness] of actions within itself analogous to the divine action; and that therefore the Spirit of God truly bears witness to the Spirit of Man, even as vice versâ the awakened Spirit will bear witness to the Spirit of God. Suppose a dull impression from a Seal prefixed anew by that Seal—it's recovered characters bear witness to the Seal, even as the Seal had borne witness to the latent yet existing Impression. . . .

9 Waterloo Plains, Ramsgate,
November 9, 1828.

My Dear Sir,

It is a not unfrequent tragico-whimsical fancy with
me to imagine myself as the survivor of

> This breathing House not built with hands,
> This body that does me grievous wrong—

and an Assessor at it's dissection—infusing, as spirits
may be supposed to have the power of doing, this and
that thought into the mind of the Anatomist. *Ex. gr.* Be
so good as to give a cut just *there,* right across the um-
bilical region—there lurks the fellow that for so many
years tormented me on my first waking! or—a stab *there,*
I beseech you, it was the seat and source of that dreaded
subsultus which so often threw my Book out of my hand,
or drove my pen in a blur over the paper on which I was
writing! . . . O if in addition to the disturbing accidents
and Taxes on my Time resulting from my almost consti-
tutional pain and difficulty in uttering and in persisting
to utter, NO! if in addition to the distractions of narrow
and embarrassed Circumstances, and of a poor man con-
strained to be under obligation to generous and affec-
tionate Friends only one degree richer than himself, the
calls of the day forcing me away in my most genial
hours from a work in which my very heart and soul were
buried, to a five guinea task, which fifty persons might
have done better, at least, more effectually for the pur-
pose; if in addition to these, and half a score other in-
trusive Draw-backs, it were possible to convey without
inflicting the sensations, which (suspended by the stim-
ulus of earnest conversation or of rapid motion) annoy

and at times overwhelm me as soon as I sit down alone, with my pen in my hand, and my head bending and body compressed, over my table (I cannot say, desk)— I dare believe that in the mind of a competent Judge what I have performed will excite more surprize than what I have omitted to do, or failed in doing. Enough of this. . . . I need not tell you, that pecuniary motives either do not act at all—or are of that class of stimulants which act only as Narcotics: and as to what *people* in *general* think about me, my mind and spirit are too awefully occupied with the concerns of another Tribunal, before which I stand momently, to be much affected by it one way or other. . . .

SELECTIONS FROM *Anima Poetae*

Our quaint metaphysical opinions, in an hour of anguish, are like playthings by the bedside of a child deadly sick.
(1798?)

The elder languages were fitter for poetry because they expressed only prominent ideas with clearness, the others but darkly. . . . Poetry gives most pleasure when only generally and not perfectly understood. It was so by me with Gray's "Bard" and Collins' Odes. The "Bard" once intoxicated me, and now I read it without pleasure. From this cause it is that what I call metaphysical poetry gives me so much delight.

Poetry which excites us to artificial feelings makes us callous to real ones.

The immoveableness of all things through which so many men were moving—a harsh contrast compared with the universal motion, the harmonious system of motions in the country, and everywhere in Nature. In the dim light London appeared to be a huge place of sepulchres through which hosts of spirits were gliding.
(Friday evening, November 27, 1799)

Not only words, as far as relates to speaking, but the knowledge of words as distinct component parts, which we learn by learning to read—what an immense effect it must have on our reasoning faculties! Logical in opposition to real.

Hot-headed men confuse, your cool-headed gentry jumble. The man of warm feelings only produces order and true connection.

To *think* of a thing is different from to *perceive* it, as "to walk" is from to "feel the ground under you"; perhaps in the same way too—namely, a succession of perceptions accompanied by a sense of *nisus* and purpose.

Materialists unwilling to admit the mysterious element of our nature make it all mysterious—nothing mysterious in nerves, eyes, etc., but that nerves think, etc.! Stir up the sediment into the transparent water, and so make all opaque.

> "—and the deep power of Joy
> We see into the Life of Things."

By deep feeling we make our *ideas dim*, and this is what we mean by our life, ourselves. I think of the wall —it is before me a distinct image. Here I necessarily think of the *idea* and the thinking *I* as two distinct and opposite things. Now let me think of *myself*, of the thinking being. The idea becomes dim, whatever it be—so dim that I know not what it is; but the feeling is deep and steady, and this I call *I*—identifying the percipient and the perceived.

Hartley, looking out of my study window, fixed his eyes steadily and for some time on the opposite prospect and said, "Will yon mountains *always* be?" I shewed him the whole magnificent prospect in a looking-glass, and held it up, so that the whole was like a canopy or ceiling over his head, and he struggled to express himself concerning the difference between the thing and the image almost with convulsive effort. I never before saw such an abstract of *thinking* as a pure act and energy— of thinking as distinguished from thought.

(March 17, 1801, Tuesday)

Quaere, whether or no too great definiteness of terms in any language may not consume too much of the vital and idea-creating force in distinct, clear, full-made images, and so prevent originality. For original might be distinguished from positive thought.

Metaphysics make all one's thoughts equally corrosive on the body, by introducing a habit of making momently and common thought the subject of uncommon interest and intellectual energy.

(1802)

The unspeakable comfort to a good man's mind, nay, even to a criminal, to be *understood*—to have some one that understands one—and who does not feel that, on earth, no one does? The hope of this, always more or less disappointed—gives the passion to friendship.

Hartley, at Mr. Clarkson's, sent for a candle. The *seems* made him miserable. "What do you mean, my love?" "The seems, the seems. What seems to be and is not, men and faces, and I do not (know) what, ugly,

and sometimes pretty, and these turn ugly, and they
seem when my eyes are open and worse when they are
shut—and the candle cures the *seems*."

(October, 1802)

We imagine ourselves discoverers, and that we have
struck a light, when, in reality, at most, we have but
snuffed a candle.

The great federal republic of the universe.

The rocks and stones put on a vital resemblance and
life itself seemed, thereby, to forego its restlessness, to
anticipate in its own nature an infinite repose, and to
become, as it were, compatible with immoveability.

"He who cannot wait for his reward has, in reality, not
earned it." These words I uttered in a dream, in which a
lecture I was giving—a very profound one, as I thought
—was not listened to, but I was quizzed.

A smile, as foreign or alien to, as detached from the
gloom of the countenance, as I have seen a small spot
of light travel slowly and sadly along the mountain's
breast, when all beside has been dark with the storm.

(October, 1803)

The sunny mist, the luminous gloom of Plato.

Nothing affects me much at the moment it happens.
It either stupifies me, and I, perhaps, look at a merry-
make and dance-the-hay of flies, or listen entirely to the
loud click of the great clock, or I am simply indifferent,
not without some sense of philosophical self-compla-
cency. For a thing at the moment is but a thing of the

moment; it must be taken up into the mind, diffuse it-self through the whole multitude of shapes and thoughts, not one of which it leaves untinged, between (not one of) which and it some new thought is not engendered. Now this is a work of time, but the body feels it quicker with me.

What is it that I employ my metaphysics on? To per-plex our clearest notions and living moral instincts? To extinguish the light of love and of conscience, to put out the life of arbitrement, to make myself and others *worth-less, soulless, Godless?* No, to expose the folly and the legerdemain of those who have thus abused the blessed organ of language, to support all old and venerable truths, to support, to kindle, to project, to make the rea-son spread light over our feelings, to make our feelings diffuse vital warmth through our reason—these are my objects and these my subjects. Is this the metaphysic that bad spirits in hell delight in?

My nature requires another nature for its support, and reposes only in another from the necessary indigence of its being. Intensely similar yet not the same (must that other be); or, may I venture to say, the same indeed, but dissimilar, as the same breath sent with the same force, the same pauses, and the same melody pre-imaged in the mind, into the flute and the clarion shall be the same *soul diversely incarnate.*

Abstruse reasoning is to the inductions of common sense what reaping is to delving. But the implements with which we reap, how are they gained? by delving. Besides, what is common sense now was abstract reason-ing with earlier ages.

The soul within the body—can I, any way, compare this to the reflection of the fire seen through my window on the solid wall, seeming, of course, within the solid wall, as deep within as the distance of the fire from the wall. I fear I can make nothing out of it; but why do I always hurry away from any interesting thought to do something uninteresting? As, for instance, when this thought struck me, I turned off my attention suddenly and went to look for the copy of Wolff which I had missed. Is it a cowardice of all deep feeling, even though pleasurable? or is it laziness? or is it something less obvious than either? Is it connected with my epistolary embarrassments?

I have only to shut my eyes to feel how ignorant I am whence these forms and coloured forms, and colours distinguishable beyond what I can distinguish, derive their birth. These varying and infinite co-present colours, what are they? I ask, to what do they belong in my waking remembrance? and almost never receive an answer. Only I perceive and know that whatever I change, in any part of me, produces some change in these eye-spectra; as, for instance, if I press my legs or change sides.

(December 19, 1803, morning)

There are thoughts that seem to give me a power over my own life. I could kill myself by persevering in the thought. Mem., to describe as accurately as may be the approximating symptoms.

This evening, and indeed all this day, I ought to have been reading and filling the margins of Malthus.

I had begun and found it pleasant. Why did I neglect

it? Because I ought not to have done this. The same applies to the reading and writing of letters, essays, etc. Surely this is well worth a serious analysis, that, by understanding, I may attempt to heal it. For it is a deep and wide disease in my moral nature, at once elm-and-oak-rooted. Is it love of liberty, of spontaneity or what? These all express, but do not explain the fact.

After I had got into bed last night I said to myself that I had been pompously enunciating as a difficulty, a problem of easy and common solution—viz., that it was the effect of association. From infancy up to manhood, under parents, schoolmasters, inspectors, etc., our pleasures and pleasant self-chosen pursuits (self-chosen because pleasant, and not originally pleasant because self-chosen) have been forcibly interrupted, and dull, unintelligible rudiments, or painful tasks imposed upon us instead. Now all duty is felt as a *command*, and every command is of the nature of an offence. Duty, therefore, by the law of association being felt as a command from without, would naturally call up the sensation of the pain roused from the commands of parents and schoolmasters. But I awoke this morning at half-past one, and as soon as disease permitted me to think at all, the shallowness and sophistry of this solution flashed upon me at once. I saw that the phenomenon occurred far, far too early: I have observed it in infants of two or three months old, and in Hartley I have seen it turned up and layed bare to the unarmed eye of the merest common sense. The fact is that interruption of itself is painful, because and as far as it acts as *disruption*. And thus without any reference to or distinct recollection of my former theory I saw great reason to attribute the effect, wholly, to the streamy nature of the associative faculty, and the more, as it is evident that they labour under this defect who are most reverie-ish and streamy—Hartley, for instance, and myself. This seems to me no common corrob-oration of my former thought on the origin of moral evil in general.

(Tuesday morning, January 10, 1804)

It is related by D. Unzer, an authority wholly to be relied on, that an *ohrwurm* (earwig) cut in half ate its own hinder part! Will it be the reverse with Great Britain and America?

One travels along with the lines of a mountain. Years ago I wanted to make Wordsworth sensible of this. How fine is Keswick vale! Would I repose, my soul lies and is quiet upon the broad level vale. Would it act? it darts up into the mountain-top like a kite, and like a chamois-goat runs along the ridge—or like a boy that makes a sport on the road of running along a wall or narrow fence!

One of the most noticeable and fruitful facts in psy-chology is the modification of the same feeling by differ-ence of form. The Heaven lifts up my soul, the sight of the ocean seems to widen it. We feel the same force at work, but the difference, whether in mind or body that we should feel in actual travelling horizontally or in direct ascent, *that* we feel in fancy. For what are our feelings of this kind but a motion imagined, (together) with the feelings that would accompany that motion, (but) less distinguished, more blended, more rapid, more confused, and, thereby, co-adunated? Just as white is the very emblem of one in being the confusion of all.

How opposite to nature and the fact to talk of the "one moment" of Hume, of our whole being an aggre-gate of successive single sensations! Who ever felt a

single sensation? Is not every one at the same moment
conscious that there co-exist a thousand others, a darker
shade, or less light, even as when I fix my attention on
a white house or a grey bare hill or rather long ridge that
runs out of sight each way (how often I want the Ger-
man *unübersekbar!*) (untranslatable)—the pretended
sight-sensation, is it anything more than the light-point
in every picture either of nature or of a good painter?
and, again, subordinately, in every component part of
the picture? And what is a moment? Succession with in-
terspace? Absurdity! It is evidently only the *licht-punct*
in the indivisible undivided duration.

There are two sorts of talkative fellows whom it would
be injurious to confound, and I, S. T. Coleridge, am the
latter. The first sort is of those who use five hundred
words more than needs to express an idea—that is not
my case. Few men, I will be bold to say, put more mean-
ing into their words than I, or choose them more de-
liberately and discriminately. The second sort is of those
who use five hundred more ideas, images, reasons, etc.,
than there is any need of to arrive at their object, till the
only object arrived at is that the mind's eye of the by-
stander is dazzled with colours succeeding so rapidly as
to leave one vague impression that there has been a
great blaze of colours all about something. Now this is
my case, and a grievous fault it is. My illustrations swal-
low up my thesis. I feel too intensely the omnipresence
of all in each, platonically speaking; or, psychologically,
my brain-fibres, or the spiritual light which abides in
the brain-marrow, as visible light appears to do in sundry
rotten mackerel and other *smashy* matters, is of too gen-
eral an affinity with all things, and though it perceives
the *difference* of things, yet is eternally pursuing the
likenesses, or, rather, that which is common (between

them). Bring me two things that seem the very same, and then I am quick enough (not only) to show the difference, even to hair-splitting, but to go on from circle to circle till I break against the shore of my hearers' patience, or have my concentricals dashed to nothing by a snore. That is my ordinary mishap. At Malta, however, no one can charge me with one or the other. I have earned the general character of being a quiet well-meaning man, rather dull indeed! and who would have thought that he had been a *poet!* "O, a very wretched poetaster, ma'am! As to the reviews, 'tis well known he half-ruined himself in paying cleverer fellows than himself to write them," etc.

How far might one imagine all the theory of association out of a system of growth, by applying to the brain and soul what we know of an embryo? One tiny particle combines with another its like, and, so, lengthens and thickens, and this is, at once, memory and increasing vividness of impression. One might make a very amusing allegory of an embryo soul up to birth! Try! it is promising! You have not above three hundred volumes to write before you come to it, and as you write, perhaps, a volume once in ten years, you have ample time.

My dear fellow! never be ashamed of scheming—you can't think of living less than 4000 years, and that would nearly suffice for your present schemes. To be sure, if they go on in the same ratio to the performance, then a small difficulty arises; but never mind! look at the bright side always and die in a dream! Oh!

In the preface of my metaphysical works, I should say —"Once for all, read Kant, Fichte, etc., and then you will trace, or, if you are on the hunt, track me." Why, then, not acknowledge your obligations step by step?

Because I could not do so in a multitude of glaring
resemblances without a lie, for they had been mine,
formed and full-formed, before I had ever heard of these
writers, because to have fixed on the particular instances
in which I have really been indebted to these writers
would have been hard, if possible, to me who read for
truth and self-satisfaction, and not to make a book, and
who always rejoiced and was jubilant when I found my
own ideas well expressed by others—and, lastly, let me
say, because (I am proud, perhaps, but) I seem to know
that much of the *matter* remains my own, and that the
soul is mine. I fear not him for a critic who can confound
a fellow-thinker with a compiler.

In all processes of the understanding the shortest way
will be discovered the last; and this, perhaps, while it
constitutes the great advantage of having a teacher to
put us on the shortest road at the first, yet sometimes
occasions a difficulty in the comprehension, inasmuch as
the longest way is more near to the existing state of the
mind, nearer to what if left to myself, on starting the
thought, I should have thought next. The shortest way
gives me the *knowledge* best, but the longest makes me
more *knowing*.

If one thought leads to another, so often does it blot
out another. This I find when having lain musing on my
sofa, a number of interesting thoughts having suggested
themselves, I conquer my bodily indolence, and rise to
record them in these books, alas! my only confidants. The
first thought leads me on indeed to new ones; but noth-
ing but the faint memory of having had these remains
of the other, which had been even more interesting to
me. I do not know whether this be an idiosyncrasy, a

peculiar disease, of *my* particular memory—but so it is with *me*—my thoughts crowd each other to death.

The first man of science was he who looked into a thing, not to learn whether it could furnish him with food, or shelter, or weapons, or tools, or ornaments, or *playwiths,* but who sought to know it for the gratification of *knowing;* while he that first sought to *know* in order to *be* was the first philosopher. I have read of two rivers passing through the same lake, yet all the way preserving their streams visibly distinct—if I mistake not, the Rhone and the Adar, through the Lake of Geneva. In a far finer distinction, yet in a subtler union, such, for the contemplative mind, are the streams of knowing and being. The lake is formed by the two streams in man and nature as it exists in and for man; and up this lake the philosopher sails on the junction-line of the constituent streams, still pushing upward and sounding as he goes, towards the common fountain-head of both, the mysterious source whose being is knowledge, whose knowledge is being—the adorable I AM IN THAT I AM. (1814)

SELECTIONS FROM *Table Talk*

A single thought is that which it is from other thoughts, as a wave of the sea takes its form and shape from the waves which precede and follow it. (From T. Allsop)

April 30, 1830

Plato's works are preparatory exercises for the mind. He leads you to see, that propositions involving in themselves contradictory conceptions, are nevertheless true; and which, therefore, must belong to a higher logic— that of ideas. They are contradictory only in the Aristotelian logic, which is the instrument of the understanding. I have read most of the works of Plato several times with profound attention, but not all his writings. In fact, I soon found that I had read Plato by anticipation. He was a consummate genius.

July 26, 1830

John Thelwall had something very good about him. We were once sitting in a beautiful recess in the Quantocks, when I said to him, "Citizen John, this is a fine place to talk treason in!"—"Nay! Citizen Samuel," replied he, "it is rather a place to make a man forget that there is any necessity for treason!"

Thelwall thought it very unfair to influence a child's mind by inculcating any opinions before it should have come to years of discretion, and be able to choose for itself. I showed him my garden, and told him it was my botanical garden. "How so?" said he, "it is covered with weeds."—"Oh," I replied, "*that* is only because it has not yet come to its age of discretion and choice. The weeds, you see, have taken the liberty to grow, and I thought it unfair in me to prejudice the soil towards roses and strawberries."

September 21, 1830

. . . He told me that facts gave birth to, and were the absolute ground of principles; to which I said, that unless he had a principle of selection, he would not have taken notice of those facts upon which he grounded his principle. You must have a lantern in your hand to give light, otherwise all the materials in the world are useless, for you could not arrange them. "But then," said Mr.

——, *"that* principle of selection came from facts!"—
"To be sure!" I replied; "but there must have been
again an antecedent light to see those antecedent facts.
The relapse may be carried in imagination backwards for
ever,—but go back as you may, you cannot come to a
man without a previous aim or principle." He then asked
me what I had to say to Bacon's induction: I told him I
had a good deal to say, if need were; but that it was
perhaps enough for the occasion to remark, that what
he was evidently taking for the Baconian *in*duction was
mere *de*duction—a very different thing.

June 28, 1834

You may not understand my system, or any given part
of it,—or by a determined act of wilfulness, you may,
even though perceiving a ray of light, reject it in anger
and disgust:—but this I will say,—that if you once mas-
ter it, or any part of it, you cannot hesitate to acknowl-
edge it as the truth. You cannot be sceptical about it.

The metaphysical disquisition at the end of the first
volume of the "Biographia Literaria" is unformed and
immature;—it contains the fragments of the truth, but
it is not fully thought out. It is wonderful to myself to
think how infinitely more profound my views now are,
and yet how much clearer they are withal. The circle is
completing; the idea is coming round to, and to be, the
common sense.

POLITICS

Address Delivered at Bristol[1]
(1795)

(From *The Friend*, First Section, Essay **XVI**, 1795)

Ἀεὶ γὰρ τῆς ἐλευθερίας ἐφίεμαι· πόλλα δὲ ἐν καὶ τοῖς
φιλελευθέροις μισητά, ἀντελεύθερα.

*For I am always a lover of liberty; but in those who would
appropriate the title, I find too many points destructive of
liberty and hateful to her genuine advocates.*

Companies resembling the present will, from a variety
of circumstances, consist chiefly of the zealous advocates
for freedom. It will therefore be our endeavour, not so
much to excite the torpid, as to regulate the feelings of
the ardent: and above all, to evince the necessity of bot-
toming on fixed principles, that so we may not be the
unstable patriots of passion or accident, nor hurried
away by names of which we have not sifted the meaning,
and by tenets of which we have not examined the con-
sequences. The times are trying; and in order to be pre-
pared against their difficulties, we should have acquired
a prompt facility of adverting in all our doubts to some
grand and comprehensive truth. In a deep and strong
soil must that tree fix its roots, the height of which is to
*reach to heaven, and the sight of it to the ends of all the
earth.*

The example of France is indeed a warning to Britain.

[1] For the setting of this speech, see pp. 242–43.

A nation wading to its rights through blood, and marking the track of freedom by devastation! Yet let us not embattle our feelings against our reason. Let us not indulge our malignant passions under the mask of humanity. Instead of railing with infuriate declamation against these excesses, we shall be more profitably employed in tracing them to their sources. French freedom is the beacon which if it guides to equality should shew us likewise the dangers that throng the road.

The annals of the French revolution have recorded in letters of blood, that the knowledge of the few cannot counteract the ignorance of the many; that the light of philosophy, when it is confined to a small minority, points out the possessors as the victims, rather than the illuminators, of the multitude. The patriots of France either hastened into the dangerous and gigantic error of making certain evil the means of contingent good, or were sacrificed by the mob, with whose prejudices and ferocity their unbending virtue forbade them to assimilate. Like Samson, the people were strong—like Samson the people were blind. "Those two massy pillars" of the temple of oppression, their monarchy and aristocracy,

> With horrible·convulsion to and fro
> *They* tugg'd, *they* shook—till down they came and drew
> The whole roof after them with burst of thunder
> Upon the heads of all who sat beneath,
> Lords, ladies, captains, counsellors, *and* priests,
> Their choice nobility!

The Girondists, who were the first republicans in power, were men of enlarged views and great literary attainments; but they seem to have been deficient in that vigour and daring activity, which circumstances made necessary. Men of genius are rarely either prompt in action or consistent in general conduct. Their early habits have been those of contemplative indolence; and the day-dreams, with which they have been accustomed to amuse their solitude, adapt them for splendid speculation, not temperate and practicable counsels. Brissot, the leader of the Gironde party, is entitled to the character of a virtuous man, and an eloquent speaker; but he was rather a sublime visionary, than a quick-eyed politician; and his excellences equally with his faults rendered him unfit for the helm in the stormy hour of revolution. Robespierre, who displaced him, possessed a glowing ardour that still remembered the end, and a cool ferocity that never either overlooked or scrupled the means. What that end was, is not known: that it was a wicked one, has by no means been proved. I rather think, that the distant prospect, to which he was travelling, appeared to him grand and beautiful; but that he fixed his eye on it with such intense eagerness as to neglect the foulness of the road. If, however, his first intentions were pure, his subsequent enormities yield us a melancholy proof, that it is not the character of the possessor which directs the power, but the power which shapes and depraves the character of the possessor. In Robespierre, its influence was assisted by the properties of his disposition.—Enthusiasm, even in the gentlest temper, will frequently generate sensations of an unkindly order. If we clearly perceive any one thing to be of vast and infinite importance to ourselves and all mankind, our first feelings impel us to turn with angry contempt from those, who doubt and oppose it. The ardour of undisciplined benevolence seduces us into malignity: and whenever our hearts are warm, and our objects great and excellent, intolerance is the sin that does most easily beset us. But this enthusiasm in Robespierre was blended with gloom, and suspiciousness, and inordinate vanity. His dark imagination was still brooding over supposed plots against freedom;—to prevent tyranny he became a tyrant,—and having realised the evils which he suspected, a wild and dreadful tyrant.—And thus, his ear deafened to the whispers of conscience by the clamorous plaudits of the mob, he despotized in all the pomp of patriotism, and masqueraded on the bloody stage of revolution, a Caligula with the cap of liberty on his head.

It has been affirmed, and I believe with truth, that the system of terrorism by suspending the struggles of contrarient factions communicated an energy to the operations of the republic, which had been hitherto unknown, and without which it could not have been preserved. The system depended for its existence on the general sense of its necessity, and when it had answered its end, it was soon destroyed by the same power that had given it birth—popular opinion. It must not however be disguised, that at all times, but more especially when the public feelings are wavy and tumultuous, artful demagogues may create this opinion: and they, who are inclined to tolerate evil as the means of contingent good, should reflect, that if the excesses of terrorism gave to the republic that efficiency and repulsive force which its circumstances made necessary, they likewise afforded to the hostile courts the most powerful support, and excited that indignation and horror which every where precipitated the subject into the designs of the ruler. Nor let it be forgotten that these excesses perpetuated the war in La Vendée and made it more terrible, both by the accession of numerous partizans, who had fled from the persecution of Robespierre, and by inspiring the Chouans with fresh fury, and an unsubmitting spirit of revenge and desperation.

Revolutions are sudden to the unthinking only. Strange rumblings and confused noises still precede these earthquakes and hurricanes of the moral world.

The process of revolution in France has been dreadful, and should incite us to examine with an anxious eye the motives and manners of those, whose conduct and opinions seem calculated to forward a similar event in our own country. The oppositionists to "things as they are," are divided into many and different classes. To delineate them with an unflattering accuracy may be a delicate, but it is a necessary, task, in order that we may enlighten, or at least be aware of, the misguided men who have enlisted under the banners of liberty, from no principles or with bad ones: whether they be those, who

> admire they know not what,
> And know not whom, but as one leads to the other;—

or whether those,

> Whose end is private hate, not help to freedom,
> Adverse and turbulent when she would lead
> To virtue.

The majority of democrats appear to me to have attained that portion of knowledge in politics, which infidels possess in religion. I would by no means be supposed to imply that the objections of both are equally unfounded, but that they both attribute to the system which they reject, all the evils existing under it; and that both contemplating truth and justice in the nakedness of abstraction, condemn constitutions and dispensations without having sufficiently examined the natures, circumstances, and capacities of their recipients.

The first class among the professed friends of liberty is composed of men, who unaccustomed to the labour of thorough investigation, and not particularly oppressed by the burthens of state, are yet impelled by their feelings to disapprove of its grosser depravities, and prepared to give an indolent vote in favour of reform. Their

sensibilities not braced by the co-operation of fixed prin-
ciples, they offer no sacrifices to the divinity of active
virtue. Their political opinions depend with weather-
cock uncertainty on the winds of rumour, that blow from
France. On the report of French victories they blaze into
republicanism, at a tale of French excesses they darken
into aristocrats. These dough-baked patriots are not how-
ever useless. This oscillation of political opinion will
retard the day of revolution, and it will operate as a
preventive to its excesses. Indecisiveness of character,
though the effect of timidity, is almost always associated
with benevolence.

Wilder features characterize the second class. Suffi-
ciently possessed of natural sense to despise the priest,
and of natural feeling to hate the oppressor, they listen
only to the inflammatory harangues of some mad-headed
enthusiast, and imbibe from them poison, not food; rage,
not liberty. Unillumined by philosophy, and stimulated
to a lust of revenge by aggravated wrongs, they would
make the altar of freedom stream with blood, while the
grass grew in the desolated halls of justice.

We contemplate those principles with horror. Yet
they possess a kind of wild justice well calculated to
spread them among the grossly ignorant. To unen-
lightened minds, there are terrible charms in the idea
of retribution, however savagely it be inculcated. The
groans of the oppressors make fearful yet pleasant music
to the ear of him, whose mind is darkness, and into
whose soul the iron has entered.

This class, at present, is comparatively small—yet
soon to form an overwhelming majority, unless great
and immediate efforts are used to lessen the intolerable
grievances of our poor brethren, and infuse into their
sorely wounded hearts the healing qualities of knowl-
edge. For can we wonder that men should want human-

ity, who want all the circumstances of life that humanize? Can we wonder that with the ignorance of brutes they should unite their ferocity? Peace and comfort be with these! But let us shudder to hear from men of dissimilar opportunities sentiments of similar revengefulness. The purifying alchemy of education may transmute the fierceness of an ignorant man into virtuous energy; but what remedy shall we apply to him whom plenty has not softened, whom knowledge has not taught benevolence? This is one among the many fatal effects which result from the want of fixed principles.

There is a third class among the friends of freedom, who possess not the wavering character of the first description, nor the ferocity last delineated. They pursue the interests of freedom steadily, but with narrow and self-centering views: they anticipate with exultation the abolition of privileged orders, and of acts that persecute by exclusion from the right of citizenship. Whatever is above them they are most willing to drag down; but every proposed alteration that would elevate their poorer brethren, they rank among the dreams of visionaries: as if there were any thing in the superiority of lord to gentleman so mortifying in the barrier, so fatal to happiness in the consequences, as the more real distinction of master and servant, of rich man and of poor. Wherein am I made worse by my ennobled neighbour? Do the childish titles of aristocracy detract from my domestic comforts, or prevent my intellectual acquisitions? But those institutions of society which should condemn me to the necessity of twelve hours' daily toil, would make my soul a slave, and sink the rational being in the mere animal. It is a mockery of our fellow-creatures' wrongs to call them equal in rights, when by the bitter compulsion of their wants we make them inferior to us in all that can soften the heart, or dignify the understanding. Let us not say

that this is the work of time—that it is impracticable
at present, unless we each in our individual capacities
do strenuously and perseveringly endeavour to diffuse
among our domestics those comforts and that illumina-
tion which far beyond all political ordinances are the
true equalizers of men.

We turn with pleasure to the contemplation of that
small but glorious band, whom we may truly distinguish
by the name of thinking and disinterested patriots. These
are the men who have encouraged the sympathetic pas-
sions till they have become irresistible habits, and made
their duty a necessary part of their self-interest, by th·'
long-continued cultivation of that moral taste which de-
rives our most exquisite pleasures from the contempla-
tion of possible perfection, and proportionate pain from
the perception of existing depravity. Accustomed to re-
gard all the affairs of man as a process, they never hurry
and they never pause. Theirs is not that twilight of politi-
cal knowledge which gives us just light enough to place
one foot before the other; as they advance the scene still
opens upon them, and they press right onward with a
vast and various landscape of existence around them.
Calmness and energy mark all their actions. Convinced
that vice originates not in the man, but in the surround-
ing circumstances; not in the heart, but in the under-
standing; the Christian patriot is hopeless concerning no
one;—to correct a vice or generate a virtuous conduct
he pollutes not his hands with the scourge of coercion;
but by endeavouring to alter circumstances would re-
move, or by strengthening the intellect disarm, the
temptation. . . .

But if we hope to instruct others, we should familiar-
ize our own minds to some fixed and determinate prin-
ciples of action. The world is a vast labyrinth, in which
almost every one is running a different way, and almost

every one manifesting hatred to those who do not run the
same way. A few indeed stand motionless, and not seek-
ing to lead themselves or others out of the maze, laugh
at the failures of their brethren. Yet with little reason:
for more grossly than the most bewildered wanderer does
he err, who never aims to go right. It is more honourable
to the head, as well as to the heart, to be misled by our
eagerness in the pursuit of truth, than to be safe from
blundering by contempt of it. The happiness of man-
kind is the end of virtue, and truth is the knowledge of
the means; which he will never seriously attempt to dis-
cover, who has not habitually interested himself in the
welfare of others. The searcher after truth must love and
be beloved; for general benevolence is a necessary mo-
tive to constancy of pursuit; and this general benevo-
lence is begotten and rendered permanent by social and
domestic affections. Let us beware of that proud philos-
ophy, which affects to inculcate philanthropy while it
denounces every home-born feeling by which it is pro-
duced and nurtured. The paternal and filial duties dis-
cipline the heart and prepare it for the love of all
mankind. The intensity of private attachments encour-
ages, not prevents, universal benevolence. The nearer
we approach to the sun, the more intense his heat: yet
what corner of the system does he not cheer and vivify?

The man who would find truth, must likewise seek it
with a humble and simple heart, otherwise he will be
precipitate and overlook it; or he will be prejudiced, and
refuse to see it. To emancipate itself from the tyranny
of association, is the most arduous effort of the mind,
particularly in religious and political disquisitions. The
assertors of the system have associated with it the preser-
vation of order and public virtue; the oppugners, im-
posture and wars and rapine. Hence, when they dispute,
each trembles at the consequences of the other's opinions

instead of attending to his train of arguments. Of this however we may be certain, whether we be Christians or infidels, aristocrats or republicans, that our minds are in a state insusceptible of knowledge, when we feel an eagerness to detect the falsehood of an adversary's reasonings, not a sincere wish to discover if there be truth in them;—when we examine an argument in order that we may answer it, instead of answering because we have examined it.

Our opponents are chiefly successful in confuting the theory of freedom by the practices of its advocates: from our lives they draw the most forcible arguments against our doctrines. Nor have they adopted an unfair mode of reasoning. In a science the evidence suffers neither diminution nor increase from the actions of its professors; but the comparative wisdom of political systems depends necessarily on the manners and capacities of the recipients. Why should all things be thrown into confusion to acquire that liberty which a faction of sensualists and gamblers will neither be able nor willing to preserve?

A system of fundamental reform will scarcely be effected by massacres mechanized into revolution. We cannot therefore inculcate on the minds of each other too often or with too great earnestness the necessity of cultivating benevolent affections. We should be cautious how we indulge the feelings even of virtuous indignation. Indignation is the handsome brother of anger and hatred. The temple of despotism, like that of Tescalipoca, the Mexican deity, is built of human skulls, and cemented with human blood;—let us beware that we be not transported into revenge while we are levelling the loathsome pile; lest when we erect the edifice of freedom we but vary the style of architecture, not change the materials. Let us not wantonly offend even the prejudices of our weaker brethren, nor by ill-timed and vehement declarations of opinion excite in them malignant feelings towards us. The energies of the mind are wasted in these intemperate effusions. Those materials of projectile force, which now carelessly scattered explode with an offensive and useless noise, directed by wisdom and union might heave rocks from their base,—or perhaps (apart from the metaphor) might produce the desired effect without the convulsion.

For this subdued sobriety of temper a practical faith in the doctrine of philosophical necessity seems the only preparative. That vice is the effect of error and the off-spring of surrounding circumstances, the object therefore of condolence not of anger, is a proposition easily under-stood, and as easily demonstrated. But to make it spread from the understanding to the affections, to call it into action, not only in the great exertions of patriotism, but in the daily and hourly occurrences of social life, requires the most watchful attentions of the most energetic mind. It is not enough that we have once swallowed these truths;—we must feed on them, as insects on a leaf, till the whole heart be coloured by their qualities, and shew its food in every the minutest fibre.[1]

Finally, in the spirit of the Apostle,

Watch ye! Stand fast in the principles of which ye have been convinced! Quit yourselves like men! Be strong! Yet let all things be done in the spirit of love!

---

[1] I hope that this last paragraph, in all the fulness of its contrast with my present convictions, will start up before me whenever I speak, think, or feel intolerantly of persons on account of their doctrines and opinions. 30th Oct. 1818. —S. T. C

On the Principles
of Political Knowledge

(From *The Friend*, First Section, Essays I and III, 1810)

ESSAY I

All the different philosophical systems of political jus-
tice, all the theories on the rightful origin of govern-
ment, are reducible in the end to three classes, corre-
spondent to the three different points of view, in which
the human being itself may be contemplated. The first
denies all truth and distinct meaning to the words, right
and duty; and affirming that the human mind consists
of nothing but manifold modifications of passive sensa-
tion, considers men as the highest sort of animals in-
deed, but at the same time the most wretched; inasmuch
as their defenceless nature forces them into society:
while such is the multiplicity of wants engendered by
the social state, that the wishes of one are sure to be in
contradiction to those of some other. The assertors of
this system consequently ascribe the origin and continu-
ance of government to fear, or the power of the stronger,
aided by the force of custom. This is the system of
Hobbes. Its statement is its confutation. It is, indeed, in
the literal sense of the word preposterous: for fear pre-
supposes conquest, and conquest a previous union and
agreement between the conquerors. A vast empire may
perhaps be governed by fear; at least the supposition is
not absolutely inconceivable, under circumstances which
prevent the consciousness of a common strength. A mil-

lion of men united by mutual confidence and free inter-
course of thoughts form one power, and this is as much
a real thing as a steam engine; but a million of insulated
individuals is only an abstraction of the mind, and but
one told so many times over without addition, as an idiot
would tell the clock at noon—one, one, one. But when,
in the first instances, the descendants of one family
joined together to attack those of another family, it is
impossible that their chief or leader should have ap-
peared to them stronger than all the rest together; they
must therefore have chosen him, and this as for particu-
lar purposes, so doubtless under particular conditions,
expressed or understood. Such we know to be the case
with the North American tribes at present; such, we are
informed by history, was the case with our own remote
ancestors. Therefore, even on the system of those who,
in contempt of the oldest and most authentic records,
consider the savage as the first and natural state of man,
government must have originated in choice and an
agreement. The apparent exceptions in Africa and Asia
are, if possible, still more subversive of this system: for
they will be found to have originated in religious im-
posture, and the first chiefs to have secured a willing
and enthusiastic obedience to themselves as delegates of
the Deity.

But the whole theory is baseless. We are told by his-
tory, we learn from our experience, we know from our
own hearts, that fear, of itself, is utterly incapable of
producing any regular, continuous, and calculable effect,
even on an individual; and that the fear, which does
act systematically upon the mind, always presupposes a
sense of duty, as its cause. The most cowardly of the
European nations, the Neapolitans and Sicilians, those
among whom the fear of death exercises the most tyran-
nous influence relatively to their own persons, are the

very men who least fear to take away the life of a fellow-citizen by poison or assassination; while in Great Britain, a tyrant, who has abused the power, which a vast property has given him, to oppress a whole neighbourhood, can walk in safety unarmed and unattended, amid a hundred men, each of whom feels his heart burn with rage and indignation at the sight of him. It was this man who broke my father's heart; or, it is through him that my children are clad in rags, and cry for the food which I am no longer able to provide for them. And yet they dare not touch a hair of his head! Whence does this arise? Is it from a cowardice of sensibility that makes the injured man shudder at the thought of shedding blood? Or from a cowardice of selfishness which makes him afraid of hazarding his own life? Neither the one nor the other! The field of Waterloo, as the most recent of a hundred equal proofs, has borne witness that,—

——bring a *Briton* frae his hill,
.   .   .   .

Say, such is royal George's will,
        An' there's the foe,
He has nae thought but how to kill
        Twa at a blow.

Nae cauld, faint-hearted doubtings tease him;
Death comes, wi' fearless eye he sees him;
Wi' bluidy hand, a welcome gies him;
        And when he fa's,
His latest draught o' breathin leaves him
        In faint huzzas.

Whence then arises the difference of feeling in the former case? To what does the oppressor owe his safety? To the spirit-quelling thought;—the laws of God and of my country have made his life sacred! I dare not touch a hair of his head!—'Tis conscience that makes cowards

of us all,—but oh! it is conscience too which makes
heroes of us all. . . .

ESSAY III

The second system corresponds to the second point of
view under which the human being may be considered,
namely, as an animal gifted with understanding, or the
faculty of suiting measures to circumstances. According
to this theory, every institution of national origin needs
no other justification than a proof, that under the par-
ticular circumstances it is expedient. Having in my
former essays expressed myself,—so at least I am con-
scious I shall have appeared to do to many persons;—
with comparative slight of the understanding considered
as the sole guide of human conduct, and even with some-
thing like contempt and reprobation of the maxims of
expedience, when represented as the only steady light of
the conscience, and the absolute foundation of all moral-
ity; I shall perhaps seem guilty of an inconsistency, in
declaring myself an adherent' of this second system, a
zealous advocate for deriving the various forms and
modes of government from human prudence, and of
deeming that to be just which experience has proved to
be expedient. From this charge of inconsistency I shall
best exculpate myself by the full statement of the third
system, and by the exposition of its grounds and conse-
quences.

The third and last system, then, denies all rightful
origin to government, except as far as it is derivable
from principles contained in the reason of man, and
judges all the relations of man in society by the laws of
moral necessity, according to ideas.—I here use the word
in its highest and primitive sense, and as nearly synony-

mous with the modern word ideal,—according to arche-
typal ideas co-essential with the reason, the conscious-
ness of these ideas being indeed the sign and necessary
product of the full development of the reason. The fol-
lowing then is the fundamental principle of this theory:
Nothing is to be deemed rightful in civil society, or to be
tolerated as such, but what is capable of being demon-
strated out of the original laws of the pure reason. Of
course, as there is but one system of geometry, so accord-
ing to this theory there can be but one constitution and
one system of legislation, and this consists in the free-
dom, which is the common right of all men, under the
controul of that moral necessity, which is the common
duty of all men. Whatever is not every where necessary,
is no where right. On this assumption the whole theory
is built. To state it nakedly is to confute it satisfactorily.
So at least it should seem. But in how winning and spe-
cious a manner this system may be represented even to
minds of the loftiest order, if undisciplined and unhum-
bled by practical experience, has been proved by the
general impassioned admiration and momentous effects
of Rousseau's *Du Contrat Social,* and the writings of the
French economists, or, as they more appropriately en-
titled themselves, physiocratic philosophers: and in how
tempting and dangerous a manner it may be represented
to the populace, has been made too evident in our coun-
try by the temporary effects of Paine's Rights of Man.
Relatively, however, to this latter work it should be ob-
served, that it is not a legitimate offspring of any one
theory, but a confusion of the immorality of the first sys-
tem with the misapplied universal principles of the last:
and in this union, or rather lawless alternation, consists
the essence of Jacobinism, as far as Jacobinism is any-
thing but a term of abuse, or has any meaning of its own
distinct from democracy and sedition.

A constitution equally suited to China and America, or to Russia and Great Britain, must surely be equally unfit for both, and deserve as little respect in political, as a quack's panacea in medical, practice. Yet there are three weighty motives for a distinct exposition of this theory, and of the ground on which its pretensions are bottomed: and I dare affirm, that for the same reasons there are few subjects which in the present state of the world have a fairer claim to the attention of every serious Englishman, who is likely, directly or indirectly, as partizan or as opponent, to interest himself in schemes of reform.

The first motive is derived from the propensity of mankind to mistake the abhorrence occasioned by the unhappy effects or accompaniments of a particular system for an insight into the falsehood of its principles. And it is the latter only, a clear insight, not any vehement emotion, that can secure its permanent rejection. . . . That man has reflected little on human nature who does not perceive that the detestable maxims and correspondent crimes of the existing French despotism, have already dimmed the recollections of the democratic phrenzy in the minds of men; by little and little, have drawn off to other objects the electric force of the feelings, which had massed and upholden those recollections; and that a favourable concurrence of occasions is alone wanting to awaken the thunder and precipitate the lightning from the opposite quarter of the political heaven. The true origin of human events is so little susceptible of that kind of evidence which can compel our belief even against our will; and so many are the disturbing forces which modify the motion given by the first projection; and every age has, or imagines it has, its own circumstances which render past experience no longer applicable to the present case; that there will never be want-

ing answers and explanations, and specious flatteries
of hope. I well remember, that when the examples of
former Jacobins, Julius Cæsar, Cromwell, &c., were ad-
duced in France and England at the commencement of
the French Consulate, it was ridiculed as pedantry and
pedants' ignorance, to fear a repetition of such usurpa-
tion at the close of the enlightened eighteenth century.
Those who possess the *Moniteurs* of that date will find
set proofs, that such results were little less than impos-
sible, and that it was an insult to so philosophical an age,
and so enlightened a nation, to dare direct the public eye
towards them as lights of admonition and warning.

It is a common weakness with official statesmen, and
with those who deem themselves honoured by their
acquaintance, to attribute great national events to the
influence of particular persons, to the errors of one man
and to the intrigues of another, to any possible spark of
a particular occasion, rather than to the true cause, the
predominant state of public opinion. I have known men
who, with most significant nods, and the civil contempt
of pitying half smiles, have declared the natural explana-
tion of the French revolution to be the mere fancies of
garretteers, and then, with the solemnity of cabinet min-
isters, have proceeded to explain the whole by anecdotes.
It is so stimulant to the pride of a vulgar mind, to be
persuaded that it knows what few others know, and that
it is the important depository of a sort of state secret, by
communicating which it confers an obligation on others!
But I have likewise met with men of intelligence, who at
the commencement of the revolution were travelling on
foot through the French provinces, and they bear wit-
ness, that in the remotest villages every tongue was
employed in echoing and enforcing the doctrines of
the Parisian journalists; that the public highways were
crowded with enthusiasts, some shouting the watch-

words of the revolution, others disputing on the most abstract principles of the universal constitution, which they fully believed, that all the nations of the earth were shortly to adopt; the most ignorant among them confident of his fitness for the highest duties of a legislator; and all prepared to shed their blood in the defence of the inalienable sovereignty of the self-governed people. The more abstract the notions were, with the closer affinity did they combine with the most fervent feelings, and all the immediate impulses to action. The Lord Chancellor Bacon lived in an age of court intrigues, and was familiarly acquainted with all the secrets of personal influence. He, if any man, was qualified to take the gauge and measurement of their comparative power; and he has told us, that there is one, and but one infallible source of political prophecy, the knowledge of the predominant opinions and the speculative principles of men in general, between the age of twenty and thirty. Sir Philip Sidney,—the favourite of Queen Elizabeth, the paramount gentleman of Europe, the nephew, and —as far as a good man could be—the confidant of the intriguing and dark-minded Earl of Leicester,—was so deeply convinced that the principles diffused through the majority of a nation are the true oracles from whence statesmen are to learn wisdom, and that when the people speak loudly it is from their being strongly possessed either by the godhead or the dæmon, that in the revolution of the Netherlands he considered the universal adoption of one set of principles, as a proof of the divine presence. "If Her Majesty," says he, "were the fountain, I would fear, considering what I daily find, that we should wax dry. But she is but a means which God useth." But if my readers wish to see the question of the efficacy of principles and popular opinions for evil and for good proved and illustrated with an eloquence worthy of the subject, I can refer them with the hardiest anticipation of their thanks, to the late work concerning the relations of Great Britain, Spain, and Portugal, by my honoured friend, William Wordsworth, *quem quoties lego, non verba mihi videor audire, sed tonitrua.*

That erroneous political notions—they having become general and a part of the popular creed—have practical consequences, and these, of course, of a most fearful nature, is a truth as certain as historic evidence can make it: and that when the feelings excited by these calamities have passed away, and the interest in them has been displaced by more recent events, the same errors are likely to be started afresh, pregnant with the same calamities, is an evil rooted in human nature in the present state of general information, for which we have hitherto found no adequate remedy. It may, perhaps in the scheme of providence, be proper and conducive to its ends, that no adequate remedy should exist: for the folly of men is the wisdom of God. But if there be any means, if not of preventing, yet of palliating, the disease, and, in the more favoured nations, of checking its progress at the first symptoms; and if these means are to be at all compatible with the civil and intellectual freedom of mankind; they are to be found only in an intelligible and thorough exposure of the error, and, through that discovery, of the source, from which it derives its speciousness and powers of influence on the human mind. This therefore is my first motive for undertaking the disquisition.

The second is, that though the French code of revolutionary principles is now generally rejected as a system, yet every where in the speeches and writings of the English reformers, nay, not seldom in those of their opponents, ſ find certain maxims asserted or appealed to, which are not tenable, except as constituent parts of that system. Many of the most specious arguments in proof of the imperfection and injustice of the present constitution of our legislature will be found, on closer examination, to pre-suppose the truth of certain principles, from which the adducers of these arguments loudly profess their dissent. But in political changes no permanence can be hoped for in the edifice, without consistency in the foundation.

The third motive is, that by detecting the true source of the influence of these principles, we shall at the same time discover their natural place and object; and that in themselves they are not only truths, but most important and sublime truths; and that their falsehood and their danger consists altogether in their misapplication. Thus the dignity of human nature will be secured, and at the same time a lesson of humility taught to each individual, when we are made to see that the universal necessary laws, and pure ideas of reason, were given us, not for the purpose of flattering our pride and enabling us to become national legislators; but that, by an energy of continued self-conquest, we might establish a free and yet absolute government in our own spirits.

THEOLOGICO-METAPHYSICAL

On Method

(From *The Friend,* Second Section, Essays IV–XI, 1818)

ESSAY IV

Ὃ δὲ μετὰ ταῦτα δίκαιόν ἐστι ποιεῖν, ἄκουε, ἵνα σοι καὶ
ἀποκρίνωμαι ὃ σὺ ἐρωτᾷς, πῶς χρὴ ἔχειν ἐμὲ καὶ σὲ πρὸς ἀλλήλους.
Εἰ μὲν ὅλως φιλοσοφίας καταπεφρόνηκας, ἔᾳν χαίρειν· εἰ δὲ
παρ᾽ ἑτέρου ἀκήκοας ἢ αὐτὸς βελτίονα εὕρηκας τῶν παρ᾽ ἐμοί,
ἐκεῖνα τίμα· εἰ δ᾽ ἄρα τὰ παρ᾽ ἡμῶν σοι ἀρέσκει, τιμητέον καὶ ἐμὲ
μάλιστα.   PLATO

*Hear then what are the terms on which you and I ought
to stand toward each other. If you hold philosophy altogether
in contempt, bid it farewell. Or if you have heard from any
other person, or have yourself found out a better than mine,
then give honour to that, which ever it be. But if the doctrine
taught in these our works please you, then it is but just that
you should honour me too in the same proportion.*

What is that which first strikes us, and strikes us at
once, in a man of education, and which, among educated
men, so instantly distinguishes the man of superior mind,
that (as was observed with eminent propriety of the late
Edmund Burke) "we cannot stand under the same arch-
way during a shower of rain, without finding him out"?
Not the weight or novelty of his remarks; not any un-
usual interest of facts communicated by him; for we may

suppose both the one and the other precluded by the shortness of our intercourse, and the triviality of the subjects. The difference will be impressed and felt, though the conversation should be confined to the state of the weather or the pavement. Still less will it arise from any peculiarity in his words and phrases. For if he be, as we now assume, a well-educated man as well as a man of superior powers, he will not fail to follow the golden rule of Julius Cæsar, *insolens verbum, tanquam scopulum, evitare.* Unless where new things necessitate new terms, he will avoid an unusual word as a rock. It must have been among the earliest lessons of his youth, that the breach of this precept, at all times hazardous, becomes ridiculous in the topics of ordinary conversation. There remains but one other point of distinction possible; and this must be, and in fact is, the true cause of the impression made on us. It is the unpremeditated and evidently habitual arrangement of his words, grounded on the habit of foreseeing, in each integral part, or (more plainly) in every sentence, the whole that he then intends to communicate. However irregular and desultory his talk, there is method in the fragments.

Listen, on the other hand, to an ignorant man, though perhaps shrewd and able in his particular calling, whether he be describing or relating. We immediately perceive, that his memory alone is called into action; and that the objects and events recur in the narration in the same order, and with the same accompaniments, however accidental or impertinent, in which they had first occurred to the narrator. The necessity of taking breath, the efforts of recollection, and the abrupt rectification of its failures, produce all his pauses; and with exception of the "and then," the "and there," and the still less significant, "and so," they constitute likewise all his connections.

Our discussion, however, is confined to method as employed in the formation of the understanding, and in the constructions of science and literature. It would indeed be superfluous to attempt a proof of its importance in the business and economy of active or domestic life. From the cotter's hearth or the workshop of the artizan to the palace or the arsenal, the first merit, that which admits neither substitute nor equivalent, is, that every thing be in its place. Where this charm is wanting, every other merit either loses its name, or becomes an additional ground of accusation and regret. Of one, by whom it is eminently possessed, we say proverbially, he is like clock-work. The resemblance extends beyond the point of regularity, and yet falls short of the truth. Both do, indeed, at once divide and announce the silent and otherwise indistinguishable lapse of time. But the man of methodical industry and honourable pursuits does more; he realizes its ideal divisions, and gives a character and individuality to its moments. If the idle are described as killing time, he may be justly said to call it into life and moral being, while he makes it the distinct object not only of the consciousness, but of the conscience. He organizes the hours, and gives them a soul; and that, the very essence of which is to fleet away, and evermore to have been, he takes up into his own permanence, and communicates to it the imperishableness of a spiritual nature. Of the *good and faithful servant*, whose energies, thus directed, are thus methodized, it is less truly affirmed, that he lives in time, than that time lives in him. His days, months, and years, as the stops and punctual marks in the records of duties performed, will survive the wreck of worlds, and remain extant when time itself shall be no more. . . .

The difference between the products of a well-disciplined and those of an uncultivated understanding, in relation to what we will now venture to call the science of method, is often and admirably exhibited by our great dramatist. I scarcely need refer my readers to the Clown's evidence, in the first scene of the second act of *Measure for Measure*, or to the Nurse in *Romeo and Juliet*. But not to leave the position, without an instance to illustrate it, I will take the easy-yielding Mrs. Quickly's relation of the circumstances of Sir John Falstaff's debt to her:—

FALSTAFF. What is the gross sum that I owe thee?
HOSTESS. Marry, if thou wert an honest man, thyself and the money too. Thou didst swear to me upon a parcel-gilt goblet, sitting in my Dolphin chamber, at the round table, by a sea-coal fire, upon Wednesday in Whitsun week, when the prince broke thy head for liking his father to a singing-man of Windsor; thou didst swear to me then, as I was washing thy wound, to marry me and make me my lady thy wife. Canst thou deny it? Did not goodwife Keech, the butcher's wife, come in then and call me gossip Quickly?—coming in to borrow a mess of vinegar; telling us she had a good dish of prawns; whereby thou didst desire to eat some; whereby I told thee they were ill for a green wound, &c.

And this, be it observed, is so far from being carried beyond the bounds of a fair imitation, that the poor soul's thoughts and sentences are more closely inter-linked than the truth of nature would have required, but that the connections and sequence, which the habit of method can alone give, have in this instance a substitute in the fusion of passion. For the absence of method, which characterizes the uneducated, is occasioned by an habitual submission of the understanding to mere events and images as such, and independent of any power in the mind to classify or appropriate them. The general accompaniments of time and place are the only relations which persons of this class appear to regard in their statements. As this constitutes their leading feature, the contrary excellence, as distinguishing the well-educated man, must be referred to the contrary habit. Method, therefore, becomes natural to the mind which has been accustomed to contemplate not things only, or for their own sake alone, but likewise and chiefly the relations of things, either their relations to each other, or to the observer, or to the state and apprehension of the hearers. To enumerate and analyze these relations, with the conditions under which alone they are discoverable, is to teach the science of method.

The enviable results of this science, when knowledge has been ripened into those habits which at once secure and evince its possession, can scarcely be exhibited more forcibly as well as more pleasingly, than by contrasting with the former extract from Shakespeare the narration given by Hamlet to Horatio of the occurrences during his proposed transportation to England, and the events that interrupted his voyage:—

HAMLET. Sir, in my heart there was a kind of fighting
That would not let me sleep; methought, I lay
Worse than the mutines in the bilboes. Rashly,
And praised be rashness for it——Let us know,
Our indiscretion sometimes serves us well,
When our deep plots do fail: and that should teach us,
There's a divinity that shapes our ends,
Rough-hew them how we will.
HORATIO. That is most certain.
HAMLET. Up from my cabin,
My sea-gown scarf'd about me, in the dark
Grop'd I to find out them; had my desire;
Finger'd their packet; and, in fine, withdrew
To my own room again: making so bold,
My fears forgetting manners, to unseal
Their grand commission; where I found, Horatio,
A royal knavery; an exact command—

Larded with many several sorts of reasons,
Importing Denmark's health, and England's too,
With, ho! such bugs and goblins in my life—
That on the supervise, no leisure bated,
No, not to stay the grinding of the axe,
My head should be struck off!
HORATIO. Is't possible?
HAMLET. Here's the commission; read it at more leisure.

Here the events, with the circumstances of time and place, are all stated with equal compression and rapidity, not one introduced which could have been omitted without injury to the intelligibility of the whole process. If any tendency is discoverable, as far as the mere facts are in question, it is the tendency to omission: and, accordingly, the reader will observe in the following quotation that the attention of the narrator is called back to one material circumstance, which he was hurrying by, by a direct question from the friend to whom the story is communicated, "How was this sealed?" But by a trait which is indeed peculiarly characteristic of Hamlet's mind, ever disposed to generalize, and meditative if to excess (but which, with due abatement and reduction, is distinctive of every powerful and methodizing intellect), all the digressions and enlargements consist of reflections, truths, and principles of general and permanent interest, either directly expressed or disguised in playful satire.

　　　　　　　　I sat me down;
Devis'd a new commission; wrote it fair.
I once did hold it, as our statists do,
A baseness to write fair, and laboured much
How to forget that learning; but, sir, now
It did me yeoman's service. Wilt thou know
The effect of what I wrote?
HORATIO. Ay, good my lord,
HAMLET. An earnest conjuration from the king,—

As England was his faithful tributary;
As love between them, like the palm, might flourish;
As peace should still her wheaten garland wear,
And stand a comma 'tween their amities,
And many such like ases of great charge—
That on the view and knowing of these contents,
Without debatement further, more or less,
He should the bearers put to sudden death,
No shriving time allowed.

HORATIO. How was this seal'd?

HAMLET. Why, even in that was heaven ordinant.
I had my father's signet in my purse,
Which was the model of that Danish seal:
Folded the writ up in the form of the other;
Subscribed it; gave't the impression; placed it safely,
The changeling never known. Now, the next day
Was our sea-fight; and what to this was sequent,
Thou know'st already.

HORATIO. So Guildenstern and Rosencrantz go to't?

HAMLET. Why, man, they did make love to this employment.
They are not near my conscience: their defeat
Doth by their own insinuation grow.
'Tis dangerous when the baser nature comes
Between the pass and fell incensed points
Of mighty opposites.

It would, perhaps, be sufficient to remark of the preceding passage, in connection with the humorous specimen of narration,

> Fermenting o'er with frothy circumstance.

in *Henry IV.*, that if, overlooking the different value of the matter in each, we considered the form alone, we should find both immethodical,—Hamlet from the excess, Mrs. Quickly from the want, of reflection and generalization; and that method, therefore, must result from the due mean or balance between our passive impressions and the mind's own re-action on the same. Whether this re-action do not suppose or imply a primary act positively originating in the mind itself, and prior to the object in order of nature, though co-instantaneous with it in its manifestation, will be hereafter discussed. But I had a further purpose in thus contrasting these extracts from our myriad-minded bard, μυριονοῦς ἄνηρ. I wished to bring forward, each for itself, these two elements of method, or, to adopt an arithmetical term, its two main factors.

Instances of the want of generalization are of no rare occurrence in real life: and the narrations of Shakespeare's Hostess and the Tapster differ from those of the ignorant and unthinking in general by their superior humour, the poet's own gift and infusion, not by their want of method, which is not greater than we often meet with in that class, of which they are the dramatic representatives. Instances of the opposite fault, arising from the excess of generalization and reflection in minds of the opposite class, will, like the minds themselves, occur less frequently in the course of our own personal experience. Yet they will not have been wanting to our readers, nor will they have passed unobserved, though the great poet himself (ὁ τὴν ἑαυτοῦ ψυχὴν ὥσει ὕλην τινα ἀσώματον μορφαῖς ποικιλαῖς μορφώσας[1]) has more conveniently supplied the illustrations. To complete, therefore, the purpose aforementioned, that of presenting each of the two components as separately as possible, I chose an instance in which, by the surplus of its own activity, Hamlet's mind disturbs the arrangement, of which that very activity had been the cause and impulse.

Thus exuberance of mind, on the one hand, interferes

---

[1] He that moulded his own soul as some incorporeal material, into various forms.—THEMISTIUS—*S. T. C.*

with the forms of method; but sterility of mind, on the other, wanting the spring and impulse to mental action, is wholly destructive of method itself. For in attending too exclusively to the relations which the past or passing events and objects bear to general truth, and the moods of his own thought, the most intelligent man is sometimes in danger of overlooking that other relation, in which they are likewise to be placed to the apprehension and sympathies of his hearers. His discourse appears like soliloquy intermixed with dialogue. But the uneducated and unreflecting talker overlooks all mental relations, both logical and psychological; and consequently precludes all method which is not purely accidental. Hence the nearer the things and incidents in time and place, the more distant, disjointed, and impertinent to each other, and to any common purpose, will they appear in his narration: and this from the want of a staple, or starting-post, in the narrator himself; from the absence of the leading thought, which, borrowing a phrase from the nomenclature of legislation, I may not inaptly call the initiative. On the contrary, where the habit of method is present and effective, things the most remote and diverse in time, place, and outward circumstance, are brought into mental contiguity and succession, the more striking as the less expected. But while I would impress the necessity of this habit, the illustrations adduced give proof that in undue preponderance, and when the prerogative of the mind is stretched into despotism, the discourse may degenerate into the grotesque or the fantastical. . . .

It is Shakespeare's peculiar excellence, that throughout the whole of his splendid picture-gallery (the reader will excuse the acknowledged inadequacy of this metaphor), we find individuality every where, mere portrait

no where. In all his various characters, we still feel our-
selves communing with the same nature, which is every
where present as the vegetable sap in the branches,
sprays, leaves, buds, blossoms, and fruits, their shapes,
tastes, and odours. Speaking of the effect, that is, his
works themselves, we may define the excellence of their
method as consisting in that just proportion, that union
and interpenetration, of the universal and the particular,
which must ever pervade all works of decided genius and
true science. For method implies a progressive transi-
tion, and it is the meaning of the word in the original
language. The Greek μέθοδος is literally a way or path
of transit. Thus we extol the *Elements* of Euclid, or
Socrates' discourse with the slave in the *Menon* of Plato,
as methodical, a term which no one who holds himself
bound to think or speak correctly, would apply to the
alphabetical order or arrangement of a common diction-
ary. But as without continuous transition there can be no
method, so without a preconception there can be no
transition with continuity. The term, method, cannot
therefore, otherwise than by abuse, be applied to a mere
dead arrangement, containing in itself no principle of
progression.

ESSAY V

*Scientiis idem quod plantis. Si planta aliqua uti in animo
habeas, de radice quid fiat, nil refert: si vero transferre cupias
in aliud solum, tutius est radicibus uti quam surculis. Sic
traditio, quæ nunc in usu est, exhibet plane tanquam truncos
(pulchros illos quidem) scientiarum; sed tamen absque radici-
bus fabro lignario certe commodos, at plantatori inutiles.
Quod si, disciplinæ ut crescant, tibi cordi sit, de truncis
minus sis solicitus: ad id curam adhibe, ut radices illæsæ,
etiam cum aliquantulo terræ adhærentis, extrahantur: dum-*

modo hoc pacto et scientiam propriam revisere, vestigiaque
cognitionis tuæ remetiri possis; et eam sic transplantare in
animum alienum, sicut crevit in tuo.   BACON.[1]

It is with sciences as with trees. If it be your purpose to make
some particular use of the tree, you need not concern yourself
about the roots. But if you wish to transfer it into another
soil, it is then safer to employ the roots than the scions. Thus
the mode of teaching most common at present exhibits clearly
enough the trunks, as it were, of the sciences, and those too
of handsome growth; but nevertheless, without the roots,
valuable and convenient as they undoubtedly are to the car-
penter, they are useless to the planter. But if you have at
heart the advancement of education, as that which proposes
to itself the general discipline of the mind for its end and
aim, be less anxious concerning the trunks, and let it be your
care, that the roots should be extracted entire, even though
a small portion of the soil should adhere to them: so that at
all events you may be able, by this mean, both to review your
own scientific acquirements, re-measuring as it were the
steps of your knowledge for your own satisfaction, and at
the same time to transplant it into the minds of others, just
as it grew in your own.

It has been observed, in a preceding page, that the
relations of objects are prime materials of method, and
that the contemplation of relations is the indispensable
condition of thinking methodically. It becomes necessary
therefore to add, that there are two kinds of relation,
in which objects of mind may be contemplated. The first
is that of law, which, in its absolute perfection, is con-
ceivable only of the Supreme Being, whose creative idea
not only appoints to each thing its position, but in that
position, and in consequence of that position, gives it
its qualities, yea, gives it its very existence, as that partic-
ular thing. Yet in whatever science the relation of the

[1] *De Augment. Scient.* vi. c. 2, with some verbal altera-
tions and transposition.—*H. N. Coleridge*

parts to each other and to the whole is predetermined
by a truth originating in the mind, and not abstracted
or generalized from observation of the parts, there we
affirm the presence of a law, if we are speaking of the
physical sciences, as of astronomy for instance; or the
presence of fundamental ideas, if our discourse be upon
those sciences, the truths of which, as truths absolute,
not merely have an independent origin in the mind, but
continue to exist in and for the mind alone. Such, for
instance, is geometry, and such are the ideas of a perfect
circle, of asymptotes, and the like.

I have thus assigned the first place in the science of
method to law; and first of the first, to law, as the abso-
lute kind, which comprehending in itself the substance
of every possible degree precludes from its conception all
degree, not by generalization, but by its own plenitude.
As such, therefore, and as the sufficient cause of the
reality correspondent thereto, I contemplate it as exclu-
sively an attribute of the Supreme Being, inseparable
from the idea of God; adding, however, that from the
contemplation of law in this its only perfect form, must
be derived all true insight into all other grounds and
principles necessary to method, as the science common
to all sciences, which in each, in the words of Plato,
τυγχάνει ὄν ἄλλο αὐτῆς τῆς ἐπιστήμης. Alienated from
this intuition or stedfast faith, ingenious men may pro-
duce schemes conducive to the peculiar purposes of par-
ticular sciences, but no scientific system.

But though I cannot enter on the proof of this assertion,
I dare not remain exposed to the suspicion of having
obtruded a mere private opinion, as a fundamental truth.
The authorities are such that my only difficulty is occa-
sioned by their number. The following extract from
Aristocles (preserved with other interesting fragments of
the same writer by Eusebius of Cæsarea) is as explicit

as peremptory. Ἐφιλοσόφησε δὲ Πλάτων, εἰ καί τις ἄλλος τῶν πώποτε, γνησίως καὶ τελείως. Ἠξίου δὲ μὴ δύνασθαι τὰ ἀνθρώπινα κατιδεῖν ἡμᾶς, εἰ μὴ τὰ θεῖα πρότερον ὀφθείη.[1] And Plato himself in his *Republic*, happily still extant, evidently alludes to the same doctrine. For personating Socrates in the discussion of a most important problem, namely, whether political justice is or is not the same as private honesty, after many inductions, and much analytic reasoning, he breaks off with these words—καὶ εὖ γ᾽ ἴσθι, ὦ Γλαύκων, ὡς ἡ ἐμὴ δόξα, ἀκριβῶς μὲν τοῦτο ἐκ τοιούτων μεθόδων, οἵαις νῦν ἐν τοῖς λόγοις χρώμεθα, οὐ μή ποτε λάβωμεν· ἀλλὰ γὰρ μακροτέρα καὶ πλείων ὁδὸς ἡ ἐπὶ τοῦτο ἄγουσα[2]—not however, he adds precluding the former (the analytic, and inductive, to wit) which have their place likewise, in which (but as subordinate to the other) they are both useful and requisite. If any doubt could be entertained as to the purport of these words, it would be removed by the fact stated by Aristotle, that Plato had discussed the problem, whether in order to scientific ends we must set out from principles or ascend towards them: in other words, whether the synthetic or analytic be the right method. But as no such question is directly discussed

[1] *Præparat. Evangel.* xi. c. 3. Plato, who philosophized legitimately and perfectively, if ever any man did in any age, held it for an axiom, that it is not possible for us to have an insight into things human (that is, the nature and relations of man, and the objects presented by nature for his investigation), without a previous contemplation or intellectual vision of things divine, that is, of truths that are to be affirmed concerning the absolute, as far as they can be made known to us.—*H. N. Coleridge*

[2] *De Republica,* iv. But know well, O Glaucon, as my firm persuasion, that by such methods as we have hitherto used in this inquisition, we can never attain to a satisfactory insight: for it is a longer and ampler way that conducts to this.
—*H. N. Coleridge*

in the published works of the great master, Aristotle,
must either have received it orally from Plato himself,
or have found it in the ἄγραφα δόγματα, the private text-
books or manuals constructed by his select disciples, and
intelligible to those only who like themselves had been
entrusted with the esoteric, or interior and unveiled, doc-
trines of Platonism. Comparing this therefore with the
writings, which he held it safe or not profane to make
public, we may safely conclude, that Plato considered
the investigation of truth *a posteriori* as that which is
employed in explaining the results of a more scientific
process to those, for whom the knowledge of the results
was alone requisite and sufficient; or in preparing the
mind for legitimate method, by exposing the insuffi-
ciency or self-contradictions of the proofs and results
obtained by the contrary process. . . .

ESSAY VI

ʹΑπάντων ζητοῦντες λόγον ἔξωθεν ἀναιροῦσι λόγον.

The second relation is that of theory, in which the
existing forms and qualities of objects, discovered by
observation or experiment, suggest a given arrangement
of many under one point of view; and this not merely or
principally in order to facilitate the remembrance, recol-
lection, or communication of the same; but for the pur-
poses of understanding, and in most instances of con-
trolling, them. In other words, all theory supposes the
general idea of cause and effect. The scientific arts of
medicine, chemistry, and physiology in general, are ex-
amples of a method hitherto founded on this second sort
of relation. . . .

These truths I have (as the most pleasing and popular
mode of introducing the subject) hitherto illustrated

from Shakespeare. But the same truths, namely the ne-
cessity of a mental initiative to all method, as well as
a careful attention to the conduct of the mind in the
exercise of method itself, may be equally, and here per-
haps more characteristically, proved from the most fa-
miliar of the sciences. We may draw our elucidation
even from those which are at present fashionable among
us; from botany or from chemistry. In the lowest attempt
at a methodical arrangement of the former science, that
of artificial classification for the preparatory purpose of
a nomenclature, some antecedent must have been con-
tributed by the mind itself; some purpose must be in
view; or some question at least must have been proposed
to nature, grounded, as all questions are, upon some idea
of the answer; as for instance, the assumption that—
"two great sexes animate the world." [1] For no man can
confidently conceive a fact to be universally true who
does not with equal confidence anticipate its necessity,
and who does not believe that necessity to be demon-
strable by an insight into its nature, whenever and
wherever such insight can be obtained. . . . What is
botany at this present hour? Little more than an enor-
mous nomenclature; a huge catalogue, well arranged,
and yearly and monthly augmented, in various editions,
each with its own scheme of technical memory and its
own conveniences of reference. . . . The terms system,
method, science, are mere improprieties of courtesy,
when applied to a mass enlarging by endless appositions,
but without a nerve that oscillates, or a pulse that throbs,
in sign of growth or inward sympathy. The innocent
amusement, the healthful occupation, the ornamental
accomplishment of amateurs (most honourable indeed
and deserving of all praise as a preventive substitute for

[1] *Paradise Lost,* viii. 151.—*H. N. Coleridge*

the stall, the kennel, and the subscription-room), it has yet to expect the devotion and energies of the philosopher.

So long back as the first appearance of Dr. Darwin's *Phytologia,* I, then[1] in earliest manhood, presumed to hazard the opinion, that the physiological botanists were hunting in a false direction, and sought for analogy where they should have looked for antithesis. I saw, or thought I saw, that the harmony between the vegetable and animal world, was not a harmony of resemblance, but of contrast; and that their relation to each other was that of corresponding opposites. They seemed to me, whose mind had been formed by observation, unaided, but at the same time unenthralled, by partial experiment, as two streams from the same fountain indeed, but flowing the one due west, and the other direct east, and that consequently, the resemblance would be as the proximity, greatest in the first and rudimental products of vegetable and animal organization. Whereas, according to the received notion, the highest and most perfect vegetable, and the lowest and rudest animal forms, ought to have seemed the links of the two systems, which is contrary to fact. Since that time, the same idea has dawned in the minds of philosophers capable of demonstrating its objective truth by induction of facts in an unbroken series of correspondences in nature. From these men, or from minds enkindled by their labours, we may hope hereafter to receive it, or rather the yet higher idea to which it refers us, matured into laws of organic nature, and thence to have one other splendid proof, that with the knowledge of law alone dwell power and prophecy, decisive experiment, and, lastly, a scientific method, that dissipating with its earliest rays the gnomes of hy-

[1] 1801. The *Zoonomia* was published in 1793.—*H. N. Coleridge.*

pothesis and the mists of theory may, within a single generation, open out on the philosophic seer discoveries that had baffled the gigantic, but blind and guideless, industry of ages.

Such, too, is the case with the assumed indecomponible substances of the laboratory. They are the symbols of elementary powers, and the exponents of a law, which, as the root of all these powers, the chemical philosopher, whatever his theory may be, is instinctively labouring to extract. This instinct, again, is itself but the form, in which the idea, the mental correlative of the law, first announces its incipient germination in his own mind: and hence proceeds the striving after unity of principle through all the diversity of forms, with a feeling resembling that which accompanies our endeavours to recollect a forgotten name; when we seem at once to have and not to have it; which the memory feels but cannot find. Thus, as "the lunatic, the lover, and the poet," suggest each the other to Shakespeare's Theseus, as soon as his thoughts present to him the one form, of which they are but varieties; so water and flame, the diamond, the charcoal, and the mantling champagne, with its ebullient sparkles, are convoked and fraternized by the theory of the chemist. This is, in truth, the first charm of chemistry, and the secret of the almost universal interest excited by its discoveries. The serious complacency which is afforded by the sense of truth, utility, permanence, and progression, blends with and ennobles the exhilarating surprise and the pleasurable sting of curiosity, which accompany the propounding and the solving of an enigma. It is the sense of a principle of connection given by the mind, and sanctioned by the correspondency of nature. Hence the strong hold which in all ages chemistry has had on the imagination. If in Shakespeare we find nature idealized into poetry,

through the creative power of a profound yet observant
meditation, so through the meditative observation of a
Davy, a Wollaston, or a Hatchett;

> By some connatural force,
> Powerful at greatest distance to unite
> With secret amity things of like kind,

we find poetry, as it were, substantiated and realized
in nature,—yea, nature itself disclosed to us, *geminam
istam naturam, quæ fit et facit, et creat et creatur,* as at
once the poet and the poem.

ESSAY VII

Ταυτῇ τοινῦν διαίρω χῶρις μὲν, οὓς νῦν δὴ ἔλεγες φιλοθεάμονάς τε,
καὶ φιλοτέχνους, καὶ πρακτίκους, καὶ χῶρις αὖ περὶ ὧν ὁ λόγος,
οὓς μόνους ἀν τὶς ὀρθῶς προσείποι φιλοσόφους, ὡς μὲν γιγνώσκοντας,
τίνος ἔστιν ἐπιστήμη ἐκάστη τούτων τῶν ἐπιστήμων, ὁ τυγχάνει
ὄν ἄλλο αὐτῆς τῆς ἐπιστημης.   PLATO.[1]

*In the following then I distinguish, first, those whom you
indeed may call philotheorists, or philotechnists, or practi-
cians, and secondly those whom alone you may rightly de-
nominate philosophers, as knowing what the science of all
these branches of science is, which may prove to be some-
thing more than the mere aggregate of the knowledges in any
particular science.*

From Shakespeare to Plato, from the philosophic poet
to the poetic philosopher, the transition is easy, and the
road is crowded with illustrations of our present subject.
For of Plato's works, the larger and more valuable por-
tion have all one common end, which comprehends and
shines through the particular purpose of each several

---

[1] The above quotation appears to be compounded of two
or more independent passages. The opening clause is from
The Republic, Bk. v. (ii. 476. Steph.)—*H. N. Coleridge*

dialogue; and this is to establish the sources, to evolve the principles, and exemplify the art of method. This is the clue, without which it would be difficult to exculpate the noblest productions of the divine philosopher from the charge of being tortuous and labyrinthine in their progress, and unsatisfactory in their ostensible results. The latter indeed appear not seldom to have been drawn for the purpose of starting a new problem, rather than that of solving the one proposed as the subject of the previous discussion. But with the clear insight that the purpose of the writer is not so much to establish any particular truth, as to remove the obstacles, the continuance of which is preclusive of all truth, the whole scheme assumes a different aspect, and justifies itself in all its dimensions. We see, that to open anew a well of springing water, not to cleanse the stagnant tank, or fill, bucket by bucket, the leaden cistern; that the education of the intellect, by awakening the principle and method of self-development, was his proposed object, not any specific information that can be conveyed into it from without;—not to assist in storing the passive mind with the various sorts of knowledge most in request, as if the human soul were a mere repository or banqueting-room, but to place it in such relations of circumstance as should gradually excite the germinal power that craves no knowledge but what it can take up into itself, what it can appropriate, and reproduce in fruits of its own. To shape, to dye, to paint over, and to mechanize the mind, he resigned, as their proper trade, to the sophists, against whom he waged open and unremitting war. For the ancients, as well as the moderns, had their machinery for the extemporaneous mintage of intellects, by means of which, off-hand, as it were, the scholar was enabled to make a figure on any and all subjects, on any and all occasions. . . .

ESSAY VIII

The soul doth give
Brightness to the eye: and some say, that the sun
If not enlighten'd by th' Intelligence
That doth inhabit it, would shine no more
Than a dull clod of earth.

CARTWRIGHT's *Lady-Errant*, Act III, scene iv.

It is strange, yet characteristic of the spirit that was at work during the latter half of the last century, and of which the French revolution was, I hope, the closing monsoon, that the writings of Plato should be accused of estranging the mind from sober experience and substantial matter of fact, and of debauching it by fictions and generalities;—Plato, whose method is inductive throughout, who argues on all subjects not only from, but in and by, inductions of facts;—who warns us indeed against that usurpation of the senses, which quenching the *lumen siccum* of the mind, sends it astray after individual cases for their own sakes,—against that *tenuem et manipularem experientiam,* which remains ignorant even of the transitory relations, to which the *pauca particularia* of its idolatry not seldom owe their fluxional existence;—but who so far oftener, and with such unmitigated hostility, pursues the assumptions, abstractions, generalities, and verbal legerdemain of the sophists! Strange, but still more strange, that a notion so groundless should be entitled to plead in its behalf the authority of Lord Bacon, from whom the Latin words in the preceding sentence are taken, and whose scheme of logic, as applied to the contemplation of nature, is Platonic throughout, and differing only in the mode, which in Lord Bacon is dogmatic, that is, assertory, in Plato tentative, and (to adopt the Socratic phrase) obstetric. I am not the first, or even among the first, who have considered Bacon's studied depreciation of the ancients, with his silence, or worse than silence, concerning the merits of his contemporaries, as the least amiable, the least exhilarating, side in the character of our illustrious countryman. His detractions from the divine Plato it is more easy to explain than to justify or even to palliate; and that he has merely retaliated Aristotle's own unfair treatment of his predecessors and contemporaries, may lessen the pain, but should not blind us to the injustice of the aspersions on the name and works of that philosopher. . . .

I yield to none in grateful veneration of Lord Bacon's philosophical writings. I am proud of his very name, as a lover of knowledge; and as an Englishman, I am almost vain of it. But I may not permit the honest workings of national attachment to degenerate into the jealous and indiscriminate partiality of clanship. Unawed by such as praise and abuse by wholesale, I dare avow that there are points in the character of our Verulam, from which I turn to the life and labours of John Kepler,[1] as from gloom to sunshine. The beginning and the close of his life were clouded by poverty and domestic troubles, while the intermediate years were comprised within the most tumultuous period of the history of his country, when the furies of religious and political discord had left neither eye, ear, nor heart for the muses. But Kepler seemed born to prove that true genius can overpower all obstacles. If he gives an account of his modes of proceeding, and of the views under which they first occurred to his mind, how unostentatiously and *in transitu*, as it were, does he introduce himself to our notice; and yet never fails to present the living germ out of which the genuine method, as the inner form of the tree of science, springs up! With what affectionate reverence

[1] Born 1571, ten years after Lord Bacon: died 1630, four years after the death of Bacon.—*S. T. C.*

does he express himself of his master and immediate predecessor, Tycho Brahe;—with what zeal does he vindicate his services against posthumous detraction! How often and how gladly does he speak of Copernicus;—and with what fervent tones of faith and consolation does he proclaim the historic fact that the great men of all ages have prepared the way for each other, as pioneers and heralds! Equally just to the ancients and to his contemporaries, how circumstantially, and with what exactness of detail, does Kepler demonstrate that Euclid Copernicises—ὡς πρὸ τοῦ Κοπερνίκου κοπερνικίζει Εὐκλείδης,—how elegant the compliments which he addresses to Porta, and with what cordiality he thanks him for the invention of the *camera obscura*, as enlarging his views into the laws of vision! But while I cannot avoid contrasting this generous enthusiasm with Lord Bacon's cold and invidious treatment of Gilbert, and his assertion that the works of Plato and Aristotle had been carried down the stream of time, like straws, by their levity alone, when things of weight and worth had sunk to the bottom;—still in the founder of a revolution, scarcely less important for the scientific, and even for the commercial, world than that of Luther for the world of religion and politics, we must allow much to the heat of protestation, much to the vehemence of hope, and much to the vividness of novelty. Still more must we attribute to the then existing and actual state of the Platonic and Peripatetic philosophies, or rather to the dreams or verbiage which then passed current as such. . . . And this historical interpretation is rendered the more necessary by his fondness for point and antithesis in his style, where we must often disturb the sound in order to arrive at the sense. But with these precautions;—and if, in collating the philosophical works of Lord Bacon with those of Plato, we, in both cases alike, separate the

grounds and essential principles of their philosophic sys-
tems from the inductions themselves; no inconsiderable
portion of which, in the British sage, as well as in the
divine Athenian, is neither more nor less crude and erro-
neous than might be anticipated from the infant state
of natural history, chemistry, and physiology, in their
several ages; and if we moreover separate the principles
from their practical application, which in both is not sel-
dom impracticable, and, in our countryman, not always
reconcileable with the principles themselves;—we shall
not only extract that from each which is for all ages, and
which constitutes their true systems of philosophy, but
shall convince ourselves that they are radically one and
the same system;—in that, namely, which is of universal
and imperishable worth, the science of method, and the
grounds and conditions of the science of method.

ESSAY IX

*A great authority may be a poor proof, but it is an excellent
presumption: and few things give a wise man a truer delight
than to reconcile two great authorities, that had been com-
monly but falsely held to be dissonant.*—STAPYLTON.

Under a deep impression of the importance of the
truths I have essayed to develop, I would fain remove
every prejudice that does not originate in the heart
rather than in the understanding. For truth, says the
wise man, will not enter a malevolent spirit. . . .

In the first instance, Lord Bacon equally with myself
demands what I have ventured to call the intellectual
or mental initiative, as the motive and guide of every
philosophical experiment; some well-grounded purpose,
some distinct impression of the probable results, some
self-consistent anticipation, as the ground of the *prudens
quæstio,* the forethoughtful query, which he affirms to be

the prior half of the knowledge sought, *dimidium scientiæ*. With him, therefore, as with me, an idea is an experiment proposed, an experiment is an idea realized. . . . In this indeed we find the great object both of Plato's and of Lord Bacon's labours. They both saw that there could be no hope of any fruitful and secure method, while forms merely subjective were presumed as the true and proper moulds of objective truth. This is the sense in which Lord Bacon uses the phrases, *intellectus humanus, mens hominis*, so profoundly and justly characterized in the preliminary essay to the *Novum Organum*. And with all right and propriety did he so apply them: for this was, in fact, the sense in which the phrases were applied by the teachers, whom he is controverting; by the doctors of the schools, and the visionaries of the laboratory. To adopt the bold but happy phrase of a late ingenious French writer, it is the *homme particulier*, as contrasted with *l'homme général*, against which, Heraclitus and Plato, among the ancients, and among the moderns, Bacon and Stewart (rightly understood), warn and pre-admonish the sincere inquirer. Most truly, and in strict consonance with his two great predecessors, does our immortal Verulam teach, that the human understanding, even independently of the causes that always, previously to its purification by philosophy, render it more or less turbid or uneven, *sicut speculum inæquale rerum radios ex figura et sectione propria immutat:* that our understanding not only reflects the objects subjectively, that is, substitutes for the inherent laws and properties of the objects the relations which the objects bear to its own particular constitution; but that in all its conscious presentations and reflexes, it is itself only a *phænomenon* of the inner sense, and requires the same corrections as the appearances transmitted by the outward senses. But that there is potentially, if not actually, in every rational being, a somewhat, call it what you will, the pure reason, the spirit, *lumen siccum*, νοῦς, φῶς νοερὸν, intellectual intuition, or the like,—and that in this are to be found the indispensable conditions of all science, and scientific research, whether meditative, contemplative, or experimental,—is often expressed, and every where supposed, by Lord Bacon. And that this is not only the right but the possible nature of the human mind, to which it is capable of being restored, is implied in the various remedies prescribed by him for its diseases, and in the various means of neutralizing or converting into useful instrumentality the imperfections which cannot be removed. There is a sublime truth contained in his favourite phrase, *idola intellectus*. He thus tells us, that the mind of man is an edifice not built with human hands, which needs only be purged of its idols and idolatrous services to become the temple of the true and living Light. Nay, he has shown and established the true criterion between the ideas and the *idola* of the mind; namely, that the former are manifested by their adequacy to those ideas in nature, which in and through them are contemplated. . . .

We can now, as men furnished with fit and respectable credentials, proceed to the historic importance and practical application of method, under the deep and solemn conviction, that without this guiding light neither can the sciences attain to their full evolution, as the organs of one vital and harmonious body, nor that most weighty and concerning of all sciences, the science of education, be understood in its first elements, much less display its powers, as the *nisus formativus* of social man, as the appointed protoplast of true humanity. Never can society comprehend fully, and in its whole practical extent, the permanent distinction, and the occasional contrast, between cultivation and civilization; never can it attain to

a due insight into the momentous fact, fearfully as it
has been, and even now is, exemplified in a neighbour
country, that a nation can never be a too cultivated, but
may easily become an over-civilized, race: never, I re-
peat, can this sanative and preventive knowledge take
up its abode among us, while we oppose ourselves volun-
tarily to that grand prerogative of our nature, a hunger-
ing and thirsting after truth, as the appropriate end of
our intelligential, and its point of union with our moral,
nature; but therefore after truth, that must be found
within us before it can be intelligibly reflected back on
the mind from without, and a religious regard to which
is indispensable, both as a guide and object to the just
formation of the human being, poor and rich: while, in
a word, we are blind to the master-light, which I have
already presented in various points of view, and recom-
mended by whatever is of highest authority with the
venerators of the ancient, and the adherents of modern,
philosophy.

ESSAY X

Πολυμαθίη νοόν οὐ διδάσκει.——Εἶναι γὰρ ἓν τὸ σοφὸν, ἐπίστασθαι
γνώμην ἥτε ἐγκυβερνήσει πάντα διὰ πάντων.——HERACLITUS.

*The effective education of the reason is not to be supplied
by multifarious acquirements: for there is but one knowl-
edge that merits to be called wisdom, a knowledge that is
one with a law which shall govern all in and through all.*

. . . In a self-conscious and thence reflecting being,
no instinct can exist without engendering the belief of
an object corresponding to it, either present or future,
real or capable of being realized; much less the instinct,
in which humanity itself is grounded;——that by which,
in every act of conscious perception, we at once identify
our being with that of the world without us, and yet

place ourselves in contra-distinction to that world. Least of all can this mysterious pre-disposition exist without evolving a belief that the productive power,[1] which in nature acts as nature, is essentially one (that is, of one kind) with the intelligence, which is in the human mind above nature; however disfigured this belief may become by accidental forms or accompaniments, and though like heat in the thawing of ice, it may appear only in its effects. So universally has this conviction leavened the very substance of all discourse, that there is no language on earth in which a man can abjure it as a prejudice, without employing terms and conjunctions that suppose its reality, with a feeling very different from that which accompanies a figurative or metaphorical use of words. In all aggregates of construction therefore, which we contemplate as wholes, whether as integral parts or as a system, we assume an intention, as the initiative, of which the end is the correlative. . . .

I am aware that it is with our cognitions as with our

[1] Obscure from too great compression. The sense is, that the productive power, or *vis naturans*, which in the sensible world, or *natura naturata*, is what we mean by the word, nature, when we speak of the same as an agent, is essentially one, &c. In other words, idea and law are the subjective and objective poles of the same magnet, that is, of the same living and energizing reason. What an idea is in the subject, that is, in the mind, is a law in the object, that is, in nature. But throughout these Essays the want of illustrative examples, and varied exposition is, I am conscious, the main defect, and it was occasioned by the haunting dread of being tedious. But O! the cold water that was thrown on me, chiefly from those from whom I ought to have received warmth and encouragement! "Who, do you expect, will read this," &c.— But, vanity as it may appear, it is nevertheless true, and uttered with feelings the most unlike those of self conceit, that it has been my mistake through life to be looking up to those whom I ought to have been looking at, nay (in some instances) down upon. June 23rd, 1829.—*S. T. C.*

children. There is a period in which the method of
nature is working for them; a period of aimless activ-
ity and unregulated accumulation, during which it is
enough if we can preserve them in health and out of
harm's way. Again, there is a period of orderliness, or
circumspection, of discipline, in which we purify, sepa-
rate, define, select, arrange, and settle the nomenclature
of communication. There is also a period of dawning
and twilight, a period of anticipation, affording trials of
strength. And all these, both in growth of the sciences
and in the mind of a rightly-educated individual, will
precede the attainment of a scientific method. But, not-
withstanding this, unless the importance of the latter be
felt and acknowledged, unless its attainment be looked
forward to and from the very beginning prepared for,
there is little hope and small chance that any education
will be conducted aright; or will ever prove in reality
worth the name.

Much labour, much wealth may have been expended,
yet the final result will too probably warrant the sarcasm
of the Scythian traveller: *Væ! quantum nihili!* and draw
from a wise man the earnest recommendation of a full
draught from Lethe, as the first and indispensable pre-
parative for the waters of the true Helicon. Alas! how
many examples are now present to my memory, of young
men the most anxiously and expensively be-school-mas-
tered, be-tutored, be-lectured, any thing but educated;
who have received arms and ammunition, instead of
skill, strength, and courage; varnished rather than pol-
ished; perilously over-civilized, and most pitiably un-
cultivated! And all from inattention to the method dic-
tated by nature herself, to the simple truth, that as the
forms in all organized existence, so must all true and
living knowledge proceed from within; that it may be

trained, supported, fed, excited, but can never be in-
fused or impressed.

Look back on the history of the sciences. Review the
method in which Providence has brought the more fa-
voured portion of mankind to their present state. Lord
Bacon has justly remarked, *antiquitas sæculi juventus
mundi* [1]—antiquity of time is the youth of the world
and of science. In the childhood of the human race, its
education commenced with the cultivation of the moral
sense; the object proposed being such as the mind only
could apprehend, and the principle of obedience being
placed in the will. The appeal in both was made to
the inward man. *Through faith we understand that the
worlds were framed by the word of God; so that things
which are seen were not made of things which do ap-
pear.* [2] The solution of *phænomena* can never be derived
from *phænomena*. Upon this ground, the writer of the
epistle to the Hebrews (c. xi.) is not less philosophical
than eloquent. The aim, the method throughout was, in
the first place, to awaken, to cultivate, and to mature
the truly human in human nature, in and through itself,
or as independently as possible of the notices derived
from sense, and of the motives that had reference to the
sensations; till the time should arrive when the senses
themselves might be allowed to present symbols and
attestations of truths, learnt previously from deeper and
inner sources. Thus the first period of the education of
our race was evidently assigned to the cultivation of hu-
manity itself, or of that in man, which of all known em-
bodied creatures he alone possesses, the pure reason, as
designed to regulate the will. And by what method was
this done? First, by the excitement of the idea of their

[1] *Advancement of Learning*, Book I.—*H. N. Coleridge*
[2] Hebrews 11:3.

Creator as a spirit, of an idea which they were strictly forbidden to realize to themselves under any image; and, secondly, by the injunction of obedience to the will of a super-sensual Being. Nor did the method stop here. For, unless we are equally to contradict Moses and the New Testament, in compliment to the paradox of a Warburton, the rewards of their obedience were placed at a distance. For the time present they equally with us were to endure, as seeing him who is invisible. Their bodies they were taught to consider as fleshly tents, which as pilgrims they were bound to pitch wherever the invisible Director of their route should appoint, however barren or thorny the spot might appear. *Few and evil have the days of the years of my life been,*[1] says the aged Israel. But that life was but his pilgrimage, and he trusted in the promises.

Thus were the very first lessons in the divine school assigned to the cultivation of the reason and of the will; or rather of both as united in faith. The common and ultimate object of the will and of the reason was purely spiritual, and to be present in the mind of the disciple— μόνον ἐν ἰδέᾳ, μηδαμῆ εἰδωλικῶς, that is, in the idea alone, and never as an image or imagination. The means too, by which the idea was to *be* excited, as well as the symbols by which it was to be communicated, were to be, as far as possible, intellectual.

Those, on the contrary, who wilfully chose a mode opposite to this method, who determined to shape their convictions and deduce their knowledge from without, by exclusive observation of outward and sensible things as the only realities, became, it appears, rapidly civilized. They built cities, invented musical instruments, were artificers in brass and iron, and refined on the means of

[1] Genesis 47:9.

sensual gratification, and the conveniences of courtly intercourse. They became the great masters of the agreeable, which fraternized readily with cruelty and rapacity; these being, indeed, but alternate moods of the same sensual selfishness. Thus, both before and after the flood, the vicious of mankind receded from all true cultivation, as they hurried towards civilization. Finally, as it was not in their power to make themselves wholly beasts, or to remain without a semblance of religion; and yet continuing faithful to their original maxim, and determined to receive nothing as true, but what they derived, or believed themselves to derive from their senses, or (in modern phrase) what they could prove *a posteriori*, they became idolators of the heavens and the material elements. From the harmony of operation they concluded a certain unity of nature and design, but were incapable of finding in the facts any proof of a unity of person. They did not, in this respect, pretend to find what they must themselves have first assumed. Having thrown away the clusters, which had grown in the vineyard of revelation, they could not, as later reasoners, by being born in a Christian country, have been enabled to do, hang the grapes on thorns, and then pluck them as the native growth of the bushes. But the men of sense of the patriarchal times, neglecting reason and having rejected faith, adopted what the facts seemed to involve and the most obvious analogies to suggest. They acknowledged a whole bee-hive of natural gods; but while they were employed in building a temple consecrated to the material heavens, it pleased divine wisdom to send on them a confusion of lip, accompanied with the usual embitterment of controversy, where all parties are in the wrong, and the grounds of quarrel are equally plausible on all sides. . . .

ESSAY XI

Sapimus animo, fruimur anima: sine animo anima est debilis.
                                        L. Accii Fragmenta.

As there are two wants connatural to man, so are
there two main directions of human activity, pervading
in modern times the whole civilized world; and constitut-
ing and sustaining that nationality which yet it is their
tendency, and, more or less, their effect, to transcend
and to moderate,—trade and literature. These were they,
which, after the dismemberment of the old Roman
world, gradually reduced the conquerors and the con-
quered at once into several nations and a common Chris-
tendom. The natural law of increase and the instincts of
family may produce tribes, and, under rare and peculiar
circumstances, settlements and neighbourhoods; and
conquest may form empires. But without trade and lit-
erature, mutually commingled, there can be no nation;
without commerce and science, no bond of nations. As
the one hath for its object the wants of the body, real
or artificial, the desires for which are for the greater part,
nay, as far as the origination of trade and commerce is
concerned, altogether excited from without; so the other
has for its origin, as well as for its object, the wants of
the mind, the gratification of which is a natural and nec-
essary condition of its growth and sanity. And the man
(or the nation, considered according to its predominant
character as one man) may be regarded under these cir-
cumstances, as acting in two forms of method, insep-
arably co-existent, yet producing very different effects
accordingly as one or the other obtains the primacy; the
senses, the memory, and the understanding, (that is, the
retentive, reflective, and judicial functions of his mind)
being common to both methods. As is the rank assigned

to each in the theory and practice of the governing classes, and, according to its prevalence in forming the foundation of their public habits and opinions, so will be the outward and inward life of the people at large: such will the nation be. In tracing the epochs, and alternations of their relative sovereignty or subjection, consists the philosophy of history. In the power of distinguishing and appreciating their several results consists the historic sense. And that under the ascendancy of the mental and moral character the commercial relations may thrive to the utmost desirable point, while the reverse is ruinous to both, and sooner or later effectuates the fall or debasement of the country itself—this is the richest truth obtained for mankind by historic research; though unhappily it is the truth, to which a rich and commercial nation listens with most reluctance and receives with least faith. . . .

In the pursuits of commerce the man is called into action from without, in order to appropriate the outward world, as far as he can bring it within his reach, to the purposes of his senses and sensual nature. His ultimate end is appearance and enjoyment. Where on the other hand the nurture and evolution of humanity is the final aim, there will soon be seen a general tendency toward, an earnest seeking after, some ground common to the world and to man, therein to find the one principle of permanence and identity, the rock of strength and refuge, to which the soul may cling amid the fleeting surge-like objects of the senses. Disturbed as by the obscure quickening of an inward birth; made restless by swarming thoughts, that, like bees when they first miss the queen and mother of the hive, with vain discursion seek each in the other what is the common need of all; man sallies forth into nature—in nature, as in the shadows and reflections of a clear river, to discover the originals of the forms presented to him in his own intellect. Over these shadows, as if they were the substantial powers and presiding spirits of the stream, Narcissus-like, he hangs delighted: till finding nowhere a representative of that free agency which yet is a fact of immediate consciousness sanctioned and made fearfully significant by his prophetic conscience, he learns at last that what he seeks he has left behind, and that he but lengthens the distance as he prolongs the search. Under the tutorage of scientific analysis, haply first given to him by express revelation,

> *E cœlo descendit,* Γνῶθι σεαυτὸν,

he separates the relations that are wholly the creatures of his own abstracting and comparing intellect, and at once discovers and recoils from the discovery, that the reality, the objective truth, of the objects he has been adoring, derives its whole and sole evidence from an obscure sensation, which he is alike unable to resist or to comprehend, which compels him to contemplate as without and independent of himself what yet he could not contemplate at all, were it not a modification of his own being.

> Earth fills her lap with pleasures of her own;
> Yearnings she hath in her own natural kind,
> And, even with something of a mother's mind,
>   And no unworthy aim,
>   The homely nurse doth all she can
> To make her foster-child, her inmate man,
>   Forget the glories he hath known,
> And that imperial palace whence he came.

> . . .

>   O joy! that in our embers
>   Is something that doth live,
>   That nature yet remembers
>   What was so fugitive!

The thought of our past years in me doth breed
Perpetual benedictions: not indeed
For that which is most worthy to be blest;
Delight and liberty, the simple creed
Of childhood, whether busy or at rest,
With new-fledged hope still fluttering in his breast:—
        Not for these I raise
          The song of thanks and praise;
       But for those obstinate questionings
        Of sense and outward things,
        Fallings from us, vanishings;
        Blank misgivings of a creature
Moving about in worlds not realized,
High instincts, before which our mortal nature
Did tremble like a guilty thing surprized!
        But for those first affections,
        Those shadowy recollections,
          Which, be they what they may,
Are yet the fountain light of all our day,
Are yet a master light of all our seeing;
        Uphold us—cherish—and have power to make
Our noisy years seem moments in the being
Of the eternal silence: truths that wake,
          To perish never;
Which neither listlessness, nor mad endeavour,
          Nor man nor boy,
Nor all that is at enmity with joy,
Can utterly abolish or destroy!
        Hence, in a season of calm weather,
          Though inland far we be,
Our souls have sight of that immortal sea
          Which brought us hither;
          Can in a moment travel thither—
And see the children sport upon the shore,
And hear the mighty waters rolling evermore.
                    WORDSWORTH

Long indeed will man strive to satisfy the inward
querist with the phrase, laws of nature. But though the

individual may rest content with the seemly metaphor, the race cannot. If a law of nature be a mere generaliza-tion, it is included in the above as an act of the mind. But if it be other and more, and yet manifestable only in and to an intelligent spirit, it must in act and substance be itself spiritual: for things utterly heterogeneous can have no intercommunion. In order therefore to the recog-nition of himself in nature man must first learn to com-prehend nature in himself, and its laws in the ground of his own existence. Then only can he reduce *phæ-nomena* to principles; then only will he have achieved the method, the self-unravelling clue, which alone can securely guide him to the conquest of the former;—when he has discovered in the basis of their union the necessity of their differences, in the principle of their continuance the solution of their changes. It is the idea alone of the common centre, of the universal law, by which all power manifests itself in opposite yet interdependent forces— (ἡ γὰρ δυὰς ἀεὶ παρὰ μονάδι κάθηται, καὶ νοεραῖς ἀςτράπτει τομαῖς)—which enlightening inquiry, multi-plying experiment, and at once inspiring humility and perseverance will lead him to comprehend gradually and progressively the relation of each to the other, of each to all, and of all to each.

Imagine the unlettered African, or rude yet musing Indian, poring over an illuminated manuscript of the inspired volume, with the vague yet deep impression that his fates and fortunes are in some unknown manner connected with its contents. Every tint, every group of characters, has its several dream. Say that after long and dissatisfying toils, he begins to sort, first the para-graphs that appear to resemble each other, then the lines, the words—nay, that he has at length discovered that the whole is formed by the recurrence and inter-changes of a limited number of cyphers, letters, marks, and points, which, however, in the very height and utmost perfection of his attainment, he makes twenty-fold more numerous than they are, by classing every different form of the same character, intentional or accidental, as a separate element. And the whole is without soul or substance, a talisman of superstition, a mockery of science: or employed perhaps at last to feather the arrows of death, or to shine and flutter amid the plumes of savage vanity. The poor Indian too truly represents the state of learned and systematic ignorance—arrangement guided by the light of no leading idea, mere orderliness without method.

But see! the friendly missionary arrives. He explains to him the nature of written words, translates them for him into his native sounds, and thence into the thoughts of his heart—how many of these thoughts then first evolved into consciousness, which yet the awakening disciple receives, and not as aliens! Henceforward, the book is unsealed for him; the depth is opened out; he communes with the spirit of the volume as with a living oracle. The words become transparent, and he sees them as though he saw them not.

I have thus delineated the two great directions of man and society with their several objects and ends. Concerning the conditions and principles of method appertaining to each, I have affirmed (for the facts hitherto adduced have been rather for illustration than for evidence, to make the position distinctly understood rather than to enforce the conviction of its truth;) that in both there must be a mental antecedent; but that in the one it may be an image or conception received through the senses, and originating from without, the inspiriting passion or desire being alone the immediate and proper offspring of the mind; while in the other the initiative thought, the intellectual seed, must itself have its birth-place within, whatever excitement from without may be necessary for its germination. Will the soul thus awakened neglect or undervalue the outward and conditional causes of her growth? Far rather, might I dare borrow a wild fancy from the Mantuan bard, or the poet of Arno, will it be with her, as if a stem or trunk, suddenly endued with sense and reflection, should contemplate its green shoots, their leafits and budding blossoms, wondered at as then first noticed, but welcomed nevertheless as its own growth: while yet with undiminished gratitude, and a deepened sense of dependency, it would bless the dews and the sunshine from without, deprived of the awakening and fostering excitement of which, its own productivity would have remained for ever hidden from itself, or felt only as the obscure trouble of a baffled instinct.

Hast thou ever raised thy mind to the consideration of existence, in and by itself, as the mere act of existing? Hast thou ever said to thyself thoughtfully, It is! heedless in that moment, whether it were a man before thee, or a flower, or a grain of sand,—without reference, in short, to this or that particular mode or form of existence? If thou hast indeed attained to this, thou wilt have felt the presence of a mystery, which must have fixed thy spirit in awe and wonder. The very words,—There is nothing! or,—There was a time, when there was nothing! are self-contradictory. There is that within us which repels the proposition with as full and instantaneous a light, as if it bore evidence against the fact in the right of its own eternity.

Not to be, then, is impossible: to be, incomprehensible. If thou hast mastered this intuition of absolute existence, thou wilt have learnt likewise, that it was this, and no other, which in the earlier ages seized the nobler minds, the elect among men, with a sort of sacred horror.

This it was which first caused them to feel within themselves a something ineffably greater than their own individual nature. It was this which, raising them aloft, and projecting them to an ideal distance from themselves, prepared them to become the lights and awakening voices of other men, the founders of law and religion, the educators and foster-gods of mankind. The power, which evolved this idea of being, being in its essence, being limitless, comprehending its own limits in its dilatation, and condensing itself into its own apparent mounds [moulds?]—how shall we name it? The idea itself, which like a mighty billow at once overwhelms and bears aloft—what is it? Whence did it come? In vain would we derive it from the organs of sense: for these supply only surfaces, undulations, phantoms. In vain from the instruments of sensation: for these furnish only the chaos, the shapeless elements of sense. And least of all may we hope to find its origin, or sufficient cause, in the moulds and mechanism of the understanding, the whole purport and functions of which consist in individualization, in outlines and differencings by quantity and relation. It were wiser to seek substance in shadow, than absolute fulness in mere negation.

I have asked then for its birth-place in all that constitutes our relative individuality, in all that each man calls exclusively himself. It is an alien of which they know not: and for them the question itself is purposeless, and the very words that convey it are as sounds in an unknown language, or as the vision of heaven and earth expanded by the rising sun, which falls but as warmth on the eye-lids of the blind. To no class of *phænomena* or particulars can it be referred, itself being none; therefore, to no faculty by which these alone are apprehended. As little dare we refer it to any form of abstraction or generalization; for it has neither co-ordi-

nate nor *analogon;* it is absolutely one; and that it is,
and affirms itself to be, is its only predicate. And yet this
power, nevertheless, is;—in supremacy of being it is;—
and he for whom it manifests itself in its adequate idea,
dare as little arrogate it to himself as his own, can as
little appropriate it either totally or by partition, as he
can claim ownership in the breathing air, or make an
inclosure in the cope of heaven. He bears witness of it
to his own mind, even as he describes life and light: and,
with the silence of light, it describes itself and dwells in
us only as far as we dwell in it. The truths which it mani-
fests are such as it alone can manifest, and in all truth
it manifests itself. By what name then canst thou call a
truth so manifested? Is it not revelation? Ask thyself
whether thou canst attach to that latter word any con-
sistent meaning not included in the idea of the former.
And the manifesting power, the source and the correla-
tive of the idea thus manifested—is it not God? Either
thou knowest it to be God, or thou hast called an idol
by that awful name. Therefore in the most appropriate,
no less than in the highest, sense of the word were the
earliest teachers of humanity inspired. They alone were
the true seers of God, and therefore prophets of the hu-
man race.

Look round you, and you behold everywhere an
adaptation of means to ends. Meditate on the nature of
a being whose ideas are creative, and consequently more
real, more substantial than the things that, at the height
of their creaturely state, are but their dim reflexes; and
the intuitive conviction will arise that in such a being
there could exist no motive to the creation of a machine
for its own sake; that, therefore, the material world must
have been made for the sake of man, at once the high-
priest and representative of the Creator, as far as he
partakes of that reason in which the essences of all things

co-exist in all their distinctions yet as one and indivisible. But I speak of man in his idea, and as subsumed in the divine humanity, in whom alone God loved the world.

In all inferior things from the grass on the house top to the giant tree of the forest; from the gnats that swarm in its shade, and the mole that burrows amid its roots to the eagle which builds in its summit, and the elephant which browses on its branches, we behold—first, a sub-jection to universal laws by which each thing belongs to the whole, as interpenetrated by the powers of the whole; and, secondly, the intervention of particular laws by which the universal laws are suspended or tempered for the weal and sustenance of each particular class. Hence and thus we see too that each species, and each individual of every species, becomes a system, a world of its own. If then we behold this economy everywhere in the irrational creation, shall we not hold it probable that by some analogous intervention a similar tempera-ment will have been effected for the rational and moral? Are we not entitled to expect some appropriate agency in behalf of the presiding and alone progressive creature? To presume some especial provision for the permanent interest of the creature destined to move and grow to-wards that divine humanity which we have learnt to contemplate as the final cause of all creation, and the centre in which all its lines converge?

To discover the mode of intervention requisite for man's development and progression we must seek then for some general law, by the untempered and uncounter-acted action of which man's development and progres-sion would be prevented and endangered. But this we shall find in that law of his understanding and fancy, by which he is impelled to abstract the changes and out-ward relations of matter and to arrange them under the form of causes and effects. And this was necessary, as the condition under which alone experience and intellectual growth are possible. But, on the other hand, by the same law he is inevitably tempted to misinterpret a constant precedence into positive causation, and thus to break and scatter the one divine and invisible life of nature into countless idols of the sense; and falling prostrate before lifeless images, the creatures of his own abstraction, is himself sensualized, and becomes a slave to the things of which he was formed to be the conqueror and sovereign. From the fetisch of the imbruted African to the soul-debasing errors of the proud fact-hunting materialist, we may trace the various ceremonials of the same idolatry, and shall find selfishness, hate, and servitude as the results. If therefore by the over-ruling and suspension of the phantom-cause of this superstition, if by separating effects from their natural antecedents, if by presenting the *phænomena* of time (as far as is possible) in the absolute forms of eternity, the nursling of experience should, in the early period of his pupilage, be compelled by a more impressive experience to seek in the invisible life alone for the true cause and invisible *nexus* of the things that are seen; we shall not demand the evidences of ordinary experience for that which, if it ever existed, existed as its anthithesis and for its counteraction. Was it an appropriate mean to a necessary end? Has it been attested by lovers of truth; has it been believed by lovers of wisdom? Do we see throughout all nature the occasional intervention of particular agencies in countercheck of universal laws? (And of what other definition is a miracle susceptible?) These are the questions: and if to these our answer must be affirmative, then we too will acquiesce in the traditions of humanity, and yielding as to a high interest of our own being, will discipline ourselves to the reverential and kindly faith, that the guides and teachers of mankind were the hands

of power, no less than the voices of inspiration: and
little anxious concerning the particular forms, proofs,
and circumstances of each manifestation we will give
an historic credence to the historic fact, that men sent
by God have come with signs and wonders on the earth.

If it be objected, that in nature, as distinguished from
man, this intervention of particular laws is, or with the
increase of science will be, resolvable into the universal
laws which they had appeared to counterbalance, we
will reply: Even so it may be in the case of miracles; but
wisdom forbids her children to antedate their knowl-
edge, or to act and feel otherwise or further than they
know. But should that time arrive, the sole difference,
that could result from such an enlargement of our view,
would be this;—that what we now consider as miracles
in opposition to ordinary experience, we should then
reverence with a yet higher devotion as harmonious
parts of one great complex miracle, when the antithesis
between experience and belief would itself be taken up
into the unity of intuitive reason.

And what purpose of philosophy can this acquiescence
answer? A gracious purpose, a most valuable end; if
it prevent the energies of philosophy from being idly
wasted, by removing the contrariety without confound-
ing the distinction between philosophy and faith. The
philosopher will remain a man in sympathy with his
fellow men. The head will not be disjoined from the
heart, nor will speculative truth be alienated from prac-
tical wisdom. And vainly without the union of both shall
we expect an opening of the inward eye to the glorious
vision of that existence which admits of no question out
of itself, acknowledges no predicate but the I AM IN
THAT I AM Θαυμάζοντες φιλοσοφοῦμεν· φιλοσοφήσαντες
θαμβοῦμεν. In wonder (τῷ θαυμάζειν) says Aristotle,
does philosophy begin: and in astoundment (τῷ θαμβεῖν)

says Plato, does all true philosophy finish. As every faculty, with every the minutest organ of our nature, owes its whole reality and comprehensibility to an existence incomprehensible and groundless, because the ground of all comprehension; not without the union of all that is essential in all the functions of our spirit, not without an emotion tranquil from its very intensity, shall we worthily contemplate in the magnitude and integrity of the world that life-ebullient stream which breaks through every momentary embankment, again indeed, and evermore to embank itself, but within no banks to stagnate or be imprisoned.

But here it behoves us to bear in mind, that all true reality has both its ground and its evidence in the will, without which as its complement science itself is but an elaborate game of shadows, begins in abstractions and ends in perplexity. For considered merely intellectually, individuality, as individuality, is only conceivable as with and in the universal and infinite, neither before nor after it. No transition is possible from one to the other, as from the architect to the house, or the watch to its maker. The finite form can neither be laid hold of by, nor can it appear to, the mere speculative intellect, as any thing of itself real, but merely as an apprehension, a frame-work which the human imagination forms by its own limits, as the foot measures itself on the snow; and the sole truth of which we must again refer to the divine imagination, in virtue of its own omniformity. For even as thou art capable of beholding the transparent air as little during the absence as during the presence of light, so canst thou behold the finite things as actually existing neither with nor without the substance. Not without,— for then the forms cease to be, and are lost in night: not with it,—for it is the light, the substance shining through it, which thou canst alone really see.

The ground-work, therefore, of all pure speculation is the full apprehension of the difference between the contemplation of reason, namely, that intuition of things which arises when we possess ourselves, as one with the whole, which is substantial knowledge, and that which presents itself when transferring reality to the negations of reality, to the ever varying frame-work of the uniform life, we think of ourselves as separated beings, and place nature in antithesis to the mind, as object to subject, thing to thought, death to life. This is abstract knowledge, or the science of the mere understanding. By the former, we know that existence is its own predicate, self-affirmation, the one attribute in which all others are contained, not as parts, but as manifestations. It is an eternal and infinite self-rejoicing, self-loving, with a joy unfathomable, with a love all comprehensive. It is absolute; and the absolute is neither singly that which affirms, nor that which is affirmed; but the identity and living *copula* of both.

On the other hand, by the abstract knowledge which belongs to us as finite beings, and which leads to a science of delusion then only, when it would exist for itself instead of being the instrument of the former (even as the former is equally hollow and yet more perilously delusive, where it is not radicated in a deeper ground)— when it would itself, I say, be its own life and verity, instead of being, as it were, a translation of the living word into a dead language, for the purposes of memory, arrangement, and general communication,—it is by this abstract knowledge that the understanding distinguishes the affirmed from the affirming. Well if it distinguish without dividing! Well if by distinction it add clearness to fulness, and prepare for the intellectual re-union of the all in one in that eternal Reason whose fulness hath no opacity, whose transparency hath no *vacuum.*

If we thoughtfully review the three preceding paragraphs, we shall find the conclusion to be;—that the dialectic intellect by the exertion of its own powers exclusively can lead us to a general affirmation of the supreme reality, of an absolute being. But here it stops. It is utterly incapable of communicating insight or conviction concerning the existence or possibility of the world, as different from Deity. It finds itself constrained to identify, more truly to confound, the Creator with the aggregate of his creatures, and, cutting the knot which it cannot untwist, to deny altogether the reality of all finite existence, and then to shelter itself from its own dissatisfaction, its own importunate queries, in the wretched evasion that of nothings, no solution can be required: till pain haply, and anguish, and remorse, with bitter scoff and moody laughter inquire;—Are we then indeed nothings?—till through every organ of sense nature herself asks;—How and whence did this sterile and pertinacious nothing acquire its plural number?—*Unde quæso, hæc nihili in nihila tam portentosa transnihilatio?* —and lastly;—What is that inward mirror, in and for which these nothings have at least relative existence? The inevitable result of all consequent reasoning, in which the intellect refuses to acknowledge a higher or deeper ground than it can itself supply, and weens to possess within itself the centre of its own system, is— and from Zeno the Eleatic to Spinosa, and from Spinosa to the Schellings, Okens and their adherents, of the present day, ever has been—pantheism under one or other of its modes, the least repulsive of which differs from the rest, not in its consequences, which are one and the same in all, and in all alike are practically atheistic, but only as it may express the striving of the philosopher himself to hide these consequences from his own mind. This, therefore, I repeat, is the final conclusion. All speculative disquisition must begin with postulates, which the conscience alone can at once authorize and substantiate: and from whichever point the reason may start, from the things which are seen to the one invisible, or from the idea of the absolute one to the things that are seen, it will find a chasm, which the moral being only, which the spirit and religion of man alone, can fill up.

Thus I prefaced my inquiry into the science of method with a principle deeper than science, more certain than demonstration. For that the very ground, saith Aristotle, is groundless or self-grounded, is an identical proposition. From the indemonstrable flows the sap that circulates through every branch and spray of the demonstration. To this principle I referred the choice of the final object, the control over time, or, to comprise all in one, the method of the will. From this I started, or rather seemed to start; for it still moved before me, as an invisible guardian and guide, and it is this the re-appearance of which announces the conclusion of the circuit, and welcomes me at the goal. Yea (saith an enlightened physician), there is but one principle, which alone reconciles the man with himself, with others and with the world; which regulates all relations, tempers all passions, gives power to overcome or support all suffering, and which is not to be shaken by aught earthly, for it belongs not to the earth; namely, the principle of religion, the living and substantial faith *which passeth all understanding,* as the cloud-piercing rock, which overhangs the stronghold of which it had been the quarry and remains the foundation. This elevation of the spirit above the semblances of custom and the senses to a world of spirit, this life in the idea, even in the supreme and godlike, which alone merits the name of life, and without which our organic life is but a state of somnambulism; this it is which affords the sole sure anchorage in the storm, and at the same time the substantiating principle of all true wisdom, the satisfactory solution of all the contradictions of human nature, of the whole riddle of the world. This alone belongs to and speaks intelligibly to all alike, the learned and the ignorant, if but the heart listens. For alike present in all, it may be awakened, but it cannot be given. But let it not be supposed, that it is a sort of knowledge: no! it is a form of BEING, or indeed it is the only knowledge that truly *is*, and all other science is real only as far as it is symbolical of this. The material universe, saith a Greek philosopher, is but one vast complex *mythus*, that is, symbolical representation, and mythology the *apex* and complement of all genuine physiology. But as this principle cannot be implanted by the discipline of logic, so neither can it be excited or evolved by the arts of rhetoric. For it is an immutable truth, that what comes from the heart, that alone goes to the heart: what proceeds from a divine impulse, that the godlike alone can awaken.

SELECTIONS FROM
The Statesman's Manual

. . . To the immense majority of men, even in civilized countries, speculative philosophy has ever been, and must ever remain, a *terra incognita*. Yet it is not the less true, that all the epoch-forming revolutions of the Christian world, the revolutions of religion and with them the civil, social, and domestic habits of the nations concerned, have coincided with the rise and fall of metaphysical systems. So few are the minds that really govern the machine of society, and so incomparably more numerous and more important are the indirect consequences of things than their foreseen and direct effects.

. . . Nothing great was ever achieved without enthusiasm. For what is enthusiasm but the oblivion and swallowing-up of self in an object dearer than self, or in an idea more vivid? . . . in the genuine enthusiasm of morals, religion, and patriotism, this enlargement and elevation of the soul above its mere self attest the presence, and accompany the intuition, of ultimate principles alone. These alone can interest the undegraded human spirit deeply and enduringly, because these alone belong to its essence, and will remain with it permanently.

Notions, the depthless abstractions of fleeting *phæ-nomena,* the shadows of sailing vapors, the colorless repetitions of rainbows, have effected their utmost when they have added to the distinctness of our knowledge. For this very cause they are of themselves adverse to lofty emotion, and it requires the influence of a light and warmth, not their own, to make them crystallize into a semblance of growth. But every principle is actualized by an idea; and every idea is living, productive, partaketh of infinity, and (as Bacon has sublimely observed) containeth an endless power of semination. Hence it is, that science, which consists wholly in ideas and principles, is power.

. . . At the annunciation of principles, of ideas, the soul of man awakes and starts up, as an exile in a far distant land at the unexpected sounds of his native language, when after long years of absence, and almost of oblivion, he is suddenly addressed in his own mother-tongue.

Eheu! paupertina philosophia in paupertinam religionem ducit:—A hunger-bitten and idea-less philosophy naturally produces a starveling and comfortless religion. It is among the miseries of the present age that it recognizes no *medium* between literal and metaphorical. Faith is either to be buried in the dead letter, or its name and honors usurped by a counterfeit product of the mechanical understanding, which in the blindness of self-complacency confounds symbols with allegories. Now an allegory is but a translation of abstract notions into a picture-language, which is itself nothing but an abstraction from objects of the senses; the principal being more worthless even than its phantom proxy, both alike unsubstantial, and the former shapeless to boot. On the other hand a symbol (ὁ ἔστι ἀεὶ ταυτηγόρικον) is characterized by a translucence of the special in the individual, or of the general in the special, or of the universal in the general; above all by the translucence of the eternal through and in the temporal. It always partakes of the reality which it renders intelligible; and while it enunciates the whole, abides itself as a living part in that unity of which it is the representative. The others are but empty echoes which the fancy arbitrarily associates with apparitions of matter, less beautiful but not less shadowy than the sloping orchard of hillside pasture-field seen in the transparent lake below. Alas, for the flocks that are to be led forth to such pastures!

FROM APPENDIX B

There exists in the human being, at least in man fully developed, no mean symbol of tri-unity in reason, religion, and the will. For each of the three, though a distinct agency, implies and demands the other two, and loses its own nature at the moment that from distinction it passes into division or separation. The perfect frame of a man is the perfect frame of a state: and in the light of this idea we must read Plato's *Republic*.[1]

The comprehension, impartiality, and far-sightedness of reason, (the legislative of our nature) taken singly and exclusively, becomes mere visionariness in intellect, and indolence or hard-heartedness in morals. It is the science of cosmopolitism without country, of philanthropy without neighbourliness or consanguinity, in short, of all the impostures of that philosophy of the French Revolution, which would sacrifice each to the shadowy idol of all. For Jacobinism is *monstrum hybridum*, made up in part of despotism, or the lust of rule grounded in selfness; and in part of abstract reason misapplied to objects that belong entirely to experience and the understanding. Its instincts and mode of action are in strict correspondence with its origin. In all places, Jacobinism betrays its mixed parentage and nature by applying to the brute passions and physical force of the multitude (that is, to man as a mere animal), in order to build up government and the frame of society on natural rights instead of social privileges, on the universals of abstract reason instead of positive institutions, the lights of specific experience, and the modifications of existing circumstances. Right in its most proper sense is the creature of law and statute, and only in the technical language of the courts has it any substantial and independent sense. In morals, right is a word without meaning except as the correlative of duty.

From all this it follows, that reason as the science of all as a whole must be interpenetrated by a power, that represents the concentration of all in each—a power that

[1] If I judge rightly, this celebrated work is to *The History of the Town of Man-soul*, what Plato was to John Bunyan. —S. T. C.

acts by a contraction of universal truths into individual duties, such contraction being the only form in which those truths can attain life and reality. Now this is religion, which is the executive of our nature, and on this account the name of highest dignity, and the symbol of sovereignty. To the same purport I have elsewhere defined religion as philosophy evolved from idea into act and fact by the superinduction of the extrinsic conditions of reality.

Yet even religion itself, if ever in its too exclusive devotion to the specific and individual it neglects to interpose the contemplation of the universal, changes its being into superstition, and becoming more and more earthly and servile, as more and more estranged from the one in all, goes wandering at length with its pack of amulets, bead-rolls, periapts, fetisches, and the like pedlary, on pilgrimages to Loretto, Mecca, or the temple of Jaggernaut, arm in arm with sensuality on one side and self-torture on the other, followed by a motley group of friars, pardoners, faquirs, gamesters, flagellants, mountebanks, and harlots.

But neither can reason or religion exist or co-exist as reason and religion, except as far as they are actuated by the will (the Platonic θυμὸς,) which is the sustaining, coercive and ministerial power, the functions of which in the individual correspond to the officers of war and police in the ideal Republic of Plato. In its state of immanence or indwelling in reason and religion, the will appears indifferently as wisdom or as love: two names of the same power, the former more intelligential, the latter more spiritual, the former more frequent in the Old, the latter in the New, Testament. But in its utmost abstraction and consequent state of reprobation, the will becomes Satanic pride and rebellious self-idolatry in the relations of the spirit to itself, and remorseless despotism relatively to others; the more hopeless as the more obdurate by its subjugation of sensual impulses, by its superiority to toil and pain and pleasure; in short, by the fearful resolve to find in itself alone the one absolute motive of action, under which all other motives from within and from without must be either subordinated or crushed.

This is the character which Milton has so philosophically as well as sublimely embodied in the Satan of his *Paradise Lost*. Alas! too often has it been embodied in real life. Too often has it given a dark and savage grandeur to the historic page. And wherever it has appeared, under whatever circumstances of time and country, the same ingredients have gone to its composition; and it has been identified by the same attributes. Hope in which there is no cheerfulness; stedfastness within and immovable resolve, with outward restlessness and whirling activity; violence with guile; temerity with cunning; and, as the result of all, interminableness of object with perfect indifference of means; these are the qualities that have constituted the commanding genius; these are the marks, that have characterized the masters of mischief, the liberticides, and mighty hunters of mankind, from Nimrod to Buonaparte. And from inattention to the possibility of such a character as well as from ignorance of its elements, even men of honest intentions too frequently become fascinated. Nay, whole nations have been so far duped by this want of insight and reflection as to regard with palliative admiration, instead of wonder and abhorrence, the Molochs of human nature, who are indebted for the larger portion of their meteoric success to their total want of principle, and who surpass the generality of their fellow creatures in one act of courage only, that of daring to say with their whole heart, "Evil, be thou my good!"—All system so far is power; and a systematic criminal, self-consistent and entire in wickedness, who entrenches villany within villany, and barricadoes crime by crime, has removed a world of obstacles by the mere decision, that he will have no obstacles, but those of force and brute matter.

I have only to add a few sentences, in completion of this comment, on the conscience and on the understanding. The conscience is neither reason, religion, or will, but an experience *sui generis* of the coincidence of the human will with reason and religion. It might, perhaps be called a spiritual sensation; but that there lurks a contradiction in the terms, and that it is often deceptive to give a common or generic name to that, which being unique, can have no fair analogy. In strictness, therefore, the conscience is neither a sensation nor a sense; but a testifying state, best described in the words of Scripture, as *the peace of God that passeth all understanding.* . . .

If you have accompanied me thus far, thoughtful reader, let it not weary you if I digress for a few moments to another book, likewise a revelation of God —the great book of his servant Nature. That in its obvious sense and literal interpretation it declares the being and attributes of the Almighty Father, none but the fool in heart has ever dared gainsay. But it has been the music of gentle and pious minds in all ages, it is the poetry of all human nature, to read it likewise in a figurative sense, and to find therein correspondencies and symbols of the spiritual world.

I have at this moment before me, in the flowery meadow, on which my eye is now reposing, one of its most soothing chapters, in which there is no lamenting word, no one character of guilt or anguish. For never can I look and meditate on the vegetable creation without a feeling similar to that with which we gaze at a

beautiful infant that has fed itself asleep at its mother's
bosom, and smiles in its strange dream of obscure yet
happy sensations. The same tender and genial pleasure
takes possession of me, and this pleasure is checked and
drawn inward by the like aching melancholy, by the
same whispered remonstrance, and made restless by a
similar impulse of aspiration. It seems as if the soul said
to herself: From this state hast thou fallen! Such shouldst
thou still become, thy self all permeable to a holier
power! thy self at once hidden and glorified by its own
transparency, as the accidental and dividuous in this
quiet and harmonious object is subjected to the life and
light of nature; to that life and light of nature, I say,
which shines in every plant and flower, even as the trans-
mitted power, love and wisdom of God over all fills, and
shines through, nature! But what the plant is by an act
not its own and unconsciously—that must thou make
thyself to become—must by prayer and by a watchful
and unresisting spirit, join at least with the preventive
and assisting grace to make thyself, in that light of con-
science which inflameth not, and with that knowledge
which puffeth not up!

But further, and with particular reference to that un-
divided reason, neither merely speculative or merely
practical, but both in one, which I have in this annota-
tion endeavoured to contra-distinguish from the under-
standing, I seem to myself to behold in the quiet objects,
on which I am gazing, more than an arbitrary illustra-
tion, more than a mere *simile,* the work of my own fancy.
I feel an awe, as if there were before my eyes the same
power as that of the reason—the same power in a lower
dignity, and therefore a symbol established in the truth
of things. I feel it alike, whether I contemplate a single
tree or flower, or meditate on vegetation throughout the
world, as one of the great organs of the life of nature.

Lo!—with the rising sun it commences its outward life and enters into open communion with all the elements, at once assimilating them to itself and to each other. At the same moment it strikes its roots and unfolds its leaves, absorbs and respires, steams forth its cooling vapour and finer fragrance, and breathes a repairing spirit, at once the food and tone of the atmosphere, into the atmosphere that feeds it. Lo!—at the touch of light how it returns an air akin to light, and yet with the same pulse effectuates its own secret growth, still contracting to fix what expanding it had refined. Lo!—how upholding the ceaseless plastic motion of the parts in the profoundest rest of the whole it becomes the visible *organismus* of the entire silent or elementary life of nature and, therefore, in incorporating the one extreme becomes the symbol of the other; the natural symbol of that higher life of reason, in which the whole series (known to us in our present state of being) is perfected, in which, therefore, all the subordinate gradations recur, and are re-ordained *in more abundant honor.* . . .

FROM *Aids to Reflection*

Life is the one universal soul, which, by virtue of the enlivening BREATH, and the informing WORD, all organized bodies have in common, each *after its kind.* This, therefore, all animals possess, and man as an animal. But, in addition to this, God transfused into man a higher gift, and specially inbreathed:—even a living (that is, self-subsisting) soul, a soul having its life in itself. "And man became a living soul." He did not merely *possess* it, he *became* it. It was his proper *being,* his truest *self, the* man *in* the man. None then, not one of human kind, so poor and destitute, but there is provided for him, even in his present state, *a house not built with hands.* Aye, and spite of the philosophy (falsely so called) which mistakes the causes, the conditions, and the occasions of our becoming *conscious* of certain truths and realities for the truths and realities themselves—a house gloriously furnished. Nothing is wanted but the eye, which is the light of this house, the light which is the eye of this soul. This *seeing* light, this *enlightening* eye, is Reflection.[1] It is more, indeed, than is ordinarily meant by that word; but it is what a *Christian* ought to mean by it, and to know too, whence it first came, and still continues to come—of what light even this light is *but* a reflection. This, too, is THOUGHT; and all thought is but unthinking that does not flow out of this, or tend towards it.

Aphorism IX

---

[1] The διάνοια of St. John, I Epistle 5:20, inaccurately rendered *Understanding* in our translation. To exhibit the full force of the Greek word, we must say *a power of discernment by Reason.*—S. T. C.

Poetry and Religion

It is impossible to pay a higher compliment to poetry, than to consider the effects it produces in common with religion, yet distinct (as far as distinction can be, where there is no division) in those qualities which religion exercises and diffuses over all mankind, as far as they are subject to its influence.

I have often thought that religion (speaking of it only as it accords with poetry, without reference to its more serious impressions) is the poetry of mankind, both having for their objects:—

1. To generalise our notions; to prevent men from confining their attention solely, or chiefly, to their own narrow sphere of action, and to their own individual circumstances. By placing them in certain awful relations it merges the individual man in the whole species, and makes it impossible for any one man to think of his future lot, or indeed of his present condition, without at the same time comprising in his view his fellow-creatures.

2. That both poetry and religion throw the object of deepest interest to a distance from us, and thereby not only aid our imagination, but in a most important manner subserve the interest of our virtues; for that man is indeed a slave, who is a slave to his own senses, and whose mind and imagination cannot carry him beyond the distance which his hand can touch, or even his eye can reach.

3. The grandest point of resemblance between them is, that both have for their object (I hardly know whether the English language supplies an appropriate word) the perfecting, and the pointing out to us the indefinite improvement of our nature, and fixing our attention upon that. They bid us, while we are sitting in the dark at our little fire, look at the mountain-tops, struggling with darkness, and announcing that light which shall be common to all, in which individual interests shall resolve into one common good, and every man shall find in his fellow man more than a brother.

Such being the case, we need not wonder that it has pleased Providence, that the divine truths of religion should have been revealed to us in the form of poetry; and that at all times poets, not the slaves of any particular sectarian opinions, should have joined to support all those delicate sentiments of the heart (often when they were most opposed to the reigning philosophy of the day) which may be called the feeding streams of religion.

I have heard it said that an undevout astronomer is mad. In the strict sense of the word, every being capable of understanding must be mad, who remains, as it were, fixed in the ground on which he treads—who, gifted with the divine faculties of indefinite hope and fear, born with them, yet settles his faith upon that, in which neither hope nor fear has any proper field for display. Much more truly, however, might it be said that, an undevout poet is mad: in the strict sense of the word, an undevout poet is an impossibility. . . .

From Lecture VIII, 1811–12

Allegory

Substitute a simile for the thing it resembles, instead of annexing it, and it becomes a metaphor: thus if in speaking of the Duke of Wellington's campaign in Portugal against Massena we should say, "At length he left his mountain strongholds and fell on the rear of the retreating army, as a cloud from the hill tops," it is a simile; if more briefly we say, "At length the cloud descended from its hill and discharged itself in thunder and lightning on the plain," it becomes a metaphor, and a metaphor is a fragment of an allegory. But if it be asked, how do you define an allegory so as to distinguish it from a fable, I can reply only by a confession of my ignorance and inability. The fact is, that allegory must be used in two senses—the one including, while the other is defined by excluding, fable. Fable is a shorter and simpler sort of allegory—this is the past sense—and again whatever of this kind is not a fable, not only is, but is called, an allegory. So a pony is a smaller sort of horse: and horses that are not ponies are called horses. A shrub is a smaller sort of tree: and we are in no risk of being misunderstood when we say, the laurel is but a shrub in this country, but in the south of Europe it is a tree. It may indeed be justly said, that in a fable no allegoric agent or image should be used which has not had some one paramount quality universally attributed to it beforehand, while in an allegory the resemblance may have been presented for the first time by the writer. This is the true cause why animals, the heathen gods, and trees, the properties of which are recalled by their very names, are almost the only proper *dramatis personae* of a fable. A bear, a fox, a tiger, a

lion, Diana, an oak, a willow, are *every man's* metaphor
for clumsiness, cunning, ferocious or magnanimous cour-
age, chastity, unbendingness, and flexibility, and it
would be a safe rule that what would not be at once
and generally intelligible in a metaphor may be intro-
duced in an allegory, but ought not to be in a fable.
This, however, is one of the conditions of a good fable
rather than a definition of a fable generally, and fortu-
nately the difficulty of defining a thing or term is almost
always in an inverse proportion to the necessity. Lin-
naeus found no difficulty in establishing discriminating
characters of the different tribes of apes, but very great
in scientific contra-distinctions between the genera man
and ape; but it is to be hoped that he had not met with
many individuals of either kind that had produced any
practical hesitation in determining his judgment.

We may then safely define allegoric writing as the
employment of one set of agents and images with ac-
tions and accompaniments· correspondent, so as to con-
vey, while in disguise, either moral qualities or concep-
tions of the mind that are not in themselves objects of
the senses, or other images, agents, actions, fortunes,
and circumstances, so that the difference is everywhere
presented to the eye or imagination while the likeness
is suggested to the mind; and this connectedly so that
the parts combine to form a consistent whole.

The most beautiful allegory ever composed, the Tale
of Cupid and Psyche, tho' composed by an heathen, was
subsequent to the general spread of Christianity, and
written by one of those philosophers who attempted to
Christianize a sort of Oriental and Egyptian Platonism
enough to set it up against Christianity; but the first
allegory completely modern in its form is the *Psycho-
machia* or *Battle of the Soul* by Prudentius, a Christian
poet of the fifth century—facts that fully explain both

the origin and nature of narrative allegory, as a sub-
stitute for the mythological imagery of polytheism, and
differing from it only in the more obvious and inten-
tional distinction of the sense from the symbol, and the
known unreality of the latter—so as to be a kind of
intermediate step between actual persons and mere per-
sonifications. But for this very cause it is incapable of
exciting any lively interest for any length of time, for
if the allegoric personage be strongly individualized so
as to interest us, we cease to think of it as allegory; and
if it does not interest us, it had better be away. The
dullest and most defective parts of Spenser are those in
which we are compelled to think of his agents as alle-
gories—and how far the Sin and Death of Milton are
exceptions to this censure, is a delicate problem which
I shall attempt to solve in another lecture; but in that
admirable allegory, the first Part of *Pilgrim's Progress,*
which delights every one, the interest is so great that
[in] spite of all the writer's attempts to force the alle-
goric purpose on the reader's mind by his strange names
—Old Stupidity of the Tower of Honesty, etc., etc.—
his piety was baffled by his genius, and the Bunyan of
Parnassus had the better of Bunyan of the conventicle;
and with the same illusion as we read any tale known to
be fictitious, as a novel, we go on with his characters as
real persons, who had been nicknamed by their neigh-
bours. But the most decisive verdict against narrative
allegory is to be found in Tasso's own account of what
he would have the reader understand by the persons
and events of his Jerusalem. Apollo be praised! not a
thought like it would ever enter of its own accord into
any mortal mind; and what is an additional good fea-
ture, when put there, it will not stay, having the very
opposite quality that snakes have—they come out of
their holes into open view at the sound of sweet music,

while the allegoric meaning slinks off at the very first
notes, and lurks in murkiest oblivion—and utter in-
visibility.

The Education of Children

In the education of children, love is first to be in-
stilled, and out of love obedience is to be educed. Then
impulse and power should be given to the intellect, and
the ends of a moral being be exhibited. For this object
thus much is effected by works of imagination;—that
they carry the mind out of self, and show the possible
of the good and the great in the human character. The
height, whatever it may be, of the imaginative standard
will do no harm; we are commanded to imitate one who
is inimitable. We should address ourselves to those
faculties in a child's mind, which are first awakened by
nature, and consequently first admit of cultivation, that
is to say, the memory and the imagination. The com-
paring power, the judgment, is not at that age active,
and ought not to be forcibly excited, as is too frequently
and mistakenly done in the modern systems of educa-
tion, which can only lead to selfish views, debtor and
creditor principles of virtue, and an inflated sense of
merit. In the imagination of man exist the seeds of all
moral and scientific improvement; chemistry was first
alchemy, and out of astrology sprang astronomy. In the
childhood of those sciences the imagination opened a
way, and furnished materials, on which the ratiocinative
powers in a maturer state operated with success. The
imagination is the distinguishing characteristic of man
as a progressive being; and I repeat that it ought to be
carefully guided and strengthened as the indispensable
means and instrument of continued amelioration and re-

finement. Men of genius and goodness are generally restless in their minds in the present, and this, because they are by a law of their nature unremittingly regarding themselves in the future, and contemplating the possible of moral and intellectual advance towards perfection. Thus we live by hope and faith; thus we are for the most part able to realize what we will, and thus we accomplish the end of our being. The contemplation of futurity inspires humility of soul in our judgment of the present.

I think the memory of children cannot, in reason, be too much stored with the objects and facts of natural history. God opens the images of nature, like the leaves of a book, before the eyes of his creature, Man—and teaches him all that is grand and beautiful in the foaming cataract, the glassy lake, and the floating mist.

The common modern novel, in which there is no imagination, but a miserable struggle to excite and gratify mere curiosity, ought, in my judgment, to be wholly forbidden to children. Novel-reading of this sort is especially injurious to the growth of the imagination, the judgment, and the morals, especially to the latter, because it excites mere feelings without at the same time ministering an impulse to action. Women are good novelists, but indifferent poets; and this because they rarely or never thoroughly distinguish between fact and fiction. In the jumble of the two lies the secret of the modern novel, which is the *medium aliquid* between them, having just so much of fiction as to obscure the fact, and so much of fact as to render the fiction insipid. The perusal of a fashionable lady's novel is to me very much like looking at the scenery and decorations of a theatre by broad daylight. The source of the common fondness for novels of this sort rests in that dislike of vacancy and that love of sloth, which are inherent in the human mind; they afford excitement without producing reaction. By reaction I mean an activity of the intellectual faculties, which shows itself in consequent reasoning and observation, and originates action and conduct according to a principle. Thus, the act of thinking presents two sides for contemplation,—that of external causality, in which the train of thought may be considered as the result of outward impressions, of accidental combinations, of fancy, or the associations of the memory,—and on the other hand, that of internal causality, or of the energy of the will on the mind itself. Thought, therefore, might thus be regarded as passive or active; and the same faculties may in a popular sense be expressed as perception or observation, fancy or imagination, memory or recollection.

Dreams and Apparitions

. . . I have thought it a mistake, tho' a very general one, that in ordinary dreams we judge the objects to be real. The fact is that we simply do not determine that they are unreal; and the sensations, which they seem to occasion, are in truth the causes and occasions of the images—of which there are two obvious proofs: first, that the strangest and most sudden transformations do not produce any sensation of surprise; and the second, that [in dreaming of] the most dreadful images, which during the dream were accompanied with agonies of terror, we merely wake or even turn round on the other side, and off fly both image and agony, which would be impossible if the sensations were produced by the images. This has always appeared to me absolute demonstration of the true nature of ghosts and apparitions, such of the tribe as were not pure lies. Fifty years ago, and to this day in the ruder parts of Great Britain and Ireland, in almost every kitchen, and in many parlours, you might meet persons who would assure you in the most solemn manner, so that you could not doubt of their *veracity* at least, that they had seen an apparition of such and such a person—in many cases, that the apparition had spoken to them; and they describe themselves as in an agony of terror. "But how were you in health the hour after?"—"Oh, there was nothing the matter with my health." Now take the other class of facts, in which real ghosts have appeared. I mean tricks and dressed up figures for the purpose of passing for an apparition. In every instance I have known or heard of (and I have collected very many) the consequence has been either sudden death, or fits, or idiocy, or mania, or a brain fever. Whence comes the difference? Evidently from this—that in the one case the whole of the nervous system has been by slight internal causes, gradually and all together, brought into a certain state, the sensation of which is extravagantly exaggerated during sleep, and of which the images are the mere effects and exponents, as the motions of the weathercock are of the wind; while in the other case, the image, rushing thro' the senses upon a nervous system wholly unprepared, actually causes the sensation, which is sometimes powerful enough to produce a total check, and almost always lesion or inflammation. Who has not witnessed the difference in shock when we have leaped down half a dozen steps intentionally, and that of having missed a single stair? How comparatively severe the latter is! To return to dreams, however, I not only believe, from the reasons given, but have more than once actually experienced, that the most fearful forms, when produced simply by association, instead of causing pain, produce no other effect than the same would do if they had passed

thro' my mind as thoughts, while I was composing a
fairy tale. The whole depends on the wise and gracious
law in our nature that the actual bodily sensations called
forth according to the law of association by thoughts
and images of the mind, never greatly transcend the
limits of pleasurable feeling in a tolerably healthy frame,
unless where an act of judgment supervenes and inter-
prets them as purporting instant danger to ourselves, as
for instance in the case of the King in *Hamlet*.

The fact really is, as to apparitions, that the terror
produces the image instead of the contrary; for *in om-
nem actum perceptionis influit imaginatio*, as says Wolfe.

O, strange is the self-power of the imagination—when
painful sensations have made it their interpreter, or re-
turning gladsomeness or convalescence has made its
chilled and evanished figures and landscape bud, blos-
som, and live in scarlet, green, and snowy white (like
the fire-screen inscribed with the nitrate and muriate of
cobalt)—strange is the power to represent the events
and circumstances, even to the anguish or the triumph
of the *quasi*-credent soul, while the necessary conditions,
the only possible causes of such contingencies, are known
to be in fact quite hopeless;—yea, when the pure mind
would recoil from the eve-lengthened shadow of an ap-
proaching hope, as from a crime;—and yet the effect
shall have place, and substance, and living energy, and,
on a blue islet of ether, in a whole sky of blackest cloud-
age, shine like a firstling of creation!

Dante

Born at Florence, 1265—Died 1321

. . . *The Divina Commedia* is a system of moral,
political, and theological truths, with arbitrary personal

exemplifications, which are not, in my opinion, allegorical. I do not even feel convinced that the punishments in the Inferno are strictly allegorical. I rather take them to have been in Dante's mind *quasi*-allegorical, or conceived in analogy to pure allegory.

I have said, that a combination of poetry with doctrines, is one of the characteristics of the Christian muse; but I think Dante has not succeeded in effecting this combination nearly so well as Milton.

This comparative failure of Dante, as also some other peculiarities of his mind, *in malam partem,* must be immediately attributed to the state of North Italy in his time, which is vividly represented in Dante's life; a state of intense democratical partizanship, in which an exaggerated importance was attached to individuals, and which whilst it afforded a vast field for the intellect, opened also a boundless arena for the passions, and in which envy, jealousy, hatred, and other malignant feelings, could and did assume the form of patriotism, even to the individual's own conscience.

All this common, and, as it were, natural partizanship was aggravated and coloured by the Guelf and Ghibelline factions; and, in part explanation of Dante's adherence to the latter, you must particularly remark, that the Pope had recently territorialized his authority to a great extent, and that this increase of territorial power in the church, was by no means the same beneficial movement for the citizens of free republics, as the parallel advance in other countries was for those who groaned as vassals under the oppression of the circumjacent baronial castles.

By way of preparation to a satisfactory perusal of the *Divina Commedia,* I will now proceed to state what I consider to be Dante's chief excellences as a poet. And I begin with

1. Style—the vividness, logical connexion, strength

and energy of which cannot be surpassed. In this I
think Dante superior to Milton; and his style is accord-
ingly more imitable than Milton's, and does to this day
exercise a greater influence on the literature of his coun-
try. You cannot read Dante without feeling a gush of
manliness of thought within you. Dante was very sen-
sible of his own excellence in this particular, and speaks
of poets as guardians of the vast armory of language,
which is the intermediate something between matter and
spirit.[1] Indeed there was a passion and a miracle of
words in the twelfth and thirteenth centuries, after the
long slumber of language in barbarism, which gave an
almost romantic character, a virtuous quality and power,
to what was read in a book, independently of the
thoughts or images contained in it. This feeling is very
often perceptible in Dante.

II. The Images in Dante are not only taken from
obvious nature, and are all intelligible to all, but are ever
conjoined with the universal feeling received from na-
ture, and therefore affect the general feelings of all men.
And in this respect, Dante's excellence is very great, and
may be contrasted with the idiosyncracies of some meri-
torious modern poets, who attempt an eruditeness, the
result of particular feelings. Consider the simplicity, I
may say plainness, of the following simile, and how dif-
ferently we should in all probability deal with it at the
present day:

> *Quale i fioretti dal notturno gelo*
> *Chinati e chiusi, poi che 'l sol gl' imbianca,*
> *Si drizzan tutti aperti in loro stelo,—*
> *Tal mi fec' io di mia virtute stanca:*
> Inferno, canto 2, v. 127–31

[1] See *Inferno*, canto 1, v. 79–87.

As florets, by the frosty air of night
Bent down and clos'd, when day has blanch'd their leaves,
Rise all unfolded on their spiry stems,—
So was my fainting vigour new restor'd.

CARY

III. Consider the wonderful profoundness of the whole third canto of the Inferno; and especially of the inscription over Hell gate: *"Per me si va,"* etc.[1] which can only be explained by a meditation on the true nature of religion; that is,—reason *plus* the understanding. I say profoundness rather than sublimity; for Dante does not so much elevate your thoughts as send them down deeper. In this canto all the images are distinct, and even vividly distinct; but there is a total impression of infinity; the wholeness is not in vision or conception, but in an inner feeling of totality, and absolute being.

IV. In picturesqueness, Dante is beyond all other poets, modern or ancient, and more in the stern style of Pindar, than of any other. Michel Angelo is said to have made a design for every page of the *Divina Commedia*. As superexcellent in this respect, I would note the conclusion of the third canto of the Inferno [and canto 22, v. 127–144].

V. Very closely connected with this picturesqueness, is the topographic reality of Dante's journey through Hell. You should note and dwell on this as one of his great charms, and which gives a striking peculiarity to his poetic power. He thus takes the thousand delusive forms of a nature worse than chaos, having no reality but from the passions which they excite, and compels them into the service of the permanent. . . .

VI. For Dante's power,—his absolute mastery over, although rare exhibition of, the pathetic, I can do no more than refer to the passages on Francesca di Rimini

[1] Inferno, canto 3, v. 1 ff.

(Inferno, canto 5, v. 73 to the end) and on Ugolino
(Inferno, canto 33, v. 1 to 75). They are so well known,
and rightly so admired, that it would be pedantry to
analyze their composition; but you will note that the
first is the pathos of passion, the second that of affection;
and yet even in the first, you seem to perceive that the
lovers have sacrificed their passion to the cherishing of a
deep and rememberable impression.

VII. As to going into the endless subtle beauties of
Dante, that is impossible; but I cannot help citing the
first triplet of the twenty-ninth canto of the Inferno:

> *La molta gente e le diverse piaghe*
> *Avean le luci mie sì inebriate,*
> *Che dello stare a piangere eran vaghe.*

So were mine eyes inebriate with the view
Of the vast multitude, whom various wounds
Disfigur'd, that they long'd to stay and weep.

CARY

Nor have I now room for any specific comparison of
Dante with Milton. But if I had, I would institute it upon
the ground of the last canto of the Inferno from the first
to the sixty-ninth line, and from the 106th to the end.
And in this comparison I should notice Dante's occa-
sional fault of becoming grotesque from being too
graphic without imagination; as in his Lucifer compared
with Milton's Satan. Indeed he is sometimes horrible
rather than terrible,—falling into the μισητόν instead of
the δεινόν of Longinus; in other words, many of his im-
ages excite bodily disgust, and not moral fear. But here,
as in other cases, you may perceive that the faults of
great authors are generally excellencies carried to an
excess.

From Lecture X, 1818

Shakespeare

THE POWER OF THE IDEA

. . . What had a grammatical and logical consistency for the ear, what could be put together and represented to the eye, these poets [Jonson, Fletcher, Massinger] took from the ear and eye, unchecked by any intuition of an inward impossibility, just as a man might fit together a quarter of an orange, a quarter of an apple, and the like of a lemon and of a pomegranate, and make it look like one round diverse colored fruit. But nature, who works from within by evolution and assimilation according to a law, cannot do it. Nor could Shakespeare, for he too worked in the spirit of nature, by evolving the germ within by the imaginative power according to an idea—for as the power of seeing is to light, so is an idea in mind to a law in nature. They are correlatives that suppose each other. Doubtless from mere observation, or from the occasional similarity of the writer's own character, more or less will happen to be in correspondence with nature, and still more in apparent compatibility; but yet the false source is always discoverable, first by the gross contradictions to nature in so many other parts, and secondly, by the want of the impression, which Shakespeare makes, that the thing said not only might have been said, but that nothing else could be substituted to excite the same sense of its exquisite propriety. . . .

But there is a diversity of the most dangerous kind here. Shakespeare shaped his characters out of the nature within; but we cannot so safely say, out of *his own*

nature, as an *individual person*. No! this latter is itself
but a *natura naturata*, an effect, a product, not a *power*.
It was Shakespeare's prerogative to have the *universal*
which is potentially in each *particular*, opened out to
him in the *homo generalis*, not as an abstraction of obser-
vation from a variety of men, but as the substance capa-
ble of endless modifications, of which his own personal
existence was but one, and to use *this one* as the eye that
beheld the other, and as the tongue that could convey
the discovery. [There is] no greater or more common
vice in dramatic writers than to draw out of themselves.
How I—alone and in the self-sufficiency of my study,
as all men are apt to be proud in their dreams—should
like to be talking king! I am the king who would bully
the kings. Tut! Shakespeare in composing had no *I* but
the *I* representative.

From Lecture VII, 1818

A DAY DREAM

O, when I think of [the] inexhaustible mine of virgin
treasure in our Shakespeare, that I have been almost
daily reading him since I was ten years old, that the
thirty intervening years have been not fruitlessly and
unintermittingly employed in the study of Greek, Latin,
English, Italian, Spanish, and German *belle lettrists*, and
for the last fifteen years far more intensely to the analysis
of the laws of life and reason as they exist in man, and
that every step I have made forward in taste, number of
facts, from history or my own observation, and in the
knowledge of [the different laws] and the apparent ex-
ceptions [from] accidental collision [of] the disturbing
forces of them, and know that at every new accession of
knowledge, after every successful exercise of meditation,
every fresh presentation of experience, I have unfailingly

discovered a proportionate increase of wisdom and intui-
tion in Shakespeare—when I know this, and know too
that by a conceivable and possible, tho' hardly to be
expected, arrangement of the British theatres, so large—
not all indeed—but so large a proportion of this indefi-
nite *all* (which no comprehension has yet drawn the
line of circumscription so as to say to itself, I have seen
the whole), might be sent into the heads and hearts,
into the very souls, of the mass of mankind, to whom
except by this living comment and interpretation it must
remain for ever a sealed-up volume, a deep well without
a wheel or windlass—it seems to me a pardonable enthu-
siasm to steal away from sober likelihood and share so
rich a feast in the faery world of possibility! Yet even in
the sober cheerfulness of a circumspect hope, much, very
much, might be done—enough, assuredly, to furnish a
kind and strenuous nature with ample motives for the
attempt to effect what may be effected.

Such, honored sirs! were the thoughts and feelings in-
spired by the general view of the subject. Yonder in the
distance see that rich and varied country and the splen-
did palace or temple which commands it, and nothing
insurmountable in the interspace to stop us in our road
toward it. We descend from the mountain (pity that we
cannot make a crow's flight toward it), and then we dis-
cover the Stygian pools or morasses, or even park walls
and gates with reformer-traps and spring-guns threatened
to trespassers, thickest hedges, and miry lanes—and so
at length tread back our road, tired, way-worn, sick
at heart, with torn clothes, . . . [?] scratches and . . .
[?] with a thorn.

1812(?)

SHAKESPEARE'S POETRY

. . . We have examined with what armour clothed and with what titles authorized Shakespeare came forward as a poet to demand the throne of fame, as the dramatic poet of England; we have now to observe and retrace the excellencies which compelled even his contemporaries to seat him on that throne, altho' there were giants in those days contending for the same honor. Hereafter we shall endeavor to make out the title of the English drama, as created by and existing in Shakespeare, and its right to the supremacy of dramatic excellence in general. I have endeavoured to prove that he had shewn himself a *poet,* previously to his appearance [as] a dramatic poet—and that had no *Lear,* no *Othello,* no *Henry the Fourth,* no *Twelfth Night* appeared, we must have admitted that Shakespeare possessed the chief if not all the requisites of a poet—namely, deep feeling and exquisite sense of beauty, both as exhibited to the eye in combinations of form, and to the ear in sweet and appropriate melody (with the exception of Spenser he is [the sweetest of English poets?]); that these feelings were under the command of *his own will*—that in his very first productions he projected his mind out of his own particular being, and felt and made others feel, on subjects [in] no way connected with himself, except by force of contemplation, and that sublime faculty, by which a great mind becomes that which it meditates on. To this we are to add the affectionate love of nature and natural objects, without which no man could have observed so steadily, or painted so truly and passionately the very minutest beauties of the external world. Next, we have shewn that he possessed fancy, considered as the faculty of bringing together [images dissimilar in the main by some one point or more of likeness distinguished].

> Full gently now she takes him by the hand,
> A lily prison'd in a gaol of snow,
> Or ivory in an alabaster band;
> So white a friend engirts so white a foe.
>
> *Venus and Adonis,* 361–64.

Still mounting, we find undoubted proof in his mind of imagination, or the power by which one image or feeling is made to modify many others and by a sort of *fusion to force many into one*—that which after shewed itself in such might and energy in *Lear,* where the deep anguish of a father spreads the feeling of ingratitude and cruelty over the very elements of heaven. Various are the workings of this greatest faculty of the human mind—both passionate and tranquil. In its tranquil and purely pleasurable operation, it acts chiefly by producing out of many things, as they would have appeared in the description of an ordinary mind, described slowly and in unimpassioned succession, a oneness, even as nature, the greatest of poets, acts upon us when we open our eyes upon an extended prospect. Thus the flight of Adonis from the enamoured goddess in the dusk of the evening—

> Look! how a bright star shooteth from the sky,
> So glides he in the night from Venus' eye.

How many images and feelings are here brought together without effort and without discord—the beauty of Adonis—the rapidity of his flight—the yearning yet hopelessness of the enamoured gazer—and a shadowy ideal character thrown over the whole.—Or it acts by impressing the stamp of humanity, of human feeling, over inanimate objects—

The pines shorn by the sea wind and seen in twilight[1]

(1808)

ROMEO AND JULIET

In a former lecture I endeavoured to point out the union of the Poet and the Philosopher, or rather the warm embrace between them, in the *Venus and Adonis* and *Lucrece* of Shakespeare. From thence I passed on to *Love's Labour's Lost,* as the link between his character as a Poet, and his art as a Dramatist; and I shewed that, although in that work the former was still predominant, yet that the germs of his subsequent dramatic power were easily discernible.

I will now, as I promised in my last, proceed to *Romeo and Juliet,* not because it is the earliest, or among the earliest of Shakespeare's works of that kind, but because in it are to be found specimens, in degree, of all the excellences which he afterwards displayed in his more perfect dramas, but differing from them in being less forcibly evidenced, and less happily combined: all the parts are more or less present, but they are not united with the same harmony.

There are, however, in *Romeo and Juliet* passages where the poet's whole excellence is evinced, so that nothing superior to them can be met with in the productions of his after years. The main distinction between this play and others is, as I said, that the parts are less happily combined, or to borrow a phrase from the painter, the whole work is less in keeping. Grand portions are produced: we have limbs of giant growth; but the production, as a whole, in which each part gives de-

---

[1] See *Biographia Literaria,* chapter xv.

light for itself, and the whole, consisting of these delightful parts, communicates the highest intellectual pleasure and satisfaction, is the result of the application of judgment and taste. These are not to be attained but by painful study, and to the sacrifice of the stronger pleasures derived from the dazzling light which a man of genius throws over every circumstance, and where we are chiefly struck by vivid and distinct images. Taste is an attainment after a poet has been disciplined by experience, and has added to genius that talent by which he knows what part of his genius he can make acceptable, and intelligible to the portion of mankind for which he writes.

In my mind it would be a hopeless symptom, as regards genius, if I found a young man with anything like perfect taste. In the earlier works of Shakespeare we have a profusion of double epithets, and sometimes even the coarsest terms are employed, if they convey a more vivid image; but by degrees the associations are connected with the image they are designed to impress, and the poet descends from the ideal into the real world so far as to conjoin both—to give a sphere of active operations to the ideal, and to elevate and refine the real.

In *Romeo and Juliet* the principal characters may be divided into two classes: in one class passion—the passion of love—is drawn and drawn truly, as well as beautifully; but the persons are not individualised farther than as the actor appears on the stage. It is a very just description and development of love, without giving, if I may so express myself, the philosophical history of it—without shewing how the man became acted upon by that particular passion, but leading it through all the incidents of the drama, and rendering it predominant.

Tybalt is, in himself, a common-place personage. And here allow me to remark upon a great distinction between Shakespeare, and all who have written in imitation of him. I know no character in his plays, (unless indeed Pistol be an exception) which can be called the mere portrait of an individual: while the reader feels all the satisfaction arising from individuality, yet that very individual is a sort of class character, and this circumstance renders Shakespeare the poet of all ages.

Tybalt is a man abandoned to his passions—with all the pride of family, only because he thought it belonged to him as a member of that family, and valuing himself highly, simply because he does not care for death. This indifference to death is perhaps more common than any other feeling: men are apt to flatter themselves extravagantly, merely because they possess a quality which it is a disgrace not to have, but which a wise man never puts forward, but when it is necessary.

Jeremy Taylor in one part of his voluminous works, speaking of a great man, says that he was naturally a coward, as indeed most men are, knowing the value of life, but the power of his reason enabled him, when required, to conduct himself with uniform courage and hardihood. The good bishop, perhaps, had in his mind a story, told by one of the ancients, of a Philosopher and a Coxcomb, on board the same ship during a storm: the Coxcomb reviled the Philosopher for betraying marks of fear: "Why are you so frightened? I am not afraid of being drowned: I do not care a farthing for my life."—"You are perfectly right," said the Philosopher, "for your life is not worth a farthing."

Shakespeare never takes pains to make his characters win your esteem, but leaves it to the general command of the passions, and to poetic justice. It is most beautiful to observe, in *Romeo and Juliet,* that the characters principally engaged in the incidents are preserved innocent from all that could lower them in our opinion, while the

rest of the personages, deserving little interest in them-
selves, derive it from being instrumental in those situa-
tions in which the more important personages develope
their thoughts and passions.

Look at Capulet—a worthy, noble-minded old man
of high rank, with all the impatience that is likely to
accompany it. It is delightful to see all the sensibilities
of our nature so exquisitely called forth; as if the poet
had the hundred arms of the polypus, and had thrown
them out in all directions to catch the predominant feel-
ing. We may see in Capulet the manner in which anger
seizes hold of everything that comes in its way, in order
to express itself, as in the lines where he reproves Tybalt
for his fierceness of behaviour, which led him to wish to
insult a Montague, and disturb the merriment.—

> Go to, go to;
> You are a saucy boy. Is't so, indeed?
> This trick may chance to scath you;—I know what.
> You must contrary me! marry, 'tis time.—
> Well said, my hearts!—You are a princox: go:
> Be quiet or—More light, more light!—For shame!
> I'll make you quiet.—What! cheerly, my hearts!
>   Act I, Scene 5.

The line

> This trick may chance to scath you;—I know what,

was an allusion to the legacy Tybalt might expect; and
then, seeing the lights burn dimly, Capulet turns his
anger against the servants. Thus we see that no one
passion is so predominant, but that it includes all the
parts of the character, and the reader never has a mere
abstract of a passion, as of wrath or ambition, but the
whole man is presented to him—the one predominant
passion acting, if I may so say, as the leader of the band
to the rest.

It could not be expected that the poet should introduce such a character as Hamlet into every play; but even in those personages, which are subordinate to a hero so eminently philosophical, the passion is at least rendered instructive, and induces the reader to look with a keener eye, and a finer judgment into human nature.

Shakespeare has this advantage over all other dramatists—that he has availed himself of his psychological genius to develope all the minutiæ of the human heart: shewing us the thing that, to common observers, he seems solely intent upon, he makes visible what we should not otherwise have seen: just as, after looking at distant objects through a telescope, when we behold them subsequently with the naked eye, we see them with greater distinctness, and in more detail, than we should otherwise have done.

Mercutio is one of our poet's truly Shakespearian characters; for throughout his plays, but especially in those of the highest order, it is plain that the personages were drawn rather from meditation than from observation, or to speak correctly, more from observation, the child of meditation. It is comparatively easy for a man to go about the world, as if with a pocket-book in his hand, carefully noting down what he sees and hears: by practice he acquires considerable facility in representing what he has observed, himself frequently unconscious of its worth, or its bearings. This is entirely different from the observation of a mind, which, having formed a theory and a system upon its own nature, remarks all things that are examples of its truth, confirming it in that truth, and, above all, enabling it to convey the truths of philosophy, as mere effects derived from, what we may call, the outward watchings of life.

Hence it is that Shakespeare's favourite characters are full of such lively intellect. Mercutio is a man possessing all the elements of a poet: the whole world was, as it were, subject to his law of association. Whenever he wishes to impress anything, all things become his servants for the purpose: all things tell the same tale, and sound in unison. This faculty, moreover, is combined with the manners and feelings of a perfect gentleman, himself utterly unconscious of his powers. By his loss it was contrived that the whole catastrophe of the tragedy should be brought about: it endears him to Romeo, and gives to the death of Mercutio an importance which it could not otherwise have acquired.

I say this in answer to an observation, I think by Dryden, (to which indeed Dr. Johnson has fully replied) that Shakespeare having carried the part of Mercutio as far as he could, till his genius was exhausted, had killed him in the third Act, to get him out of the way. What shallow nonsense! As I have remarked, upon the death of Mercutio the whole catastrophe depends; it is produced by it. The scene in which it occurs serves to show how indifference to any subject but one, and aversion to activity on the part of Romeo, may be overcome and roused to the most resolute and determined conduct. Had not Mercutio been rendered so amiable and so interesting, we could not have felt so strongly the necessity for Romeo's interference, connecting it immediately, and passionately, with the future fortunes of the lover and his mistress.

But what am I to say of the Nurse? We have been told that her character is the mere fruit of observation —that it is like Swift's *Polite Conversation,* certainly the most stupendous work of human memory, and of unceasingly active attention to what passes around us, upon record. The Nurse in *Romeo and Juliet* has sometimes been compared to a portrait by Gerard Dow, in which every hair was so exquisitely painted, that it would bear the test of the microscope. Now, I appeal confidently to my hearers whether the closest observation of the manners of one or two old nurses would have enabled Shakespeare to draw this character of admirable generalisation? Surely not. Let any man conjure up in his mind all the qualities and peculiarities that can possibly belong to a nurse, and he will find them in Shakespeare's picture of the old woman: nothing is omitted. This effect is not produced by mere observation. The great prerogative of genius (and Shakespeare felt and availed himself of it) is now to swell itself to the dignity of a god, and now to subdue and keep dormant some part of that lofty nature, and to descend even to the lowest character—to become everything, in fact, but the vicious.

Thus, in the Nurse you have all the garrulity of old age, and all its fondness; for the affection of old-age is one of the greatest consolations of humanity. I have often thought what a melancholy world this would be without children, and what an inhuman world without the aged.

You have also in the Nurse the arrogance of ignorance, with the pride of meanness at being connected with a great family. You have the grossness, too, which that situation never removes, though it sometimes suspends it; and, arising from that grossness, the little low vices attendant upon it, which, indeed, in such minds are scarcely vices.—Romeo at one time was the most delightful and excellent young man, and the Nurse all willingness to assist him; but her disposition soon turns in favour of Paris, for whom she professes precisely the same admiration. How wonderfully are these low peculiarities contrasted with a young and pure mind, educated under different circumstances!

Another point ought to be mentioned as characteristic of the ignorance of the Nurse:—it is, that in all her recollections, she assists herself by the remembrance of

visual circumstances. The great difference, in this re-
spect, between the cultivated and the uncultivated mind
is this—that the cultivated mind will be found to recall
the past by certain regular trains of cause and effect;
whereas, with the uncultivated mind, the past is recalled
wholly by coincident images, or facts which happened
at the same time. This position is fully exemplified in the
following passages put into the mouth of the Nurse:—

> Even or odd, of all days in the year,
> Come Lammas eve at night shall she be fourteen.
> Susan and she—God rest all Christian souls!—
> Were of an age.—Well, Susan is with God;
> She was too good for me. But, as I said,
> On Lammas eve at night shall she be fourteen;
> That shall she, marry: I remember it well.
> 'Tis since the earthquake now eleven years;
> And she was wean'd,—I never shall forget it,—
> Of all the days of the year, upon that day;
> For I had then laid wormwood to my dug,
> Sitting in the sun under the dove-house wall:
> My lord and you were then at Mantua.—
> Nay, I do bear a brain:—but, as I said,
> When it did taste the wormwood on the nipple
> Of my dug, and felt it bitter, pretty fool,
> To see it tetchy, and fall out with the dug!
> Shake, quoth the dove-house: 'twas no need, I trow,
> To bid me trudge.
> And since that time it is eleven years
> For then she could stand alone.

                                              Act I, Scene 3.

She afterwards goes on with similar visual impres-
sions, so true to the character.—More is here brought
into one portrait than could have been ascertained by
one man's mere observation, and without the introduc-
tion of a single incongruous point.

I honour, I love, the works of Fielding as much, or perhaps more, than those of any other writer of fiction of that kind: take Fielding in his characters of postillions, landlords, and landladies, waiters, or indeed, of any-body who had come before his eye, and nothing can be more true, more happy, or more humorous; but in all his chief personages, Tom Jones for instance, where Fielding was not directed by observation, where he could not assist himself by the close copying of what he saw, where it is necessary that something should take place, some words be spoken, or some object described, which he could not have witnessed, (his soliloquies for example, or the interview between the hero and Sophia Western before the reconciliation) and I will venture to say, loving and honouring the man and his productions as I do, that nothing can be more forced and unnatural: the language is without vivacity or spirit, the whole matter is incongruous, and totally destitute of psychological truth.

On the other hand, look at Shakespeare: where can any character be produced that does not speak the language of nature? where does he not put into the mouths of his *dramatis personæ*, be they high or low, Kings or Constables, precisely what they must have said? Where, from observation, could he learn the language proper to Sovereigns, Queens, Noblemen or Generals? yet he invariably uses it.—Where, from observation, could he have learned such lines as these, which are put into the mouth of Othello, when he is talking to Iago of Brabantio?

> Let him do his spite:
> My services, which I have done the signiory,
> Shall out-tongue his complaints. 'Tis yet to know,
> Which, when I know that boasting is an honour,

I shall promulgate, I fetch my life and being
From men of royal siege; and my demerits
May speak, unbonneted, to as proud a fortune
As this that I have reach'd: for know, Iago,
But that I love the gentle Desdemona,
I would not my unhoused free condition
Put into circumscription and confine
For the sea's worth.

Act I, Scene 2.

I ask where was Shakespeare to observe such language as this? If he did observe it, it was with the inward eye of meditation upon his own nature: for the time, he became Othello, and spoke as Othello, in such circumstances, must have spoken. . . .

(1811–12)

HAMLET

Compare the easy language of common life in which this drama opens, with the wild wayward lyric of the opening of *Macbeth*. The language is familiar: no poetic descriptions of night, no elaborate information conveyed by one speaker to another of what both had before their immediate perceptions (such as the first distich in Addison's *Cato*,[1] which is a translation into poetry of "Past four o'clock, and a damp morning")—yet nothing bordering on the comic on the one hand, and no striving of the intellect on the other. It is the language of *sensation* among men who feared no charge of effeminacy for feeling what they felt no want of resolution to bear. Yet the armour, the dead silence, the watchfulness that first interrupts it, the welcome relief of guard, the cold, the

---

[1] PORT. The dawn is over-cast, the morning lours,
And heavily in clouds brings on the day.

broken expressions as of a man's compelled attention to
bodily feelings allowed no man,—all excellently accord
with and prepare for the after gradual rise into tragedy
—but above all into a tragedy the interest of which is
eminently *ad et apud intra,* as *Macbeth* . . . [?] is *ad
extra.*

The preparation *informative* of the audience [is] just
as much as was precisely necessary: how gradual first,
and with the uncertainty appertaining to a question—

> What, has *this thing* appeared *again* to-night.

Even the word "again" has its *credibilizing* effect. Then
the representative of the ignorance of the audience,
Horatio (not himself but [quoted by] Marcellus to Ber-
nardo) anticipates the common solution, "'tis but our
phantasy." But Marcellus rises secondly into "[this]
dreaded sight." Then this "thing" becomes at once an
"apparition," and that too an intelligent spirit that is to
be *spoken* to.

> Tush, tush! 'twill not appear.

Then the shivery feeling, at such a time, with two eye-
witnesses, of sitting down to hear a story of a ghost, and
this, too, a ghost that had appeared two nights before
[at] about this very time. The effort of the narrator to
master his own imaginative terrors; the consequent ele-
vation of the style, itself a continuation of this effort; the
turning off to an *outward* object, "yon same star." O
heaven! words are wasted to those that feel and to those
who do not feel the exquisite judgement of Shakespeare.

Hume himself could not but have faith in *this* Ghost
dramatically, let his anti-ghostism be as strong as Sam-
son against ghosts less powerfully raised.

[I, i, 70–72.

MARCELLUS. Good now, sit down, and tell me, he that knows,
Why this same strict and most observant watch
So nightly toils the subject of the land.]

The exquisitely natural transit into the narration retro-
spective. [When the Ghost re-appears, note] Horatio's
increased courage from having translated the late indi-
vidual spectre into thought and past experience, and
Marcellus' and Bernardo's sympathy with it [Horatio's
courage] in daring to strike, while yet the former feeling
returns in

We do it wrong [being so majestical,
To offer it the show of violence.]

[I, i, 149–52.   I have heard,
The cock, that is the trumpet to the morn,
Doth with his lofty and shrill-sounding throat
Awake the god of day.]

No Addison more careful to be poetical in diction than
Shakespeare in providing the grounds and sources of its
propriety. But *how* to elevate a thing almost mean by its
familiarity, young poets may learn in the cock-crow. . . .

Hamlet.—Polonius.—Hamlet's character is the preva-
lence of the abstracting and generalizing habit over the
practical. He does not want courage, skill, will, or oppor-
tunity; but every incident sets him thinking; and it is
curious, and at the same time, strictly natural, that Ham-
let, who all the play seems reason itself, should be im-
pelled, at last, by mere accident to effect his object. I
have a smack of Hamlet myself, if I may say so.

A Maxim is a conclusion upon observation of matters
of fact, and is merely retrospective: an Idea, or, if you
like, a Principle, carries knowledge within itself, and is

prospective. Polonius is a man of maxims. Whilst he is descanting on matters of past experience, as in that excellent speech to Laertes before he sets out on his travels, he is admirable; but when he comes to advise or project, he is a mere dotard. You see Hamlet, as the man of ideas, despises him.

A man of maxims only is like a Cyclops with one eye, and that eye placed in the back of his head. . . .

From Coleridge's notes in his own copy of Shakespeare

Milton

Born in London, 1608.—Died, 1674.

If we divide the period from the accession of Elizabeth to the Protectorate of Cromwell into two unequal portions, the first ending with the death of James I. the other comprehending the reign of Charles and the brief glories of the Republic, we are forcibly struck with a difference in the character of the illustrious actors, by whom each period is rendered severally memorable. Or rather, the difference in the characters of the great men in each period, leads us to make this division. Eminent as the intellectual powers were that were displayed in both; yet in the number of great men, in the various sorts of excellence, and not merely in the variety but almost diversity of talents united in the same individual, the age of Charles falls short of its predecessor; and the stars of the Parliament, keen as their radiance was, in fulness and richness of lustre, yield to the constellation at the court of Elizabeth;—which can only be paralleled by Greece in her brightest moment, when the titles of the poet, the philosopher, the historian, the statesman and the general not seldom formed a garland round the same head, as in the instances of our Sidneys and Raleighs. But then, on the other hand, there was a vehemence of will, an enthusiasm of principle, a depth and an earnestness of spirit, which the charms of individual fame and personal aggrandisement could not pacify,—an aspiration after reality, permanence, and general good,—in short, a moral grandeur in the latter period, with which the low intrigues, Machiavellic maxims, and selfish and servile ambition of the former, stand in painful contrast.

The causes of this it belongs not to the present occasion to detail at length; but a mere allusion to the quick succession of revolutions in religion, breeding a political indifference in the mass of men to religion itself, the enormous increase of the royal power in consequence of the humiliation of the nobility and the clergy—the transference of the papal authority to the crown,—the unfixed state of Elizabeth's own opinions, whose inclinations were as popish as her interests were protestant—the controversial extravagance and practical imbecility of her successor—will help to explain the former period; and the persecutions that had given a life and soul-interest to the disputes so imprudently fostered by James,—the ardour of a conscious increase of power in the commons, and the greater austerity of manners and maxims, the natural product and most formidable weapon of religious disputation, not merely in conjunction, but in closest combination, with newly awakened political and republican zeal, these perhaps account for the character of the latter aera.

In the close of the former period, and during the bloom of the latter, the poet Milton was educated and formed; and he survived the latter, and all the fond hopes and aspirations which had been its life; and so in evil days, standing as the representative of the combined

excellence of both periods, he produced the *Paradise
Lost* as by an after-throe of nature. "There are some per-
sons (observes a divine, a contemporary of Milton's) of
whom the grace of God takes early hold, and the good
spirit inhabiting them, carries them on in an even con-
stancy through innocence into virtue, their Christianity
bearing equal date with their manhood, and reason and
religion, like warp and woof, running together, make up
one web of a wise and exemplary life. This (he adds) is
a most happy case, wherever it happens; for, besides that
there is no sweeter or more lovely thing on earth than
the early buds of piety, which drew from our Saviour
signal affection to the beloved disciple, it is better to
have no wound than to experience the most sovereign
balsam, which, if it work a cure, yet usually leaves a scar
behind." Although it was and is my intention to defer
the consideration of Milton's own character to the con-
clusion of this Lecture, yet I could not prevail on myself
to approach the *Paradise Lost* without impressing on
your minds the conditions under which such a work was
in fact producible at all, the original genius having been
assumed as the immediate agent and efficient cause; and
these conditions I find in the character of the times and
in his own character. The age in which the foundations
of his mind were laid, was congenial to it as one golden
aera of profound erudition and individual genius;—that
in which the superstructure was carried up, was no less
favourable to it by a sternness of discipline and a show
of self-control, highly flattering to the imaginative dignity
of an heir of fame, and which won Milton over from the
dear-loved delights of academic groves and cathedral
aisles to the anti-prelatic party. It acted on him, too, no
doubt, and modified his studies by a characteristic con-
troversial spirit, (his presentation of God is tinted with
it)—a spirit not less busy indeed in political than in the-

ological and ecclesiastical dispute, but carrying on the
former almost always, more or less, in the guise of the
latter. And so far as Pope's censure of our poet,—that he
makes God the Father a school divine—is just, we must
attribute it to the character of his age, from which the
men of genius, who escaped, escaped by a worse disease,
the licentious indifference of a Frenchified court.

Such was the *nidus* or soil, which constituted, in the
strict sense of the word, the circumstances of Milton's
mind. In his mind itself there were purity and piety ab-
solute; an imagination to which neither the past nor the
present were interesting, except as far as they called
forth and enlivened the great ideal, in which and for
which he lived; a keen love of truth, which, after many
weary pursuits, found a harbour in a sublime listening to
the still voice in his own spirit, and as keen a love of his
country, which, after a disappointment still more depres-
sive, expanded and soared into a love of man as a pro-
bationer of immortality. These were, these alone could
be, the conditions under which such a work as the *Para-
dise Lost* could be conceived and accomplished. By a
life-long study Milton had known—

> What was of use to know,
> What best to say could say, to do had done.
> His actions to his words agreed, his words
> To his large heart gave utterance due, his heart
> Contain'd of good, wise, fair, the perfect shape;[1]

[1] Coleridge is adapting a passage from *Paradise Regained*,
iii, 7–11.

> —what is of use to know,
> What best to say canst say, to do canst do;
> Thy actions to thy words accord; thy words
> To thy large heart give utterance due; thy heart
> Contains of good, wise, just, the perfect shape.
>   —*T. M. Raysor*

and he left the imperishable total, as a bequest to the
ages coming, in the PARADISE LOST.[1] . . .

From Lecture X, 1818

---

[1] "Not perhaps here, but towards, or as, the conclusion, to
chastise the fashionable notion that poetry is a relaxation or
amusement, one of the superfluous toys and luxuries of the
intellect! To contrast the permanence of poems with the
transiency and fleeting moral effects of empires, and what
are called, great events."—S. T. C.

From BIOGRAPHIA LITERARIA

Chapter I

The motives of the present work—Reception of the Author's first publication—The discipline of his taste at school—The effect of contemporary writers on youthful minds—Bowles's sonnets—Comparison between the Poets before and since Mr. Pope.

It has been my lot to have had my name introduced, both in conversation, and in print, more frequently than I find it easy to explain, whether I consider the fewness, unimportance, and limited circulation of my writings, or the retirement and distance in which I have lived, both from the literary and political world. Most often it has been connected with some charge which I could not acknowledge, or some principle which I had never entertained. Nevertheless, had I had no other motive or incitement, the reader would not have been troubled with this exculpation. What my additional purposes were, will be seen in the following pages. It will be found, that the least of what I have written concerns myself personally. I have used the narration chiefly for the purpose of giving a continuity to the work, in part for the sake of the miscellaneous reflections suggested to me by particular events, but still more as introductory to the statement of my principles in Politics, Religion, and Philosophy, and an application of the rules, deduced from philosophical principles, to poetry and criticism. But of the objects, which I proposed to myself, it was not the least important to effect, as far as possible, a settlement of the long continued controversy concerning the true nature of poetic diction; and at the same time to define with the utmost impartiality the real *poetic* character of the poet, by whose writings this controversy was first kindled, and has been since fuelled and fanned.

In 1794, when I had barely passed the verge of manhood, I published a small volume of juvenile poems. They were received with a degree of favor, which, young as I was, I well know was bestowed on them not so much for any positive merit, as because they were considered buds of hope, and promises of better works to come. The critics of that day, the most flattering equally with the severest, concurred in objecting to them obscurity, a general turgidness of diction, and a profusion of new coined double epithets. The first is the fault which a writer is the least able to detect in his own compositions: and my mind was not then sufficiently disciplined to receive the authority of others, as a substitute for my own conviction. Satisfied that the thoughts, such as they were, could not have been expressed otherwise, or at least more perspicuously, I forgot to enquire, whether the thoughts themselves did not demand a degree of attention unsuitable to the nature and objects of poetry. This remark however applies chiefly, though not exclusively, to the *Religious Musings*. The remainder of the charge I admitted to its full extent, and not without sincere acknowledgments both to my private and public censors for their friendly admonitions. In the after editions, I pruned the double epithets with no sparing hand, and used my best efforts to tame the swell and glitter both of thought and diction; though in truth, these parasite plants of youthful poetry had insinuated themselves into my longer poems with such intricacy of union, that I was often obliged to omit disentangling the weed, from the fear of snapping the flower. From that period to the date of the present work I have published nothing, with my name, which could by any possibility have come before the board of anonymous criticism. Even the three or four poems, printed with the works of a friend, as far as they were censured at all, were charged with the same or similar defects, though I am persuaded not with equal justice: with an EXCESS OF ORNAMENT, in addition to STRAINED AND ELABORATE DICTION. (*Vide the criticisms on the "Ancient Mariner" in the* Monthly *and* Critical Reviews *of the first volume of the* Lyrical Ballads.) May I be permitted to add, that, even at the early period of my juvenile poems, I saw and admitted the superiority of an austerer and more natural style, with an insight not less clear, than I at present possess. My judgement was stronger, than were my powers of realizing its dictates; and the faults of my language, though indeed partly owing to a wrong choice of subjects, and the desire of giving a poetic colouring to abstract and metaphysical truths, in which a new world then seemed to open upon me, did yet, in part likewise, originate in unfeigned diffidence of my own comparative talent.—During several years of my youth and early manhood, I reverenced those, who had reintroduced the manly simplicity of the Greek, and of our own elder poets, with such enthusiasm as made the hope seem presumptuous of writing successfully in the same style. Perhaps a similar process has happened to others; but my earliest poems were marked by an ease and simplicity, which I have studied, perhaps with inferior success, to impress on my later compositions.

At school I enjoyed the inestimable advantage of a very sensible, though at the same time a very severe

master. He[1] early moulded my taste to the preference of
Demosthenes to Cicero, of Homer and Theocritus to Virgil, and again of Virgil to Ovid. He habituated me to
compare Lucretius, (in such extracts as I then read)
Terence, and above all the chaster poems of Catullus,
not only with the Roman poets of the, so called, silver
and brazen ages; but with even those of the Augustan
era: and on grounds of plain sense and universal logic
to see and assert the superiority of the former in the
truth and nativeness, both of their thoughts and diction.
At the same time that we were studying the Greek
Tragic Poets, he made us read Shakespeare and Milton
as lessons: and they were the lessons too, which required
most time and trouble to *bring up,* so as to escape his
censure. I learnt from him, that Poetry, even that of the
loftiest and, seemingly, that of the wildest odes, had a
logic of its own, as severe as that of science; and more
difficult, because more subtle, more complex, and dependent on more, and more fugitive causes. In the truly
great poets, he would say, there is a reason assignable,
not only for every word, but for the position of every
word; and I well remember that, availing himself of the
synonimes to the Homer of Didymus, he made us attempt to show, with regard to each, *why* it would not
have answered the same purpose; and *wherein* consisted
the peculiar fitness of the word in the original text.

In our own English compositions, (at least for the
last three years of our school education,) he showed no
mercy to phrase, metaphor, or image, unsupported by a
sound sense, or where the same sense might have been
conveyed with equal force and dignity in plainer words.
Lute, harp, and lyre, muse, muses, and inspirations,

[1] The Rev. James Bowyer, many years Head Master of the
Grammar School, Christ's Hospital.—*S. T. C.*

Pegasus, Parnassus, and Hippocrene were all an abomination to him. In fancy I can almost hear him now, exclaiming *"Harp? Harp? Lyre? Pen and ink, boy, you mean! Muse, boy, Muse? Your Nurse's daughter, you mean! Pierian spring? Oh aye! the cloister-pump, I suppose!"* Nay, certain introductions, similes, and examples, were placed by name on a list of interdiction. Among the similes, there was, I remember, that of the Manchineel fruit, as suiting equally well with too many subjects; in which however it yielded the palm at once to the example of Alexander and Clytus, which was equally good and apt, whatever might be the theme. Was it ambition? Alexander and Clytus!—Flattery? Alexander and Clytus! —Anger? Drunkenness? Pride? Friendship? Ingratitude? Late repentance? Still, still Alexander and Clytus! At length, the praises of agriculture having been exemplified in the sagacious observation, that, had Alexander been holding the plough, he would not have run his friend Clytus through with a spear, this tried and serviceable old friend was banished by public edict in secula seculorum. I have sometimes ventured to think, that a list of this kind, or an index expurgatorius of certain well known and ever returning phrases, both introductory, and transitional, including a large assortment of modest egoisms, and flattering illeisms, &c., &c., might be hung up in our low-courts, and both houses of parliament, with great advantage to the public, as an important saving of national time, an incalculable relief to his Majesty's ministers, but above all, as insuring the thanks of country attornies, and their clients, who have private bills to carry through the house.

Be this as it may, there was one custom of our master's, which I cannot pass over in silence, because I think it imitable and worthy of imitation. He would often permit our exercises, under some pretext of want of time, to accumulate, till each lad had four or five to be looked over. Then placing the whole number *abreast* on his desk, he would ask the writer, why this or that sentence might not have found as appropriate a place under this or that other thesis: and if no satisfying answer could be returned, and two faults of the same kind were found in one exercise, the irrevocable verdict followed, the exercise was torn up, and another on the same subject to be produced, in addition to the tasks of the day. The reader will, I trust, excuse this tribute of recollection to a man, whose severities, even now, not seldom furnish the dreams, by which the blind fancy would fain interpret to the mind the painful sensations of distempered sleep; but neither lessen nor dim the deep sense of my moral and intellectual obligations. He sent us to the University excellent Latin and Greek scholars, and tolerable Hebraists. Yet our classical knowledge was the least of the good gifts, which we derived from his zealous and conscientious tutorage. He is now gone to his final reward, full of years, and full of honors, even of those honors, which were dearest to his heart, as gratefully bestowed by that school, and still binding him to the interests of that school, in which he had been himself educated, and to which during his whole life he was a dedicated thing.

From causes, which this is not the place to investigate, no models of past times, however perfect, can have the same vivid effect on the youthful mind, as the productions of contemporary genius. The Discipline, my mind had undergone, "Ne falleretur rotundo sono et versuum cursu, concinnis et floribus; sed ut inspiceret quidnam subesset, quæ sedes, quod firmamentum, quis fundus verbis; an figuræ essent mera ornatura et orationis fucus; vel sanguinis e materiæ ipsius corde effluentis rubor quidam nativus et incalescentia genuina"; removed all obstacles to the appreciation of excellence in style without diminishing my delight. That I was thus prepared for the perusal of Mr. Bowles's sonnets and earlier poems, at once increased *their* influence, and *my* enthusiasm. The great works of past ages seem to a young man things of another race, in respect to which his faculties must remain passive and submiss, even as to the stars and mountains. But the writings of a contemporary, perhaps not many years older than himself, surrounded by the same circumstances, and disciplined by the same manners, possess a *reality* for him, and inspire an actual friendship as of a man for a man. His very admiration is the wind which fans and feeds his hope. The poems themselves assume the properties of flesh and blood. To recite, to extol, to contend for them is but the payment of a debt due to one, who exists to receive it.

There are indeed modes of teaching which have produced, and are producing, youths of a very different stamp; modes of teaching, in comparison with which we have been called on to despise our great public schools, and universities

> in whose halls are hung
> Armoury of the invincible knights of old—

modes, by which children are to be metamorphosed into prodigies. And prodigies with a vengeance have I known thus produced! Prodigies of self-conceit, shallowness, arrogance, and infidelity! Instead of storing the memory, during the period when the memory is the predominant faculty, with facts for the after exercise of the judgement; and instead of awakening by the noblest models the fond and unmixed Love and Admiration, which is the natural and graceful temper of early youth; *these* nurselings of improved pedagogy are taught to dispute and decide; to suspect all, but their own and their lec-

turer's wisdom; and to hold nothing sacred from their
contempt, but their own contemptible arrogance: boy-
graduates in all the technicals, and in all the dirty pas-
sions and impudence of anonymous criticism. . . .

I had just entered on my seventeenth year, when the
sonnets of Mr. Bowles, twenty in number, and just then
published in a quarto pamphlet, were first made known
and presented to me, by a schoolfellow who had quitted
us for the University, and who, during the whole time
that he was in our first form (or in our school language
a GRECIAN,) had been my patron and protector. I refer
to Dr. Middleton, the truly learned, and every way ex-
cellent Bishop of Calcutta.

It was a double pleasure to me, and still remains a
tender recollection, that I should have received from a
friend so revered the first knowledge of a poet, by whose
works, year after year, I was so enthusiastically delighted
and inspired. My earliest acquaintances will not have
forgotten the undisciplined eagerness and impetuous
zeal, with which I laboured to make proselytes, not only
of my companions, but of all with whom I conversed, of
whatever rank, and in whatever place. As my school
finances did not permit me to purchase copies, I made,
within less than a year and a half, more than forty tran-
scriptions, as the best presents I could offer to those, who
had in any way won my regard. And with almost equal
delight did I receive the three or four following publica-
tions of the same author.

Though I have seen and known enough of mankind to
be well aware, that I shall perhaps stand alone in my
creed, and that it will be well, if I subject myself to no
worse charge than that of singularity; I am not therefore
deterred from avowing, that I regard, and ever have re-
garded the obligations of intellect among the most sacred
of the claims of gratitude. A valuable thought, or a par-

ticular train of thoughts, gives me additional pleasure, when I can safely refer and attribute it to the conversation or correspondence of another. My obligations to Mr. Bowles were indeed important, and for radical good. At a very premature age, even before my fifteenth year, I had bewildered myself in metaphysicks, and in theological controversy. Nothing else pleased me. History, and particular facts, lost all interest in my mind. Poetry (though for a school-boy of that age, I was above par in English versification, and had already produced two or three compositions which, I may venture to say, without reference to my age, were somewhat above mediocrity, and which had gained me more credit than the sound, good sense of my old master was at all pleased with,) poetry itself, yea, novels and romances, became insipid to me. In my friendless wanderings on our *leave-days*,[1] (for I was an orphan, and had scarcely any connections in London,) highly was I delighted, if any passenger, especially if he were drest in black, would enter into conversation with me. For I soon found the means of directing it to my favorite subjects

> Of providence, fore-knowledge, will, and fate,
> Fix'd fate, free will, fore-knowledge absolute,
> And found no end in wandering mazes lost.

This preposterous pursuit was, beyond doubt, injurious both to my natural powers, and to the progress of my education. It would perhaps have been destructive, had it been continued; but from this I was auspiciously withdrawn, partly indeed by an accidental introduction to an amiable family, chiefly however, by the genial influence of a style of poetry, so tender and yet so manly, so nat-

[1] The Christ's Hospital phrase, not for holidays altogether, but for those on which the boys are permitted to go beyond the precincts of the school.—*S. T. C.*

ural and real, and yet so dignified and harmonious, as
the sonnets &c. of Mr. Bowles! Well were it for me, per-
haps, had I never relapsed into the same mental disease;
if I had continued to pluck the flower and reap the har-
vest from the cultivated surface, instead of delving in the
unwholesome quicksilver mines of metaphysic depths.
But if in after time I have sought a refuge from bodily
pain and mismanaged sensibility in abstruse researches,
which exercised the strength and subtlety of the under-
standing without awakening the feelings of the heart;
still there was a long and blessed interval, during which
my natural faculties were allowed to expand, and my
original tendencies to develope themselves: my fancy,
and the love of nature, and the sense of beauty in forms
and sounds.

The second advantage, which I owe to my early pe-
rusal, and admiration of these poems, (to which let me
add, though known to me at a somewhat later period,
the "Lewsdon Hill" of Mr. Crow) bears more immedi-
ately on my present subject. Among those with whom I
conversed, there were, of course, very many who had
formed their taste, and their notions of poetry, from the
writings of Mr. Pope and his followers: or to speak more
generally, in that school of French poetry, condensed
and invigorated by English understanding, which had
predominated from the last century. I was not blind to
the merits of the school, yet as from inexperience of the
world, and consequent want of sympathy with the gen-
eral subjects of these poems, they gave me little pleasure,
I doubtless undervalued the *kind,* and with the presump-
tion of youth withheld from its masters the legitimate
name of poets. I saw that the excellence of this kind
consisted in just and acute observations on men and
manners in an artificial state of society, as its matter and
substance: and in the logic of wit, conveyed in smooth

and strong epigrammatic couplets, as its *form*. Even when the subject was addressed to the fancy, or the intellect, as in the *Rape of the Lock,* or the *Essay on Man;* nay, when it was a consecutive narration, as in that astonishing product of matchless talent and ingenuity, Pope's Translation of the *Iliad;* still a *point* was looked for at the end of each second line, and the whole was as it were a sorites, or, if I may exchange a logical for a grammatical metaphor, a *conjunction disjunctive,* of epigrams. Meantime the matter and diction seemed to me characterized not so much by poetic thoughts, as by thoughts *translated* into the language of poetry. On this last point, I had occasion to render my own thoughts gradually more and more plain to myself, by frequent amicable disputes concerning Darwin's BOTANIC GARDEN, which, for some years, was greatly extolled, not only by the *reading* public in general, but even by those, whose genius and natural robustness of understanding enabled them afterwards to act foremost in dissipating these "painted mists" that occasionally rise from the marshes at the foot of Parnassus. During my first Cambridge vacation, I assisted a friend in a contribution for a literary society in Devonshire: and in this I remember to have compared Darwin's work to the Russian palace of ice, glittering, cold and transitory. In the same essay too, I assigned sundry reasons, chiefly drawn from a comparison of passages in the Latin poets with the original Greek, from which they were borrowed, for the preference of Collins' odes to those of Gray; and of the simile in Shakespeare

> How like a younker or a prodigal,
> The skarfed bark puts from her native bay,
> Hugg'd and embraced by the strumpet wind!
> How like the prodigal doth she return,

> With over-weather'd ribs and ragged sails,
> Lean, rent, and beggar'd by the strumpet wind!

to the imitation in the Bard;

> Fair laughs the morn, and soft the zephyr blows,
> While proudly riding o'er the azure realm
> In gallant trim the gilded vessel goes,
> YOUTH at the prow and PLEASURE at the helm;
> Regardless of the sweeping whirlwind's sway,
> That hush'd in grim repose, expects its evening prey.

(In which, by the bye, the words "realm" and "sway" are rhymes dearly purchased.) I preferred the original on the ground, that in the imitation it depended wholly on the compositor's putting, or not putting, a *small Capital*, both in this, and in many other passages of the same poet, whether the words should be personifications, or mere abstractions. 1 mention this, because, in referring various lines in Gray to their original in Shakespeare and Milton; and in the clear perception how completely all the propriety was lost in the transfer; I was, at that early period, led to a conjecture, which, many years afterwards was recalled to me from the same thought having been started in conversation, but far more ably, and developed more fully, by Mr. Wordsworth; namely, that this style of poetry, which I have characterised above, as translations of prose thoughts into poetic language, had been kept up by, if it did not wholly arise from, the custom of writing Latin verses, and the great importance attached to these exercises, in our public schools. Whatever might have been the case in the fifteenth century, when the use of the Latin tongue was so general among learned men, that Erasmus is said to have forgotten his native language; yet in the present day it is not to be supposed, that a youth can *think* in Latin, or that he can have any other reliance on the force or fitness of his phrases, but the authority of the writer from whence he has adopted them. Consequently he must first prepare his thoughts, and then pick out, from Virgil, Horace, Ovid, or perhaps more compendiously from his Gradus,[1] halves and quarters of lines, in which to embody them.

I never object to a certain degree of disputatiousness in a young man from the age of seventeen to that of four or five and twenty, provided I find him always arguing on one side of the question. The controversies, occasioned by my unfeigned zeal for the honor of a favorite contemporary, then known to me only by his works, were of great advantage in the formation and establishment of my taste and critical opinions. In my defence of the lines running into each other, instead of closing at each couplet, and of natural language, neither bookish, nor vulgar, neither redolent of the lamp, nor of the kennel, such as *I will remember thee;* instead of the same thought tricked up in the rag-fair finery of

> ———Thy image on her wing
> Before my FANCY's eye shall MEMORY bring,

I had continually to adduce the metre and diction of the Greek Poets from Homer to Theocritus inclusive; and still more of our elder English poets from Chaucer to Milton. Nor was this all. But as it was my constant reply

[1] In the "Nutricia" of Politian there occurs this line:

"*Pura coloratos interstrepit unda lapillos.*"

Casting my eye on a University prize-poem, I met this line:

"*Lactea purpureos interstrepit unda lapillos.*"

Now look out in the Gradus for *Purus,* and you find as the first synonime, *lacteus;* for *coloratus,* and the first synonime is *purpureus.* I mention this by way of elucidating one of the most ordinary processes in the *ferrumination* of these centos. —*S. T. C.*

to authorities brought against me from later poets of great name, that no authority could avail in opposition to TRUTH, NATURE, LOGIC, and the LAWS of UNIVERSAL GRAMMAR; actuated too by my former passion for metaphysical investigations; I labored at a solid foundation, on which permanently to ground my opinions, in the component faculties of the human mind itself, and their comparative dignity and importance. According to the faculty or source, from which the pleasure given by any poem or passage was derived, I estimated the merit of such poem or passage. As the result of all my reading and meditation, I abstracted two critical aphorisms, deeming them to comprise the conditions and criteria of poetic style; first, that not the poem which we have *read,* but that to which we *return,* with the greatest pleasure, possesses the genuine power, and claims the name of *essential poetry.* Second, that whatever lines can be translated into other words of the same language, without diminution of their significance, either in sense, or association, or in any worthy feeling, are so far vicious in their diction. Be it however observed, that I excluded from the list of worthy feelings, the pleasure derived from mere novelty in the reader, and the desire of exciting wonderment at his powers in the author. Oftentimes since then, in pursuing French tragedies, I have fancied two marks of admiration at the end of each line, as hieroglyphics of the author's own admiration at his own cleverness. Our genuine admiration of a great poet is a continuous *under-current* of feeling; it is everywhere present, but seldom anywhere as a separate excitement. I was wont boldly to affirm, that it would be scarcely more difficult to push a stone out from the pyramids with the bare hand, than to alter a word, or the position of a word, in Milton or Shakespeare, (in their most important works at least,) without making the author say something else, or something worse, than he does say. One great distinction, I appeared to myself to see plainly, between, even the characteristic faults of our elder poets, and the false beauty of the moderns. In the former, from DONNE to COWLEY, we find the most fantastic out-of-the-way thoughts, but in the most pure and genuine mother English; in the latter, the most obvious thoughts, in language the most fantastic and arbitrary. Our faulty elder poets sacrificed the passion and passionate flow of poetry, to the subtleties of intellect, and to the starts of wit; the moderns to the glare and glitter of a perpetual, yet broken and heterogeneous imagery, or rather to an amphibious something, made up, half of image, and half of abstract[1] meaning. The one sacrificed the heart to the head; the other both heart and head to point and drapery.

The reader must make himself acquainted with the general style of composition that was at that time deemed poetry, in order to understand and account for the effect produced on me by the SONNETS, the MONODY at MATLOCK, and the HOPE, of Mr. Bowles; for it is peculiar to original genius to become less and less *striking,* in proportion to its success in improving the taste and judgement of its contemporaries. The poems of WEST, indeed, had the merit of chaste and manly diction, but they were cold, and, if I may so express it, only *dead-coloured;* while in the best of Warton's there is a stiffness, which too often gives them the appearance of imitations from the Greek. Whatever relation therefore of cause or impulse Percy's collection of Ballads may bear to the most *popular* poems of the present day; yet

[1] I remember a ludicrous instance in the poem of a young tradesman:

"No more will I endure love's pleasing pain,
   Or round my *heart's leg* tie his galling chain."

in the more sustained and elevated style, of the then living poets, Bowles and Cowper were, to the best of my knowledge, the first who combined natural thoughts with natural diction; the first who reconciled the heart with the head. . . .

Chapter II

Supposed irritability of men of Genius—Brought to the test of facts—Causes and Occasions of the charge—Its Injustice.

I have often thought, that it would be neither uninstructive nor unamusing to analyze, and bring forward into distinct consciousness, that complex feeling, with which readers in general take part against the author, in favor of the critic; and the readiness with which they apply to *all* poets the old sarcasm of Horace upon the scribblers of his time: "Genus irritabile vatum." A debility and dimness of the imaginative power, and a consequent necessity of reliance on the immediate impressions of the senses, do, we well know, render the mind liable to superstition and fanaticism. Having a deficient portion of internal and proper warmth, minds of this class seek in the crowd *circum fana* for a warmth in common, which they do not possess singly. Cold and phlegmatic in their own nature, like damp hay, they heat and inflame by co-acervation; or like bees they become restless and irritable through the increased temperature of collected multitudes. Hence the German word for fanaticism, (such at least was its original import,) is derived from the swarming of bees, namely, Schwärmen, Schwärmerei. The passion being in an inverse proportion to the insight, *that* the more vivid, as *this* the less distinct; anger is the inevitable consequence. The absense of all

foundation within their own minds for that, which they
yet believe both true and indispensable for their safety
and happiness, cannot but produce an uneasy state of
feeling, an involuntary sense of fear from which nature
has no means of rescuing herself but by anger. Experi-
ence informs us that the first defence of weak minds is
to recriminate.

> There's no Philosopher but sees,
> That rage and fear are one disease,
> Tho' that may burn, and this may freeze,
> They're both alike the ague.
>
> *Mad Ox.*

But where the ideas are vivid, and there exists an endless
power of combining and modifying them, the feelings
and affections blend more easily and intimately with
these ideal creations than with the objects of the senses;
the mind is affected by thoughts, rather than by things;
and only then feels the requisite interest even for the
most important events and accidents, when by means of
meditation they have passed into *thoughts.* The sanity
of the mind is between superstition with fanaticism on
the one hand, and enthusiasm with indifference and a
diseased slowness to action on the other. For the concep-
tions of the mind may be so vivid and adequate, as to
preclude that impulse to the realizing of them, which is
strongest and most restless in those, who possess more
than mere *talent,* (or the faculty of appropriating and
applying the knowledge of others,) yet still want some-
thing of the creative, and self-sufficing power of absolute
Genius. For this reason therefore, they are men of *com-
manding* genius. While the former rest content between
thought and reality, as it were in an intermundium of
which their own living spirit supplies the *substance,* and
their imagination the ever-varying *form;* the latter must

impress their preconceptions on the world without, in
order to present them back to their own view with the
satisfying degree of clearness, distinctness, and individ-
uality. These in tranquil times are formed to exhibit a
perfect poem in palace, or temple, or landscape-garden;
or a tale of romance in canals that join sea with sea, or
in walls of rock, which, shouldering back the billows,
imitate the power, and supply the benevolence of nature
to sheltered navies; or in aqueducts that, arching the
wide vale from mountain to mountain, give a Palmyra
to the desert. But alas! in times of tumult they are the
men destined to come forth as the shaping spirit of Ruin,
to destroy the wisdom of ages in order to substitute the
fancies of a day, and to change kings and kingdoms, as
the wind shifts and shapes the clouds.[1] The records of
biography seem to confirm this theory. The men of the
greatest genius, as far as we can judge from their own
works or from the accounts of their contemporaries, ap-
pear to have been of calm and tranquil temper in all
that related to themselves. In the inward assurance of
permanent fame, they seem to have been either indiffer-
ent or resigned, with regard to immediate reputation.
Through all the works of Chaucer there reigns a chear-
fulness, a manly hilarity, which makes it almost impos-
sible to doubt a correspondent habit of feeling in the
author himself. Shakespeare's evenness and sweetness of
temper were almost proverbial in his own age. That this

[1] Of old things all are over old,
Of good things none are good enough:—
We'll show that we can help to frame
A world of other stuff.

I too will have my kings, that take
From me the sign of life and death:
Kingdoms shall shift about, like clouds,
Obedient to my breath.
                    Wordsworth's *Rob Roy*—S. T. C.

did not arise from ignorance of his own comparative greatness, we have abundant proof in his Sonnets, which could scarcely have been known to Mr. Pope, when he asserted that our great bard "grew immortal in his own despite." . . .

In Spenser, indeed, we trace a mind constitutionally tender, delicate, and, in comparison with his three great compeers, I had almost said, *effeminate;* and this additionally saddened by the unjust persecution of Burleigh, and the severe calamities, which overwhelmed his latter days. These causes have diffused over all his compositions "a melancholy grace," and have drawn forth occasional strains, the more pathetic from their gentleness. But no where do we find the least trace of irritability, and still less of quarrelsome or affected contempt of his censurers.

The same calmness, and even greater self-possession, may be affirmed of Milton, as far as his poems, and poetic character are concerned. He reserved his anger for the enemies of religion, freedom, and his country. My mind is not capable of forming a more august conception, than arises from the contemplation of this great man in his latter days: poor, sick, old, blind, slandered, persecuted,

> Darkness before, and danger's voice behind,—

in an age in which he was as little understood by the party, *for* whom, as by that, *against* whom he had contended; and among men before whom he strode so far as to *dwarf* himself by the distance; yet still listening to the music of his own thoughts, or if additionally cheered, yet cheered only by the prophetic faith of two or three solitary individuals, he did nevertheless

> ———Argue not
> Against Heaven's hand or will, nor bate a jot

> Of heart or hope; but still bore up and steer'd
> Right onward.

From others only do we derive our knowledge that Milton, in his latter day, had his scorners and detractors; and even in his day of youth and hope, that he had enemies would have been unknown to us, had they not been likewise the enemies of his country.

I am well aware, that in advanced stages of literature, when there exist many and excellent models, a high degree of talent, combined with taste and judgement, and employed in works of imagination, will acquire for a man the *name* of a great genius; though even that *analogon* of genius, which, in certain states of society, may even render his writings more popular than the absolute reality could have done, would be sought for in vain in the mind and temper of the author himself. Yet even in instances of this kind, a close examination will often detect, that the irritability, which has been attributed to the author's *genius* as its cause, did really originate in an ill conformation of body, obtuse pain, or constitutional defect of pleasurable sensation. What is charged to the *author*, belongs to the *man*, who would probably have been still more impatient, but for the humanizing influences of the very pursuit, which yet bears the blame of his irritability.

How then are we to explain the easy credence generally given to this charge, if the charge itself be not, as I have endeavoured to show, supported by experience? This seems to me of no very difficult solution. In whatever country literature is widely diffused, there will be many who mistake an intense desire to possess the reputation of poetic genius, for the actual powers, and original tendencies which constitute it. But men, whose dearest wishes are fixed on objects wholly out of their own power, become in all cases more or less impatient and prone to anger. Besides, though it may be paradoxical to assert, that a man can know one thing and believe the opposite, yet assuredly a vain person may have so habitually indulged the wish, and persevered in the attempt, to appear what he is not, as to become himself one of his own proselytes. Still, as this counterfeit and artificial persuasion must differ, even in the person's own feelings, from a real sense of inward power, what can be more natural, than that this difference should betray itself in suspicious and jealous irritability? Even as the flowery sod, which covers a hollow, may be often detected by its shaking and trembling. . . .

For myself, if from my own feelings, or from the less suspicious test of the observations of others, I had been made aware of any literary testiness or jealousy; I trust, that I should have been, however, neither silly nor arrogant enough to have burthened the imperfection on GENIUS. But an experience (and I should not need documents in abundance to prove my words, if I added) a tried experience of twenty years, has taught me, that the original sin of my character consists in a careless indifference to public opinion, and to the attacks of those who influence it; that praise and admiration have become yearly less and less desirable, except as marks of sympathy; nay that it is difficult and distressing to me, to think with any interest even about the sale and profit of my works, important as, in my present circumstances, such considerations must needs be. Yet it never occurred to me to believe or fancy, that the quantum of intellectual power bestowed on me by nature or education was in any way connected with this habit of my feelings; or that it needed any other parents or fosterers than constitutional indolence, aggravated into languor by ill-health; the accumulating embarrassments of procrastination; the mental cowardice, which is the inseparable companion of procrastination, and which makes us anxious to think and converse on any thing rather than on what concerns ourselves; in fine, all those close vexations, whether chargeable on my faults or my fortunes, which leave me but little grief to spare for evils comparatively distant and alien.

Indignation at literary wrongs I leave to men born under happier stars. I cannot *afford it*. But so far from condemning those who can, I deem it a writer's duty, and think it creditable to his heart, to feel and express a resentment proportioned to the grossness of the provocation, and the importance of the object. There is no profession on earth, which requires an attention so early, so long, or so unintermitting as that of poetry; and indeed as that of literary composition in general, if it be such as at all satisfies the demands both of taste and of sound logic. How difficult and delicate a task even the mere mechanism of verse is, may be conjectured from the failure of those, who have attempted poetry late in life. Where then a man has, from his earliest youth, devoted his whole being to an object, which by the admission of all civilized nations in all ages is honorable as a pursuit, and glorious as an attainment; what of all that relates to himself and his family, if only we except his moral character, can have fairer claims to his protection, or more authorize acts of self-defence, than the elaborate products of his intellect and intellectual industry? Prudence itself would command us to *show*, even if defect or diversion of natural sensibility had prevented us from *feeling*, a due interest and qualified anxiety for the offspring and representatives of our nobler being. I know it, alas! by woeful experience! I have laid too many eggs in the hot sands of this wilderness, the world, with ostrich carelessness and ostrich oblivion. The greater part indeed have been trod under foot, and are forgotten; but yet no small number have crept forth into life, some to furnish feathers for the caps of others, and still more to plume the shafts in the quivers of my enemies, of them that unprovoked have lain in wait against my soul.

Sic vos, non vobis, mellificatis, apes!

Chapter III

The author's obligations to critics, and the probable occasion —Principles of modern criticism.

To anonymous critics in reviews, magazines, and news-journals of various name and rank, and to satirists with or without a name in verse or prose, or in verse-text aided by prose-comment, I do seriously believe and profess, that I owe full two thirds of whatever reputation and publicity I happen to possess. For when the name of an individual has occurred so frequently, in so many works, for so great a length of time, the readers of these works (which with a shelf or two of BEAUTIES, ELEGANT EXTRACTS and ANAS, form nine-tenths of the reading of the reading public[1]) cannot but be familiar with the

---

[1] For as to the devotees of the circulating libraries, I dare not compliment their *pass-time*, or rather *kill-time*, with the name of *reading*. Call it rather a sort of beggarly day-dreaming, during which the mind of the dreamer furnishes for itself nothing but laziness, and a little mawkish sensibility; while the whole *materiel* and imagery of the dose is supplied *ab extra* by a sort of mental *camera obscura* manufactured at the printing office, which *pro tempore* fixes, reflects, and transmits the moving phantasms of one man's delirium, so as

name, without distinctly remembering whether it was introduced for an eulogy or for censure. And this becomes the more likely, if (as I believe) the habit of perusing periodical works may be properly added to Averrhoe's[1] catalogue of ANTI-MNEMONICS, or weakeners of the memory. But where this has not been the case, yet the reader will be apt to suspect, that there must be something more than usually strong and extensive in a reputation, that could either require or stand so merciless and long-continued a cannonading. Without any feeling

---

to people the barrenness of a hundred other brains afflicted with the same trance or suspension of all common sense and all definite purpose. We should therefore transfer this species of *amusement* (if indeed those can be said to retire *a musis,* who were never in their company, or relaxation be attributable to those, whose bows are never bent) from the genus, *reading,* to that comprehensive class characterized by the power of reconciling the two contrary yet co-existing propensities of human nature, namely, indulgence of sloth, and hatred of vacancy. In addition to novels and tales of chivalry in prose or rhyme, (by which last I mean neither rhythm nor metre), this genus comprises as its species, gaming, swinging, or swaying on a chair or gate; spitting over a bridge; smoking; snuff-taking; tête-à-tête quarrels after dinner between husband and wife; conning word by word all the advertisements of a daily newspaper in a public house on a rainy day, &c. &c. &c.—*S. T. C.*

[1] Ex gr. Pediculos e capillis excerptos in arenam jacere incontusos: eating of unripe fruit; gazing on the clouds, and (in genere) on moveable things suspended in the air; riding among a multitude of camels; frequent laughter; listening to a series of jests and humorous anecdotes, as when (so to modernize the learned Saracen's meaning) one man's droll story of an Irishman inevitably occasions another's droll story of a Scotchman, which again, by the same sort of conjunction disjunctive, leads to some étouderie of a Welshman, and that again to some sly hit of a Yorkshireman; the habit of reading tombstones in church-yards, &c. By the bye, this catalogue, strange as it may appear, is not insusceptible of a sound psychological commentary.—*S. T. C.*

of *anger* therefore (for which indeed, on my own account, I have no pretext) I may yet be allowed to express some degree of *surprize*, that, after having run the critical gauntlet for a certain class of faults which I *had*, nothing having come before the judgement-seat in the interim, I should, year after year, quarter after quarter, month after month (not to mention sundry petty periodicals of still quicker revolution, "or weekly or diurnal") have been, for at least 17 years consecutively dragged forth by them into the foremost ranks of the *proscribed*, and forced to abide the brunt of abuse, for faults directly opposite, and which I certainly had not. . . .

Whatever may have been the case with others, I certainly cannot attribute this persecution to personal dislike, or to envy, or to feelings of vindictive animosity. Not to the former, for with the exception of a very few who are my intimate friends, and were so before they were known as authors, I have had little other acquaintance with literary characters, than what may be implied in an accidental introduction, or casual meeting in a mixt company. And, as far as words and looks can be trusted, I must believe that, even in these instances, I had excited no unfriendly disposition.[1] Neither by let-

[1] Some years ago, a gentleman, the chief writer and conductor of a celebrated review, distinguished by its hostility to Mr. Southey, spent a day or two at Keswick. That he was, without diminution on this account, treated with every hospitable attention by Mr. Southey and myself, I trust I need not say. But one thing I may venture to notice; that at no period of my life do I remember to have received so many, and such high coloured compliments in so short a space of time. He was likewise circumstantially informed by what series of accidents it had happened, that Mr. Wordsworth, Mr. Southey, and I had become neighbours; and how utterly unfounded was the supposition, that we considered ourselves, as belonging to any common school, but that of good sense

ter, or in conversation, have I ever had dispute or con-
troversy beyond the common social interchange of opin-
ions. Nay, where I had reason to suppose my convic-
tions fundamentally different, it has been my habit, and
I may add, the impulse of my nature, to assign the
grounds of my belief, rather than the belief itself; and
not to express dissent, till I could establish some points
of complete sympathy, some grounds common to both
sides, from which to commence its explanation.

Still less can I place these attacks to the charge of
envy. The few pages which I have published, are of too
distant a date; and the extent of their sale a proof too

---

confirmed by the long-established models of the best times
of Greece, Rome, Italy, and England; and still more ground-
less the notion, that Mr. Southey (for as to myself I have
published so little, and that little of so little importance, as
to make it ludicrous to mention my name at all) could have
been concerned in the formation of a poetic sect with Mr.
Wordsworth, when so many of his works had been published
not only previously to any acquaintance between them; but
before Mr. Wordsworth himself had written anything but
in a diction ornate, and uniformly sustained; when too the
slightest examination will make it evident, that between those
and the after writings of Mr. Southey, there exists no other
difference than that of a progressive degree of excellence
from progressive developement of power, and progressive
facility from habit and increase of experience. Yet among
the first articles which this man wrote after his return from
Keswick, we were characterized as "the School of whining
and hypochondiacal poets that haunt the Lakes." In reply
to a letter from the same gentleman, in which he had asked
me, whether I was in earnest in preferring the style of Hooker
to that of Dr. Johnson; and Jeremy Taylor to Burke; I stated,
somewhat at large, the comparative excellences and defects,
which characterized our best prose writers, from the reforma-
tion, to the first half of Charles 2nd; and that of those who
had flourished during the present reign, and the preceding
one. About twelve months afterwards, a review appeared on
the same subject, in the concluding paragraph of which the
reviewer asserts, that his chief motive for entering into the

conclusive against their having been popular at any time; to render probable, I had almost said possible, the excitement of envy on *their* account; and the man who should envy me on any *other,* verily he must be *envy-mad!*

Lastly, with as little semblance of reason, could I suspect any animosity towards me from vindictive feelings as the cause. I have before said, that my acquaintance with literary men has been limited and distant; and that I have had neither dispute nor controversy. From my first entrance into life, I have, with few and short inter-

---

discussion was to separate a rational and qualified admiration of our elder writers, from the indiscriminate enthusiasm of a recent school, who praised what they did not understand, and caricatured what they were unable to imitate. And, that no doubt might be left concerning the persons alluded to, the writer annexes the names of Miss BAILLIE, W. SOUTHEY, WORDSWORTH and COLERIDGE. For that which follows, I have only hearsay evidence; but yet such as demands my belief; viz. that on being questioned concerning this apparently wanton attack, more especially with regard to Miss Bailie, the writer had stated as his motives, that this lady, when at Edinburgh had declined a proposal of introducing him to her; that Mr. Southey had written against him; and Mr. Wordsworth had talked contemptuously of ʰim; but that as to *Coleridge* he had noticed him merely because the names of Southey and Wordsworth and Coleridge always went together. But if it were worth while to mix together, as ingredients, half the anecdotes which I either myself know to be true, or which I have received from men incapable of intentional falsehood, concerning the characters, qualifications, and motives of our anonymous critics, whose decisions are oracles for our reading public, I might safely borrow the words of the apocryphal Daniel, *"Give me leave,* O SOVEREIGN PUBLIC, *and I shall slay this dragon without sword or staff."* For the compound would be as the "Pitch, and fat, and hair which Daniel took, and did seethe them together, and made lumps thereof, and put into the dragon's mouth, and so the dragon burst in sunder; and Daniel said, 'LO, THESE ARE THE GODS YE WORSHIP.'"
—S. T. C.

vals, lived either abroad or in retirement. My different essays on subjects of national interest, published at different times, first in the Morning Post and then in the Courier, with my courses of lectures on the principles of criticism as applied to Shakespeare and Milton, constitute my whole publicity; the only occasions on which I *could* offend any member of the republic of letters. With one solitary exception in which my words were first misstated and then wantonly applied to an individual, I could never learn, that I had excited the displeasure of any among my literary contemporaries. Having announced my intention to give a course of lectures on the characteristic merits and defects of English poetry in its different æras; first, from Chaucer to Milton; second, from Dryden inclusive to Thompson; and third, from Cowper to the present day; I changed my plan, and confined my disquisition to the two former æras, that I might furnish no possible pretext for the unthinking to misconstrue, or the malignant to misapply my words, and having stampt their own meaning on them, to pass them as current coin in the marts of garrulity or detraction.

Praises of the unworthy are felt by ardent minds as robberies of the deserving; and it is too true, and too frequent, that Bacon, Harrington, Machiavel, and Spinosa, are *not* read, because Hume, Condillac, and Voltaire *are*. But in promiscuous company no prudent man will oppugn the merits of a contemporary in his own supposed department; contenting himself with praising in his turn those whom *he* deems excellent. If I should ever deem it my duty at all to oppose the pretensions of individuals, I would oppose them in books which could be weighed and answered, in which I could evolve the whole of my reasons and feelings, with their requisite limits and modifications; not in irrecoverable conversation, where however strong the reasons might be, the feelings that prompted them would assuredly be attributed by some one or other to envy and discontent. Besides I well know, and I trust, have acted on that knowledge, that it must be the ignorant and injudicious who extol the unworthy; and the eulogies of critics without taste or judgement are the natural reward of authors without feeling or genius. "Sint unicuique sua præmia."

How then, dismissing, as I do, these three causes, am I to account for attacks, the long continuance and inveteracy of which it would require all three to explain? The solution may seem to have been given, or at least suggested, in a note to a preceding page. *I was in habits of intimacy with Mr. Wordsworth and Mr. Southey!* This, however, transfers, rather than removes the difficulty. Be it, that, by an unconscionable extension of the old adage, "noscitur a socio," my literary friends are never under the water-fall of criticism, but I must be wet through with the spray; yet how came the torrent to descend upon *them?*

First then, with regard to Mr. Southey. I well remember the general reception of his earlier publications: viz. the poems published with Mr. Lovell under the names of Moschus and Bion; the two volumes of poems under his own name, and the Joan of Arc. The censures of the critics by profession are extant, and may be easily referred to:—careless lines, inequality in the merit of the different poems, and (in the lighter works) a predilection for the strange and whimsical; in short, such faults as might have been anticipated in a young and rapid writer, were indeed sufficiently enforced. Nor was there at that time wanting a party spirit to aggravate the defects of a poet, who with all the courage of uncorrupted youth had avowed his zeal for a

cause, which he deemed that of liberty, and his abhor-
rence of oppression by whatever name consecrated. But
it was as little objected by others, as dreamt of by the
poet himself, that he *preferred* careless and prosaic
lines on rule and of forethought, or indeed that he
pretended to any other art or theory of poetic diction,
besides that which we may all learn from Horace, Quinc-
tilian, the admirable dialogue de Causis Corruptæ Elo-
quentiæ, or Strada's Prolusions; if indeed natural good
sense and the early study of the best models in his own
language had not infused the same maxims more
securely, and, if I may venture the expression, more
vitally. All that could have been fairly deduced was,
that in his taste and estimation of writers Mr. Southey
agreed far more with Warton, than with Johnson. Nor
do I mean to deny, that at all times Mr. Southey was
of the same mind with Sir Philip Sidney in preferring
an excellent ballad in the *humblest* style of poetry to
twenty indifferent poems that strutted in the *highest*.
And by what have his works, published since then, been
characterized, each more strikingly than the preceding,
but by greater splendor, a deeper pathos, profounder
reflections, and a more sustained dignity of language
and of metre? Distant may the period be, but whenever
the time shall come, when all his works shall be col-
lected by some editor worthy to be his biographer, I
trust that an excerpta of all the passages, in which his
writings, name, and character have been attacked, from
the pamphlets and periodical works of the last twenty
years, may be an accompaniment. Yet that it would
prove medicinal in after times I dare not hope; for as
long as there are readers to be delighted with calumny,
there will be found reviewers to calumniate. And such
readers will become in all probability more numerous,
in proportion as a still greater diffusion of literature

shall produce an increase of sciolists, and sciolism bring with it petulance and presumption. In times of old, books were as religious oracles; as literature advanced, they next became venerable preceptors; they then descended to the rank of instructive friends; and, as their numbers increased, they sunk still lower to that of entertaining companions; and at present they seem degraded into culprits to hold up their hands at the bar of every self-elected, yet not the less peremptory, judge, who chuses to write from humour or interest, from enmity or arrogance, and to abide the decision (in the words of Jeremy Taylor) "of him that reads in malice, or him that reads after dinner."

The same gradual retrograde movement may be traced, in the relation which the authors themselves have assumed towards their readers. From the lofty address of Bacon: "these are the meditations of Francis of Verulam, which that posterity should be possessed of, he deemed *their* interest:" or from dedication to Monarch or Pontiff, in which the honor given was asserted in equipoise to the patronage acknowledged . . . there was a gradual sinking in the etiquette or allowed style of pretension.

Poets and Philosophers, rendered diffident by their very number, addressed themselves to *"learned* readers;" then, aimed to conciliate the graces of "the *candid* reader;" till, the critic still rising as the author sunk, the amateurs of literature collectively were erected into a municipality of judges, and addressed as THE TOWN! And now, finally, all men being supposed able to read, and all readers able to judge, the multitudinous PUBLIC, shaped into personal unity by the magic of abstraction, sits nominal despot on the throne of criticism. But, alas! as in other despotisms, it but echoes the decisions of its invisible ministers, whose intellectual claims to the guardianship of the muses seem, for the greater part, analogous to the physical qualifications which adapt their oriental brethren for the superintendence of the Harem. Thus it is said, that St. Nepomuc was installed the guardian of bridges, because he had fallen over one, and sunk out of sight; thus too St. Cecilia is said to have been first propitiated by musicians, because, having failed in her own attempts, she had taken a dislike to the art, and all its successful professors. But I shall probably have occasion hereafter to deliver my convictions more at large concerning this state of things, and its influences on taste, genius, and morality.

In the "Thalaba," the "Madoc," and still more evidently in the unique[1] "Cid," in the "Kehama," and, as last, so best, the "Don Roderick"; Southey has given abundant proof, "se cogitâsse quám sit magnum dare aliquid in manus hominum, nec persuadere sibi posse, non sæpe tractandum quod placere et semper et omnibus cupiat." Plin. Ep., Lib. 7, Ep. 17. But on the other hand, I guess, that Mr. Southey was quite unable to comprehend, wherein could consist the crime or mischief of printing half a dozen or more playful poems; or to speak more generally, compositions which would be enjoyed or passed over, according as the taste and humour of the reader might chance to be; provided they contained nothing immoral. In the present age "peri-

[1] I have ventured to call it "unique"; not only because I know no work of the kind in our language (if we except a few chapters of the old translation of Froissart) none, which uniting the charms of romance and history, keeps the imagination so constantly on the wing, and yet leaves so much for after reflection; but likewise, and chiefly, because it is a compilation which, in the various excellencies of translation, selection, and arrangement, required and proves greater genius in the compiler, as living in the present state of society, than in the original composers.—*S. T. C.*

turæ parcere chartæ" is emphatically an unreasonable demand. The merest trifle, he ever sent abroad, had tenfold better claims to its ink and paper, than all the silly criticisms, which prove no more, than that the critic was not one of those, for whom the trifle was written; and than all the grave exhortations to a greater reverence for the public. As if the passive page of a book, by having an epigram or doggrel tale impressed on it, instantly assumed at once loco-motive power and a sort of ubiquity, so as to flutter and buz in the ear of the public to the sore annoyance of the said mysterious personage. But what gives an additional and more ludicrous absurdity to these lamentations is the curious fact, that if in a volume of poetry the critic should find poem or passage which he deems more especially worthless, he is sure to select and reprint it in the review; by which, on his own grounds, he wastes as much more paper than the author, as the copies of a fashionable review are more numerous than those of the original book; in some, and those the most prominent instances, as ten thousand to five hundred. I know nothing that surpasses the vileness of deciding on the merits of a poet or painter, (not by characteristic defects; for where there is genius, *these* always point to his characteristic *beauties;* but) by accidental failures or faulty passages; except the impudence of defending it, as the proper duty, and most instructive part, of criticism. Omit or pass slightly over the expression, grace, and grouping of Raphael's *figures;* but ridicule in *detail* the knitting-needles and broom-twigs, that are to represent trees in his back grounds; and never let him hear the last of his *galli-pots!* Admit that the Allegro and Penseroso of Milton are not *without merit;* but repay yourself for this concession, by reprinting at length the *two poems on the University Carrier!* As a fair specimen of his Son-

nets, quote "*A Book was writ of late called Tetrachor-
don*"; and, as characteristic of his rhythm and metre,
cite his literal translation of the first and second psalm!
In order to justify yourself, you need only assert, that
had you dwelt chiefly on the beauties and excellencies
of the poet, the admiration of these might seduce the
attention of future writers from the objects of their love
and wonder, to an imitation of the few poems and pas-
sages in which the poet was most unlike himself.

But till reviews are conducted on far other prin-
ciples, and with far other motives; till in the place of
arbitrary dictation and petulant sneers, the reviewers
support their decisions by reference to fixed canons of
criticism, previously established and deduced from the
nature of man; reflecting minds will pronounce it arro-
gance in them thus to announce themselves to men of
letters, as the guides of their taste and judgement. To
the purchaser and mere reader it is, at all events, an
injustice. He who tells me that there are *defects* in a
new work, tells me nothing which I should not have
taken for granted without his information. But he, who
points out and elucidates the *beauties* of an original
work, does indeed give me interesting information, such
as experience would not have authorized me in antici-
pating. . . .

Chapter IV

The Lyrical Ballads *with the preface—Mr. Wordsworth's
earlier poems—On fancy and imagination—The investiga-
tion of the distinction important to the fine arts.*

I have wandered far from the object in view, but as I
fancied to myself readers who would respect the feelings
that had tempted me from the main road; so I dare cal-

culate on not a few, who will warmly sympathize with
them. At present it will be sufficient for my purpose, if
I have proved, that Mr. Southey's writings no more than
my own furnished the original occasion to this fiction of
a *new school* of poetry, and to the clamors against its
supposed founders and proselytes.

As little do I believe that "Mr. WORDSWORTH's Lyrical
Ballads" were in *themselves* the cause. I speak exclu-
sively of the two volumes so entitled. A careful and re-
peated examination of these confirms me in the belief,
that the omission of less than an hundred lines would
have precluded nine-tenths of the criticism on this work.
I hazard this declaration, however, on the supposition,
that the reader has taken it up, as he would have done
any other collection of poems purporting to derive their
subjects or interests from the incidents of domestic or
ordinary life, intermingled with higher strains of medita-
tion which the poet utters in his own person and char-
acter; with the proviso, that they were perused without
knowledge of, or reference to, the author's peculiar opin-
ions, and that the reader had not had his attention previ-
ously directed to those peculiarities. In these, as was
actually the case with Mr. Southey's earlier works, the
lines and passages which might have offended the gen-
eral taste, would have been considered as mere inequal-
ities, and attributed to inattention, not to perversity of
judgement. The men of business who had passed their
lives chiefly in cities, and who might therefore be ex-
pected to derive the highest pleasure from acute notices
of men and manners conveyed in easy, yet correct and
pointed language; and all those who, reading but little
poetry, are most stimulated with that species of it, which
seems most distant from prose, would probably have
passed by the volume altogether. Others more catholic in
their taste, and yet habituated to be most pleased when

most excited, would have contented themselves with de-
ciding, that the author had been successful in proportion
to the elevation of his style and subject. Not a few per-
haps, might by their admiration of "the lines written near
Tintern Abbey," those "left upon a Seat under a Yew
Tree," the "old Cumberland beggar," and "Ruth," have
been gradually led to peruse with kindred feeling the
"Brothers," the "Hart leap well," and whatever other
poems in that collection may be described as holding a
middle place between those written in the highest and
those in the humblest style; as for instance between the
"Tintern Abbey," and "The Thorn," or the "Simon Lee."
Should their taste submit to no further change, and still
remain unreconciled to the colloquial phrases, or the
imitations of them, that are, more or less, scattered
through the class last mentioned; yet even from the small
number of the latter, they would have deemed them but
an inconsiderable subtraction from the merit of the
whole work; or, what is sometimes not unpleasing in
the publication of a new writer, as serving to ascertain
the natural tendency, and consequently the proper direc-
tion of the author's genius.

In the critical remarks, therefore, prefixed and an-
nexed to the *Lyrical Ballads,* I believe that we may
safely rest, as the true origin of the unexampled opposi-
tion which Mr. Wordsworth's writings have been since
doomed to encounter. The humbler passages in the
poems themselves were dwelt on and cited to justify
the rejection of the theory. What in and for themselves
would have been either forgotten or forgiven as imper-
fections, or at least comparative failures, provoked direct
hostility when announced as intentional, as the result of
choice after full deliberation. Thus the poems, admitted
by *all* as excellent, joined with those which had pleased
the far *greater* number, though they formed two-thirds

of the whole work, instead of being deemed (as in all right they should have been, even if we take for granted that the reader judged aright) an atonement for the few exceptions, gave wind and fuel to the animosity against both the poems and the poet. In all perplexity there is a portion of fear, which predisposes the mind to anger. Not able to deny that the author possessed both genius and a powerful intellect, they felt *very positive,* but were not *quite certain,* that he might not be in the right, and they themselves in the wrong; an unquiet state of mind, which seeks alleviation by quarrelling with the occasion of it, and by wondering at the perverseness of the man, who had written a long and argumentative essay to persuade them, that

> Fair is foul, and foul is fair;

in other words, that they had been all their lives admiring without judgement, and were now about to censure without reason.[1]

---

[1] In opinions of long continuance, and in which we have never before been molested by a single doubt, to be suddenly *convinced* of an *error,* is almost like being *convicted* of a fault. There is a state of mind, which is the direct antithesis of that, which takes place when we *make a bull. The bull* namely consists in the bringing together two incompatible thoughts, with the *sensation,* but without the *sense,* of their connection. The psychological condition, or that which constitutes the possibility of this state, being such disproportionate vividness of two distant thoughts, as extinguishes or obscures the consciousness of the intermediate images or conceptions, or wholly abstracts the attention from them. Thus in the well known bull, *"I was a fine child, but they changed me;"* the first conception expressed in the word *"I,"* is that of personal identity—*Ego contemplans:* the second expressed in the word *"me,"* is the visual image or object by which the mind represents to itself its past condition, or rather, its personal identity under the form in which it imagined itself

That this conjecture is not wide from the mark, I am induced to believe from the noticeable fact, which I can state on my own knowledge, that the same general censure should have been grounded by almost every different person on some different poem. Among those, whose candour and judgement I estimate highly, I distinctly remember six who expressed their objections to the *Lyrical Ballads* almost in the same words, and altogether to the same purport, at the same time admitting, that several of the poems had given them great pleasure; and, strange as it might seem, the composition which one cited as execrable, another quoted as his favorite. I am indeed convinced in my own mind, that could the same experiment have been tried with these volumes, as was made in the well known story of the picture, the result

---

previously to have existed,—*Ego contemplatus.* Now the change of one visual image for another involves in itself no absurdity, and becomes absurd only by its immediate juxtaposition with the first thought, which is rendered possible by the whole attention being successively absorbed in each singly, so as not to notice the interjacent notion, "changed," which by its incongruity with the first thought, "*I,*" constitutes the bull. Add only, that this process is facilitated by the circumstance of the words "*I*" and "*me,*" being sometimes equivalent, and sometimes having a distinct meaning; sometimes, namely, signifying the act of self-consciousness, sometimes the external image in and by which the mind represents that act to itself, the result and symbol of its individuality. Now suppose the direct contrary state, and you will have a distinct sense of the connection between two conceptions, without that *sensation* of such connection which is supplied by habit. The man *feels* as if he were standing on his head, though he cannot but *see*, that he is truly standing on his feet. This, as a painful sensation, will of course have a tendency to associate itself with the person who occasions it; even as persons, who have been by painful means restored from derangement, are known to feel an involuntary dislike towards their physician.—S. T. C.

would have been the same; the parts which had been covered by the number of the black spots on the one day, would be found equally *albo lapide notatæ* on the succeeding.

However this may be, it is assuredly hard and unjust to fix the attention on a few separate and insulated poems with as much aversion, as if they had been so many plague-spots on the whole work, instead of passing them over in silence, as so much blank paper, or leaves of a bookseller's catalogue; especially, as no one pretends to have found any immorality or indelicacy; and the poems, therefore, at the worst, could only be regarded as so many light or inferior coins in a roleau of gold, not as so much alloy in a weight of bullion. A friend whose *talents* I hold in the highest respect, but whose *judgement* and strong sound sense I have had almost continued occasion to *revere,* making the usual complaints to me concerning both the style and subjects of Mr. Wordsworth's minor poems; I admitted that there were some few of the tales and incidents, in which I could not myself find a sufficient cause for their having been recorded in metre. I mentioned the "Alice Fell" as an instance; "nay," replied my friend with more than usual quickness of manner, "I cannot agree with you *there!* that, I own, *does* seem to me a remarkably pleasing poem." In the *Lyrical Ballads,* (for my experience does not enable me to extend the remark equally unqualified to the two subsequent volumes,) I have heard at different times, and from different individuals every single poem *extolled* and *reprobated,* with the exception of those of loftier kind, which as was before observed, seem to have won universal praise. This fact of itself would have made me diffident in my censures, had not a still stronger ground been furnished by the strange contrast of the heat and long continuance of the opposition, with the nature of the faults stated as justifying it. The seductive faults, the dulcia vitia of Cowley, Marini, or Darwin might reasonably be thought capable of corrupting the public judgement for half a century, and require a twenty years' war, campaign after campaign, in order to dethrone the usurper and re-establish the legitimate taste. But that a downright simpleness, under the affectation of simplicity, prosaic words in feeble metre, silly thoughts in childish phrases, and a preference of mean, degrading, or at best trivial associations and characters, should succeed in forming a school of imitators, a company of almost *religious* admirers, and this too among young men of ardent minds, liberal education, and not

with academic laurels unbestowed;

and that this bare and bald *counterfeit* of poetry, which is characterized as *below* criticism, should for nearly twenty years have well-nigh *engrossed* criticism, as the main, if not the only, *butt* of review, magazine, pamphlet, poem, and paragraph;—this is indeed matter of wonder! . . .

During the last year of my residence at Cambridge, I became acquainted with Mr. Wordsworth's first publication entitled "Descriptive Sketches"; and seldom, if ever, was the emergence of an original poetic genius above the literary horizon more evidently announced. In the form, style, and manner of the whole poem, and in the structure of the particular lines and periods, there is an harshness and acerbity connected and combined with words and images all a-glow, which might recall those products of the vegetable world, where gorgeous blossoms rise out of the hard and thorny rind and shell, within which the rich fruit was elaborating. The language was not only peculiar and strong, but at times knotty and contorted, as by its own impatient strength;

while the novelty and struggling crowd of images, acting in conjunction with the difficulties of the style, demanded always a greater closeness of attention, than poetry, (at all events, than descriptive poetry) has a right to claim. It not seldom therefore justified the complaint of obscurity. In the following extract I have sometimes fancied, that I saw an emblem of the poem itself, and of the author's genius as it was then displayed.

'Tis storm; and hid in mist from hour to hour,
All day the floods a deepening murmur pour;
The sky is veiled, and every cheerful sight:
Dark is the region as with coming night;
And yet what frequent bursts of overpowering light!
Triumphant on the bosom of the storm,
Glances the fire-clad eagle's wheeling form;
Eastward, in long perspective glittering, shine
The wood-crowned cliffs that o'er the lake recline;
Wide o'er the Alps a hundred streams unfold,
At once to pillars turn'd that flame with gold;
Behind his sail the peasant strives to shun
The West, that burns like one dilated sun,
Where in a mighty crucible expire
The mountains, glowing hot, like coals of fire.

The poetic PSYCHE, in its process to full developement, undergoes as many changes as its Greek name-sake, the butterfly.[1] And it is remarkable how soon genius clears

[1] The fact, that in Greek Psyche is the common name for the soul, and the butterfly, is thus alluded to in the following stanzas from an unpublished poem of the author:

The butterfly the ancient Grecians made
The soul's fair emblem, and its only name—
But of the soul, escaped the slavish trade
Of mortal life! For in this earthly frame
Our's is the reptile's lot, much toil, much blame,
Manifold motions making little speed,
And to deform and kill the things, whereon we feed.
—S. T. C.

and purifies itself from the faults and errors of its earliest
products; faults which, in its earliest compositions, are
the more obtrusive and confluent, because as heteroge-
neous elements, which had only a temporary use, they
constitute the very *ferment,* by which themselves are
carried off. Or we may compare them to some diseases,
which must work on the humours, and be thrown out on
the surface, in order to secure the patient from their fu-
ture recurrence. I was in my twenty-fourth year, when
I had the happiness of knowing Mr. Wordsworth per-
sonally, and while memory lasts, I shall hardly forget the
sudden effect produced on my mind, by his recitation
of a manuscript poem, which still remains unpublished,
but of which the stanza, and tone of style, were the
same as those of the "Female Vagrant," as originally
printed in the first volume of the *Lyrical Ballads.*
There was here no mark of strained thought, or forced
diction, no crowd or turbulence of imagery; and, as the
poet hath himself well described in his lines "on re-visit-
ing the Wye," manly reflection, and human associations
had given both variety, and an additional interest to
natural objects, which in the passion and appetite of the
first love they had seemed to him neither to need or per-
mit. The occasional obscurities, which had risen from
an imperfect controul over the resources of his native
language, had almost wholly disappeared, together with
that worse defect of arbitrary and illogical phrases, at
once hackneyed, and fantastic, which hold so distin-
guished a place in the *technique* of ordinary poetry,
and will, more or less, alloy the earlier poems of the
truest genius, unless the attention has been specifically
directed to their worthlessness and incongruity.[1] I did

[1] Mr. Wordsworth, even in his two earliest, "the Evening
Walk and the Descriptive Sketches," is more free from this
latter defect than most of the young poets his contempo-

not perceive anything particular in the mere style of the
poem alluded to during its recitation, except indeed such
difference as was not separable from the thought and
manner; and the Spenserian stanza, which always, more
or less, recalls to the reader's mind Spenser's own style,
would doubtless have authorized, in my then opinion, a
more frequent descent to the phrases of ordinary life,
than could without an ill effect have been hazarded in
the heroic couplet. It was not however the freedom from
false taste, whether as to common defects, or to those
more properly his own, which made so unusual an im-
pression on my feelings immediately, and subsequently
on my judgement. It was the union of deep feeling with
profound thought; the fine balance of truth in observing,
with the imaginative faculty in modifying the objects
observed; and above all the original gift of spreading
the tone, the *atmosphere,* and with it the depth and
height of the ideal world around forms, incidents, and
situations, of which, for the common view, custom had
bedimmed all the lustre, had dried up the sparkle and

---

raries. It may however be exemplified, together with the
harsh and obscure construction, in which he more often of-
fended, in the following lines:—

> 'Mid stormy vapours ever driving by,
> Where ospreys, cormorants, and herons cry;
> Where hardly given the hopeless waste to cheer,
> Denied the bread of life, the foodful ear,
> Dwindles the pear on autumn's latest spray,
> And *apple sickens* pale in summer's ray;
> *Ev'n here content has fixed her smiling reign*
> *With independence, child of high disdain.*

I hope, I need not say, that I have quoted these lines for no
other purpose than to make my meaning fully understood.
It is to be regretted that Mr. Wordsworth has not republished
these two poems entire.—*S. T. C.*

the dew drops. "To find no contradiction in the union of old and new; to contemplate the ANCIENT of days and all his works with feelings as fresh, as if all had then sprang forth at the first creative fiat; characterizes the mind that feels the riddle of the world, and may help to unravel it. To carry on the feelings of childhood into the powers of manhood; to combine the child's sense of wonder and novelty with the appearances, which every day for perhaps forty years had rendered familiar;

> With sun and moon and stars throughout the year,
> And man and woman;

this is the character and privilege of genius, and one of the marks which distinguish genius from talents. And therefore is it the prime merit of genius and its most unequivocal mode of manifestation, so to represent familiar objects as to awaken in the minds of others a kindred feeling concerning them and that freshness of sensation which is the constant accompaniment of mental, no less than of bodily, convalescence. Who has not a thousand times seen snow fall on water? Who has not watched it with a new feeling, from the time that he has read Burns' comparison of sensual pleasure

> To snow that falls upon a river
> A moment white—then gone for ever!

In poems, equally as in philosophic disquisitions, genius produces the strongest impressions of novelty, while it rescues the most admitted truths from the impotence caused by the very circumstance of their universal admission. Truths of all others the most awful and mysterious, yet being at the same time of universal interest, are too often considered as *so* true, that they lose all the life and efficiency of truth, and lie bed-ridden in the dormitory of the soul, side by side with the most despised and exploded errors."—*The Friend*,[1] p. 76, No. 5.

This excellence, which in all Mr. Wordsworth's writings is more or less predominant, and which constitutes the character of his mind, I no sooner felt, than I sought to understand. Repeated meditations led me first to suspect, (and a more intimate analysis of the human faculties, their appropriate marks, functions, and effects matured my conjecture into full conviction,) that fancy and imagination were two distinct and widely different faculties, instead of being, according to the general belief, either two names with one meaning, or, at furthest, the lower and higher degree of one and the same power. It is not, I own, easy to conceive a more opposite translation of the Greek *Phantasia* than the Latin *Imaginatio*; but it is equally true that in all societies there exists an instinct of growth, a certain collective, unconscious good sense working progressively to desynonymize[2] those

[1] As *The Friend* was printed on stampt sheets, and sent only by the post to a very limited number of subscribers, the author has felt less objection to quote from it, though a work of his own. To the public at large indeed it is the same as a volume in manuscript.—S. T. C.

[2] This is effected either by giving to the one word a general, and to the other an exclusive use; as "to put on the back" and "to indorse;" or by an actual distinction of meanings, as "naturalist," and "physician;" or by difference of relation, as "I" and "Me" (each of which the rustics of our different provinces still use in all the cases singular of the first personal pronoun). Even the mere difference, or corruption, in the *pronunciation* of the same word, if it have become general, will produce a new word with a distinct signification; thus "property" and "propriety;" the latter of which, even to the time of Charles II was the *written* word for all the senses of both. Thus too "mister" and "master," both hasty pronunciations of the same word "magister," "mistress," and "miss," "if" and "give," &c. &c. There is a sort of *minim immortal* among the animalcula infusoria which has not nat-

words originally of the same meaning, which the con-
flux of dialects had supplied to the more homogeneous
languages, as the Greek and German: and which the
same cause, joined with accidents of translation from
original works of different countries, occasion in mixt
languages like our own. The first and most important
point to be proved is, that two conceptions perfectly dis-
tinct are confused under one and the same word, and
(this done) to appropriate that word exclusively to one
meaning, and the synonyme (should there be one) to
the other. But if (as will be often the case in the arts
and sciences) no synonyme exists, we must either invent
or borrow a word. In the present instance the appropria-
tion has already begun, and been legitimated in the
derivative adjective: Milton had a highly *imaginative,*
Cowley a very *fanciful* mind. If therefore I should suc-
ceed in establishing the actual existences of two faculties
generally different, the nomenclature would be at once
determined. To the faculty by which I had characterized
Milton, we should confine the term *imagination;* while
the other would be contra-distinguished as *fancy.* Now
were it once fully ascertained, that this division is no less

---

urally either birth, or death, absolute beginning, or absolute
end: for at a certain period a small point appears on its back,
which deepens and lengthens till the creature divides into
two, and the same process recommences in each of the halves
now become integral. This may be a fanciful, but it is by no
means a bad emblem of the formation of words, and may
facilitate the conception, how immense a nomenclature may
be organized from a few simple sounds by rational beings in
a social state. For each new application, or excitement of the
same sound, will call forth a different sensation, which can-
not but affect the pronunciation. The after recollection of the
sound, without the same vivid sensation, will modify it still
further; till at length all trace of the original likeness is worn
away.—*S. T. C.*

grounded in nature, than that of delirium from mania, or Otway's

> Lutes, lobsters, seas of milk, and ships of amber,

from Shakespear's

> What! have his daughters brought him to this pass?

or from the preceding apostrophe to the elements; the theory of the fine arts, and of poetry in particular, could not, I thought, but derive some additional and important light. It would in its immediate effects furnish a torch of guidance to the philosophical critic; and ultimately to the poet himself. In energetic minds, truth soon changes by domestication into power; and from directing in the discrimination and appraisal of the product, becomes influencive in the production. To admire on principle, is the only way to imitate without loss of originality.

It has been already hinted, that metaphysics and psychology have long been my hobby-horse. But to have a hobby-horse, and to be vain of it, are so commonly found together, that they pass almost for the same. I trust therefore, that there will be more good humour than contempt, in the smile with which the reader chastises my self-complacency, if I confess myself uncertain, whether the satisfaction from the perception of a truth new to myself may not have been rendered more poignant by the conceit, that it would be equally so to the public. There was a time, certainly, in which I took some little credit to myself, in the belief that I had been the first of my countrymen, who had pointed out the diverse meaning of which the two terms were capable, and analyzed the faculties to which they should be appropriated. Mr. W. Taylor's recent volume of synonymes I have not yet seen;[1] but his specification of the terms in

[1] I ought to have added, with the exception of a single sheet which I accidentally met with at the printer's. Even from this scanty specimen, I found it impossible to doubt the talent, or not to admire the ingenuity of the author. That his distinctions were for the greater part unsatisfactory to *my* mind, proves nothing against their accuracy; but it may possibly be serviceable to him, in case of a second edition, if I take this opportunity of suggesting the query; whether he may not have been occasionally misled, by having assumed, as to me he appeared to have done, the non-existence of *any* absolute synonymes in our language? Now I cannot but think, that there are many which remain for our posterity to distinguish and appropriate, and which I regard as so much reversionary wealth in our mother-tongue. When two distinct meanings are confounded under one or more words, (and such must be the case, as sure as our knowledge is progressive and of course imperfect) erroneous consequences will be drawn, and what is true in one sense of the word will be affirmed as true in toto. Men of research, startled by the consequences, seek in the things themselves (whether in or out of the mind) for a knowledge of the fact, and having discovered the difference, remove the equivocation either by the substitution of a new word, or by the appropriation of one of the two or more words, that had before been used promiscuously. When this distinction has been so naturalized and of such general currency that the language itself does as it were *think* for us (like the sliding rule which is the mechanic's safe substitute for arithmetical knowledge) we then say, that it is evident to *common sense*. Common sense, therefore, differs in different ages. What was born and christened in the schools passes by degrees into the world at large, and becomes the property of the market and the tea-table. At least I can discover no other meaning of the term, *common sense*, if it is to convey any specific difference from sense and judgement in genere, and where it is not used scholastically for the *universal reason*. Thus in the reign of Charles II, the philosophic world was called to arms by the moral sophisms of Hobbs, and the ablest writers exerted themselves in the detection of an error, which a school-boy would now be able to confute by the mere recollection, that *compulsion* and *obligation* conveyed

question has been clearly shown to be both insufficient and erroneous by Mr. Wordsworth in the Preface added to the late collection of his *Lyrical Ballads and Other Poems*. The explanation which Mr. Wordsworth has himself given will be found to differ from mine, chiefly perhaps, as our objects are different. It could scarcely indeed happen otherwise, from the advantage I have enjoyed of frequent conversation with him on a subject to which a poem of his own first directed my attention, and my conclusions concerning which, he had made more lucid to myself by many happy instances drawn from the operation of natural objects on the mind. But it was Mr. Wordsworth's purpose to consider the influences of fancy and imagination as they are manifested in poetry, and from the different effects to conclude their diversity in kind; while it is my object to investigate the seminal principle, and then from the kind to deduce the degree. My friend has drawn a masterly sketch of the branches with their *poetic fruitage*. I wish to add the trunk, and even the roots as far as they lift themselves above ground, and are visible to the naked eye of our common consciousness.

Yet even in this attempt I am aware, that I shall be obliged to draw more largely on the reader's attention, than so immethodical a miscellany can authorize; when in such a work (the *Ecclesiastical Polity*) of such a mind as Hooker's, the judicious author, though no less admirable for the perspicuity than for the port and dignity of his language; and though he wrote for men of learning in a learned age; saw nevertheless occasion to anticipate and guard against "complaints of obscurity," as often as he was about to trace his subject "to the highest well-

---

two ideas perfectly disparate, and that what appertained to the one, had been falsely transferred to the other by a mere confusion of terms.—*S. T. C.*

spring and fountain." Which, (continues he) "because men are not accustomed to, the pains we take are more needful a great deal, than acceptable; and the matters we handle, seem by reason of newness (till the mind grow better acquainted with them) dark and intricate." I would gladly therefore spare both myself and others this labor, if I knew how without it to present an intelligible statement of my poetic creed; not as my *opinions,* which weigh for nothing, but as deductions from established premises conveyed in such a form, as is calculated either to effect a fundamental conviction, or to receive a fundamental confutation. If I may dare once more adopt the words of Hooker, "they, unto whom we shall seem tedious, are in no wise injured by us, because it is in their own hands to spare that labor, which they are not willing to endure." Those at least, let me be permitted to add, who have taken so much pains to render me ridiculous for a perversion of taste, and have supported the charge by attributing strange notions to me on no other authority than their own conjectures, owe it to themselves as well as to me not to refuse their attention to my own statement of the theory, which I *do* acknowledge; or shrink from the trouble of examining the grounds on which I rest it, or the arguments which I offer in its justification.

Chapter V

On the law of association—Its history traced from Aristotle to Hartley.

There have been men in all ages, who have been impelled as by an instinct to propose their own nature as

a problem, and who devote their attempts to its solu-
tion. The first step was to construct a table of distinc-
tions, which they seem to have formed on the principle
of the absence or presence of the WILL. Our various
sensations, perceptions, and movements were classed as
active or passive, or as media partaking of both. A still
finer distinction was soon established between the vol-
untary and the spontaneous. In our perceptions we seem
to ourselves merely passive to an external power,
whether as a mirror reflecting the landscape, or as a
blank canvas on which some unknown hand paints it.
For it is worthy of notice, that the latter, or the system
of idealism may be traced to sources equally remote
with the former, or materialism; and Berkeley can boast
an ancestry at least as venerable as Gassendi or Hobbs.
These conjectures, however, concerning the mode in
which our perceptions originated, could not alter the
natural difference of *things* and *thoughts*. In the former,
the cause appeared wholly external, while in the latter,
sometimes our will interfered as the producing or de-
termining cause, and sometimes our nature seemed to
act by a mechanism of its own, without any conscious
effort of the will, or even against it. Our inward experi-
ences were thus arranged in three separate classes, the
passive sense, or what the school-men call the merely
receptive quality of the mind; the voluntary; and the
spontaneous, which holds the middle place between
both. But it is not in human nature to meditate on any
mode of action, without enquiring after the law that
governs it; and in the explanation of the spontaneous
movements of our being, the metaphysician took the
lead of the anatomist and natural philosopher. In Egypt,
Palestine, Greece, and India the analysis of the mind
had reached its noon and manhood, while experimental
research was still in its dawn and infancy. For many,

very many centuries, it has been difficult to advance a
new truth, or even a new error, in the philosophy of the
intellect or morals. With regard, however, to the laws
that direct the spontaneous movements of thought and
the principle of their intellectual mechanism there ex-
ists, it has been asserted, an important exception most
honorable to the moderns, and in the merit of which
our own country claims the largest share. Sir James
Mackintosh, (who amid the variety of his talents and
attainments is not of less repute for the depth and
accuracy of his philosophical enquiries than for the
eloquence with which he is said to render their most
difficult results perspicuous, and the driest attractive,)
affirmed in the lectures, delivered by him in Lincoln's
Inn Hall, that the law of association as established in
the contemporaneity of the original impressions, formed
the basis of all true psychology; and any ontological or
metaphysical science, not contained in such (i. e. em-
pirical) psychology, was but a web of abstractions and
generalizations. Of this prolific truth, of this great fun-
damental law, he declared HOBBS to have been the
original *discoverer,* while its full application to the
whole intellectual system we owed to David Hartley;
who stood in the same relation to Hobbs as Newton
to Kepler; the law of association being that to the mind,
which gravitation is to matter.

Of the former clause in this assertion, as it respects
the comparative merits of the ancient metaphysicians,
including their commentators, the school-men, and of
the modern French and British philosophers from
Hobbs to Hume, Hartley, and Condillac, this is not the
place to speak. So wide indeed is the chasm between
this gentleman's philosophical creed and mine, that so
far from being able to join hands, we could scarcely
make our voices intelligible to each other: and to *bridge*

it over, would require more time, skill, and power than
I believe myself to possess. But the latter clause in-
volves for the greater part a mere question of fact and
history, and the accuracy of the statement is to be tried
by documents rather than reasoning.

First, then, I deny Hobbs's claim in toto: for he had
been anticipated by Des Cartes, whose work "De
Methodo," preceded Hobbs's "De Natura Humana," by
more than a year. But what is of much more impor-
tance, Hobbs builds nothing on the principle which he
had announced. He does not even announce it, as dif-
fering in any respect from the general laws of material
motion and impact: nor was it, indeed, possible for him
so to do, compatibly with his system, which was exclu-
sively material and mechanical. Far otherwise is it with
Des Cartes; greatly as he too in his after writings (and
still more egregiously his followers De la Forge, and
others) obscured the truth by their attempts to explain
it on the theory of nervous fluids, and material con-
figurations. But, in his interesting work, "De Methodo,"
Des Cartes relates the circumstance which first led him
to meditate on this subject, and which since then has
been often noticed and employed as an instance and
illustration of the law. A child who with its eyes band-
aged had lost several of his fingers by amputation, con-
tinued to complain for many days successively of pains,
now in this joint and now in that, of the very fingers
which had been cut off. Des Cartes was led by this
incident to reflect on the uncertainty with which we
attribute any particular place to any inward pain or un-
easiness, and proceeded after long consideration to es-
tablish it as a general law; that contemporaneous im-
pressions, whether images or sensations, recall each other
mechanically. On this principle, as a ground work, he
built up the whole system of human language, as one

continued process of association. He showed in what sense not only general terms, but generic images (under the name of abstract ideas) actually existed, and in what consists their nature and power. As one word may become the general exponent of many, so by association a simple image may represent a whole class. But in truth Hobbs himself makes no claims to any discovery, and introduces this law of association, or (in his own language) discursûs mentalis, as an admitted fact, in the *solution* alone of which, this by causes purely physiological, he arrogates any originality. His system is briefly this; whenever the senses are impinged on by external objects, whether by the rays of light reflected from them, or by effluxes of their finer particles, there results a correspondent motion of the innermost and subtlest organs. This motion constitutes a *representation,* and there remains an *impression* of the same, or a certain disposition to repeat the same motion. Whenever we feel several objects at the same time, the *impressions* that are left, (or in the language of Mr. Hume, the *ideas,*) are linked together. Whenever therefore any one of the movements, which constitute a complex impression, is renewed through the senses, the others succeed mechanically. It follows of necessity therefore that Hobbs as well as Hartley and all others who derive association from the connection and interdependence of the supposed matter, the movements of which constitute our thoughts, *must* have reduced all its forms to the one law of time. But even the merit of announcing this law with philosophic precision cannot be fairly conceded to him. For the objects of any two ideas[1] need not have co-

---

[1] I here use the word "idea" in Mr. Hume's sense on account of its general currency amongst the English metaphysicians; though against my own judgement, for I believe that the vague use of this word has been the cause of much error

existed in the same sensation in order to become mutu-
ally associable. The same result will follow when one

---

and more confusion. The word, ἰδέα, in its original sense as
used by Pindar, Aristophanes, and in the Gospel of St. Mat-
thew, represented the visual abstraction of a distant object,
when we see the whole without distinguishing its parts.
Plato adopted it as a technical term, and as the antithesis to
εἴδωλα, or sensuous images; the transient and perishable em-
blems, or mental words, of ideas. The ideas themselves he
considered as mysterious powers, living, seminal, formative,
and exempt from time. In this sense the word became the
property of the Platonic school; and it seldom occurs in
Aristotle, without some such phrase annexed to it, as accord-
ing to Plato, or as Plato says. Our English writers to the end
of Charles 2nd's reign, or somewhat later, employed it either
in the original sense, or platonically, or in a sense nearly
correspondent to our present use of the substantive, Ideal,
always however opposing it, more or less, to image, whether
of present or absent objects. The reader will not be displeased
with the following interesting exemplification from Bishop
Jeremy Taylor. "St. Lewis the King sent Ivo Bishop of
Chartres on an embassy, and he told, that he met a grave and
stately matron on the way with a censer of fire in one hand,
and a vessel of water in the other; and observing her to have
a melancholy, religious, and phantastic deportment and look,
he asked her what those symbols meant, and what she meant
to do with her fire and water; she answered, my purpose is
with the fire to burn paradise, and with my water to quench
the flames of hell, that men may serve God purely for the
love of God. But we rarely meet with such spirits which love
virtue so metaphysically as *to abstract her from all sensible
compositions, and love the purity of the idea.*" Des Cartes
having introduced into his philosophy the fanciful hypothe-
sis of *material ideas,* or certain configurations of the brain,
which were as so many moulds to the influxes of the external
world; Mr. Locke adopted the term, but extended its signifi-
cation to whatever is the immediate object of the mind's
attention or consciousness. Mr. Hume, distinguishing those
representations which are accompanied with a sense of a
present object, from those reproduced by the mind itself,
designated the former by *impressions,* and confined the word
idea to the latter.—*S. T. C.*

only of the two ideas has been represented by the senses, and the other by the memory.

Long however before either Hobbs or Des Cartes the law of association had been defined, and its important functions set forth by Melanchthon, Ammerbach, and Ludovicus Vives; more especially by the last. Phantasia, it is to be noticed, is employed by Vives to express the mental power of comprehension, or the *active* function of the mind; and imaginatio for the receptivity (vis receptiva) of impressions, or for the *passive* perception. The power of combination he appropriates to the· former: "quæ singula et simpliciter acceperat imaginatio, ea conjungit et disjungit phantasia." And the law by which the thoughts are spontaneously presented follows thus: "quæ simul sunt a phantasia comprehensa, si alterutrum occurrat, solet secum alterum repræsentare." To time therefore he subordinates all the other exciting causes of association. The soul proceeds "a causa ad effectum, ab hoc ad instrumentum, a parte ad totum"; thence to the place, from place to person, and from this to whatever preceded or followed, all as being parts of a total impression, each of which may recall the other. The apparent springs "Saltus vel transitus etiam longissimos," he explains by the same thought having been a component part of two or more total impressions. Thus "ex Scipione venio in cogitationem potentiæ Turcicæ, propter victorias ejus in eâ parte Asiæ in qua regnabat Antiochus."

But from Vives I pass at once to the source of his doctrines, and (as far as we can judge from the remains yet extant of Greek philosophy) as to the first, so to the fullest and most perfect enunciation of the associative principle, viz. to the writings of Aristotle; and of these in particular to the books "De Anima," "De Memoria," and that which is entitled in the old translations "Parva

Naturalia." In as much as later writers have either deviated from, or added to his doctrines, they appear to me to have introduced either error or groundless supposition.

•In the first place it is to be observed, that Aristotle's positions on this subject are unmixed with fiction. The wise Stagyrite speaks of no successive particles propagating motion like billiard balls, (as Hobbs); nor of nervous or animal spirits, where inanimate and irrational solids are thawed down, and distilled, or filtrated by ascension, into living and intelligent fluids, that etch and re-etch engravings on the brain, (as the followers of Des Cartes, and the humoral pathologists in general); nor of an oscillating ether which was to effect the same service for the nerves of the brain considered as solid fibres, as the animal spirits perform for them under the notion of hollow tubes (as *Hartley* teaches)—nor finally, (with yet more recent dreamers) of chemical compositions by elective affinity, or of an electric light at once the immediate object and the ultimate organ of inward vision, which rises to the brain like an Aurora Borealis, and there disporting in various shapes (as the balance of plus and minus, or negative and positive, is destroyed or re-established) images out both past and present. Aristotle delivers a just *theory* without pretending to an *hypothesis;* or in other words a comprehensive survey of the different facts, and of their relations to each other without *supposition,* i.e. a fact *placed under* a number of facts, as their common support and explanation; though in the majority of instances these hypotheses or suppositions better deserve the name of ὑποποιήσεις, or *suffictions.* He uses indeed the word κινήσεις, to express what we call representations or ideas, but he carefully distinguishes them from material motion, designating the latter always by annexing the words ἐν τόπῳ, or κατὰ τόπον. On the contrary, in his treatise "De Anima," he excludes place and motion from all the operations of thought, whether representations or volitions, as attributes utterly and absurdly heterogeneous.

The *general law* of association, or, more accurately, the *common condition* under which all exciting causes act, and in which they may be generalized, according to Aristotle is this. Ideas by having been together acquire a power of recalling each other; or every partial representation awakes the total representation of which it had been a part. In the practical determination of this common principle to particular recollections, he admits five agents or occasioning causes: 1st, connection in time, whether simultaneous, preceding, or successive; 2nd, vicinity or connection in space; 3rd, interdependence or necessary connection, as cause and effect; 4th, likeness; and 5th, contrast. As an additional solution of the occasional seeming chasms in the continuity of reproduction he proves, that movements or ideas possessing one or the other of these five characters had passed through the mind as intermediate links, sufficiently clear to recall other parts of the same total impressions with which they had co-existed, though not vivid enough to excite that degree of attention which is requisite for distinct recollection, or as we may aptly express it, *after-consciousness*. In association then consists the whole mechanism of the reproduction of impressions, in the Aristotelian Psychology. It is the universal law of the *passive* fancy and *mechanical* memory; that which supplies to all other faculties their objects, to all thought the elements of its materials.

In consulting the excellent commentary of St. Thomas

Aquinas on the Parva Naturalia of Aristotle, I was struck at once with its close resemblance to Hume's Essay on association. The main thoughts were the same in both, the *order* of the thoughts was the same, and even the illustrations differed only by Hume's occasional substitution of more modern examples. I mentioned the circumstance to several of my literary acquaintances, who admitted the closeness of the resemblance, and that it seemed too great to be explained by mere coincidence; but they thought it improbable that Hume should have held the pages of the angelic Doctor worth turning over. But some time after Mr. Payne, of the King's mews, shewed Sir James Mackintosh some odd volumes of St. Thomas Aquinas, partly perhaps from having heard that Sir James (then Mr.) Mackintosh had in his lectures passed a high encomium on this canonized philosopher, but chiefly from the fact, that the volumes had belonged to Mr. Hume, and had here and there marginal marks and notes of reference in his own hand writing. Among these volumes was that which contains the *Parva Naturalia,* in the old Latin version, swathed and swaddled in the commentary afore mentioned!

It remains then for me, first to state wherein Hartley differs from Aristotle; then, to exhibit the grounds of my conviction, that he differed only to err; and next as the result, to shew, by what influences of the choice and judgement the associative power becomes either memory or fancy; and, in conclusion, to appropriate the remaining offices of the mind to the reason, and the imagination. With my best efforts to be as perspicuous as the nature of language will permit on such a subject, I earnestly solicit the good wishes and friendly patience of my readers, while I thus go "sounding on my dim and perilous way."

Chapter VII

Of the original mistake or equivocation which procured admission for the Hartleian theory—Memoria Technica.

. . . The attention will be more profitably employed in attempting to discover and expose the paralogisms, by the magic of which such a faith could find admission into minds framed for a nobler creed. These, it appears to me, may be all reduced to one sophism as their common genus; the mistaking the *conditions* of a thing for its *causes* and *essence;* and the process, by which we arrive at the knowledge of a faculty, for the faculty itself. The air I breathe is the *condition* of my life, not its cause. We could never have learnt that we had eyes but by the process of seeing; yet having seen we know that the eyes must have pre-existed in order to render the process of sight possible. Let us cross-examine Hartley's scheme under the guidance of this distinction; and we shall discover, that contemporaneity, (Leibnitz's *Lex Continui,*) is the *limit and condition* of the laws of mind, itself being rather a law of matter, at least of phænomena considered as material. At the utmost, it is to *thought* the same, as the law of gravitation is to loco-motion. In every voluntary movement we first counteract gravitation, in order to avail ourselves of it. It must exist, that there may be a something to be counteracted, and which, by its re-action, may aid the force that is exerted to resist it. Let us consider what we do when we leap. We first resist the gravitating power by an act purely voluntary, and then by another act, voluntary in part, we yield to it in order to light on the spot, which we had previously proposed to our-

selves. Now let a man watch his mind while he is com-
posing; or, to take a still more common case, while he
is trying to recollect a name; and he will find the proc-
ess completely analogous. Most of my readers will have
observed a small water-insect on the surface of rivulets,
which throws a cinque-spotted shadow fringed with
prismatic colours on the sunny bottom of the brook;
and will have noticed, how the little animal *wins* its
way up against the stream, by alternate pulses of active
and passive motion, now resisting the current, and now
yielding to it in order to gather strength and a momen-
tary *fulcrum* for a further propulsion. This is no unapt
emblem of the mind's self-experience in the act of think-
ing. There are evidently two powers at work, which
relatively to each other are active and passive; and this
is not possible without an intermediate faculty, which is
at once both active and passive. (In philosophical lan-
guage, we must denominate this intermediate faculty
in all its degrees and determinatons, the IMAGINATION.
But, in common language, and especially on the subject
of poetry, we appropriate the name to a superior degree
of the faculty, joined to a superior voluntary controul
over it.)

Contemporaneity, then, being the common condition
of all the laws of association, and a component element
in all the materia subjecta, the parts of which are to be
associated, must needs be co-present with all. Nothing,
therefore, can be more easy than to pass off on an in-
cautious mind this constant companion of each, for the
essential substance of all. But if we appeal to our own
consciousness, we shall find that even time itself, as the
cause of a *particular* act of association, is distinct from
contemporaneity, as the *condition* of *all* association. See-
ing a mackerel, it may happen, that I immediately think
of gooseberries, because I at the same time ate mackerel

with gooseberries as the sauce. The first syllable of the
latter word, being that which had co-existed with the
image of the bird so called, I may then think of a
goose. In the next moment the image of a swan may
arise before me, though I had never seen the two birds
together. In the two former instances, I am conscious
that their co-existence in *time* was the circumstance,
that enabled me to recollect them; and equally con-
scious am I that the latter was recalled to me by the
joint operation of likeness and contrast. So it is with
cause and *effect;* so too with *order.* So I am able to dis-
tinguish whether it was proximity in time, or continuity
in space, that occasioned me to recall B. on the mention
of A. They cannot be indeed *separated* from contem-
poraneity; for that would be to separate them from the
mind itself. The act of consciousness is indeed identical
with *time* considered in its essence. (I mean *time* per
se, as contra-distinguished from our *notion* of time; for
this is always blended with the idea of space, which, as
the *contrary* of time, is therefore its *measure.*) Never-
theless the accident of seeing two objects at the same
moment acts as a distinguishable cause from that of
having seen them at the same place: and the true prac-
tical general law of association is this; that whatever
makes certain parts of a total impression more vivid or
distinct than the rest, will determine the mind to recall
these in preference to others equally linked together by
the common condition of contemporaneity, or (what
I deem a more appropriate and philosophical term) of
continuity. But the will itself by confining and intensify-
ing[1] the attention may arbitrarily give vividness or dis-

[1] I am aware, that this word occurs neither in Johnson's
Dictionary or in any classical writer. But the word, "*to
intend,*" which Newton and others before him employ in this
sense, is now so completely appropriated to another meaning,

tinctness to any object whatsoever; and from hence we may deduce the uselessness, if not the absurdity, of certain recent schemes which *promise* an artificial *memory*, but which in reality can only produce a confusion and debasement of the *fancy*. Sound logic, as the habitual subordination of the individual to the species, and of the species to the genus; philosophical knowledge of facts under the relation of cause and effect; a chearful and communicative temper disposing us to notice the similarities and contrasts of things, that we may be able to illustrate the one by the other; a quiet conscience; a condition free from anxieties; sound health, and above all (as far as relates to passive remembrance) a healthy digestion; *these* are the best, these are the only ARTS OF MEMORY.

Chapter X

A chapter of digression and anecdotes, as an interlude preceding that on the nature and genesis of the imagination or plastic power—On pedantry and pedantic expressions—Various anecdotes of the author's literary life, and the progress of his opinions in religion and politics.

"*Esemplastic. The word is not in Johnson, nor have I met with it elsewhere.*" Neither have I. I constructed it myself from the Greek words, εἰς ἓν πλάττειν, to shape

---

that I could not use it without ambiguity: while to paraphrase the sense, as by *render intense,* would often break up the sentence and destroy that harmony of the position of words with the logical position of the thoughts, which is a beauty in all composition, and more especially desirable in a close philosophical investigation. I have therefore hazarded the word, *intensify:* though, I confess, it sounds uncouth to my own ear.—*S. T. C.*

into one; because, having to convey a new sense, I
thought that a new term would both aid the recollection
of my meaning, and prevent its being confounded with
the usual import of the word, imagination. *"But this is
pedantry!"* Not necessarily so, I hope. If I am not mis-
informed, pedantry consists in the use of words unsuit-
able to the time, place, and company. The language of
the market would be in the schools as *pedantic,* though
it might not be reprobated by that name, as the language
of the schools in the market. The mere man of the world,
who insists that no other terms but such as occur in com-
mon conversation should be employed in a scientific dis-
quisition, and with no greater precision, is as truly a
pedant as the man of letters, who either over-rating the
acquirements of his auditors, or misled by his own famil-
iarity with technical or scholastic terms, converses at the
wine-table with his mind fixed on his musæum or labora-
tory; even though the latter pedant instead of desiring
his wife to *make the tea* should bid her add to the quant.
suff. of thea Sinensis the oxyd of hydrogen saturated
with caloric. To use the colloquial (and in truth some-
what *vulgar*) metaphor, if the pedant of the cloyster,
and the pedant of the lobby, both *smell equally of the
shop,* yet the odour from the Russian binding of good old
authentic-looking folios and quartos is less annoying than
the steams from the tavern or bagnio. Nay, though the
pedantry of the scholar should betray a little ostentation,
yet a well-conditioned mind would more easily, me-
thinks, tolerate the *fox brush* of learned vanity, than the
sans culotterie of a contemptuous ignorance, that as-
sumes a merit from mutilation in the self-consoling sneer
at the pompous incumbrance of tails.

The first lesson of philosophic discipline is to wean
the student's attention from the DEGREES of things, which
alone form the vocabulary of common life, and to direct

it to the KIND abstracted from *degree*. Thus the chemical student is taught not to be startled at disquisitions on the heat in ice, or on latent and fixible light. In such discourse the instructor has no other alternative than either to use old words with new meanings (the plan adopted by Darwin in his Zoonomia;) or to introduce new terms, after the example of Linnæus, and the framers of the present chemical nomenclature. The latter mode is evidently preferable, were it only that the former demands a twofold exertion of thought in one and the same act. For the reader, or hearer, is required not only to learn and bear in mind the new definition; but to unlearn, and keep out of his view, the old and habitual meaning; a far more difficult and perplexing task, and for which the mere *semblance* of eschewing pedantry seems to me an inadequate compensation. Where, indeed, it is in our power to recall an unappropriate term that had without sufficient reason become obsolete, it is doubtless a less evil to restore than to coin anew. Thus to express in one word, all that appertains to the perception, considered as passive, and merely recipient, I have adopted from our elder classics the word *sensuous;* because *sensual* is not at present used, except in a bad sense, or at least as a *moral* distinction; while *sensitive* and *sensible* would each convey a different meaning. Thus too I have followed Hooker, Sanderson, Milton, &c., in designating the *immediateness* of any act or object of knowledge by the word *intuition,* used sometimes subjectively, sometimes objectively, even as we use the word, thought, now as *the* thought, or act of thinking, and now as *a* thought, or the object of our reflection; and we do this without confusion or obscurity. The very words, *objective* and *subjective,* of such constant recurrence in the schools of yore, I have ventured to re-introduce, because I could not so briefly or conveniently by any more familiar terms distinguish the percipere from the percipi. Lastly, I have cautiously discriminated the terms, THE REASON, and THE UNDERSTANDING, encouraged and confirmed by the authority of our genuine divines and philosophers, before the revolution.

> ———"both life, and sense,
> Fancy, and *understanding;* whence the soul
> *Reason* receives, and REASON is her *being,*
> DISCURSIVE or INTUITIVE: discourse[1]
> Is oftest your's, the latter most is our's,
> Differing but in *degree,* in *kind* the same."
> *Paradise Lost,* Book V.

I say, that I was *confirmed* by authority so venerable: for I had previous and higher motives in my own conviction of the importance, nay, of the necessity of the distinction, as both an indispensable condition and a vital part of all sound speculation in metaphysics, ethical or theological. . . .

All my experience from my first entrance into life to the present hour is in favor of the warning maxim, that the man, who opposes in toto the political or religious zealots of his age, is safer from their obloquy than he who differs from them but in one or two points, or perhaps only in degree. By that transfer of the feelings of private life into the discussion of public questions, which is the *queen bee* in the hive of party fanaticism, the partisan has more sympathy with an intemperate

[1] But for sundry notes on Shakespeare, &c., and other pieces which have fallen in my way, I should have deemed it unnecesary to observe, that *discourse* here, or elsewhere, does not mean what we *now* call discoursing; but the *discursion* of the *mind,* the processes of generalization and subsumption, of deduction and conclusion. Thus, Philosophy has *hitherto* been DISCURSIVE; while Geometry is *always* and *essentially* INTUITIVE.—S. T. C.

Opposite than with a moderate Friend. We now enjoy
an intermission, and long may it continue! In addition
to far higher and more important merits, our present
Bible societies and other numerous associations for na-
tional or charitable objects, may serve perhaps to carry
off the superfluous activity and fervour of stirring minds
in innocent hyperboles and the bustle of management.
But the poison-tree is not dead, though the sap may for
a season have subsided to its roots. At least let us not
be lulled into such a notion of our entire security, as not
to keep watch and ward, even on our best feelings. I
have seen gross intolerance shewn in support of tolera-
tion; sectarian antipathy most obtrusively displayed in
the promotion of an undistinguishing comprehension of
sects; and acts of cruelty, (I had almost said,) of
treachery, committed in furtherance of an object vitally
important to the cause of humanity; and all this by men
too of naturally kind dispositions and exemplary con-
duct.

The magic rod of fanaticism is preserved in the very
adyta of human nature; and needs only the re-exciting
warmth of a master hand to bud forth afresh and pro-
duce the old fruits. The horror of the peasants' war in
Germany, and the direful effects of the Anabaptists'
tenets, (which differed only from those of Jacobinism
by the substitution of theological for philosophical jar-
gon), struck all Europe for a time with affright. Yet
little more than a century was sufficient to obliterate all
effective memory of these events. The same principles
with similar though less dreadful consequences were
again at work from the imprisonment of the first Charles
to the restoration of his son. The fanatic maxim of ex-
tirpating fanaticism by persecution produced a civil
war. The war ended in the victory of the insurgents;
but the temper survived, and Milton had abundant

grounds for asserting, that "Presbyter was but OLD PRIEST writ large!" One good result, thank heaven! of this zealotry was the re-establishment of the church. And now it might have been hoped, that the mischievous spirit would have been bound for a season, "and a seal set upon him, that he might deceive the nation no more." But no! The ball of persecution was taken up with undiminished vigor by the persecuted. The same fanatic principle that, under the solemn oath and covenant, had turned cathedrals into stables, destroyed the rarest trophies of art and ancestral piety, and hunted the brightest ornaments of learning and religion into holes and corners, now marched under episcopal banners, and, having first crowded the prisons of England, emptied its whole vial of wrath on the miserable Covenanters of Scotland. (*Laing's* History of Scotland.— *Walter Scott's* bards, ballads, &c.) A merciful providence at length constrained both parties to join against a common enemy. A wise government followed; and the established church became, and now is, not only the brightest example, but our best and only sure bulwark, of toleration! the true and indispensable bank against a new inundation of persecuting zeal—ESTO PERPETUA!

A long interval of quiet succeeded; or rather, the exhaustion had produced a cold fit of the ague which was symptomatized by indifference among the many, and a tendency to infidelity or scepticism in the educated classes. At length those feelings of disgust and hatred, which for a brief while the multitude had attached to the crimes and absurdities of sectarian and democratic fanaticism, were transferred to the oppressive privileges of the noblesse, and the luxury, intrigues and favoritism of the continental courts. The same principles, dressed in the ostentatious garb of a fashionable philosophy, once more rose triumphant and effected the French revolution. And have we not within the last three or four years had reason to apprehend, that the detestable maxims and correspondent measures of the late French despotism had already bedimmed the public recollections of democratic phrensy; had drawn off to other objects the electric force of the feelings which had massed and upheld those recollections; and that a favorable concurrence of occasions was alone wanting to awaken the thunder and precipitate the lightning from the opposite quarter of the political heaven?

In part from constitutional indolence, which in the very hey-day of hope had kept my enthusiasm in check, but still more from the habits and influences of a classical education and academic pursuits, scarcely had a year elapsed from the commencement of my literary and political adventures before my mind sank into a state of thorough disgust and despondency, both with regard to the disputes and the parties disputant. With more than *poetic* feeling I exclaimed:

> The sensual and the dark rebel in vain,
> Slaves by their own compulsion! In mad game
> They break their manacles, to wear the *name*
> Of freedom, graven on a heavier chain.
> O liberty! with profitless endeavour
> Have I pursued thee many a weary hour;
> But thou nor swell'st the victor's pomp, nor ever
> Didst breathe thy soul in forms of human power!
> 　　Alike from all, howe'er they praise thee,
> 　　(Nor prayer nor boastful name delays thee)
> 　　From superstition's harpy minions
> 　　And factious blasphemy's obscener slaves,
> 　　Thou speedest on thy cherub pinions,
> The guide of homeless winds and playmate of the waves!
> 　　　　　　　　　　　France, *a Palinodia.*

I retired to a cottage in Somersetshire at the foot of Quantock, and devoted my thoughts and studies to the foundations of religion and morals. Here I found myself all afloat. Doubts rushed in; broke upon me *"from the fountains of the great deep,"* and fell *"from the windows of heaven."* The fontal truths of natural religion and the books of Revelation alike contributed to the flood; and it was long ere my ark touched on an Ararat, and rested. The *idea* of the Supreme Being appeared to me to be as necessarily implied in all particular modes of being as the idea of infinite space in all the geometrical figures by which space is limited. I was pleased with the Cartesian opinion, that the idea of God is distinguished from all other ideas by involving its *reality;* but I was not wholly satisfied. I began then to ask myself, what proof I had of the outward *existence* of anything? Of this sheet of paper for instance, as a thing in itself, separate from the phæ-nomenon or image in my perception. I saw, that in the nature of things such proof is impossible; and that of all modes of being, that are not objects of the senses, the existence is *assumed* by a logical necessity arising from the constitution of the mind itself, by the absence of all motive to doubt it, not from any absolute contradiction in the supposition of the contrary. Still the existence of a being, the ground of all existence, was not yet the existence of a moral creator, and governor. . . .

For a very long time, indeed, I could not reconcile personality with infinity; and my head was with Spin-oza, though my whole heart remained with Paul and John. . . .

Chapter XII

*A chapter of requests and premonitions concerning the pe-
rusal or omission of the chapter that follows.*

In the perusal of philosophical works I have been
greatly benefited by a resolve, which, in the antithetic
form and with the allowed quaintness of an adage or
maxim, I have been accustomed to word thus: *"until you
understand a writer's ignorance, presume yourself igno-
rant of his understanding."* This *golden rule* of mine
does, I own, resemble those of Pythagoras in its obscu-
rity rather than in its depth. If however the reader will
permit me to be my own Hierocles, I trust, that he will
find its meaning fully explained by the following in-
stances. I have now before me a treatise of a religious
fanatic, full of dreams and supernatural *experiences.* I
see clearly the writer's grounds, and their hollowness.
I have a complete insight into the causes, which through
the medium of his body has acted on his mind; and by
application of received and ascertained laws I can sat-
isfactorily explain to my own reason all the strange in-
cidents, which the writer records of himself. And this
I can do without suspecting him of any intentional false-
hood. As when in broad day-light a man tracks the steps
of a traveller, who had lost his way in a fog or by a
treacherous moonshine, even so, and with the same tran-
quil sense of certainty, can I follow the traces of this
bewildered visionary. I UNDERSTAND HIS IGNORANCE.

On the other hand, I have been re-perusing with the
best energies of my mind the *Timæus* of PLATO. What-
ever I comprehend, impresses me with a reverential
sense of the author's genius; but there is a considerable

portion of the work, to which I can attach no consistent meaning. In other treatises of the same philosopher, intended for the average comprehensions of men, I have been delighted with the masterly good sense, with the perspicuity of the language, and the aptness of the inductions. I recollect likewise, that numerous passages in this author, which I thoroughly comprehend, were formerly no less unintelligible to me, than the passages now in question. It would, I am aware, be quite *fashionable* to dismiss them at once as Platonic Jargon. But this I cannot do with satisfaction to my own mind, because I have sought in vain for causes adequate to the solution of the assumed inconsistency. I have no insight into the possibility of a man so eminently wise using words with such half-meanings to himself, as must perforce pass into no-meaning to his readers. When in addition to the motives thus suggested by my own reason, I bring into distinct remembrance the number and the series of great men, who after long and zealous study of these works had joined in honoring the name of PLATO with epithets, that almost transcend humanity, I feel, that a contemptuous verdict on my part might argue want of modesty, but would hardly be received by the judicious, as evidence of superior penetration. Therefore, utterly baffled in all my attempts to understand the ignorance of Plato, I CONCLUDE MYSELF IGNORANT OF HIS UNDERSTANDING.

In lieu of the various requests which the anxiety of authorship addresses to the unknown reader, I advance but this one; that he will either pass over the following chapter altogether, or read the whole connectedly. The fairest part of the most beautiful body will appear deformed and monstrous, if dissevered from its place in the organic Whole. Nay, on delicate subjects, where a seemingly trifling difference of more or less may constitute a difference in *kind*, even a *faithful* display of the main and supporting ideas, if yet they are separated from the forms by which they are at once cloathed and modified, may perchance present a skeleton indeed; but a skeleton to alarm and deter. Though I might find numerous precedents, I shall not desire the reader to strip his mind of all prejudices, or to keep all prior systems out of view during his examination of the present. For in truth, such requests appear to me not much unlike the advice given to hypochondriacal patients in Dr. Buchan's domestic medicine; videlicet, to preserve themselves uniformly tranquil and in good spirits. Till I had discovered the art of destroying the memory *a parte post,* without injury to its future operations, and without detriment to the judgement, I should suppress the request as premature; and therefore, however much I may *wish* to be read with an unprejudiced mind, I do not presume to state it as a necessary condition.

The extent of my daring is to suggest one criterion, by which it may be rationally conjectured before-hand, whether or no a reader would lose his time, and perhaps his temper, in the perusal of this, or any other treatise constructed on similar principles. But it would be cruelly misinterpreted, as implying the least disrespect either for the moral or intellectual qualities of the individuals thereby precluded. The criterion is this: if a man receives as fundamental facts, and therefore of course indemonstrable and incapable of further analysis, the general notions of matter, spirit, soul, body, action, passiveness, time, space, cause, and effect, consciousness, perception, memory and habit; if he feels his mind completely at rest concerning all these, and is satisfied, if only he can analyse all other notions into some one or more of these supposed elements with plausible subordination and apt arrangement: to such a mind I would

as courteously as possible convey the hint, that for him
the chapter was not written.

Vir bonus es, doctus, prudens; ast haud tibi spiro.

For these terms do in truth *include* all the difficulties,
which the human mind can propose for solution. Taking
them therefore in mass, and unexamined, it requires
only a decent apprenticeship in logic, to draw forth their
contents in all forms and colours, as the professors of
legerdemain at our village fairs pull out ribbon after
ribbon from their mouths. And not more difficult is it to
reduce them back again to their different genera. But
though this analysis is highly useful in rendering our
knowledge more distinct, it does not really add to it. It
does not increase, though it gives us a greater mastery
over, the wealth which we before possessed. For forensic
purposes, for all the established professions of society,
this is sufficient. But for philosophy in its highest sense
as the science of ultimate truths, and therefore scientia
scientiarum, this mere analysis of terms is preparative
only, though as a preparative discipline indispensable.

Still less dare a favorable perusal be anticipated from
the proselytes of that compendious philosophy, which
talking of mind but thinking of brick and mortar, or
other images equally abstracted from body, contrives a
theory of spirit by nicknaming matter, and in a few hours
can qualify its dullest disciples to explain the omne
scibile by reducing all things to impressions, ideas, and
sensations.

But it is time to tell the truth; though it requires some
courage to avow it in an age and country, in which dis-
quisitions on all subjects, not privileged to adopt tech-
nical terms or scientific symbols, must be addressed to
the PUBLIC. I say then, that it is neither possible or neces-

sary for all men, or for many, to be PHILOSOPHERS. There
is a *philosophic* (and inasmuch as it is actualized by an
effort of freedom, an *artificial*) *consciousness*, which lies
beneath or (as it were) *behind* the spontaneous con-
sciousness natural to all reflecting beings. As the elder
Romans distinguished their northern provinces into Cis-
Alpine and Trans-Alpine, so may we divide all the ob-
jects of human knowledge into those on this side, and
those on the other side of the spontaneous consciousness;
citra et trans conscientiam communem. The latter is
exclusively the domain of PURE philosophy, which is
therefore properly entitled transcendental, in order to
discriminate it at once, both from mere reflection and
re-presentation on the one hand, and on the other from
those flights of lawless speculation which, abandoned by
all distinct consciousness, because transgressing the
bounds and purposes of our intellectual faculties, are
justly condemned, as *transcendent.* The first range of
hills, that encircles the scanty vale of human life, is the
horizon for the majority of its inhabitants. On *its* ridges
the common sun is born and departs. From *them* the
stars rise, and touching *them* they vanish. By the many,
even this range, the natural limit and bulwark of the
vale, is but imperfectly known. Its higher ascents are too
often hidden by mists and clouds from uncultivated
swamps, which few have courage or curiosity to pene-
trate. To the multitude below these vapors appear, now
as the dark haunts of terrific agents, on which none may
intrude with impunity; and now all *a-glow,* with colors
not their own, they are gazed at as the splendid palaces
of happiness and power. But in all ages there have been
a few, who measuring and sounding the rivers of the
vale at the feet of their furthest inaccessible falls have
learned, that the sources must be far higher and far in-
ward; a few, who even in the level streams have detected

elements, which neither the vale itself or the surround-
ing mountains contained or could supply. How and
whence to these thoughts, these strong probabilities, the
ascertaining vision, the intuitive knowledge may finally
supervene, can be learnt only by the fact. I might oppose
to the question the words with which[1] Plotinus supposes
NATURE to answer a similar difficulty. "Should any one
interrogate her, how she works, if graciously she vouch-
safe to listen and speak, she will reply, it behoves thee
not to disquiet me with interrogatories, but to under-
stand in silence even as I am silent, and work without
words."

Likewise in the fifth book of the fifth *Ennead,* speak-
ing of the highest and intuitive knowledge as distin-
guished from the discursive, or in the language of
Wordsworth,

The vision and the faculty divine;

he says: "it is not lawful to enquire from whence it
sprang, as if it were a thing subject to place and motion,

[1] *Ennead,* III, l. 8, c. 3. The force of the Greek συνιέναι
is imperfectly expressed by "understand;" our own idiomatic
phrase *"to go along with me"* comes nearest to it. The pas-
sage, that follows, full of profound sense, appears to me
evidently corrupt; and in fact no writer more wants, better de-
serves, or is less likely to obtain, a new and more correct edi-
tion—τί οὖν συνιέναι; ὅτι τὸ γενόμενόν ἐστι θέαμα ἐμόν, σιώπησις
(*mallem,* θέαμα, ἐμοῦ σιωπώσης), καὶ φύσει γενόμενον θεώρημα,
καί μοι γενομένη ἐκ θεωρίας τῆς ὡδὶ τὴν φύσιν ἔχειν φιλοθεάμονα
ὑπάρχει. (*mallem,* καὶ μοὶ ἡ γενομένη ἐκ θεωρίας αὐτῆς ὡδὶς)
"what then are we to understand? That whatever is produced
is an intuition, I silent; and that, which is thus generated,
is by its nature a theorem, or form of contemplation; and
the birth, which results to me from this contemplation, at-
tains to have a contemplative nature." So Synesius: Ὠδὶς
ἱερά, Ἄρρητα γονά. The after comparison of the process of
the natura naturans with that of the geometrician is drawn
from the very heart of philosophy.—S. T. C.

for it neither approached hither, nor again departs from hence to some other place; but it either appears to us or it does not appear. So that we ought not to pursue it with a view of detecting its secret source, but to watch in quiet till it suddenly shines upon us; preparing ourselves for the blessed spectacle as the eye waits patiently for the rising sun." They and they only can acquire the philosophic imagination, the sacred power of self-intuition, who within themselves can interpret and understand the symbol, that the wings of the air-sylph are forming within the skin of the caterpillar; those only, who feel in their own spirits the same instinct, which impels the chrysalis of the horned fly to leave room in its involucrum for antennæ yet to come. They know and feel, that the *potential* works *in* them, even as the *actual* works on them! In short, all the organs of sense are framed for a corresponding world of sense; and we have it. All the organs of spirit are framed for a correspondent world of spirit: though the latter organs are not developed in all alike. But they exist in all, and their first appearance discloses itself in the *moral* being. How else could it be, that even worldlings, not wholly debased, will contemplate the man of simple and disinterested goodness with contradictory feelings of pity and respect? "Poor man! he is not made for *this* world." Oh! herein they utter a prophecy of universal fulfilment; for man *must* either rise or sink.

It is the essential mark of the true philosopher to rest satisfied with no imperfect light, as long as the impossibility of attaining a fuller knowledge has not been demonstrated. That the common consciousness itself will furnish proofs by its own direction, that it is connected with master-currents below the surface, I shall merely assume as a postulate pro tempore. This having been granted, though but in expectation of the argument, I can safely deduce from it the equal truth of my former assertion, that philosophy cannot be intelligible to all, even of the most learned and cultivated classes. A system, the first principle of which it is to render the mind intuitive of the *spiritual* in man (i. e. of that which lies *on the other side* of our natural consciousness) must needs have a greater obscurity for those, who have never disciplined and strengthened this ulterior consciousness. It must in truth be a land of darkness, a perfect *Anti-Goshen*, for men to whom the noblest treasures of their own being are reported only through the imperfect translation of lifeless and sightless *notions*. Perhaps, in great part, through words which are but the shadows of notions; even as the notional understanding itself is but the shadowy abstraction of living and actual truth. On the IMMEDIATE, which dwells in every man, and on the original intuition, or absolute affirmation of it, (which is likewise in every man, but does not in every man rise into consciousness) all the *certainty* of our knowledge depends; and this becomes intelligible to no man by the ministry of mere words from without. The medium, by which spirits understand each other, is not the surrounding air; but the *freedom* which they possess in common, as the common ethereal element of their being, the tremulous reciprocations of which propagate themselves even to the inmost of the soul. Where the spirit of a man is not *filled* with the consciousness of freedom (were it only from its restlessness, as of one still struggling in bondage) all spiritual intercourse is interrupted, not only with others, but even with himself. No wonder then, that he remains incomprehensible to himself as well as to others. No wonder, that, in the fearful desert of his consciousness, he wearies himself out with empty words, to which no friendly echo answers, either from his own heart, or the heart of a fellow being; or bewilders himself in the pursuit of *notional* phantoms, the mere refractions from unseen and distant truths through the distorting medium of his own unenlivened and stagnant understanding! To remain unintelligible to such a mind, exclaims Schelling on a like occasion, is honor and a good name before God and man. . . .

To an Esquimaux or New Zealander our most popular philosophy would be wholly unintelligible. The sense, the inward organ for it, is not yet born in him. So is there many a one among us, yes, and some who think themselves philosophers too, to whom the philosophic organ is entirely wanting. To such a man philosophy is a mere play of words and notions, like a theory of music to the deaf, or like the geometry of light to the blind. The connection of the parts and their logical dependencies may be seen and remembered; but the whole is groundless and hollow, unsustained by living contact, unaccompanied with any realizing intuition which exists by and in the act that affirms its existence, which is known, because it is, and is, because it is known. The words of Plotinus, in the assumed person of nature, holds true of the philosophic energy. Τὸ θεωροῦν μου θεώρημα ποιεῖ, ὥσπερ οἱ γεωμέτραι θεωροῦντες γράφουσιν· ἀλλ' ἐμοῦ μὴ γραφούσης, θεωρούσης δὲ, ὑφίστανται αἱ τῶν σωμάτων γραμμαί. With me the act of contemplation makes the thing contemplated, as the geometricians contemplating describe lines correspondent; but I not describing lines, but simply contemplating, the representative forms of things rise up into existence.

The postulate of philosophy and at the same time the test of philosophic capacity, is no other than the heaven-descended KNOW THYSELF! (*E cœlo descendit*, Γνῶθι σεαυτόν.) And this at once practically and speculatively.

For as philosophy is neither a science of the reason or understanding only, nor merely a science of morals, but the science of BEING altogether, its primary ground can be neither merely speculative or merely practical, but both in one. All knowledge rests on the coincidence of an object with a subject. . . .

If it be said, that this is Idealism, let it be remembered that it is only so far idealism, as it is at the same time, and on that very account, the truest and most binding realism. For wherein does the realism of mankind properly consist? In the assertion that there exists a something without them, what, or how, or where they know not, which occasions the objects of their perception? Oh no! This is neither connatural or universal. It is what a few have taught and learned in the schools, and which the many repeat without asking themselves concerning their own meaning. The realism common to all mankind is far elder and lies infinitely deeper than this hypothetical explanation of the origin of our perceptions, an explanation skimmed from the mere surface of mechanical philosophy. It is the table itself, which the man of common sense believes himself to see, not the phantom of a table, from which he may argumentatively deduce the reality of a table, which he does not see. If to destroy the reality of all, that we actually behold, be idealism, what can be more egregiously so, than the system of modern metaphysics, which banishes us to a land of shadows, surrounds us with apparitions, and distinguishes truth from illusion only by the majority of those who dream the same dream? "*I* asserted that the world was mad," exclaimed poor Lee, "and the world said, that I was mad, and confound them, they outvoted me."

It is to the true and original realism, that I would direct the attention. This believes and requires neither more nor less, than the object which it beholds or presents to itself, is the real and very object. In this sense, however much we may strive against it, we are all collectively born idealists, and therefore and only therefore are we at the same time realists. But of this the philosophers of the schools know nothing, or despise the faith as the prejudice of the ignorant vulgar, because they live and move in a crowd of phrases and notions from which human nature has long ago vanished. Oh, ye that reverence yourselves, and walk humbly with the divinity in your own hearts, ye are worthy of a better philosophy! Let the dead bury the dead, but do you preserve your human nature, the depth of which was never yet fathomed by a philosophy made up of notions and mere logical entities.

In the third treatise of my *Logosophia,* announced at the end of this volume, I shall give (deo volente) the demonstrations and contructions of the Dynamic Philosophy scientifically arranged. It is, according to my conviction, no other than the system of Pythagoras and of Plato revived and purified from impure mixtures. . . .

I shall now proceed to the nature and genesis of the imagination; but I must first take leave to notice, that after a more accurate perusal of Mr. Wordsworth's remarks on the imagination, in his preface to the new edition of his poems, I find that my conclusions are not so consentient with his as, I confess, I had taken for granted. In an article contributed by me to Mr. Southey's Omniana, on the soul and its organs of sense, are the following sentences. "These (the human faculties) I would arrange under the different senses and powers: as the eye, the ear, the touch, &c.; the imitative power, voluntary and automatic; the imagination, or shaping and modifying power; the fancy, or the aggregative and asso-

ciative power; the understanding, or the regulative, sub-
stantiating and realizing power; the speculative reason,
vis theoretica et scientifica, or the power by which we
produce or aim to produce unity, necessity, and uni-
versality in all our knowledge by means of principles
a priori;[1] the will, or practical reason; the faculty of
choice (*Germanice,* Willkür) and (distinct both from the
moral will and the choice,) the *sensation* of volition,
which I have found reason to include under the head of
single and double touch." To this, as far as it relates to
the subject in question, namely the words (*the aggrega-
tive and associative power*) Mr. Wordsworth's "only ob-
jection is that the definition is too general. To aggregate
and to associate, to evoke and to combine, belong as well
to the imagination as to the fancy." I reply, that if, by
the power of evoking and combining, Mr. Wordsworth
means the same as, and no more than, I meant by the
aggregative and associative, I continue to deny, that it
belongs at all to the imagination; and I am disposed to
conjecture, that he has mistaken the co-presence of fancy
with imagination for the operation of the latter singly. A
man may work with two very different tools at the same
moment; each has its share in the work, but the work
effected by each is distinct and different. But it will prob-

[1] This phrase, *a priori,* is in common, most grossly misun-
derstood, and an absurdity burdened on it, which it does not
deserve. By knowledge, *a priori,* we do not mean, that we
can know anything previously to experience, which would
be a contradiction in terms; but that having once known it
by occasion of experience (that is, something acting upon us
from without) we then know, that it must have pre-existed,
or the experience itself would have been impossible. By ex-
perience only I know, that I have eyes; but then my reason
convinces me, that I must have had eyes in order to the
experience.—S. T. C.

ably appear in the next Chapter, that deeming it neces-
sary to go back much further than Mr. Wordsworth's
subject required or permitted, I have attached a mean-
ing to both fancy and imagination, which he had not in
view, at least while he was writing that preface. He will
judge. Would to Heaven, I might meet with many such
readers. I will conclude with the words of Bishop Jeremy
Taylor: "he to whom all things are one, who draweth all
things to one, and seeth all things in one, may enjoy true
peace and rest of spirit." (*J. Taylor's* VIA PACIS.)

Chapter XIII

On the imagination, or esemplastic power.

O Adam, One Almighty is, from whom
All things proceed, and up to him return,
If not depraved from good: created all
Such to perfection, one first nature all,
Indued with various forms, various degrees
Of substance, and, in things that live, of life;
But more refin'd, more spirituous and pure,
As nearer to him plac'd, or nearer tending,
Each in their several active spheres assign'd,
Till body up to spirit work, in bounds
Proportion'd to each kind. So from the root
Springs lighter the green stalk, from thence the leaves
More airy: last the bright consummate flower
Spirits odorous breathes. Flowers and their fruit,
Man's nourishment, by gradual scale sublim'd,
To *vital* spirits aspire: to *animal:*
To *intellectual!*—give both life and sense,
Fancy and understanding; whence the soul

REASON receives, and reason is her *being*,
Discursive or intuitive.

Paradise Lost, Book v.

. . . Now the transcendental philosophy demands; first,
that two forces should be conceived which counteract
each other by their essential nature; not only not in
consequence of the accidental direction of each, but as
prior to all direction, nay, as the primary forces from
which the conditions of all possible directions are de-
rivative and deducible: secondly, that these forces
should be assumed to be both alike infinite, both alike
indestructible. The problem will then be to discover the
result or product of two such forces, as distinguished
from the result of those forces which are finite, and de-
rive their difference solely from the circumstance of
their direction. When we have formed a scheme or out-
line of these two different kinds of force, and of their
different results by the process of discursive reasoning,
it will then remain for us to elevate the Thesis from no-
tional to actual, by contemplating intuitively this one
power with its two inherent indestructible yet counter-
acting forces, and the results or generations to which
their inter-penetration gives existence, in the living
principle and in the process of our own self-conscious-
ness. By what instrument this is possible the solution
itself will discover, at the same time that it will reveal
to and for whom it is possible. Non omnia possumus
omnes. There is a philosophic no less than a poetic gen-
ius, which is differenced from the highest perfection of
talent, not by degree but by kind.

The counteraction then of the two assumed forces
does not depend on their meeting from opposite direc-
tions; the power which acts in them is indestructible; it

is therefore inexhaustibly re-ebullient; and as something must be the result of these two forces, both alike infinite, and both alike indestructible; and as rest or neutralization cannot be this result; no other conception is possible, but that the product must be a tertium aliquid, or finite generation. Consequently this conception is necessary. Now this tertium aliquid can be no other than an inter-penetration of the counteracting powers, partaking of both. . . .

The IMAGINATION then, I consider either as primary, or secondary. The primary IMAGINATION I hold to be the living Power and prime Agent of all human Perception, and as a repetition in the finite mind of the eternal act of creation in the infinite I AM. The secondary Imagination I consider as an echo of the former, co-existing with the conscious will, yet still as identical with the primary in the *kind* of its agency, and differing only in *degree*, and in the *mode* of its operation. It dissolves, diffuses, dissipates, in order to re-create; or where this process is rendered impossible, yet still at all events it struggles to idealize and to unify. It is essentially *vital*, even as all objects (*as* objects) are essentially fixed and dead.

FANCY, on the contrary, has no other counters to play with, but fixities and definites. The Fancy is indeed no other than a mode of Memory emancipated from the order of time and space; while it is blended with, and modified by that empirical phenomenon of the will, which we express by the word CHOICE. But equally with the ordinary memory the Fancy must receive all its materials ready made from the law of association. . . .

Chapter XIV

Occasion of the Lyrical Ballads, *and the objects originally proposed—Preface to the second edition—The ensuing controversy, its causes and acrimony—Philosophic definitions of a poem and poetry with scholia.*

During the first year that Mr. Wordsworth and I were neighbours, our conversations turned frequently on the two cardinal points of poetry, the power of exciting the sympathy of the reader by a faithful adherence to the truth of nature, and the power of giving the interest of novelty by the modifying colors of imagination. The sudden charm, which accidents of light and shade, which moon-light or sun-set diffused over a known and familiar landscape, appeared to represent the practicability of combining both. These are the poetry of nature. The thought suggested itself (to which of us I do not recollect) that a series of poems might be composed of two sorts. In the one, the incidents and agents were to be, in part at least, supernatural; and the excellence aimed at was to consist in the interesting of the affections by the dramatic truth of such emotions, as would naturally accompany such situations, supposing them real. And real in *this* sense they have been to every human being who, from whatever source of delusion, has at any time believed himself under supernatural agency. For the second class, subjects were to be chosen from ordinary life; the characters and incidents were to be such, as will be found in every village and its vicinity, where there is a meditative and feeling mind to seek after them, or to notice them, when they present themselves.

In this idea originated the plan of the *Lyrical Ballads;*

in which it was agreed, that my endeavours should be directed to persons and characters supernatural, or at least romantic; yet so as to transfer from our inward nature a human interest and a semblance of truth sufficient to procure for these shadows of imagination that willing suspension of disbelief for the moment, which constitutes poetic faith. Mr. Wordsworth, on the other hand, was to propose to himself as his object, to give the charm of novelty to things of every day, and to excite a feeling analogous to the supernatural, by awakening the mind's attention from the lethargy of custom, and directing it to the loveliness and the wonders of the world before us; an inexhaustible treasure, but for which, in consequence of the film of familiarity and selfish solicitude we have eyes, yet see not, ears that hear not, and hearts that neither feel nor understand.

With this view I wrote "The Ancient Mariner," and was preparing among other poems, "The Dark Ladie," and the "Christabel," in which I should have more nearly realized my ideal, than I had done in my first attempt. But Mr. Wordsworth's industry had proved so much more successful, and the number of his poems so much greater, that my compositions, instead of forming a balance, appeared rather an interpolation of heterogeneous matter. Mr. Wordsworth added two or three poems written in his own character, in the impassioned, lofty, and sustained diction, which is characteristic of his genius. In this form the *Lyrical Ballads* were published; and were presented by him, as an *experiment,* whether subjects, which from their nature rejected the usual ornaments and extra-colloquial style of poems in general, might not be so managed in the language of ordinary life as to produce the pleasureable interest, which it is the peculiar business of poetry to impart. To the second edition he added a preface of considerable length; in which, notwithstanding some passages of apparently a contrary import, he was understood to contend for the extension of this style to poetry of all kinds, and to reject as vicious and indefensible all phrases and forms of style that were not included in what he (unfortunately, I think, adopting an equivocal expression) called the language of *real* life. From this preface, prefixed to poems in which it was impossible to deny the presence of original genius, however mistaken its direction might be deemed, arose the whole long-continued controversy. For from the conjunction of perceived power with supposed heresy I explain the inveteracy and in some instances, I grieve to say, the acrimonious passions, with which the controversy has been conducted by the assailants.

Had Mr. Wordsworth's poems been the silly, the childish things, which they were for a long time described as being; had they been really distinguished from the compositions of other poets merely by meanness of language and inanity of thought; had they indeed contained nothing more than what is found in the parodies and pretended imitations of them; they must have sunk at once, a dead weight, into the slough of oblivion, and have dragged the preface along with them. But year after year increased the number of Mr. Wordsworth's admirers. They were found too not in the lower classes of the reading public, but chiefly among young men of strong sensibility and meditative minds; and their admiration (inflamed perhaps in some degree by opposition) was distinguished by its intensity, I might almost say, by its *religious* fervor. These facts, and the intellectual energy of the author, which was more or less consciously felt, where it was outwardly and even boisterously denied, meeting with sentiments of aversion to his opinions, and of alarm at their consequences, produced an eddy of criticism, which would of itself have borne up the poems by the violence, with which it whirled them round and round. With many parts of this preface, in the sense attributed to them, and which the words undoubtedly seem to authorize, I never concurred; but on the contrary objected to them as erroneous in principle, and as contradictory (in appearance at least) both to other parts of the same preface, and to the author's own practice in the greater number of the poems themselves. Mr. Wordsworth in his recent collection has, I find, degraded this prefatory disquisition to the end of his second volume, to be read or not at the reader's choice. But he has not, as far as I can discover, announced any change in his poetic creed. At all events, considering it as the source of a controversy, in which I have been honored more than I deserve by the frequent conjunction of my name with his, I think it expedient to declare once for all, in what points I coincide with his opinions, and in what points I altogether differ. But in order to render myself intelligible I must previously, in as few words as possible, explain my ideas, first, of a POEM; and secondly, of POETRY itself, in *kind,* and in *essence.*

The office of philosophical *disquisition* consists in just *distinction;* while it is the privilege of the philosopher to preserve himself constantly aware, that distinction is not division. In order to obtain adequate notions of any truth, we must intellectually separate its distinguishable parts; and this is the technical *process* of philosophy. But having so done, we must then restore them in our conceptions to the unity, in which they actually co-exist; and this is the *result* of philosophy. A poem contains the same elements as a prose composition; the difference therefore must consist in a different combination of them, in consequence of a different object being proposed. According to the difference of the object will be the difference of the combination. It is possible, that the object may be merely to facilitate the recollection of any given facts or observations by artificial arrangement; and the composition will be a poem, merely because it is distinguished from prose by metre, or by rhyme, or by both conjointly. In this, the lowest sense, a man might attribute the name of a poem to the well-known enumeration of the days in the several months;

> Thirty days hath September,
> April, June, and November, &c.

and others of the same class and purpose. And as a particular pleasure is found in anticipating the recurrence of sounds and quantities, all compositions that have this charm super-added, whatever be their contents, *may* be entitled poems.

So much for the superficial *form*. A difference of object and contents supplies an additional ground of distinction. The immediate purpose may be the communication of truths; either of truth absolute and demonstrable, as in works of science; or of facts experienced and recorded, as in history. Pleasure, and that of the highest and most permanent kind, may *result* from the *attainment* of the end; but it is not itself the immediate end. In other works the communication of pleasure may be the immediate purpose; and though truth, either moral or intellectual, ought to be the *ultimate* end, yet this will distinguish the character of the author, not the class to which the work belongs. Blest indeed is that state of society, in which the immediate purpose would be baffled by the perversion of the proper ultimate end; in which no charm of diction or imagery could exempt the Bathyllus even of an Anacreon, or the Alexis of Virgil, from disgust and aversion!

But the communication of pleasure may be the immediate object of a work not metrically composed; and that object may have been in a high degree attained, as in novels and romances. Would then the mere superaddition of metre, with or without rhyme, entitle *these* to the name of poems? The answer is, that nothing can permanently please, which does not contain in itself the reason why it is so, and not otherwise. If metre be superadded, all other parts must be made consonant with it. They must be such, as to justify the perpetual and distinct attention to each part, which an exact correspondent recurrence of accent and sound are calculated to excite. The final definition then, so deduced, may be thus worded. A poem is that species of composition, which is opposed to works of science, by proposing for its *immediate* object pleasure, not truth; and from all other species (having *this* object in common with it) it is discriminated by proposing to itself such delight from the *whole*, as is compatible with a distinct gratification from each component *part*.

Controversy is not seldom excited in consequence of the disputants attaching each a different meaning to the same word; and in few instances has this been more striking, than in disputes concerning the present subject. If a man chooses to call every composition a poem, which is rhyme, or measure, or both, I must leave his opinion uncontroverted. The distinction is at least competent to characterize the writer's intention. If it were subjoined, that the whole is likewise entertaining or affecting, as a tale, or as a series of interesting reflections, I of course admit this as another fit ingredient of a poem, and an additional merit. But if the definition sought for be that of a *legitimate* poem, I answer, it must be one, the parts of which mutually support and explain each other; all in their proportion harmonizing with, and supporting the purpose and known influences of metrical arrangement. The philosophic critics of all ages coincide with the ultimate judgement of all countries, in equally denying the praises of a just poem, on the one hand, to a series of striking lines or distiches, each of which, absorbing the whole attention of the reader to itself, disjoins it from its context, and makes it a separate whole, instead of an harmonizing part; and on the other hand, to an unsustained composition, from which the reader collects rapidly the general result, unattracted by the component parts. The reader should be carried forward, not merely or chiefly by the mechanical impulse of curiosity, or by a restless desire to arrive at the final solution; but by the pleasureable activity of mind excited by the attractions of the journey itself. Like the motion of a serpent, which the Egyptians made the emblem of intellectual power; or like the path of sound through the air; at every step he pauses and half recedes, and from the retrogressive movement collects the force which again carries him onward. "Præcipitandus est *liber* spiritus," says Petronius Arbiter most happily. The epithet, *liber*, here balances the preceding verb; and it is not easy to conceive more meaning condensed in fewer words.

But if this should be admitted as a satisfactory character of a poem, we have still to seek for a definition of poetry. The writings of PLATO, and Bishop TAYLOR, and the *Theoria Sacra* of BURNET, furnish undeniable proofs that poetry of the highest kind may exist without metre, and even without the contra-distinguishing objects of a poem. The first chapter of Isaiah (indeed a very large portion of the whole book) is poetry in the most emphatic sense; yet it would be not less irrational than strange to assert, that pleasure, and not truth, was the immediate object of the prophet. In short, whatever *specific* import we attach to the word, poetry, there will be found involed in it, as a necessary consequence, that a poem of any length neither can be, or ought to be, all poetry. Yet if an harmonious whole is to be produced, the remaining parts must be preserved *in keeping* with the poetry; and this can be no otherwise effected than by such a studïed selection and artificial arrangement, as will partake of *one*, though not *peculiar* property of poetry. And this again can be no other than the property of exciting a more continuous and equal attention than the language of prose aims at, whether colloquial or written.

My own conclusions on the nature of poetry, in the strictest use of the word, have been in part anticipated in the preceding disquisition on the fancy and imagination. What is poetry? is so nearly the same question with, what is a poet? that the answer to the one is involved in the solution of the other. For it is a distinction resulting from the poetic genius itself, which sustains and modifies the images, thoughts, and emotions of the poet's own mind.

The poet, described in *ideal* perfection, brings the whole soul of man into activity, with the subordination of its faculties to each other, according to their relative worth and dignity. He diffuses a tone and spirit of unity, that blends, and (as it were) *fuses*, each into each, by that synthetic and magical power, to which we have exclusively appropriated the name of imagination. This power, first put in action by the will and understanding, and retained under their irremissive, though gentle and unnoticed, controul (*laxis effertur habenis*) reveals itself in the balance or reconciliation of opposite or discordant qualities: of sameness, with difference; of the general, with the concrete; the idea, with the image; the individual, with the representative; the sense of novelty and freshness, with old and familiar objects; a more than usual state of emotion, with more than usual order;

judgement ever awake and steady self-possession, with
enthusiasm and feeling profound or vehement; and
while it blends and harmonizes the natural and the
artificial, still subordinates art to nature; the manner to
the matter; and our admiration of the poet to our sym-
pathy with the poetry. "Doubtless," as Sir John Davies
observes of the soul (and his words may with slight
alteration be applied, and even more appropriately, to
the poetic IMAGINATION),

> Doubtless this could not be, but that she turns
>   Bodies to spirit by sublimation strange,
> As fire converts to fire the things it burns,
>   As we our food into our nature change.
>
> From their gross matter she abstracts their forms,
>   And draws a kind of quintessence from things;
> Which to her proper nature she transforms,
>   To bear them light on her celestial wings.
>
> Thus does she, when from individual states
>   She doth abstract the universal kinds;
> Which then re-clothed in divers names and fates
>   Steal access through our senses to our minds.

Finally, GOOD SENSE is the BODY of poetic genius,
FANCY its DRAPERY, MOTION its LIFE, and IMAGINATION
the SOUL that is everywhere, and in each; and forms all
into one graceful and intelligent whole.

Chapter XV

*The specific symptoms of poetic power elucidated in a criti-
cal analysis of Shakespeare's* Venus and Adonis, *and* Lucrece.

In the application of these principles to purposes of
practical criticism as employed in the appraisal of works

more or less imperfect, I have endeavoured to discover what the qualities in a poem are, which may be deemed promises and specific symptoms of poetic power, as distinguished from general talent determined to poetic composition by accidental motives, by an act of the will, rather than by the inspiration of a genial and productive nature. In this investigation, I could not, I thought, do better, than keep before me the earliest work of the greatest genius, that perhaps human nature has yet produced, our *myriad-minded* [1] Shakespeare. I mean the *Venus and Adonis*, and the *Lucrece;* works which give at once strong promises of the strength, and yet obvious proofs of the immaturity, of his genius. From these I abstracted the following marks, as characteristics of original poetic genius in general.

1. In the *Venus and Adonis*, the first and most obvious excellence is the perfect sweetness of the versification; its adaptation to the subject; and the power displayed in varying the march of the words without passing into a loftier and more majestic rhythm than was demanded by the thoughts, or permitted by the propriety of preserving a sense of melody predominant. The delight in richness and sweetness of sound, even to a faulty excess, if it be evidently original, and not the result of an easily imitable mechanism, I regard as a highly favourable promise in the compositions of a young man. "The man that hath not music in his soul" can indeed never be a genuine poet. Imagery (even taken from nature, much more when transplanted from books, as travels, voyages, and works of natural history); af-

---

[1] Ανὴρ μυριόνους, a phrase which I have borrowed from a Greek monk, who applies it to a Patriarch of Constantinople. I might have said, that I have *reclaimed*, rather than borrowed it: for it seems to belong to Shakespeare, "de jure singulari, et ex privilegio naturæ."—*S. T. C.*

fecting incidents; just thoughts; interesting personal or
domestic feelings; and with these the art of their com-
bination or intertexture in the form of a poem; may all
by incessant effort be acquired as a trade, by a man of
talents and much reading, who, as I once before ob-
served, has mistaken an intense desire of poetic reputa-
tion for a natural poetic genius; the love of the arbitrary
end for a possession of the peculiar means. But the sense
of musical delight, with the power of producing it, is a
gift of imagination; and this together with the power of
reducing multitude into unity of effect, and modifying a
series of thoughts by some one predominant thought or
feeling, may be cultivated and improved, but can never
be learned. It is in these that "poeta nascitur non fit."

2. A second promise of genius is the choice of subjects
very remote from the private interests and circumstances
of the writer himself. At least I have found, that where
the subject is taken immediately from the author's per-
sonal sensations and experiences, the excellence of a
particular poem is but an equivocal mark, and often a
fallacious pledge, of genuine poetic power. We may
perhaps remember the tale of the statuary, who had
acquired considerable reputation for the legs of his god-
desses, though the rest of the statue accorded but indif-
ferently with ideal beauty; till his wife, elated by her
husband's praises, modestly acknowledged that she her-
self had been his constant model. In the *Venus and
Adonis* this proof of poetic power exists even to excess.
It is throughout as if a superior spirit more intuitive,
more intimately conscious, even than the characters
themselves, not only of every outward look and act, but
of the flux and reflux of the mind in all its subtlest
thoughts and feelings, were placing the whole before our
view; himself meanwhile unparticipating in the passions,
and actuated only by that pleasureable excitement,

which had resulted from the energetic fervor of his own spirit in so vividly exhibiting, what it had so accurately and profoundly contemplated. I think, I should have conjectured from these poems, that even then the great instinct, which impelled the poet to the drama, was secretly working in him, prompting him by a series and never broken chain of imagery, always vivid and, because unbroken, often minute; by the highest effort of the picturesque in words, of which words are capable, higher perhaps than was ever realized by any other poet, even Dante not excepted; to provide a substitute for that visual language, that constant intervention and running comment by tone, look and gesture, which in his dramatic works he was entitled to expect from the players. His Venus and Adonis seem at once the characters themselves, and the whole representation of those characters by the most consummate actors. You seem to be told nothing, but to see and hear everything. Hence it is, that from the perpetual activity of attention required on the part of the reader; from the rapid flow, the quick change, and the playful nature of the thoughts and images; and above all from the alienation, and, if I may hazard such an expression, the utter *aloofness* of the poet's own feelings, from those of which he is at once the painter and the analyst; that though the very subject cannot but detract from the pleasure of a delicate mind, yet never was poem less dangerous on a moral account. Instead of doing as Ariosto, and as, still more offensively, Wieland has done, instead of degrading and deforming passion into appetite, the trials of love into the struggles of concupiscence; Shakespeare has here represented the animal impulse itself, so as to preclude all sympathy with it, by dissipating the reader's notice among the thousand outward images, and now beautiful, now fanciful circumstances, which form its dresses and its scenery; or by

diverting our attention from the main subject by those
frequent witty or profound reflections, which the poet's
ever active mind has deduced from, or connected with,
the imagery and the incidents. The reader is forced into
too much action to sympathize with the merely passive
of our nature. As little can a mind thus roused and
awakened be brooded on by mean and indistinct emo-
tion, as the low, lazy mist can creep upon the surface
of a lake, while a strong gale is driving it onward in
waves and billows.

3. It has been before observed that images, however
beautiful, though faithfully copied from nature, and as
accurately represented in words, do not of themselves
characterize the poet. They become proofs of original
genius only as far as they are modified by a predominant
passion; or by associated thoughts or images awakened
by that passion; or when they have the effect of reduc-
ing multitude to unity, or succession to an instant; or
lastly, when a human and intellectual life is transferred
to them from the poet's own spirit,

> Which shoots its being through earth, sea, and air.

In the two following lines for instance, there is noth-
ing objectionable, nothing which would preclude them
from forming, in their proper place, part of a descriptive
poem:

> Behold yon row of pines, that shorn and bow'd
> Bend from the sea-blast, seen at twilight eve.

But with a small alteration of rhythm, the same words
would be equally in their place in a book of topography,
or in a descriptive tour. The same image will rise into
semblance of poetry if thus conveyed:

> Yon row of bleak and visionary pines,
> By twilight glimpse discerned, mark! how they flee

From the fierce sea-blast, all their tresses wild
Streaming before them.

I have given this as an illustration, by no means as an instance, of that particular excellence which I had in view, and in which Shakespeare even in his earliest, as in his latest, works surpasses all other poets. It is by this, that he still gives a dignity and a passion to the objects which he presents. Unaided by any previous excitement, they burst upon us at once in life and in power.

Full many a glorious morning have I seen
Flatter the mountain tops with sovereign eye.
                                        Sonnet 33.

Not mine own fears, nor the prophetic soul
Of the wide world dreaming on things to come—

.   .   .   .

.   .   .   .

The mortal moon hath her eclipse endur'd,
And the sad augurs mock their own presage;
Incertainties now crown themselves assur'd,
And Peace proclaims olives of endless age.
Now with the drops of this most balmy time
My Love looks fresh, and DEATH to me subscribes!
Since spite of him, I'll live in this poor rhyme,
While he insults o'er dull and speechless tribes.
And thou in this shalt find thy monument,
When tyrants' crests, and tombs of brass are spent.
                                        Sonnet 107.

As of higher worth, so doubtless still more characteristic of poetic genius does the imagery become, when it moulds and colors itself to the circumstances, passion, or character, present and foremost in the mind. For unrivalled instances of this excellence, the reader's own memory will refer him to the LEAR, OTHELLO, in short to which not of the *"great, ever living, dead man's"* dramatic works? "Inopem me copia fecit." How true it is to nature, he has himself finely expressed in the instance of love in Sonnet 98.

From you have I been absent in the spring,
When proud pied April drest in all its trim
Hath put a spirit of youth in every thing,
That heavy Saturn laugh'd and leap'd with him.
Yet nor the lays of birds, nor the sweet smell
Of different flowers in odour and in hue,
Could make me any summer's story tell,
Or from their proud lap pluck them, where they grew:
Nor did I wonder at the lilies white,
Nor praise the deep vermilion in the rose;
They were, tho' sweet, but figures of delight,
Drawn after you, you pattern of all those.
Yet seem'd it winter still, and, you away,
As with your shadow I with these did play!

Scarcely less sure, or if a less valuable, not less indispensable mark

Γονίμου μὲν ποιητοῦ——
——ὅστις ῥῆμα γενναῖον λάκοι,

will the imagery supply, when, with more than the power of the painter, the poet gives us the liveliest image of succession with the feeling of simultaneousness!

With this, he breaketh from the sweet embrace
Of those fair arms, that held him to her heart,
And homeward through the dark lawns runs apace:
Look! how a bright star shooteth from the sky,
So glides he in the night from Venus' eye.

4. The last character I shall mention, which would prove indeed but little, except as taken conjointly with the former; yet without which the former could scarce exist in a high degree, and (even if this were possible)

would give promises only of transitory flashes and a meteoric power; is DEPTH, and ENERGY of THOUGHT. No man was ever yet a great poet, without being at the same time a profound philosopher. For poetry is the blossom and the fragrancy of all human knowledge, human thoughts, human passions, emotions, language. In Shakespeare's *poems* the creative power and the intellectual energy wrestle as in a war embrace. Each in its excess of strength seems to threaten the extinction of the other. At length in the DRAMA they were reconciled, and fought each with its shield before the breast of the other. Or like two rapid streams, that, at their first meeting within narrow and rocky banks, mutually strive to repel each other and intermix reluctantly and in tumult; but soon finding a wider channel and more yielding shores blend, and dilate, and flow on in one current and with one voice. The *Venus and Adonis* did not perhaps allow the display of the deeper passions. But the story of Lucretia seems to favor and even demand their intensest workings. And yet we find in *Shakespeare's* management of the tale neither pathos, nor any other *dramatic* quality. There is the same minute and faithful imagery as in the former poem, in the same vivid colors, inspirited by the same impetuous vigor of thought, and diverging and contracting with the same activity of the assimilative and of the modifying faculties; and with a yet larger display, a yet wider range of knowledge and reflection; and lastly, with the same perfect dominion, often *domination,* over the whole world of language. What then shall we say? even this; that Shakespeare, no mere child of nature; no automaton of genius; no passive vehicle of inspiration possessed by the spirit, not possessing it; first studied patiently, meditated deeply, understood minutely, till knowledge, become habitual and intuitive, wedded itself to his habitual feelings, and at length gave birth to that stupendous power, by which he stands alone, with no equal or second in his own class; to that power which seated him on one of the two glory-smitten summits of the poetic mountain, with Milton as his compeer, not rival. While the former darts himself forth, and passes into all the forms of human character and passion, the one Proteus of the fire and the flood; the other attracts all forms and things to himself, into the unity of his own IDEAL. All things and modes of action shape themselves anew in the being of MILTON; while SHAKESPEARE becomes all things, yet for ever remaining himself. O what great men hast thou not produced, England! my country! truly indeed—

> Must *we* be free or die, who speak the tongue,
> Which SHAKESPEARE spake; the faith and morals hold,
> Which MILTON held. In every thing we are sprung
> Of earth's first blood, have titles manifold!
>   Wordsworth.

Chapter XVII

Examination of the tenets peculiar to Mr. Wordsworth— Rustic life (above all, low and rustic life) especially unfavorable to the formation of a human diction—The best parts of language the product of philosophers, not of clowns or shepherds—Poetry essentially ideal and generic—The language of Milton as much the language of real life, yea, incomparably more so than that of the cottager.

As far then as Mr. Wordsworth in his preface contended, and most ably contended, for a reformation in our poetic diction, as far as he has evinced the truth of passion, and the *dramatic* propriety of those figures and metaphors in the original poets, which, stripped of their justifying reasons, and converted into mere artifices of connection or ornament, constitute the characteristic falsity in the poetic style of the moderns; and as far as he has, with equal acuteness and clearness, pointed out the process by which this change was effected, and the resemblances between that state into which the reader's mind is thrown by the pleasureable confusion of thought from an unaccustomed train of words and images; and that state which is induced by the natural language of empassioned feeling; he undertook a useful task, and deserves all praise, both for the attempt and for the execution. The provocations to this remonstrance in behalf of truth and nature were still of perpetual recurrence before and after the publication of this preface. I cannot likewise but add, that the comparison of such poems of merit, as have been given to the public within the last ten or twelve years, with the majority of those produced previously to the appearance of that preface, leave no doubt on my mind, that Mr. Wordsworth is fully justified in believing his efforts to have been by no means ineffectual. Not only in the verses of those who have professed their admiration of his genius, but even of those who have distinguished themselves by hostility to his theory, and depreciation of his writings, are the impressions of his principles plainly visible. It is possible, that with these principles others may have been blended, which are not equally evident; and some which are unsteady and subvertible from the narrowness or imperfection of their basis. But it is more than possible, that these errors of defect or exaggeration, by kindling and feeding the controversy, may have conduced not only to the wider propagation of the accompanying truths, but that, by their frequent presentation to the mind in an excited state, they may have won for them a more permanent and practical result. A man will borrow a part from his opponent the more easily, if he feels himself justified in continuing to reject a part. While there remain important points in which he can still feel himself in the right, in which he still finds firm footing for continued resistance, he will gradually adopt those opinions, which were the least remote from his own convictions, as not less congruous with his own theory than with that which he reprobates. In like manner with a kind of instinctive prudence, he will abandon by little and little his weakest posts, till at length he seems to forget that they had ever belonged to him, or affects to consider them at most as accidental and "petty annexments," the removal of which leaves the citadel unhurt and unendangered.

My own differences from certain supposed parts of Mr. Wordsworth's theory ground themselves on the assumption, that his words had been rightly interpreted, as purporting that the proper diction for poetry in general consists altogether in a language taken, with due exceptions, from the mouths of men in real life, a language which actually constitutes the natural conversation of men under the influence of natural feelings. My objection is, first, that in *any* sense this rule is applicable only to *certain* classes of poetry; secondly, that even to these classes it is not applicable, except in such a sense, as hath never by any one (as far as I know or have read) been denied or doubted; and lastly, that as far as, and in that degree in which it is *practicable,* yet as a *rule* it is useless, if not injurious, and therefore either need not, or ought not to be practised. The poet informs his reader, that he had generally chosen *low and rustic* life; but not *as* low and rustic, or in order to repeat that pleasure of doubtful moral effect, which persons of elevated rank and of superior refinement oftentimes derive from a happy *imitation* of the rude unpolished manners and discourse of their inferiors. For the pleasure so derived may be traced to three exciting causes. The first is the naturalness, in *fact*, of the things represented. The second is the apparent naturalness of the *representation*, as raised and qualified by an imperceptible infusion of the author's own knowledge and talent, which infusion does, indeed, constitute it an *imitation* as distinguished from a mere *copy*. The third cause may be found in the reader's conscious feeling of his superiority awakened by the contrast presented to him; even as for the same purpose the kings and great barons of yore retained sometimes *actual* clowns and fools, but more frequently shrewd and witty fellows in that *character*. These, however, were not Mr. Wordsworth's objects. *He* chose low and rustic life, "because in that condition the essential passions of the heart find a better soil, in which they can attain their maturity, are less under restraint, and speak a plainer and more emphatic language; because in that condition of life our elementary feelings coexist in a state of greater simplicity, and consequently may be more accurately contemplated, and more forcibly communicated; because the manners of rural life germinate from those elementary feelings; and from the necessary character of rural occupations are more easily comprehended, and are more durable; and lastly, because in that condition the passions of men are incorporated with the beautiful and permanent forms of nature."

Now it is clear to me, that in the most interesting of the poems, in which the author is more or less dramatic, as "the Brothers," "Michael," "Ruth," "the Mad Mother," &c., the persons introduced are by no means taken *from low or rustic life* in the common acceptation of those words; and it is not less clear, that the sentiments and language, as far as they can be conceived to have been really transferred from the minds and conversation of such persons, are attributable to causes and circumstances not necessarily connected with "their occupations and abode." The thoughts, feelings, language, and manners of the shepherd-farmers in the vales of Cumberland and Westmoreland, as far as they are actually adopted in those poems, may be accounted for from causes, which will and do produce the same results in *every* state of life, whether in town or country. As the two principal I rank that INDEPENDENCE, which raises a man above servitude, or daily toil for the profit of others, yet not above the necessity of industry and a frugal simplicity of domestic life; and the accompanying unambitious, but solid and religious, EDUCATION, which has rendered few books familiar, but the Bible, and the liturgy or hymn book. To this latter cause, indeed, which is so far *accidental*, that it is the blessing of particular countries and a particular age, not the product of particular places or employments, the poet owes the show of probability, that his personages might really feel, think, and talk with any tolerable resemblance to his representation. It is an excellent remark of Dr. Henry More's (Enthusiasmus triumphatus, Sec. xxxv.), that "a man of confined education, but of good parts, by constant reading of the Bible will naturally form a more winning and commanding rhetoric than those that are learned; the intermixture of tongues and of artificial phrases debasing *their* style."

It is, moreover, to be considered that to the formation of healthy feelings, and a reflecting mind, *negations* involve impediments not less formidable than sophistication and vicious intermixture. I am convinced, that for the human soul to prosper in rustic life a certain vantage-ground is pre-requisite. It is not every man that is likely to be improved by a country life or by country labors. Education, or original sensibility, or both, must pre-exist, if the changes, forms, and incidents of nature are to prove a sufficient stimulant. And where these are not sufficient, the mind contracts and hardens by want of stimulants: and the man becomes selfish, sensual, gross, and hard-hearted. Let the management of the POOR LAWS in Liverpool, Manchester, or Bristol be compared with the ordinary dispensation of the poor rates in agricultural villages, where the *farmers* are the overseers and guardians of the poor. If my own experience have not been particularly unfortunate, as well as that of the many respectable country clergymen with whom I have conversed on the subject, the result would engender more than scepticism concerning the desireable influences of low and rustic life in and for itself. Whatever may be concluded on the other side, from the stronger local attachments and enterprising spirit of the Swiss, and other mountaineers, applies to a particular mode of pastoral life, under forms of property that permit and beget manners truly republican, not to rustic life in general, or to the absence of artificial cultivation. On the contrary the mountaineers, whose manners have been so often eulogized, are in general better educated and greater readers than men of equal rank elsewhere. But where this is not the case, as among the peasantry of North Wales, the ancient mountains, with all their terrors and all their glories, are pictures to the blind, and music to the deaf.

I should not have entered so much into detail upon this passage, but here seems to be the point, to which all the lines of difference converge as to their source and centre. (I mean, as far as, and in whatever respect, my poetic creed *does* differ from the doctrines promulged in this preface.) I adopt with full faith the principle of

Aristotle, that poetry as poetry is essentially[1] *ideal,* that it avoids and excludes all *accident;* that its apparent individualities of rank, character, or occupation must be *representative* of a class; and that the *persons* of poetry must be clothed with *generic* attributes, with the *common* attributes of the class: not with such as one gifted individual might *possibly* possess, but such as from his

[1] Say not that I am recommending abstractions; for these class-characteristics which constitute the instructiveness of a character, are so modified and particularized in each person of the Shakespearean Drama, that life itself does not excite more distinctly that sense of individuality which belongs to real existence. Paradoxical as it may sound, one of the essential properties of Geometry is not less essential to dramatic excellence; and Aristotle has accordingly required of the poet an involution of the universal in the individual. The chief differences are, that in Geometry it is the universal truth, which is uppermost in the consciousness; in poetry the individual form, in which the truth is clothed. With the ancients, and not less with the elder dramatists of England and France, both comedy and tragedy were considered as kinds of poetry. They neither sought in comedy to make us laugh merely; much less to make us laugh by wry faces, accidents of jargon, *slang* phrases for the day, or the clothing of common-place morals drawn from the shops or mechanic occupations of their characters. Nor did they condescend in tragedy to wheedle away the applause of the spectators, by representing before them facsimiles of their own mean selves in all their existing meanness, or to work on the sluggish sympathies by a pathos not a whit more respectable than the maudlin tears of drunkenness. Their tragic scenes were meant to *affect* us indeed; but yet within the bounds of pleasure, and in union with the activity both of our understanding and imagination. They wished to transport the mind to a sense of its possible greatness, and to implant the germs of that greatness, during the temporary oblivion of the worthless "thing we are," and of the peculiar state in which each man *happens* to be, suspending our individual recollections and lulling them to sleep amid the music of nobler thoughts.
The Friend.—S. T. C.

situation it is most probable before-hand that he *would* possess. If my premises are right and my deductions legitimate, it follows that there can be no *poetic* medium between the swains of Theocritus and those of an imaginary golden age.

The characters of the vicar and the shepherd-mariner in the poem of "THE BROTHERS," that of the shepherd of Greenhead Ghyll in the "MICHAEL," have all the verisimilitude and representative quality, that the purposes of poetry can require. They are persons of a known and abiding class, and their manners and sentiments the natural product of circumstances common to the class. Take "MICHAEL" for instance:

> An old man stout of heart, and strong of limb:
> His bodily frame had been from youth to age
> Of an unusual strength: his mind was keen,
> Intense, and frugal, apt for all affairs,
> And in his shepherd's calling he was prompt
> And watchful more than ordinary men.
> Hence he had learnt the meaning of all winds,
> Of blasts of every tone; and oftentimes
> When others heeded not, he heard the South
> Make subterraneous music, like the noise
> Of bagpipers on distant Highland hills.
> The shepherd, at such warning, of his flock
> Bethought him, and he to himself would say,
> The winds are now devising work for me!
> And truly at all times the storm, that drives
> The traveller to a shelter, summon'd him
> Up to the mountains. He had been alone
> Amid the heart of many thousand mists,
> That came to him and left him on the heights.
> So liv'd he, till his eightieth year was pass'd.
> And grossly that man errs, who should suppose
> That the green vallies, and the streams and rocks,

Were things indifferent to the shepherd's thoughts.
Fields, where with chearful spirits he had breath'd
The common air; the hills, which he so oft
Had climb'd with vigorous steps; which had impress'd
So many incidents upon his mind
Of hardship, skill or courage, joy or fear;
Which, like a book, preserved the memory
Of the dumb animals, whom he had sav'd,
Had fed or shelter'd, linking to such acts,
So grateful in themselves, the certainty
Of honorable gain; these fields, these hills
Which were his living being, even more
Than his own blood—what could they less? had laid
Strong hold on his affections, were to him
A pleasureable feeling of blind love,
The pleasure which there is in life itself.

On the other hand, in the poems which are pitched at
a lower note, as the "HARRY GILL," "IDIOT BOY," the
feelings are those of human nature in general; though
the poet has judiciously laid the *scene* in the country, in
order to place *himself* in the vicinity of interesting im-
ages, without the necessity of ascribing a sentimental
perception of their beauty to the persons of his drama.
In the "Idiot Boy," indeed, the mother's character is not
so much a real and native product of a "situation where
the essential passions of the heart find a better soil, in
which they can attain their maturity and speak a plainer
and more emphatic language," as it is an impersonation
of an instinct abandoned by judgement. Hence the two
following charges seem to me not wholly groundless:
at least, they are the only plausible objections, which I
have heard to that fine poem. The one is, that the author
has not, in the poem itself, taken sufficient care to pre-
clude from the reader's fancy the disgusting images of
ordinary morbid idiocy, which yet it was by no means

his intention to represent. He has even by the "burr, burr, burr," uncounteracted by any preceding description of the boy's beauty, assisted in recalling them. The other is, that the idiocy of the *boy* is so evenly balanced by the folly of the *mother*, as to present to the general reader rather a laughable burlesque on the blindness of anile dotage, than an analytic display of material affection in its ordinary workings.

In the "Thorn" the poet himself acknowledges in a note the necessity of an introductory poem, in which he should have pourtrayed the character of the person from whom the words of the poem are supposed to proceed: a superstitious man moderately imaginative, of slow faculties and deep feelings, "a captain of a small trading vessel, for example, who, being past the middle age of life, had retired upon an annuity, or small independent income, to some village or country town of which he was not a native, or in which he had not been accustomed to live. Such men having nothing to do become credulous and talkative from indolence." But in a poem, still more in a lyric poem (and the NURSE in Shakespeare's Romeo and Juliet alone prevents me from extending the remark even to dramatic *poetry*, if indeed the Nurse itself can be deemed altogether a case in point) it is not possible to imitate truly a dull and garrulous discourser, without repeating the effects of dullness and garrulity. However this may be, I dare assert, that the parts (and these form the far larger portion of the whole) which might as well or still better have proceeded from the poet's own imagination, and have been spoken in his own character, are those which have given, and which will continue to give, universal delight; and that the passages exclusively appropriate to the supposed narrator, such as the last couplet of the third stanza;[1] the seven last lines of the tenth;[2] and the five

[1] I've measured it from side to side;
    'Tis three feet long, and two feet wide.

[2] Nay, rack your brain—'tis all in vain,
    I'll tell you every thing I know;
    But to the Thorn, and to the Pond
    Which is a little step beyond,
    I wish that you would go:
    Perhaps when you are at the place,
    You something of her tale may trace.

I'll give you the best help I can:
Before you up the mountain go,
Up to the dreary mountain-top,
I'll tell you all I know.
'Tis now some two-and-twenty years
Since she (her name is Martha Ray)
Gave, with a maiden's true good will,
Her company to Stephen Hill;
And she was blithe and gay,
And she was happy, happy still
Whene'er she thought of Stephen Hill.

And they had fix'd the wedding day,
The morning that must wed them both;
But Stephen to another maid
Had sworn another oath;
And, with this other maid, to church
Unthinking Stephen went—
Poor Martha! on that woeful day
A pang of pitiless dismay
Into her soul was sent;
A fire was kindled in her breast,
Which might not burn itself to rest.

They say, full six months after this,
While yet the summer leaves were green,
She to the mountain-top would go,
And there was often seen.
'Tis said a child was in her womb,
As now to any eye was plain;

following stanzas, with the exception of the four admirable lines at the commencement of the fourteenth, are felt by many unprejudiced and unsophisticated hearts, as sudden and unpleasant sinkings from the height to which the poet had previously lifted them, and to which he again re-elevates both himself and his reader.

If then I am compelled to doubt the theory, by which the choice of *characters* was to be directed, not only *a priori*, from grounds of reason, but both from the few instances in which the poet himself *need* be supposed to have been governed by it, and from the comparative in-

---

She was with child, and she was mad;
Yet often she was sober sad
From her exceeding pain.
Oh me! ten thousand times I'd rather
That he had died, that cruel father!

*   *   *   *   *   *   *
*   *   *   *   *   *   *
*   *   *   *   *   *   *
*   *   *   *   *   *   *

Last Christmas when we talked of this,
Old farmer Simpson did maintain,
That in her womb the infant wrought
About its mother's heart, and brought
Her senses back again:
And, when at last her time drew near,
Her looks were calm, her senses clear.

No more I know, I wish I did,
And I would tell it all to you:
For what became of this poor child
There's none that ever knew:
And if a child was born or no,
There's no one that could ever tell;
And if 'twas born alive or dead,
There's no one knows, as I have said:
But some remember well,
That Martha Ray about this time
Would up the mountain often climb.

feriority of those instances; still more must I hesitate in
my assent to the sentence which immediately follows the
former citation; and which I can neither admit as par-
ticular fact, or as general rule. "The language too of
these men is adopted (purified indeed from what appear
to be its real defects, from all lasting and rational causes
of dislike or disgust) because such men hourly com-
municate with the best objects from which the best part
of language is originally derived; and because, from
their rank in society and the sameness and narrow circle
of their intercourse, being less under the action of social
vanity, they convey their feelings and notions in simple
and unelaborated expressions." To this I reply; that a
rustic's language, purified from all provincialism and
grossness, and so far reconstructed as to be made con-
sistent with the rules of grammar (which are in essence
no other than the laws of universal logic, applied to
psychological materials) will not differ from the lan-
guage of any other man of common-sense, however
learned or refined he may be, except as far as the
notions, which the rustic has to convey, are fewer and
more indiscriminate. This will become still clearer, if we
add the consideration (equally important though less
obvious) that the rustic, from the more imperfect devel-
opement of his faculties, and from the lower state of
their cultivation, aims almost solely to convey *insulated
facts,* either those of his scanty experience or his tradi-
tional belief; while the educated man chiefly seeks to
discover and express those *connections* of things, or
those relative *bearings* of fact to fact, from which some
more or less general law is deducible. For *facts* are valu-
able to a wise man, chiefly as they lead to the discovery
of the indwelling *law,* which is the true *being* of things,
the sole solution of their modes of existence, and in the
knowledge of which consists our dignity and our power.

546 FROM BIOGRAPHIA LITERARIA: XVII

As little can I agree with the assertion, that from the objects with which the rustic hourly communicates the best part of language is formed. For first, if to communicate with an object implies such an acquaintance with it, as renders it capable of being discriminately reflected on; the distinct knowledge of an uneducated rustic would furnish a very scanty vocabulary. The few things, and modes of action, requisite for his bodily conveniences, would alone be individualized; while all the rest of nature would be expressed by a small number of confused general terms. Secondly, I deny that the words and combinations of words derived from the objects, with which the rustic is familiar, whether with distinct or confused knowledge, can be justly said to form the *best* part of language. It is more than probable, that many classes of the brute creation possess discriminating sounds, by which they can convey to each other notices of such objects as concern their food, shelter, or safety. Yet we hesitate to call the aggregate of such sounds a language, otherwise than metaphorically. The best part of human language, properly so called, is derived from reflection on the acts of the mind itself. It is formed by a voluntary appropriation of fixed symbols to internal acts, to processes and results of imagination, the greater part of which have no place in the consciousness of uneducated man; though in civilized society, by imitation and passive remembrance of what they hear from their religious instructors and other superiors, the most uneducated share in the harvest which they neither sowed or reaped. If the history of the phrases in hourly currency among our peasants were traced, a person not previously aware of the fact would be surprised at finding so large a number, which three or four centuries ago were the exclusive property of the universities and the schools; and, at the commencement of the Reformation, had been

transferred from the school to the pulpit, and thus grad-
ually passed into common life. The extreme difficulty,
and often the impossibility, of finding words for the
simplest moral and intellectual processes of the lan-
guages of uncivilized tribes has proved perhaps the
weightiest obstacle to the progress of our most zealous
and adroit missionaries. Yet these tribes are surrounded
by the same nature as our peasants are; but in still more
impressive forms; and they are, moreover, obliged to
particularize many more of them. When, therefore,
Mr. Wordsworth adds, "accordingly, such a language"
(meaning, as before, the language of rustic life purified
from provincialism) "arising out of repeated experience
and regular feelings, is a more permanent, and a far
more philosophical language, than that which is fre-
quently substituted for it by poets, who think they are
conferring honor upon themselves and their art in pro-
portion as they indulge in arbitrary and capricious habits
of expression:" it may be answered, that the language,
which he has in view, can be attributed to rustics with
no greater right, than the style of Hooker or Bacon to
Tom Brown or Sir Roger L'Estrange. Doubtless, if what
is peculiar to each were omitted in each, the result must
needs be the same. Further, that the poet, who uses an
illogical diction, or a style fitted to excite only the low
and changeable pleasure of wonder by means of ground-
less novelty, substitutes a language of *folly* and *vanity*,
not for that of the *rustic*, but for that of *good sense* and
natural feeling.

Here let me be permitted to remind the reader, that
the positions, which I controvert, are contained in the
sentences—*"a selection of the* REAL *language of men;"*
—*"the language of these men"* (i.e. men in low and
rustic life) *"I propose to myself to imitate, and, as
far as is possible, to adopt the very language of men."*

"Between the language of prose and that of metrical composition, there neither is, nor can be any essential difference." It is against these exclusively that my opposition is directed.

I object, in the very first instance, to an equivocation in the use of the word "real." Every man's language varies, according to the extent of his knowledge, the activity of his faculties, and the depth or quickness of his feelings. Every man's language has, first, its *individualities;* secondly, the common properties of the *class* to which he belongs; and thirdly, words and phrases of *universal* use. The language of Hooker, Bacon, Bishop Taylor, and Burke differs from the common language of the learned class only by the superior number and novelty of the thoughts and relations which they had to convey. The language of Algernon Sidney differs not at all from that, which every well-educated gentleman would wish to write, and (with due allowances for the undeliberateness, and less connected train, of thinking natural and proper to conversation) such as he would wish to talk. Neither one nor the other differ half so much from the general language of cultivated society, as the language of Mr. Wordsworth's homeliest composition differs from that of a common peasant. For "real" therefore, we must substitute *ordinary,* or *lingua communis.* And this, we have proved, is no more to be found in the phraseology of low and rustic life than in that of any other class. Omit the peculiarities of each, and the result of course must be common to all. And assuredly the omissions and changes to be made in the language of rustics, before it could be transferred to any species of poem, except the drama or other professed imitation, are at least as numerous and weighty, as would be required in adapting to the same purpose the ordinary language of tradesmen and manufacturers. Not to men-

tion, that the language so highly extolled by Mr. Words-
worth varies in every county, nay in every village, ac-
cording to the accidental character of the clergyman, the
existence or non-existence of schools; or even, perhaps,
as the exciseman, publican, or barber, happen to be, or
not to be, zealous politicians, and readers of the weekly
newspaper *pro bono publico.* Anterior to cultivation, the
lingua communis of every country, as Dante has well
observed, exists every where in parts, and no where as
a whole.

Neither is the case rendered at all more tenable by
the addition of the words, *in a state of excitement.* For
the nature of a man's words, where he is strongly af-
fected by joy, grief, or anger, must necessarily depend
on the number and quality of the general truths, con-
ceptions and images, and of the words expressing them,
with which his mind had been previously stored. For
the property of passion is not to *create;* but to set in
increased activity. At least, whatever new connections
of thoughts or images, or (which is equally, if not more
than equally, the appropriate effect of strong excite-
ment) whatever generalizations of truth or experience,
the heat of passion may produce; yet the terms of their
conveyance must have pre-existed in his former conver-
sations, and are only collected and crowded together
by the unusual stimulation. It is indeed very possible to
adopt in a poem the unmeaning repetitions, habitual
phrases, and other blank counters, which an unfur-
nished or confused understanding interposes at short
intervals, in order to keep hold of his subject, which is
still slipping from him, and to give him time for recol-
lection; or in mere aid of vacancy, as in the scanty com-
panies of a country stage the same player pops back-
wards and forwards, in order to prevent the appearance
of empty spaces, in the procession of Macbeth, or Henry

VIIIth. But what assistance to the poet, or ornament to the poem, these can supply, I am at a loss to conjecture. Nothing assuredly can differ either in origin or in mode more widely from the *apparent* tautologies of intense and turbulent feeling, in which the passion is greater and of longer endurance than to be exhausted or satisfied by a single representation of the image or incident exciting it. Such repetitions I admit to be a beauty of the highest kind; as illustrated by Mr. Wordsworth himself from the song of Deborah. *"At her feet he bowed, he fell, he lay down; at her feet he bowed, he fell; where he bowed, there he fell down dead."*

Chapter XVIII

Language of metrical composition, why and wherein essentially different from that of prose—Origin and elements of metre—Its necessary consequences, and the conditions thereby imposed on the metrical writer in the choice of his diction.

I conclude, therefore, that the attempt is impracticable; and that, were it not impracticable, it would still be useless. For the very power of making the selection implies the previous possession of the language selected. Or where can the poet have lived? And by what rules could he direct his choice, which would not have enabled him to select and arrange his words by the light of his own judgement? We do not adopt the language of a class by the mere adoption of such words exclusively, as that class would use, or at least understand; but likewise by following the *order*, in which the words of such men are wont to succeed each other. Now this order, in the intercourse of uneducated men, is distinguished from the diction of their superiors in knowledge and power, by the greater *disjunction* and *separation* in the component parts of that, whatever it be, which they wish to communicate. There is a want of that prospectiveness of mind, that *surview,* which enables a man to foresee the whole of what he is to convey, appertaining to any one point; and by this means so to subordinate and arrange the different parts according to their relative importance, as to convey it at once, and as an organized whole.

Now I will take the first stanza, on which I have chanced to open, in the *Lyrical Ballads.* It is one the most simple and the least peculiar in its language.

> In distant countries have I been,
> And yet I have not often seen
> A healthy man, a man full grown,
> Weep in the public roads alone.
> But such a one, on English ground,
> And in the broad highway, I met;
> Along the broad highway he came,
> His cheeks with tears were wet:
> Sturdy he seem'd, though he was sad;
> And in his arms a lamb he had.

The words here are doubtless such as are current in all ranks of life; and of course not less so in the hamlet and cottage than in the shop, manufactory, college, or palace. But is this the *order,* in which the rustic would have placed the words? I am grievously deceived, if the following less *compact* mode of commencing the same tale be not a far more faithful copy. "I have been in a many parts, far and near, and I don't know that I ever saw before a man crying by himself in the public road; a grown man I mean, that was neither sick nor hurt,"

&c., &c. But when I turn to the following stanza in "The Thorn":

> At all times of the day and night
> This wretched woman thither goes,
> And she is known to every star,
> And every wind that blows:
> And there, beside the thorn, she sits,
> When the blue day-light's in the skies;
> And when the whirlwind's on the hill,
> Or frosty air is keen and still;
> And to herself she cries,
> Oh misery! Oh misery!
> Oh woe is me! Oh misery!

and compare this with the language of ordinary men; or with that which I can conceive at all likely to proceed, in *real* life, from *such* a narrator, as is supposed in the note to the poem; compare it either in the succession of the images or of the sentences; I am reminded of the sublime prayer and hymn of praise, which MILTON, in opposition to an established liturgy, presents as a fair *specimen* of common extemporary devotion, and such as we might expect to hear from every self-inspired minister of a conventicle! And I reflect with delight, how little a mere theory, though of his own workmanship, interferes with the processes of genuine imagination in a man of true poetic genius, who possesses, as Mr. Wordsworth, if ever man did, most assuredly does possess,

"THE VISION AND THE FACULTY DIVINE."

One point then alone remains, but that the most important; its examination having been, indeed, my chief inducement for the preceding inquisition. *"There neither is or can be any essential difference between the language of prose and metrical composition."* Such is Mr.

Wordsworth's assertion. Now prose itself, at least in all argumentative and consecutive works, differs, and ought to differ, from the language of conversation; even as reading ought to differ from talking.[1] Unless therefore the difference denied be that of the mere *words*, as materials common to all styles of writing, and not of the *style* itself in the universally admitted sense of the term, it might be naturally presumed that there must exist a

[1] It is no less an error in teachers, than a torment to the poor children, to inforce the necessity of reading as they would talk. In order to cure them of *singing* as it is called, that is, of too great a difference, the child is made to repeat the words with his eyes from off the book; and then, indeed, his tones resemble talking, as far as his fears, tears and trembling will permit. But as soon as his eye is again directed to the printed page, the spell begins anew; for an instinctive sense tells the child's feelings, that to utter its own momentary thoughts, and to recite the written thoughts of another, as of another, and a far wiser than himself, are two widely different things; and as the two acts are accompanied with widely different feelings, so must they justify different modes of enunciation. Joseph Lancaster, among his other sophistications of the excellent Dr. Bell's invaluable system, cures this fault of *singing*, by hanging fetters and chains on the child, to the music of which one of his school-fellows, who walks before, dolefully chaunts out the child's last speech and confession, birth, parentage, and education. And this soul-benumbing ignominy, this unholy and heart-hardening burlesque on the last fearful infliction of outraged law, in pronouncing the sentence to which the stern and familiarized judge not seldom bursts into tears, has been extolled as a happy and ingenious method of remedying—what? and how?—why, one extreme in order to introduce another, scarce less distant from good sense, and certainly likely to have worse moral effects, by enforcing a semblance of petulant ease and self-sufficiency, in repression, and possible after-perversion of the natural feelings. I have to beg Dr. Bell's pardon for this connection of the two names, but he knows that contrast is no less powerful a cause of association than likeness.—S. T. C.

still greater between the ordonnance of poetic composition and that of prose, than is expected to distinguish prose from ordinary conversation.

There are not, indeed, examples wanting in the history of literature, of apparent paradoxes that have summoned the public wonder as new and startling truths, but which on examination have shrunk into tame and harmless *truisms;* as the eyes of a cat, seen in the dark, have been mistaken for flames of fire. But Mr. Wordsworth is among the last men, to whom a delusion of this kind would be attributed by anyone, who had enjoyed the slightest opportunity of understanding his mind and character. Where an objection has been anticipated by such an author as natural, his answer to it must needs be interpreted in some sense which either is, or has been, or is capable of being controverted. My object then must be to discover some other meaning for the term *"essential difference"* in this place, exclusive of the indistinction and community of the words themselves. For whether there ought to exist a class of words in the English, in any degree resembling the poetic dialect of the Greek and Italian, is a question of very subordinate importance. The number of such words would be small indeed, in our language; and even in the Italian and Greek, they consist not so much of different words, as of slight differences in the *forms* of declining and conjugating the same words; forms, doubtless, which having been, at some period more or less remote, the common grammatic flexions of some tribe or province, had been accidentally appropriated to poetry by the general admiration of certain master intellects, the first established lights of inspiration, to whom that dialect happened to be native.

Essence, in its primary signification, means the principle of *individuation,* the inmost principle of the possibility of any thing, as that particular thing. It is equivalent to the *idea* of a thing, when ever we use the word, idea, with philosophic precision. Existence, on the other hand, is distinguished from essence, by the superinduction of *reality*. Thus we speak of the essence, and essential properties of a circle; but we do not therefore assert, that any thing, which really exists, is mathematically circular. Thus too, without any tautology we contend for the *existence* of the Supreme Being; that is, for a reality correspondent to the idea. There is, next, a *secondary* use of the word essence, in which it signifies the point or ground of contra-distinction between two modifications of the same substance or subject. Thus we should be allowed to say, that the style of architecture of Westminster Abbey is *essentially* different from that of St. Paul's, even though both had been built with blocks cut into the same form, and from the same quarry. Only in this latter sense of the term must it have been *denied* by Mr. Wordsworth (for in this sense alone is it *affirmed* by the general opinion) that the language of poetry (i.e. the formal construction, or architecture, of the words and phrases) is *essentially* different from that of prose. Now the burthen of the proof lies with the oppugner, not with the supporters of the common belief. Mr. Wordsworth, in consequence, assigns as the proof of his position, "that not only the language of a large portion of every good poem, even of the most elevated character, must necessarily, except with reference to the metre, in no respect differ from that of good prose, but likewise that some of the most interesting parts of the best poems will be found to be strictly the language of prose, when prose is well written. The truth of this assertion might be demonstrated by innumerable passages from almost all the poetical writings even of Milton himself." He then quotes Gray's sonnet—

In vain to me the smiling mornings shine,
And reddening Phœbus lifts his golden fire;
The birds in vain their amorous descant join,
Or chearful fields resume their green attire.
These ears, alas! for other notes repine;
A different object do these eyes require;
My lonely anguish melts no heart but mine;
And in my breast the imperfect joys expire.
Yet morning smiles the busy race to cheer,
And newborn pleasure brings to happier men:
The fields to all their wonted tribute bear,
To warm their little loves the birds complain.
I fruitless mourn to him that cannot hear,
And weep the more because I weep in vain,

and adds the following remark:—"It will easily be perceived, that the only part of this Sonnet, which is of any value, is the lines printed in italics. It is equally obvious, that, except in the rhyme, and in the use of the single word 'fruitless' for 'fruitlessly,' which is so far a defect, the language of these lines does in no respect differ from that of prose."

An idealist defending his system by the fact, that when asleep we often believe ourselves awake, was well answered by his plain neighbour, "Ah, but when awake do we ever believe ourselves asleep?"—Things identical must be convertible. The preceding passage seems to rest on a similar sophism. For the question is not, whether there may not occur in prose an order of words, which would be equally proper in a poem; nor whether there are not beautiful lines and sentences of frequent occurrence in good poems, which would be equally becoming as well as beautiful in good prose; for neither the one nor the other has ever been either denied or doubted by any one. The true question must be, whether there are not modes of expression, a *construction,* and an *order* of sentences, which are in their fit and natural place in a serious prose composition, but would be disproportionate and heterogeneous in metrical poetry; and, vice versa, whether in the language of a serious poem there may not be an arrangement both of words and sentences, and a use and selection of (what are called) *figures of speech*, both as to their kind, their frequency, and their occasions, which on a subject of equal weight would be vicious and alien in correct and manly prose. I contend that in both cases this unfitness of each for the place of the other frequently will and ought to exist.

And first from the *origin* of metre. This I would trace to the balance in the mind effected by that spontaneous effort which strives to hold in check the workings of passion. It might be easily explained likewise in what manner this salutary antagonism is assisted by the very state, which it counteracts; and how this balance of antagonists became organized into *metre* (in the usual acceptation of that term) by a supervening act of the will and judgement, consciously and for the foreseen purpose of pleasure. Assuming these principles, as the data of our argument, we deduce from them two legitimate conditions, which the critic is entitled to expect in every metrical work. First, that, as the *elements* of metre owe their existence to a state of increased excitement, so the metre itself should be accompanied by the natural language of excitement. Secondly, that as these elements are formed into metre *artificially*, by a *voluntary* act, with the design and for the purpose of blending *delight* with emotion, so the traces of present *volition* should throughout the metrical language be proportionately discernible. Now these two conditions must be reconciled and co-present. There must be not only a partnership, but a union; an interpenetration of passion and of will, of *spontaneous* impulse and of *voluntary* purpose. Again, this union can be manifested only in a frequency of forms and figures of speech (originally the offspring of passion, but now the adopted children of power) greater than would be desired or endured, where the emotion is not voluntarily encouraged and kept up for the sake of that pleasure, which such emotion, so tempered and mastered by the will, is found capable of communicating. It not only dictates, but of itself tends to produce, a more frequent employment of picturesque and vivifying language, than would be natural in any other case, in which there did not exist, as there does in the present, a previous and well understood, though tacit, *compact* between the poet and his reader, that the latter is entitled to expect, and the former bound to supply, this species and degree of pleasureable excitement. We may in some measure apply to this union the answer of POL-IXENES, in the *Winter's Tale*, to PERDITA's neglect of the streaked gilly-flowers, because she had heard it said,

> There is an art which, in their piedness, shares
> With great creating nature.
> POLIXENES.   Say there be;
> Yet nature is made better by no mean,
> But nature makes that mean; so, ev'n that art,
> Which, you say, adds to nature, is an art,
> That nature makes. You see, sweet maid, we marry
> *A gentler scyon to the wildest stock;*
> And make conceive a bark of ruder kind
> By bud of nobler race. This is an art,
> Which does mend nature—change it rather; but
> The art itself is nature.

Secondly, I argue from the EFFECTS of metre. As far as metre acts in and for itself, it tends to increase the vivacity and susceptibility both of the general feelings and of the attention. This effect it produces by the continued excitement of surprize, and by the quick reciprocations of curiosity still gratified and still re-excited, which are too slight indeed to be at any one moment objects of distinct consciousness, yet become considerable in their aggregate influence. As a medicated atmosphere, or as wine during animated conversation; they act powerfully, though themselves unnoticed. Where, therefore, correspondent food and appropriate matter are not provided for the attention and feelings thus roused, there must needs be a disappointment felt; like that of leaping in the dark from the last step of a staircase, when we had prepared our muscles for a leap of three or four.

The discussion on the powers of metre in the preface is highly ingenious and touches at all points on truth. But I cannot find any statement of its powers considered abstractly and separately. On the contrary Mr. Wordsworth seems always to estimate metre by the powers, which it exerts during (and, as I think, in *consequence of*) its combination with other elements of poetry. Thus the previous difficulty is left unanswered, *what* the elements are, with which it must be combined in order to produce its own effects to any pleasurable purpose. Double and tri-syllable rhymes, indeed, form a lower species of wit, and, attended to exclusively for their own sake, may become a source of momentary amusement; as in poor Smart's distich to the Welsh 'Squire who had promised him a hare:

> Tell me, thou son of great Cadwallader!
> Hast sent the hare? or hast thou swallow'd her?

But for any *poetic* purposes, metre resembles (if the aptness of the simile may excuse its meanness) yeast, worthless or disagreeable by itself, but giving vivacity and spirit to the liquor with which it is proportionally combined.

The reference to the "Children in the Wood," by no means satisfies my judgement. We all willingly throw ourselves back for awhile into the feelings of our childhood. This ballad, therefore, we read under such recollections of our own childish feelings, as would equally endear to us poems, which Mr. Wordsworth himself would regard as faulty in the opposite extreme of gaudy and technical ornament. Before the invention of printing, and in a still greater degree, before the introduction of writing, metre, especially *alliterative* metre (whether alliterative at the beginning of the words, as in "Pierce Plouman," or at the end as in rhymes) possessed an independent value as assisting the recollection, and consequently the preservation, of *any* series of truths or incidents. But I am not convinced by the collation of facts, that the "Children in the Wood" owes either its preservation, or its popularity, to its metrical form. Mr. Marshal's repository affords a number of tales in prose inferior in pathos and general merit, some of as old a date, and many as widely popular. "Tom Hickathrift," "Jack the Giant-killer," "Goody Two-shoes," and "Little Red Riding-hood" are formidable rivals. And that they have continued in prose, cannot be fairly explained by the assumption, that the comparative meanness of their thoughts and images precluded even the humblest forms of metre. The scene of Goody Two-shoes in the church is perfectly susceptible of metrical narration; and, among the Θαύματα θαυμαστότατα even of the present age, I do not recollect a more astonishing image than that of the *"whole rookery, that flew out of the giant's beard,"* scared by the tremendous voice, with which this monster answered the challenge of the heroic Tom Hickathrift!

If from these we turn to compositions universally, and independently of all early associations, beloved and ad-

mired; would "THE MARIA," "THE MONK," or "THE POOR
MAN'S ASS" of Sterne, be read with more delight, or have
a better chance of immortality, had they without any
change in the diction been composed in rhyme, than in
their present state? If I am not grossly mistaken, the gen-
eral reply would be in the negative. Nay, I will confess,
that, in Mr. Wordsworth's own volumes, the "ANECDOTE
FOR FATHERS," "SIMON LEE," "ALICE FELL," "THE BEG-
GARS," and "THE SAILOR'S MOTHER," notwithstanding
the beauties which are to be found in each of them
where the poet interposes the music of his own thoughts,
would have been more delightful to me in prose, told
and managed, as by Mr. Wordsworth they would have
been, in a moral essay, or pedestrian tour.

Metre in itself is simply a stimulant of the attention,
and therefore excites the question: Why is the attention
to be thus stimulated? Now the question cannot be an-
swered by the pleasure of the metre itself: for this we
have shown to be *conditional,* and dependent on the ap-
propriateness of the thoughts and expressions, to which
the metrical form is superadded. Neither can I conceive
any other answer that can be rationally given, short of
this: I write in metre, because I am about to use a lan-
guage different from that of prose. Besides, where the
language is not such, how interesting soever the reflec-
tions are, that are capable of being drawn by a philo-
sophic mind from the thoughts or incidents of the poem,
the metre itself must often become feeble. Take the last
three stanzas of "THE SAILOR'S MOTHER," for instance.
If I could for a moment abstract from the effect pro-
duced on the author's feelings, as a man, by the incident
at the time of its real occurrence, I would dare appeal to
his own judgement, whether in the *metre* itself he
found a sufficient reason for *their* being written *metri-
cally?*

And, thus continuing, she said,
I had a son, who many a day
Sailed on the seas; but he is dead;
In Denmark he was cast away:
And I have travelled far as Hull, to see
What clothes he might have left, or other property

The bird and cage they both were his:
'Twas my son's bird; and neat and trim
He kept it: many voyages
This singing-bird hath gone with him;
When last he sailed he left the bird behind;
As it might be, perhaps, from bodings of his mind.

He to a fellow-lodger's care
Had left it, to be watched and fed,
Till he came back again; and there
I found it when my son was dead;
And now, God help me for my little wit!
I trail it with me, Sir! he took so much delight in it.

If disproportioning the emphasis we read these stanzas
so as to make the rhymes perceptible, even *tri-syllable*
rhymes could scarcely produce an equal sense of oddity
and strangeness, as we feel here in finding *rhymes at all*
in sentences so exclusively colloquial. I would further
ask whether, but for that visionary state, into which the
figure of the woman and the susceptibility of his own
genius had placed the poet's imagination, (a state,
which spreads its influence and coloring over all, that
co-exists with the exciting cause, and in which

The simplest, and the most familiar things
Gain a strange power of spreading awe around [1] them,)

[1] Altered from the description of Night-Mair in the *Re-
morse*.

Oh Heaven! 'twas frightful! Now run down and stared at
By hideous shapes that cannot be remembered;

I would ask the poet whether he would not have felt an abrupt downfall in these verses from the preceding stanza?

> The ancient spirit is not dead;
> Old times, thought I, are breathing there;
> Proud was I that my country bred
> Such strength, ā dignity so fair:
> She begged an alms, like one in poor estate;
> I looked at her again, nor did my pride abate.

It must not be omitted, and is besides worthy of notice, that those stanzas furnish the only fair instance that I have been able to discover in all Mr. Wordsworth's writings, of an *actual* adoption, or true imitation, of the *real* and *very* language of *low and rustic life,* freed from provincialisms.

Thirdly, I deduce the position from all the causes elsewhere assigned, which render metre the proper form of poetry, and poetry imperfect and defective without metre. Metre therefore having been connected with *poetry* most often and by a peculiar fitness, whatever else is combined with *metre* must, though it be not itself *essentially* poetic, have nevertheless some property in common with poetry, as an intermedium of affinity, a sort (if I may dare borrow a well-known phrase from technical chemistry) of *mordaunt* between it and the super-added metre. Now poetry, Mr. Wordsworth truly affirms, does always imply PASSION: which word must be here understood in its general sense, as an excited

---

Now seeing nothing and imagining nothing;
But only being afraid—stifled with fear!
While every goodly or familiar form
Had a strange power of spreading terror round me!

N.B. Though Shakespeare has, for his own *all-justifying* purposes, introduced the Night-*Mare* with her own foals, yet Mair means a Sister, or perhaps a Hag.—*S. T. C.*

state of the feelings and faculties. And as every passion
has its proper pulse, so will it likewise have its charac-
teristic modes of expression. But where there exists that
degree of genius and talent which entitles a writer to
aim at the honors of a poet, the very *act* of poetic com-
position *itself* is, and is *allowed* to imply and to produce,
an unusual state of excitement, which of course justifies
and demands a correspondent difference of language, as
truly, though not perhaps in as marked a degree, as the
excitement of love, fear, rage, or jealousy. The vividness
of the descriptions or declamations in DONNE or DRYDEN
is as much and as often derived from the force and
fervor of the describer, as from the reflections, forms or
incidents, which constitute their subject and materials.
The wheels take fire from the mere rapidity of their
motion. To what extent, and under what modifications,
this may be admitted to act, I shall attempt to define in
an after remark on Mr. Wordsworth's reply to this ob-
jection, or rather on his objection to this reply, as already
anticipated in his preface.

Fourthly, and as intimately connected with this, if not
the same argument in a more general form, I adduce the
high spiritual instinct of the human being impelling us
to seek unity by harmonious adjustment, and thus estab-
lishing the principle, that *all* the parts of an organized
whole must be assimilated to the more *important* and
essential parts. This and the preceding arguments may
be strengthened by the reflection, that the composition
of a poem is among the *imitative* arts; and that imitation,
as opposed to copying, consists either in the interfusion
of the SAME throughout the radically DIFFERENT, or of
the different throughout a base radically the same.

Lastly, I appeal to the practice of the best poets, of
all countries and in all ages, as *authorizing* the opinion
(*deduced* from all the foregoing) that in every import

of the word ESSENTIAL, which would not here involve a mere truism, there may be, is, and ought to be an *essential* difference between the language of prose and of metrical composition.

In Mr. Wordsworth's criticism of GRAY's Sonnet, the readers' sympathy with his praise or blame of the different parts is taken for granted rather perhaps too easily. He has not, at least, attempted to win or compel it by argumentative analysis. In *my* conception at least, the lines rejected as of no value do, with the exception of the two first, differ as much and as little from the language of common life, as those which he has printed in italics as possessing genuine excellence. Of the five lines thus honourably distinguished, two of them differ from prose, even more widely than the lines which either precede or follow, in the *position* of the words.

> *A different object do these eyes require;*
> *My lonely anguish melts no heart but mine;*
> *And in my breast the imperfect joys expire.*

But were it otherwise, what would this prove, but a truth, of which no man ever doubted? Videlicet, that there are sentences, which would be equally in their place both in verse and prose. Assuredly it does not prove the point, which alone requires proof; namely, that there are not passages, which would suit the one and not suit the other. The first line of this sonnet is distinguished from the ordinary language of men by the epithet to morning. (For we will set aside, at present, the consideration, that the particular word *"smiling"* is hackneyed and (as it involves a sort of personification) not quite congruous with the common and material attribute of *shining*.) And, doubtless, this adjunction of epithets for the purpose of additional description, where no particular attention is demanded for the quality of

the thing, would be noticed as giving a poetic cast to
a man's conversation. Should the sportsman exclaim,
"*Come boys! the rosy morning calls you up,*" he will be
supposed to have some song in his head. But no one
suspects this, when he says, "A wet morning shall not
confine us to our beds." This then is either a defect in
poetry, or it is not. Whoever should decide in the *af-
firmative,* I would request him to re-peruse any one
poem of any confessedly great poet from Homer to Mil-
ton, or from Æschylus to Shakespeare; and to strike out
(in thought I mean) every instance of this kind. If the
number of these fancied erasures did not startle him; or
if he continued to deem the work improved by their
total omission; he must advance reasons of no ordinary
strength and evidence, reasons grounded in the essence
of human nature. Otherwise, I should not hesitate to
consider him as a man not so much *proof against* all
authority, as *dead to* it.

The second line,

And reddening Phœbus lifts his golden fire;

has indeed almost as many faults as words. But then it
is a bad line, not because the language is distinct from
that of prose; but because it conveys incongruous im-
ages, because it confounds the cause and the effect, the
real *thing* with the personified *representative* of the
thing; in short, because it differs from the language of
GOOD SENSE! That the "Phœbus" is hackneyed, and a
school-boy image, is an *accidental* fault, dependent on
the age in which the author wrote, and not deduced
from the nature of the thing. That it is part of an ex-
ploded mythology, is an objection more deeply grounded.
Yet when the torch of ancient learning was re-kindled,
so cheering were its beams, that our eldest poets, cut
off by Christianity from all *accredited* machinery, and

deprived of all *acknowledged* guardians and symbols of
the great objects of nature, were naturally induced to
adopt, as a *poetic* language, those fabulous personages,
those forms of the supernatural [1] in nature, which had
given them such dear delight in the poems of their great
masters. Nay, even at this day what scholar of genial
taste will not so far sympathize with them, as to read
with pleasure in PETRARCH, CHAUCER, or SPENSER, what
he would perhaps condemn as puerile in a modern poet?

I remember no poet, whose writings would safelier
stand the test of Mr. Wordsworth's theory, than SPENSER.
Yet will Mr. Wordsworth say, that the style of the fol-
lowing stanza is either undistinguished from prose, and
the language of ordinary life? Or that it is vicious, and
that the stanzas are *blots* in the *Faery Queene?*

> By this the northern waggoner had set
> His sevenfold teme behind the steadfast starre,
> That was in ocean waves yet never wet,
> But firme is fixt, and sendeth light from farre
> To all that in the wild deep wandering are:
> And chearful chanticleer with his note shrill
> Had warned once that Phœbus' fiery carre
> In haste was climbing up the easterne hill,
> Full envious that night so long his roome did fill.
>
> Book I, canto 2, stanza 2.

> At last the golden orientall gate
> Of greatest heaven gan to open fayre,
> And Phœbus fresh, as brydegrome to his mate,
> Came dauncing forth, shaking his deawie hayre,

[1] But still more by the mechanical system of philosophy
which has needlessly infected our theological opinions, and
teaching us to consider the world in its relation to God, as
of a building to its mason, leaves the idea of omnipresence
a mere abstract notion in the state-room of our reason.
—S. T. C.

And hurl'd his glist'ring beams through gloomy ayre:
Which when the wakeful elfe perceived, streightway
He started up, and did him selfe prepayre
In sun-bright armes and battailous array;
For with that pagan proud he combat will that day.

> Book I, canto 5, stanza 2.

On the contrary to how many passages, both in hymn books and in blank verse poems, could I, (were it not invidious), direct the reader's attention, the style of which is most *unpoetic, because,* and only because, it is the style of *prose?* He will not suppose me capable of having in my mind such verses, as

> I put my hat upon my head
> And walk'd into the Strand;
> And there I met another man,
> Whose hat was in his hand.

To such specimens it would indeed be a fair and full reply, that these lines are not bad, because they are *unpoetic;* but because they are empty of all sense and feeling; and that it were an idle attempt to prove that an ape is not a Newton, when it is evident that he is not a man. But the sense shall be good and weighty, the language correct and dignified, the subject interesting and treated with feeling; and yet the style shall, notwithstanding all these merits, be justly blamable as *prosaic,* and solely because the words and the order of the words would find their appropriate place in prose, but are not suitable to *metrical* composition. The "Civil Wars" of Daniel is an instructive, and even interesting work; but take the following stanzas (and from the hundred instances which abound I might probably have selected others far more striking):

> And to the end we may with better ease
> Discern the true discourse, vouchsafe to shew

What were the times foregoing near to these,
That these we may with better profit know.
Tell how the world fell into this disease;
And how so great distemperature did grow;
So shall we see with what degrees it came;
How things at full do soon wax out of frame.

Ten kings had from the Norman conqu'ror reign'd
With intermixt and variable fate,
When England to her greatest height attain'd
Of power, dominion, glory, wealth, and state;
After it had with much ado sustain'd
The violence of princes, with debate
For titles and the often mutinies
Of nobles for their ancient liberties.

For first, the Norman, conqu'ring all by might,
By might was forc'd to keep what he had got;
Mixing our customs and the form of right
With foreign constitutions he had brought;
Mast'ring the mighty, humbling the poorer wight,
By all severest means that could be wrought;
And, making the succession doubtful, rent
His new-got state, and left it turbulent.

> Book I, stanzas VII, VIII, and IX.

Will it be contended on the one side, that these lines
are mean and senseless? Or on the other, that they are
not prosaic, and for *that* reason unpoetic? This poet's
well-merited epithet is that of the *"well-languaged Dan-
iel;"* but likewise, and by the consent of his contempo-
raries no less than of all succeeding critics, the "prosaic
Daniel." Yet those, who thus designate this wise and
amiable writer, from the frequent incorrespondency of
his diction to his metre in the majority of his composi-
tions, not only deem them valuable and interesting on
other accounts; but willingly admit, that there are to be
found throughout his poems, and especially in his *Epis-*

tles and in his *Hymen's Triumph,* many and exquisite specimens of that style which, as the *neutral ground* of prose and verse, is common to both. A fine and almost faultless extract, eminent, as for other beauties, so for its perfection in this species of diction, may be seen in LAMB's Dramatic Specimens, &e., a work of various interest from the nature of the selections themselves, (all from the plays of Shakespeare's contemporaries), and deriving a high additional value from the notes, which are full of just and original criticism, expressed with all the freshness of originality.

Among the possible effects of practical adherence to a theory, that aims to *identify* the style of prose and verse, (if it does not indeed claim for the latter a yet nearer resemblance to the average style of men in the vivâ voce intercourse of real life) we might anticipate the following as not the least likely to occur. It will happen, as I have indeed before observed, that the metre itself, the sole acknowledged difference, will occasionally become metre to the eye only. The existence of *prosaisms,* and that they detract from the merit of a poem, *must* at length be conceded, when a number of successive lines can be rendered, even to the most delicate ear, unrecognizable as verse, or as having even been intended for verse, by simply transcribing them as prose; when, if the poem be in blank verse, this can be effected without any alteration, or at most by merely restoring one or two words to their proper places, from which they have been[1] transplanted for no assignable cause or

---

[1] As the ingenious gentleman under the influence of the Tragic Muse contrived to dislocate, "I wish you a good morning, Sir! Thank you, Sir, and I wish you the same," into two blank-verse heroics:—

To you a morning good, good Sir! I wish.
You, Sir! I thank: to you the same wish I.

reason but that of the author's convenience; but, if it be in rhyme, by the mere exchange of the final word of each line for some other of the same meaning, equally appropriate, dignified, and euphonic.

The answer or objection in the preface to the anticipated remark "that metre paves the way to other distinctions," is contained in the following words. "The distinction of rhyme and metre is voluntary and uniform, and not, like that produced by (what is called) poetic diction, arbitrary, and subject to infinite caprices, upon

---

In those parts of Mr. Wordsworth's works which I have thoroughly studied, I find fewer instances in which this would be practicable than I have met in many poems, where an approximation of prose has been sedulously and on system guarded against. Indeed excepting the stanzas already quoted from "THE SAILOR'S MOTHER," I can recollect but one instance: viz. a short passage of four or five lines in "THE BROTHERS," that model of English pastoral, which I have never yet read with unclouded eye.—"James, pointing to its summit, over which they had all purposed to return together, informed them that he would wait for them there. They parted, and his comrades passed that way some two hours after, but they did not find him at the appointed place, *a circumstance of which they took no heed:* but one of them, going by chance into the house, which at this time was James's house, learnt *there,* that nobody had seen him all that day." The only change which has been made is in the position of the little word *there* in two instances, the position in the original being clearly such as is not adopted in ordinary conversation. The other words printed in *italics* were so marked because, though good and genuine English, they are not the phraseology of common conversation either in the word put in apposition, or in the connection by the genitive pronoun. Men in general would have said, "but that was a circumstance they paid no attention to, or took no notice of," and the language is, on the theory of the preface, justified only by the narrator's being the *Vicar.* Yet if any ear *could* suspect, that these sentences were ever printed as metre, on these very words alone could the suspicion have been grounded.—*S. T. C.*

which no calculation whatever can be made. In the one
case the reader is utterly at the mercy of the poet re-
specting what imagery or diction he may choose to con-
nect with the passion." But is this a *poet*, of whom a
poet is speaking? No surely! rather of a fool or madman:
or at best of a vain or ignorant phantast! And might not
brains so wild and so deficient make just the same hav-
ock with rhymes and metres, as they are supposed to
effect with modes and figures of speech? How is the
reader at the *mercy* of such men? If he continue to read
their nonsense, is it not his own fault? The ultimate end
of criticism is much more to establish the principles of
writing, than to furnish *rules* how to pass judgement on
what has been written by others; if indeed it were possi-
ble that the two could be separated. But if it be asked,
by what principles the poet is to regulate his own style,
if he do not adhere closely to the sort and order of
words which he hears in the market, wake, high-road, or
plough-field? I reply; by principles, the ignorance or
neglect of which would convict him of being no *poet*,
but a silly or presumptuous usurper of the name! By the
principles of grammar, logic, psychology! In one word
by such a knowledge of the facts, material and spiritual,
that most appertain to his art, as, if it have been gov-
erned and applied by *good sense*, and rendered instinc-
tive by habit, becomes the representative and reward of
our past conscious reasonings, insights, and conclusions,
and acquires the name of TASTE. By what *rule* that does
not leave the reader at the poet's mercy, and the poet at
his own, is the latter to distinguish between the language
suitable to *suppressed*, and the language, which is char-
acteristic of *indulged*, anger? Or between that of rage
and that of jealousy? Is it obtained by wandering about
in search of angry or jealous people in uncultivated so-

ciety, in order to copy their words? Or not far rather by
the power of imagination proceeding upon the *all in
each* of human nature? By *meditation,* rather than by *ob-
servation?* And by the latter in consequence only of the
former? As eyes, for which the former has pre-deter-
mined their field of vision, and to which, as to *its* organ,
it communicates a microscopic power? There is not, I
firmly believe, a man now living, who has, from his own
inward experience, a clearer intuition, than Mr. Words-
worth himself, that the last mentioned are the true
sources of *genial* discrimination. Through the same proc-
ess and by the same creative agency will the poet dis-
tinguish the degree and kind of the excitement produced
by the very act of poetic composition. As intuitively will
he know, what differences of style it at once inspires and
justifies; what intermixture of conscious volition is nat-
ural to that state; and in what instances such figures and
colors of speech degenerate into mere creatures of an
arbitrary purpose, cold technical artifices of ornament
or connection. For, even as truth is its own light and
evidence, discovering at once itself and falsehood, so is
it the prerogative of poetic genius to distinguish by pa-
rental instinct its proper offspring from the changelings,
which the gnomes of vanity or the fairies of fashion may
have laid in its cradle or called by its names. Could a
rule be given from *without,* poetry would cease to be
poetry, and sink into a mechanical art. It would be
μόρφωσις, not ποίησις. The *rules* of the IMAGINATION are
themselves the very powers of growth and production.
The *words,* to which they are reducible, present only
the outlines and external appearance of the fruit. A de-
ceptive counterfeit of the superficial form and colors
may be elaborated; but the marble peach feels cold and
heavy, and *children* only put it to their mouths. We find

no difficulty in admitting as excellent, and the legitimate
language of poetic fervor self-impassioned, DONNE's
apostrophe to the Sun in the second stanza of his "Prog-
ress of the Soul:"

Thee, eye of heaven! this great soul envies not:
By thy male force is all, we have, begot.
In the first East thou now beginn'st to shine,
Suck'st early balm and island spices there,
And wilt anon in thy loose-rein'd career
At Tagus, Po, Seine, Thames, and Danow dine,
And see at night this western world of mine:
Yet hast thou not more nations seen than she,
Who before thee one day began to be,
And, thy frail light being quench'd, shall long, long outlive
   thee!

   Or the next stanza but one:

Great destiny, the commissary of God,
That hast mark'd out a path and period
For ev'ry thing! Who, where we offspring took,
Our ways and ends see'st at one instant: thou
Knot of all causes! Thou, whose changeless brow
Ne'er smiles or frowns! O! vouchsafe thou to look,
And shew my story in thy eternal book, &c.

   As little difficulty do we find in excluding from the
honors of unaffected warmth and elevation the madness
prepense of pseudo-poesy, or the startling *hysteric* of
weakness over-exerting itself, which bursts on the unpre-
pared reader in sundry odes and apostrophes to abstract
terms. Such are the Odes to Jealousy, to Hope, to Ob-
livion, and the like, in Dodsley's collection and the mag-
azines of that day, which seldom fail to remind me of an
Oxford copy of verses on the two SUTTONS, commencing
with

   INOCULATION, heavenly maid! descend!

It is not to be denied that men of undoubted talents, and even poets of true, though not of first-rate, genius, have from a mistaken theory deluded both themselves and others in the opposite extreme. I once read to a company of sensible and well-educated women the introductory period of Cowley's preface to his *"Pindaric Odes, written in imitation of the style and manner of the odes of Pindar."* "If, (says Cowley), a man should undertake to translate Pindar, word for word, it would be thought that one madman had translated another; as may appear, when he, that understands not the original, reads the verbal traduction of him into Latin prose, than which nothing seems more raving." I then proceeded with his own free version of the second Olympic, composed for the charitable purpose of *rationalizing* the Theban Eagle.

> Queen of all harmonious things,
> Dancing words and speaking strings,
> What God, what hero, wilt thou sing?
> What happy man to equal glories bring?
> Begin, begin thy noble choice,
> And let the hills around reflect the image of thy voice.
> Pisa does to Jove belong,
> Jove and Pisa claim thy song.
> The fair first-fruits of war, th' Olympic games,
> Alcides offer'd up to Jove;
> Alcides too thy strings may move!
> But, oh! what man to join with these can worthy prove?
> Join Theron boldly to their sacred names;
> Theron the next honor claims;
> Theron to no man gives place,
> Is first in Pisa's and in Virtue's race;
> Theron there, and he alone,
> Ev'n his own swift forefathers has outgone.

One of the company exclaimed, with the full assent of the rest, that if the original were madder than this, it must be incurably mad. I then translated the ode from the Greek, and as nearly as possible, word for word; and the impression was, that in the general movement of the periods, in the form of the connections and transitions, and in the sober majesty of lofty sense, it appeared to them to approach more nearly, than any other poetry they had heard, to the style of our Bible in the prophetic books. The first strophe will suffice as a specimen:

Ye harp-controuling hymns! (or) ye hymns the sovereigns of
    harps!
What God? what Hero?
What Man shall we celebrate?
Truly Pisa indeed is of Jove,
But the Olympiad (or the Olympic games) did Hercules
    establish,
The first-fruits of the spoils of war.
But Theron for the four-horsed car,
That bore victory to him,
It behoves us now to voice aloud:
The Just, the Hospitable,
The Bulwark of Agrigentum,
Of renowned fathers
The Flower, even him
Who preserves his native city erect and safe.

But are such rhetorical caprices condemnable only for their deviation from the language of real life? and are they by no other means to be precluded, but by the rejection of all distinctions between prose and verse, save that of metre? Surely good sense, and a moderate insight into the constitution of the human mind, would be amply sufficient to prove, that such language and such combinations are the native produce neither of the fancy nor of the imagination; that their operation consists in the excitement of surprise by the juxta-position and *apparent* reconciliation of widely different or incompatible

things. As when, for instance, the hills are made to re-
flect the image of a *voice*. Surely, no unusual taste is
requisite to see clearly, that this compulsory juxta-posi-
tion is not produced by the presentation of impressive
or delightful forms to the inward vision, nor by any sym-
pathy with the modifying powers with which the genius
of the poet had united and inspirited all the objects of
his thought; that it is therefore a species of *wit*, a pure
work of the *will*, and implies a leisure and self-possession
both of thought and of feeling, incompatible with the
steady fervor of a mind possessed and filled with the
grandeur of its subject. To sum up the whole in one sen-
tence. When a poem, or a part of a poem, shall be ad-
duced, which is evidently vicious in the figures and
contexture of its style, yet for the condemnation of which
no reason can be assigned, except that it differs from
the style in which men actually converse, then, and not
till then, can I hold this theory to be either plausible, or
practicable, or capable of furnishing either rule, guid-
ance, or precaution, that might not, more easily and
more safely, as well as more naturally, have been de-
duced in the author's own mind from considerations of
grammar, logic, and the truth and nature of things, con-
firmed by the authority of works, whose fame is not of
ONE country nor of ONE age.

Chapter XIX

*Continuation—Concerning the real object which, it is prob-
able, Mr. Wordsworth had before him in his critical preface.*

It might appear from some passages in the former
part of Mr. Wordsworth's preface, that he meant to con-
fine his theory of style, and the necessity of a close ac-

cordance with the actual language of men, to those
particular subjects from low and rustic life, which by
way of experiment he had purposed to naturalize as a
new species in our English poetry. But from the train
of argument that follows; from the reference to Milton;
and from the spirit of his critique on Gray's sonnet;
those sentences appear to have been rather courtesies
of modesty, than actual limitations of his system. Yet so
groundless does this system appear on a close examina-
tion; and so strange and over-whelming in its conse-
quences, that I cannot, and I do not, believe that the
poet did ever himself adopt it in the unqualified sense,
in which his expressions have been understood by others,
and which, indeed, according to all the common laws
of interpretation they seem to bear. What then did he
mean? I apprehend, that in the clear perception, not
unaccompanied with disgust or contempt, of the gaudy
affections of a style which passed current with too many
for poetic diction, (though in truth it had as little pre-
tensions to poetry, as to logic or, common sense), he
narrowed his view for the time; and feeling a justifiable
preference for the language of nature and of good sense,
even in its humblest and least ornamented forms, he suf-
fered himself to express, in terms at once too large and
too exclusive, his predilection for a style the most re-
mote possible from the false and showy splendour which
he wished to explode. It is possible, that this predilec-
tion, at first merely comparative, deviated for a time into
direct partiality. But the real object which he had in
view, was, I doubt not, a species of excellence which had
been long before most happily characterized by the judi-
cious and amiable GARVE, whose works are so justly be-
loved and esteemed by the Germans, in his remarks on
GELLERT, (see Sammlung einiger Abhandlungen von
Christian Garve), from which the following is literally

translated. "The talent, that is required to make excellent verses, is perhaps greater than the philosopher is ready to admit, or would find it in his power to acquire: the talent to seek only the apt expression of the thought, and yet to find at the same time with it the rhyme and the metre. Gellert possessed this happy gift, if ever any one of our poets possessed it; and nothing perhaps contributed more to the great and universal impression which his fables made on their first publication, or conduces more to their continued popularity. It was a strange and curious phenomenon, and such as in Germany had been previously unheard of, to read verses in which everything was expressed just as one would wish to talk, and yet all dignified, attractive, and interesting; and all at the same time perfectly correct as to the measure of the syllables and the rhyme. It is certain, that poetry when it has attained this excellence makes a far greater impression than prose. So much so indeed, that even the gratification which the very rhymes afford, becomes then no longer a contemptible or trifling gratification."

Chapter XX

The former subject continued.

I have no fear in declaring my conviction, that the excellence defined and exemplified in the preceding Chapter is not the characteristic excellence of Mr. Wordsworth's style; because I can add with equal sincerity, that it is precluded by higher powers. The praise of uniform adherence to genuine, logical English is undoubtedly his; nay, laying the main emphasis on the word *uniform,* I will dare add that, of all contemporary poets, it is *his alone.* For in a less absolute sense of the word, I should certainly include Mr. Bowles, Lord Byron, and, as to all his later writings, Mr. Southey, the exceptions in their work being so few and unimportant. But of the specific excellence described in the quotation from Garve, I appear to find more, and more undoubted specimens in the works of others; for instance, among the minor poems of Mr. Thomas Moore, and of our illustrious Laureate. To me it will always remain a singular and noticeable fact; that a theory which would establish this *lingua communis,* not only as the best, but as the only commendable style, should have proceeded from a poet, whose diction, next to that of Shakespeare and Milton, appears to me of all others the most *individualized* and characteristic. And let it be remembered too, that I am now interpreting the controverted passages of Mr. W's. critical preface by the purpose and object, which he may be supposed to have intended, rather than by the sense which the words themselves must convey, if they are taken without this allowance.

A person of any taste, who had but studied three or four of Shakespeare's principal plays, would without the name affixed scarcely fail to recognise as Shakespeare's a quotation from any other play, though but of a few lines. A similar peculiarity, though in a less degree, attends Mr. Wordsworth's style, whenever he speaks in his own person; or whenever, though under a feigned name, it is clear that he himself is still speaking, as in the different dramatis personæ of the "Recluse." Even in the other poems, in which he purposes to be most dramatic, there are few in which it does not occasionally burst forth. The reader might often address the poet in his own words with reference to the persons introduced:

It seems, as I retrace the ballad line by line,
That but half of it is theirs, and the better half is thine.

Who, having been previously acquainted with any considerable portion of Mr. Wordsworth's publications, and having studied them with a full feeling of the author's genius, would not at once claim as Wordsworthian the little poem on the rainbow?

> The child is father of the man, &c.

Or in the "Lucy Gray"?

> No mate, no comrade Lucy knew;
> She dwelt on a wide moor;
> *The sweetest thing that ever grew*
> *Beside a human door.*

Or in the "Idle Shepherd-boys"?

> Along the river's stony marge
> The sand-lark chaunts a joyous song;
> The thrush is busy in the wood,
> And carols loud and strong.
> A thousand lambs are on the rocks,
> All newly born! both earth and sky
> Keep jubilee, and more than all,
> Those boys with their green coronal;
> They never hear the cry,
> That plaintive cry! which up the hill
> Comes from the depth of Dungeon Gill.

Need I mention the exquisite description of the Sea Loch in the "Blind Highland Boy"? Who but a poet tells a tale in such language to the little ones by the fire-side as—

> Yet had he many a restless dream
> Both when he heard the eagle's scream,
> And when he heard the torrents roar,

And heard the water beat the shore
　　Near where their cottage stood.

Beside a lake their cottage stood,
Not small like ours, a peaceful flood,
But one of mighty size, and strange,
That, rough or smooth, is full of change,
　　And stirring in its bed.

For to this lake, by night and day,
The great sea-water finds its way
Through long, long windings of the hills,
And drinks up all the pretty rills
　　And rivers large and strong:

Then hurries back the road it came—
Returns on errand still the same;
This did it when the earth was new;
And this for evermore will do,
　　As long as earth shall last.

And with the coming of the tide,
Come boats and ships that sweetly ride,
Between the woods and lofty rocks;
And to the shepherds with their flocks
　　Bring tales of distant lands.

I might quote almost the whole of his "RUTH," but
take the following stanzas:

But, as you have before been told,
This stripling, sportive, gay, and bold,
And with his dancing crest,
So beautiful, through savage lands
Had roamed about with vagrant bands
　　Of Indians in the West.

The wind, the tempest roaring high,
The tumult of a tropic sky,
Might well be dangerous food
For him, a youth to whom was given
So much of earth, so much of heaven,
    And such impetuous blood.

Whatever in those climes he found
Irregular in sight or sound,
Did to his mind impart
A kindred impulse, seemed allied
To his own powers, and justified
    The workings of his heart.

Nor less, to feed voluptuous thought,
The beauteous forms of nature wrought,
Fair trees and lovely flowers;
The breezes their own languor lent;
The stars had feelings, which they sent
    Into those magic bowers.

Yet, in his worst pursuits, I ween
That sometimes there did intervene
Pure hopes of high intent:
For passions, linked to forms so fair
And stately, needs must have their share
    Of noble sentiment.

But from Mr. Wordsworth's more elevated compo-
sitions, which already form three-fourths of his works;
and will, I trust, constitute hereafter a still larger pro-
portion;—from these, whether in rhyme or blank-verse,
it would be difficult and almost superfluous to select
instances of a diction peculiarly his own, of a style which
cannot be imitated, without its being at once recognised

as originating in Mr. Wordsworth. It would not be easy to open on any one of his loftier strains, that does not contain examples of this; and more in proportion as the lines are more excellent, and most like the author. For those, who may happen to have been less familiar with his writings, I will give three specimens taken with little choice. The first from the lines on the "BOY OF WIN-ANDER-MERE,"—who

> Blew mimic hootings to the silent owls,
> That they might answer him. And they would shout
> Across the watery vale, and shout again,
> With long halloos and screams, and echoes loud
> Redoubled and redoubled; concourse wild
> Of mirth and jocund din. And when it chanced,
> That pauses of deep silence mock'd his skill,
> *Then sometimes in that silence, while he hung*
> *Listening, a gentle shock of mild surprize*
> *Has carried far into his heart the voice*
> *Of mountain-torrents; or the visible scene*[1]

[1] Mr. Wordsworth's having judiciously adopted *"con-course wild"* in this passage for *"a wild scene"* as it stood in the former edition, encourages me to hazard a remark, which I certainly should not have made in the works of a poet less austerely accurate in the use of the words, than he is, to his own great honor. It respects the propriety of the word *"scene,"* even in the sentence in which it is retained. DRYDEN, and he only in his more careless verses, was the first, as far as my researches have discovered, who for the convenience of rhyme used this word in the vague sense, which has been since too current even in our best writers, and which (unfortunately, I think) is given as its first explanation in Dr. Johnson's Dictionary, and therefore would be taken by an incautious reader as its proper sense. In Shakespeare and Milton the word is never used without some clear reference, proper or metaphorical, to the theatre. Thus Milton:

> Cedar, and pine, and fir, and branching palm,
> A sylvan *scene;* and, as the ranks ascend,

Would enter unawares into his mind
With all its solemn imagery, its rocks,
Its woods, and that uncertain heaven, received
Into the bosom of the steady lake.

The second shall be that noble imitation of Drayton[1]
(if it was not rather a coincidence) in the "JOANNA."

When I had gazed perhaps two minutes' space,
Joanna, looking in my eyes, beheld
That ravishment of mine, and laughed aloud.
The rock, like something starting from a sleep,
Took up the lady's voice, and laughed again!
That ancient woman seated on HELM-CRAG
Was ready with her cavern; HAMMAR-SCAR

Shade above shade, a woody *theatre*
Of stateliest view.

I object to any extension of its meaning, because the word
is already more equivocal than might be wished; inasmuch
as in the limited use, which I recommend, it may still signify
two different things; namely, the scenery, and the characters
and actions presented on the stage during the presence of
particular scenes. It can therefore be preserved from *obscurity*
only by keeping the original signification full in the mind.
Thus Milton again:
"Prepare thou for another scene."
—S. T. C.

[1] Which COPLAND scarce had spoke, but quickly every hill,
Upon her verge that stands, the neighbouring vallies fill;
HELVILLON from his height it through the mountains threw,
From whom as soon again the sound DUNBALRASE drew,
From whose stone-trophied head it on the WENDROSS went,
Which tow'rds the sea again resounded it to DENT.
That BROADWATER, therewith within her banks astound,
In sailing to the sea, told it to EGREMOUND,
Whose buildings, walks, and streets, with echoes loud and
    long,
Did mightily commend old COPLAND for her song.
DRAYTON'S POLYOLBION: *Song XXX.*—*S. T. C.*

And the tall steep of SILVER-HOW sent forth
A noise of laughter; southern LOUGHRIGG heard,
And FAIRFIELD answered with a mountain tone.
HELVELLYN far into the clear blue sky
Carried the lady's voice!—old SKIDDAW blew
His speaking trumpet!—back out of the clouds
From GLARAMARA southward came the voice:
And KIRKSTONE tossed it from his misty head!

The third, which is in rhyme, I take from the "Song
at the feast of Brougham Castle, upon the restoration
of Lord Clifford the shepherd to the estates of his an-
cestors."

Now another day is come,
Fitter hope, and nobler doom;
He hath thrown aside his crook,
And hath buried deep his book;
Armour rusting in the halls
On the blood of Clifford calls;
"Quell the Scot," exclaims the lance!
"Bear me to the heart of France,"
Is the longing of the shield—
Tell thy name, thou trembling field!—
Field of death, where'er thou be,
Groan thou with our victory!
Happy day, and mighty hour,
When our shepherd, in his power,
Mailed and horsed, with lance and sword,
To his ancestors restored,
Like a re-appearing star,
Like a glory from afar,
First shall head the flock of war!

Alas! the fervent harper did not know
That for a tranquil soul the lay was framed,

Who, long compelled in humble walks to go,
Was softened into feeling, soothed, and tamed.

Love had he found in huts where poor men lie:
His daily teachers had been woods and rills;
The silence that is in the starry sky,
The sleep that is among the lonely hills.

The words themselves, in the foregoing extracts, are no doubt sufficiently common for the greater part. (But in what poem are they not so, if we except a few mis-adventurous attempts to translate the arts and sciences into verse?) In the "Excursion" the number of poly-syllabic (or what the common people call, *dictionary*) words is more than usually great. And so must it needs be, in proportion to the number and variety of an author's conceptions, and his solicitude to express them with precision. But are those words *in those places* com-monly employed in real life to express the same thought or outward thing? Are they the style used in the ordi-nary intercourse of spoken words? No! nor are the modes of connections; and still less the breaks and transitions. Would any but a poet—at least could any one without being conscious that he had expressed himself with noticeable vivacity—have described a bird singing loud by, "The thrush is *busy* in the wood?"—or have spoken of boys with a string of club-moss round their rusty hats, as the boys *"with their green coronal?"* —or have translated a beautiful May-day into *"Both earth and sky keep jubilee?"* or have brought all the different marks and circumstances of a sea-loch before the mind, as the actions of a living and acting power? Or have represented the reflection of the sky in the water, as *"That uncertain heaven received into the bosom of the steady lake?"* Even the grammatical construction is not unfrequently peculiar; as "*The wind, the tempest roaring high, the tumult of a tropic sky,* might well be dangerous food *to him, a youth* to whom was given, &c.*" There is a peculiarity in the frequent use of the ἀσυνάρτητον (i. e. the omission of the connective particle before the last of several words, or several sentences used grammatically as single words, all being in the same case and governing or governed by the same verb) and not less in the construction of words by apposition (*to him, a youth*). In short, were there excluded from Mr. Wordsworth's poetic compositions all, that a literal adherence to the theory of his preface *would* exclude, two-thirds at least of the marked beauties of his poetry must be erased. For a far greater number of lines would be sacrificed than in any other recent poet; because the pleasure received from Wordsworth's poems being less derived either from excitement of curiosity or the rapid flow of narration, the *striking* passages form a larger proportion of their value. I do not adduce it as a fair criterion of comparative excellence, nor do I even think it such; but merely as matter of fact. I affirm, that from no contemporary writer could so many lines be quoted, without reference to the poem in which they are found, for their own independent weight or beauty. From the sphere of my own experience I can bring to my recollection three persons of no every-day powers and acquirements, who had read the poems of others with more, and more unalloyed pleasure, and had thought more highly of their authors, as poets; who yet have confessed to me, that from no modern work had so many passages started up anew in their minds at different times, and as different occasions had awakened a meditative mood.

Chapter XXII

The characteristic defects of Wordsworth's poetry, with the principles from which the judgement, that they are defects, is deduced—Their proportion to the beauties—For the greatest part characteristic of his theory only.

If Mr. Wordsworth have set forth principles of poetry which his arguments are insufficient to support, let him and those who have adopted his sentiments be set right by the confutation of these arguments, and by the substitution of more philosophical principles. And still let the due credit be given to the portion and importance of the truths, which are blended with his theory; truths, the too exclusive attention to which had occasioned its errors, by tempting him to carry those truths beyond their proper limits. If his mistaken theory have at all influenced his poetic compositions, let the effects be pointed out, and the instances given. But let it likewise be shown, how far the influence has acted; whether diffusively, or only by starts; whether the number and importance of the poems and passages thus infected be great or trifling compared with the sound portion; and lastly, whether they are inwoven into the texture of his works, or are loose and separable. The result of such a trial would evince beyond a doubt, what it is high time to announce decisively and aloud, that the *supposed* characteristics of Mr. Wordsworth's poetry, whether admired or reprobated; whether they are simplicity or simpleness; faithful adherence to essential nature, or wilful selections from human nature of its meanest forms and under the least attractive associations; are as little the *real* characteristics of his poetry at large, as of his genius and the constitution of his mind.

In a comparatively small number of poems he chose to try an experiment; and this experiment we will suppose to have failed. Yet even in these poems it is impossible not to perceive that the natural *tendency* of the poet's mind is to great objects and elevated conceptions. The poem entitled "Fidelity" is for the greater part written in language, as unraised and naked as any perhaps in the two volumes. Yet take the following stanza and compare it with the preceding stanzas of the same poem.

> There sometimes doth a leaping fish
> Send through the tarn a lonely cheer;
> The crags repeat the raven's croak,
> In symphony austere;
> Thither the rainbow comes—the cloud—
> And mists that spread the flying shroud;
> And sun-beams; and the sounding blast,
> That if it could would hurry past;
> But that enormous barrier binds it fast.

Or compare the four last lines of the concluding stanza with the former half.

> Yes, proof was plain that since the day
> On which the traveller thus had died,
> The dog had watched about the spot,
> Or by his master's side
> *How nourish'd there through such long time*
> *He knows, who gave that love sublime,*
> *And gave that strength of feeling, great*
> *Above all human estimate!*

Can any candid and intelligent mind hesitate in determining, which of these best represents the tendency and native character of the poet's genius? Will he not decide that the one was written because the poet *would*

so write, and the other because he could not so entirely
repress the force and grandeur of his mind, but that he
must in some part or other of *every* composition write
otherwise? In short, that his only disease is the being
out of his element; like the swan, that, having amused
himself, for a while, with crushing the weeds on the
river's bank, soon returns to his own majestic movements
on its reflecting and sustaining surface. Let it be ob-
served that I am here supposing the imagined judge, to
whom I appeal, to have already decided against the
poet's theory, as far as it is different from the principles
of the art, generally acknowledged.

I cannot here enter into a detailed examination of Mr.
Wordsworth's works; but I will attempt to give the main
results of my own judgement, after the acquaintance of
many years, and repeated perusals. And though, to ap-
preciate the defects of a great mind it is necessary to
understand previously its characteristic excellences, yet
I have already expressed myself with sufficient fulness,
to preclude most of the ill effects that might arise from
my pursuing a contrary arrangement. I will therefore
commence with what I deem the prominent *defects* of
his poems hitherto published.

The first *characteristic, though only occasional* defect,
which I appear to myself to find in these poems is the
INCONSTANCY of the *style*. Under this name I refer to the
sudden and unprepared transitions from lines or sen-
tences of peculiar felicity (at all events striking and
original) to a style, not only unimpassioned but undis-
tinguished. He sinks too often and too abruptly to that
style, which I should place in the second division of lan-
guage, dividing it into the three species; *first*, that which
is peculiar to poetry; *second*, that which is only proper
in prose; and *third*, the neutral or common to both.
There have been works, such as Cowley's Essay on

Cromwell, in which prose and verse are intermixed (not as in the Consolation of Boetius, or the Argenis of Barclay, by the insertion of poems supposed to have been spoken or composed on occasions previously related in prose, but) the poet passing from one to the other, as the nature of the thoughts or his own feelings dictated. Yet this mode of composition does not satisfy a cultivated taste. There is something unpleasant in the being thus obliged to alternate states of feeling so dissimilar, and this too in a species of writing, the pleasure from which is in part derived from the preparation and previous expectation of the reader. A portion of that awkwardness is felt which hangs upon the introduction of songs in our modern comic operas; and to prevent which the judicious Metastasio (as to whose exquisite *taste* there can be no hesitation, whatever doubts may be entertained as to his *poetic genius*) uniformly placed the ARIA at the end of the scene, at the same time that he almost always raises and impassions the style of the recitative immediately preceding. Even in real life, the difference is great and evident between words used as the *arbitrary marks* of thought, our smooth market-coin of intercourse, with the image and superscription worn out by currency; and those which convey pictures either borrowed from *one* outward object to enliven and particularize some *other;* or used allegorically to body forth the inward state of the person speaking; or such as are at least the exponents of his peculiar turn and unusual extent of faculty. So much so indeed, that in the social circles of private life we often find a striking use of the latter put a stop to the general flow of conversation, and by the excitement arising from concentered attention produce a sort of damp and interruption for some minutes after. But in the perusal of works of literary *art,* we *prepare* ourselves for such language; and the busi-

ness of the writer, like that of a painter whose subject
requires unusual splendor and prominence, is so to raise
the lower and neutral tints, that what in a different style
would be the *commanding* colors, are here used as the
means of that gentle *degradation* requisite in order to
produce the effect of a *whole*. Where this is not achieved
in a poem, the metre merely reminds the reader of his
claims in order to disappoint them; and where this
defect occurs frequently, his feelings are alternately
startled by anticlimax and hyperclimax.

I refer the reader to the exquisite stanzas cited for
another purpose from "the blind Highland Boy"; and
then annex, as being in my opinion instances of this
disharmony in style, the two following:

> And one, the rarest, was a shell,
> Which he, poor child, had studied well:
> The shell of a green turtle, thin
> And hollow;—you might sit therein,
> > It was so wide, and deep.

> Our Highland Boy oft visited
> The house which held this prize; and, led
> By choice or chance, did thither come
> One day, when no one was at home,
> > And found the door unbarred.

Or page 172, vol. I.

> 'Tis gone—forgotten—*let me do*
> *My best*. There was a smile or two—
> I can remember them, I see
> The smiles worth all the world to me.
> Dear Baby, I must lay thee down:
> Thou troublest me with strange alarms;
> Smiles hast thou, sweet ones of thine own;
> I cannot keep thee in my arms;
> For they confound me: *as it is*,
> I have forgot those smiles of his!

Or page 269, vol. I.

> Thou hast a nest, for thy love and thy rest,
> And though little troubled with sloth
> Drunken lark! thou would'st be loth
> To be such a traveller as I.
>   Happy, happy liver!
> *With a soul as strong as a mountain river*
> *Pouring out praise to th' Almighty giver!*
> Joy and jollity be with us both!
> Hearing thee or else some other,
>   As merry a brother
> I on the earth will go plodding on
> By myself chearfully till the day is done.

The incongruity, which I appear to find in this passage, is that of the two noble lines in italics with the preceding and following. So vol. II. page 30.

> Close by a pond, upon the further side,
> He stood alone; a minute's space, I guess,
> I watch'd him, he continuing motionless:
> To the pool's further margin then I drew,
> He being all the while before me full in view.

Compare this with the repetition of the same image, in the next stanza but two.

> And, still as I drew near with gentle pace,
> Beside the little pond or moorish flood
> Motionless as a cloud the old man stood,
> That heareth not the loud winds as they call,
> And moveth altogether, if it move at all.

Or lastly, the second of the three following stanzas, compared both with the first and the third.

> My former thoughts returned; the fear that kills;
> And hope that is unwilling to be fed;
> Cold, pain, and labour, and all fleshly ills;

And mighty poets in their misery dead.
But now, perplex'd by what the old man had said,
My question eagerly did I renew,
"How is it that you live, and what is it you do?"

He with a smile did then his words repeat;
And said, that gathering leeches far and wide
He travell'd; stirring thus about his feet
The waters of the ponds where they abide.
"Once I could meet with them on every side,
"But they have dwindled long by slow decay;
"Yet still I persevere, and find them where I may."

While he was talking thus, the lonely place,
The old man's shape, and speech, all troubled me:
In my mind's eye I seemed to see him pace
About the weary moors continually,
Wandering about alone and silently.

Indeed this fine poem is *especially* characteristic of
the author. There is scarce a defect or excellence in his
writings of which it would not present a specimen. But
it would be unjust not to repeat that this defect is only
occasional. From a careful reperusal of the two volumes
of poems, I doubt whether the objectionable passages
would amount in the whole to one hundred lines; not
the eighth part of the number of pages. In the "Excur-
sion" the feeling of incongruity is seldom excited
by the diction of any passage considered in itself, but
by the sudden superiority of some other passage form-
ing the context.

The second defect I can generalize with tolerable
accuracy, if the reader will pardon an uncouth and new-
coined word. There is, I should say, not seldom a *matter-
of-factness* in certain poems. This may be divided into,
first, a laborious minuteness and fidelity in the repre-
sentation of objects, and their positions, as they appeared
to the poet himself; *secondly,* the insertion of accidental

circumstances, in order to the full explanation of his living characters, their dispositions and actions; which circumstances might be necessary to establish the probability of a statement in real life, where nothing is taken for granted by the hearer; but appear superfluous in poetry, where the reader is willing to believe for his own sake. To this *accidentality* I object, as contravening the essence of poetry, which Aristotle pronounces to be σπουδαιότατον καὶ φιλοσοφώτατον γένος, the most intense, weighty and philosophical product of human art; adding, as the *reason*, that it is the most catholic and abstract. The following passage from Davenant's prefatory letter to Hobbs well expresses this truth. "When I considered the actions which I meant to describe, (those inferring the persons), I was again persuaded rather to choose those of a former age, than the present; and in a century so far removed, as might preserve me from their improper examinations, who know not the requisites of a poem, nor how much pleasure they lose, (and even the pleasures of heroic posey are not unprofitable), who take away the liberty of a poet, and fetter his feet in the shackles of an historian. For why should a poet doubt in story to mend the intrigues of fortune by more delightful conveyances of probable fictions, because austere historians have entered into bond to truth? An obligation, which were in poets as foolish and unnecessary, as in the bondage of false martyrs, who lie in chains for a mistaken opinion. *But by this I would imply, that truth narrative and past is the idol of historians, (who worship a dead thing), and truth operative, and by effects continually alive, is the mistress of poets, who hath not her existence in matter, but in reason.*"

For this minute accuracy in the painting of local imagery, the lines in the EXCURSION, pp. 96, 97, and 98, may be taken, if not as a striking instance, yet as an

illustration of my meaning. It must be some strong mo-
tive (as, for instance, that the description was necessary
to the intelligibility of the tale) which could induce me
to describe in a number of verses what a draughtsman
could present to the eye with incomparably greater satis-
faction by half a dozen strokes of his pencil, or the
painter with as many touches of his brush. Such descrip-
tions too often occasion in the mind of a reader, who is
determined to understand his author, a feeling of labor,
not very dissimilar to that, with which he would con-
struct a diagram, line by line, for a long geometrical
proposition. It seems to be like taking the pieces of a
dissected map out of its box. We first look at one part,
and then at another, then join and dove-tail them; and
when the successive acts of attention have been com-
pleted, there is a retrogressive effort of mind to behold
it as a whole. The poet should paint to the imagination,
not to the fancy; and I know no happier case to exem-
plify the distinction between these two faculties. Master-
pieces of the former mode of poetic painting abound in
the writings of Milton, ex. gr.

> The fig-tree; not that kind for fruit renown'd,
> But such as at this day, to Indians known,
> In Malabar or Decan spreads her arms
> Branching so broad and long, that in the ground
> The bended twigs take root, *and daughters grow*
> *About the mother tree, a pillar'd shade*
> *High over-arch'd, and* ECHOING WALKS BETWEEN:
> *There oft the Indian Herdsman, shunning heat,*
> *Shelters in cool, and tends his pasturing herds*
> *At loop holes cut through thickest shade.*
>   Milton, *Paradise Lost*, Book IX, 1100.

This is *creation* rather than *painting*, or if painting,
yet such, and with such co-presence of the whole picture
flash'd at once upon the eye, as the sun paints in a

camera obscura. But the poet must likewise understand and command what Bacon calls the *vestigia communia* of the senses, the latency of all in each, and more especially as by a magical *penna duplex,* the excitement of vision by sound and the exponents of sound. Thus "THE ECHOING WALKS BETWEEN," may be almost said to reverse the fable in tradition of the head of Memnon, in the Egyptian statue. Such may be deservedly entitled the *creative words* in the world of imagination.

The second division respects an apparent minute adherence to *matter-of-fact* in characters and incidents; *a biographical* attention to probability, and an *anxiety* of explanation and retrospect. Under this head I shall deliver, with no feigned diffidence, the results of my best reflection on the great point of controversy between Mr. Wordsworth and his objectors; namely, on THE CHOICE OF HIS CHARACTERS. I have already declared and, I trust, justified, my utter dissent from the mode of argument which his critics have hitherto employed. To *their* question, Why did you chuse such a character, or a character from such a rank of life? the poet might in my opinion fairly retort: why with the conception of my character did you make wilful choice of mean or ludicrous associations not furnished by me, but supplied from your own sickly and fastidious feelings? How was it, indeed, probable, that such arguments could have any weight with an author, whose plan, whose guiding principle, and main object it was to attack and subdue that state of association, which leads us to place the chief value on those things in which man DIFFERS from man, and to forget or disregard the high dignities, which belong to HUMAN NATURE, the sense and the feeling, which *may* be, and *ought* to be, found in *all* ranks? The feelings with which, as Christians, we contemplate a mixed congregation rising or kneeling before their common Maker:

Mr. Wordsworth would have us entertain at *all* times, as men, and as readers; and by the excitement of this lofty, yet prideless impartiality in *poetry*, he might hope to have encouraged its continuance in *real life*. The praise of good men be his! In real life, and, I trust, even in my imagination, I honor a virtuous and wise man, without reference to the presence or absence of artificial advantages. Whether in the person of an armed baron, a laurel'd bard, &c., or of an old pedlar, or still older leach-gatherer, the same qualities of head and heart must claim the same reverence. And even in poetry I am not conscious, that I have ever suffered my feelings to be disturbed or offended by any thoughts or images, which the poet himself has not presented.

But yet I object nevertheless and for the following reasons. First, because the object in view, as an *immediate* object, belongs to the moral philosopher, and would be pursued, not only more appropriately, but in my opinion with far greater probability of success, in sermons or moral essays, than in an elevated poem. It seems, indeed, to destroy the main fundamental distinction, not only between a poem and prose, but even between philosophy and works of fiction, inasmuch as it proposes *truth* for its immediate object, instead of *pleasure*. Now till the blessed time shall come, when truth itself shall be pleasure, and both shall be so united, as to be distinguishable in words only, not in feeling, it will remain the poet's office to proceed upon that state of association, which actually exists as *general;* instead of attempting first to *make* it what it ought to be, and then to let the pleasure follow. But here is unfortunately a small *Hysteron-Proteron.* For the communication of pleasure is the introductory means by which alone the poet must expect to moralize his readers. Secondly: though I were to admit, for a moment, *this* argument to be groundless: yet how is the moral effect to be produced, by merely attaching the name of some low profession to powers which are *least* likely, and to qualities which are assuredly not *more* likely, to be found in it? The poet, speaking in his own person, may at once delight and improve us by sentiments, which teach us the independence of goodness, of wisdom, and even of genius, on the favors of fortune. And having made a due reverence before the throne of Antonine, he may bow with equal awe before Epictetus among his fellow-slaves—

> ————and rejoice
> In the plain presence of his dignity.

Who is not at once delighted and improved, when the POET Wordsworth himself exclaims,

> O many are the poets that are sown
> By Nature; men endowed with highest gifts,
> The vision and the faculty divine,
> Yet wanting the accomplishment of verse,
> Nor having e'er, as life advanced, been led
> By circumstance to take unto the height
> The measure of themselves, these favor'd beings,
> All but a scatter'd few, live out their time
> Husbanding that which they possess within,
> And go to the grave unthought of. Strongest minds
> Are often those of whom the noisy world
> Hears least.
>
> *Excursion,* Book I.

To use a colloquial phrase, such sentiments, in such language, do one's heart good; though I for my part, have not the fullest faith in the *truth* of the observation. On the contrary I believe the instances to be exceedingly rare; and should feel almost as strong an objection to introduce such a character in a poetic fiction, as a pair of black swans on a lake in a fancy-landscape. When I think how many, and how much better books than Homer, or even than Herodotus, Pindar or Eschylus, could have read, are in the power of almost every man, in a country where almost every man is instructed to read and write; and how restless, how difficultly hidden, the powers of genius are; and yet find even in situations the most favorable, according to Mr. Wordsworth, for the formation of a pure and poetic language; in situations which ensure familiarity with the grandest objects of the imagination; but *one* BURNS, among the shepherds of *Scotland*, and not a single poet of humble life among those of *English* lakes and mountains; I conclude, that POETIC GENIUS is not only a very delicate but a very rare plant.

But be this as it may, the feelings with which

> I think of CHATTERTON, the marvellous boy,
> The sleepless soul, that perished in his pride;
> Of BURNS, that walk'd in glory and in joy
> Behind his plough upon the mountain-side—

are widely different from those with which I should read a *poem*, where the author, having occasion for the character of a poet and a philosopher in the fable of his narration, had chosen to make him a *chimney-sweeper;* and then, in order to remove all doubts on the subject, had *invented* an account of his birth, parentage and education, with all the strange and fortunate accidents which had concurred in making him at once poet, philosopher, and sweep! Nothing but biography can justify this. If it be admissible even in a *Novel*, it must be one in the manner of De Foe's, that were meant to pass for histories, not in the manner of Fielding's: in the life of Moll Flanders, or Colonel Jack, not in a Tom Jones, or even a Joseph Andrews. Much less then can it be legitimately introduced in a *poem*, the characters of which, amid the strongest individualization, must still remain representative. The precepts of Horace, on this point, are grounded on the nature both of poetry and of the human mind. They are not more peremptory, than wise and prudent. For in the first place a deviation from them perplexes the reader's feelings, and all the circumstances, which are feigned in order to make such accidents less improbable, divide and disquiet his faith, rather than aid and support it. Spite of all attempts, the fiction *will* appear, and unfortunately not as *fictitious* but as *false*. The reader not only *knows*, that the sentiments and language are the poet's own, and his own too in his *artificial* character, *as poet;* but by the fruitless endeavours to make him think the contrary, he is not even suffered to *forget* it. The effect is similar to that produced by an epic poet, when the fable and the characters are *derived* from Scripture history, as in the *Messiah* of Klopstock, or in Cumberland's *Calvary;* and not merely *suggested* by it, as in the *Paradise Lost* of Milton. That *illusion*, contra-distinguished from *delusion*, that *negative* faith, which simply permits the images presented to work by their own force, without either denial or affirmation of their real existence by the judgement, is rendered impossible by their immediate neighbourhood to words and facts of known and absolute truth. A faith, which transcends even historic belief, must absolutely *put out* this mere poetic Analogon of faith, as the summer sun is said to extinguish our household fires, when it shines full upon them. What would otherwise have been yielded to as pleasing fiction, is repelled as revolting falsehood. The effect produced in this latter case by the solemn belief of the reader, is in a less degree brought about in the instances, to which I have been objecting, by the baffled attempts of the author to *make* him believe.

Add to all the foregoing the seeming uselessness both of the project and of the anecdotes from which it is to derive support. Is there one word, for instance, attributed to the pedlar in the "Excursion," characteristic of a *pedlar?* One sentiment, that might not more plausibly, even without the aid of any previous explanation, have proceeded from any wise and beneficent old man, of a rank or profession in which the language of learning and refinement are natural and to be expected? Need the rank have been at all particularized, where nothing follows which the knowledge of that rank is to explain or illustrate? When on the contrary this information renders the man's language, feelings, sentiments, and information a riddle, which must itself be solved by episodes of anecdote? Finally when this, and this alone, could have induced a genuine *poet* to inweave in a poem of the loftiest style, and on subjects the loftiest and of most universal interest, such minute matters of fact, (not unlike those furnished for the obituary of a magazine by the friends of some obscure *ornament of society lately deceased* in some obscure town), as

> Among the hills of Athol he was born:
> There, on a small hereditary farm,
> An unproductive slip of rugged ground,
> His Father dwelt; and died in poverty;
> While he, whose lowly fortune I retrace,
> The youngest of three sons, was yet a babe,
> A little one—unconscious of their loss.
> But, ere he had outgrown his infant days,
> His widowed mother, for a second mate,
> Espoused the teacher of the Village School;
> Who on her offspring zealously bestowed
> Needful instruction. . . .

From his sixth year, the Boy of whom I speak,
In summer tended cattle on the hills;
But, through the inclement and the perilous days
Of long-continuing winter, he repaired
To his step-father's school,—&c.

For all the admirable passages interposed in this narration, might, with trifling alterations, have been far more appropriately, and with far greater verisimilitude, told of a poet in the character of a poet; and without incurring another defect which I shall now mention, and a sufficient illustration of which will have been here anticipated.

Third; an undue predilection for the *dramatic* form in certain poems, from which one or other of two evils result. Either the thoughts and diction are different from that of the poet, and then there arises an incongruity of style; or they are the same and indistinguishable, and then it presents a species of ventriloquism, where two are represented as talking, while in truth one man only speaks.

The fourth class of defects is closely connected with the former; but yet are such as arise likewise from an intensity of feeling disproportionate to *such* knowledge and value of the objects described, as can be fairly anticipated of men in general, even of the most cultivated classes; and with which therefore few only, and those few particularly circumstanced, can be supposed to sympathize. In this class, I comprise occasional prolixity, repetition, and an eddying, instead of progression, of thought. As instances, see pages 27, 28, and 62 of the *Poems*, Vol. I. and the first eighty lines of the Sixth Book of the *Excursion*.

Fifth and last; thoughts and images too great for the subject. This is an approximation to what might be called *mental* bombast, as distinguished from verbal: for, as in the latter there is a disproportion of the expressions to the thoughts, so in this there is a disproportion of thought to the circumstance and occasion. This, by the bye, is a fault of which none but a man of genius is capable. It is the awkwardness and strength of Hercules with the distaff of Omphale.

It is a well-known fact, that bright colors in motion both make and leave the strongest impressions on the eye. Nothing is more likely too, than that a vivid image or visual spectrum, thus originated, may become the link of association in recalling the feelings and images that had accompanied the original impression. But if we describe this in such lines, as

> They flash upon that inward eye,
> Which is the bliss of solitude!

in what words shall we describe the joy of retrospection, when the images and virtuous actions of a whole well-spent life, pass before that conscience which is indeed the *inward* eye: which is indeed *"the bliss of solitude"*? Assuredly we seem to sink most abruptly, not to say burlesquely, and almost as in a *medly,* from this couplet to—

> And then my heart with pleasure fills,
> And dances with the *daffodils.*
>
> Vol. I, p. 320.

The second instance is from Vol. II. page 12, where the poet, having gone out for a day's tour of pleasure, meets early in the morning with a knot of *gypsies,* who had pitched their blanket-tents and straw-beds, together with their children and asses, in some field by the roadside. At the close of the day on his return our tourist found them in the same place. "Twelve hours," says he,

Twelve hours, twelve bounteous hours are gone, while I
Have been a traveller under open sky,
Much witnessing of change and cheer,
Yet as I left I find them here!

Whereat the poet, without seeming to reflect that the
poor tawny wanderers might probably have been tramp-
ing for weeks together through road and lane, over moor
and mountain, and consequently must have been right
glad to rest themselves, their children and cattle, for
one whole day; and overlooking the obvious truth, that
such repose might be quite as necessary for *them*, as a
walk of the same continuance was pleasing or healthful
for the more fortunate poet; expresses his indignation in
a series of lines, the diction and imagery of which would
have been rather above, than below the mark, had they
been applied to the immense empire of China improgres-
sive for thirty centuries:

> The weary Sun betook himself to rest:—
> —Then issued Vesper from the fulgent west,
> Outshining, like a visible God,
> The glorious path in which he trod!
> And now, ascending, after one dark hour,
> And one night's diminution of her power,
> Behold the mighty Moon! this way
> She looks, as if at them—but they
> Regard not her:—oh, better wrong and strife,
> Better vain deeds or evil than such life!
> The silent Heavens have goings on:
> The Stars have tasks!—but *these* have none!

The last instance of this defect (for I know no other
than these already cited) is from the Ode, page 351,
Vol. II., where, speaking of a child, "a six years' darling
of a pigmy size," he thus addresses him:

Thou best philosopher, who yet dost keep
Thy heritage! Thou eye among the blind,
That, deaf and silent, read'st the eternal deep,
Haunted for ever by the Eternal Mind,—
Mighty Prophet! Seer blest!
On whom those truths do rest,
Which we are toiling all our lives to find!
Thou, over whom thy immortality
Broods like the day, a master o'er the slave,
A presence that is not to be put by!

Now here, not to stop at the daring spirit of metaphor
which connects the epithets "deaf and silent," with the
apostrophized *eye:* or (if we are to refer it to the preced-
ing word, philosopher) the faulty and equivocal syntax
of the passage; and without examining the propriety of
making a "master *brood* o'er a slave," or the *day* brood
at all; we will merely ask, what does all this mean? In
what sense is a child of that age a *philosopher?* In what
sense does he *read* "the eternal deep"? In what sense is
he declared to be *"for ever haunted"* by the Supreme
Being? or so inspired as to deserve the splendid titles of
a *mighty prophet,* a *blessed seer?* By reflection? by
knowledge? by conscious intuition? or by *any* form or
modification of consciousness? These would be tidings
indeed; but such as would presuppose an immediate
revelation to the inspired communicator, and require
miracles to authenticate his inspiration. Children at this
age give us no such information of themselves; and at
what time were we dipped in the Lethe, which has pro-
duced such utter oblivion of a state so godlike? There
are many of us that still possess some remembrances,
more or less distinct, respecting themselves at six years
old; pity that the worthless straws only should float,
while treasures, compared with which all the mines of

Golconda and Mexico were but straws, should be ab-
sorbed by some unknown gulf into some unknown abyss.

But if this be too wild and exorbitant to be suspected
as having been the poet's meaning; if these mysterious
gifts, faculties, and operations, are *not* accompanied with
consciousness; who *else* is conscious of them? or how can
it be called the child, if it be no part of the child's con-
scious being? For aught I know, the thinking Spirit
within me may be *substantially* one with the principle of
life, and of vital operation. For aught I know, it might
be employed as a secondary agent in the marvellous
organization and organic movements of my body. But,
surely, it would be strange language to say, that *I* con-
struct my *heart!* or that *I* propel the finer influences
through my *nerves!* or that *I* compress my brain, and
draw the curtains of sleep round my own eyes! Spinoza
and Behmen were, on different systems, both Pantheists;
and among the ancients there were philosophers, teach-
ers of the ΕΝ ΚΑΙ ΠΑΝ, who not only taught that
God was All, but that this All constituted God. Yet not
even these would confound the *part, as* a part, with the
Whole, *as* the whole. Nay, in no system is the distinction
between the individual and God, between the Modifica-
tion, and the one only Substance, more sharply drawn,
than in that of Spinoza. Jacobi indeed relates of Less-
ing, that, after a conversation with him at the house of
the poet, Gleim (the Tyrtæus and Anacreon of the
German Parnassus) in which conversation L. had
avowed privately to Jacobi his reluctance to admit any
personal existence of the Supreme Being, or the *possi-
bility* of personality except in a finite Intellect, and while
they were sitting at table, a shower of rain came on un-
expectedly. Gleim expressed his regret at the circum-
stance, because they had meant to drink their wine in
the garden: upon which Lessing in one of his half-

earnest half-joking moods, nodded to Jacobi, and said,
"It is *I*, perhaps, that am doing *that*," i.e. *raining!* and
J. answered, "or perhaps I"; Gleim contented himself
with staring at them both, without asking for any ex-
planation.

So with regard to this passage. In what sense can the
magnificent attributes, above quoted, be appropriated to
a *child*, which would not make them equally suitable to
a *bee*, or a *dog*, or a *field of corn:* or even to a ship, or
to the wind and waves that propel it? The omnipresent
Spirit works equally in them, as in the child; and the
child is equally unconscious of it as they. It cannot
surely be, that the four lines, immediately following, are
to contain the explanation?

> To whom the grave
> Is but a lonely bed without the sense or sight
> Of day or the warm light,
> A place of thought where we in waiting lie.

Surely, it cannot be that this wonder-rousing apos-
trophe is but a comment on the little poem, "We are
seven?" that the whole meaning of the passage is re-
ducible to the assertion, that a *child*, who by the bye
at six years old would have been better instructed in
most Christian families, has no other notion of death
than that of lying in a dark, cold place? And still, I hope,
not as in a *place of thought!* not the frightful notion of
lying *awake* in his grave! The analogy between death
and sleep is too simple, too natural, to render so horrid
a belief possible for children; even had they not been
in the habit, as all Christian children are, of hearing
the latter term used to express the former. But if the
child's belief be only, that "he is not dead, but sleepeth:"
wherein does it differ from that of his father and mother,
or any other adult and instructed person? To form an

idea of a thing's becoming nothing; or of nothing becoming a thing; is impossible to all finite beings alike, of whatever age, and however educated or uneducated. Thus it is with splendid paradoxes in general. If the words are taken in the common sense, they convey an absurdity; and if, in contempt of dictionaries and custom, they are so interpreted as to avoid the absurdity, the meaning dwindles into some bald truism. Thus you must at once understand the words *contrary* to their common import, in order to arrive at any *sense;* and *according* to their common import, if you are to receive from them any feeling of *sublimity* or *admiration.*

Though the instances of this defect in Mr. Wordsworth's poems are so few, that for themselves it would have been scarce just to attract the reader's attention toward them; yet I have dwelt on it, and perhaps the more for this very reason. For being so very few, they cannot sensibly detract from the reputation of an author, who is even characterized by the number of profound truths in his writings, which will stand the severest analysis; and yet few as they are, they are exactly those passages which his *blind* admirers would be most likely, and best able, to imitate. But WORDSWORTH, where he is indeed Wordsworth, may be mimicked by Copyists, he may be plundered by Plagiarists; but he can not be imitated, except by those who are not born to be imitators. For without his depth of feeling and his imaginative power his *sense* would want its vital warmth and peculiarity; and without his strong sense, his *mysticism* would become *sickly*—mere fog, and dimness!

To these defects which, as appears by the extracts, are only occasional, I may oppose, with far less fear of encountering the dissent of any candid and intelligent reader, the following (for the most part correspondent) excellences. First, an austere purity of language both

grammatically and logically; in short a perfect appro-
priateness of the words to the meaning. Of how high
value I deem this, and how particularly estimable I hold
the example at the present day, has been already stated:
and in part too the reasons on which I ground both the
moral and intellectual importance of habituating our-
selves to a strict accuracy of expression. It is noticeable,
how limited an acquaintance with the masterpieces of
art will suffice to form a correct and even a sensitive
taste, where none but master-pieces have been seen and
admired: while on the other hand, the most correct no-
tions, and the widest acquaintance with the works of
excellence of all ages and countries, will not perfectly
secure us against the contagious familiarity with the far
more numerous offspring of tastelessness or of a per-
verted taste. If this be the case, as it notoriously is, with
the arts of music and painting, much more difficult will
it be to avoid the infection of multiplied and daily ex-
amples in the practice of an art, which uses words, and
words only, as its instruments. In poetry, in which every
line, every phrase, may pass the ordeal of deliberation
and deliberate choice, it is possible, and barely possible,
to attain that ultimatum which I have ventured to pro-
pose as the infallible test of a blameless style; its *un-
translatableness* in words of the same language without
injury to the meaning. Be it observed, however, that I
include in the *meaning* of a word not only its corre-
spondent object, but likewise all the associations which it
recalls. For language is framed to convey not the object
alone, but likewise the character, mood and intentions of
the person who is representing it. In poetry it *is* prac-
ticable to preserve the diction uncorrupted by the affec-
tations and misappropriations, which promiscuous au-
thorship, and reading not promiscuous only because it is
disproportionally most conversant with the compositions

of the day, have rendered general. Yet even to the poet, composing in his own province, it is an arduous work: and as the result and pledge of a watchful good sense, of fine and luminous distinction, and of complete self-possession, may justly claim all the honor which belongs to an attainment equally difficult and valuable, and the more valuable for being rare. It is at *all* times the proper food of the understanding; but in an age of corrupt eloquence it is both food and antidote.

In prose I doubt whether it be even possible to preserve our style wholly unalloyed by the vicious phraseology which meets us everywhere, from the sermon to the newspaper, from the harangue of the legislator to the speech from the convivial chair, announcing a *toast* or sentiment. Our chains rattle, even while we are complaining of them. The poems of Boetius rise high in our estimation when we compare them with those of his contemporaries, as Sidonius Apollinarius, &c. They might even be referred to a purer age, but that the prose, in which they are set, as jewels in a crown of lead or iron, betrays the true age of the writer. Much however may be effected by education. I believe not only from grounds of reason, but from having in great measure assured myself of the fact by actual though limited experience, that, to a youth led from his first boyhood to investigate the meaning of every word and the reason of its choice and position, Logic presents itself as an old acquaintance under new names.

On some future occasion, more especially demanding such disquisition, I shall attempt to prove the close connection between veracity and habits of mental accuracy; the beneficial after-effects of verbal precision in the preclusion of fanaticism, which masters the feelings more especially by indistinct watch-words; and to display the advantages which language alone, at least which lan-

guage with incomparably greater ease and certainty than
any other means, presents to the instructor of impressing
modes of intellectual energy so constantly, so imper-
ceptibly, and as it were by such elements and atoms, as
to secure in due time the formation of a second nature.
When we reflect, that the cultivation of the judgement
is a positive command of the moral law, since the reason
can give the *principle* alone, and the conscience bears
witness only to the *motive,* while the application and
effects must depend on the judgement: when we con-
sider, that the greater part of our success and comfort
in life depends on distinguishing the similar from the
same, that which is peculiar in each thing from that
which it has in common with others, so as still to select
the most probable, instead of the merely possible or
positively unfit, we shall learn to value earnestly and
with a practical seriousness a mean, already prepared
for us by nature and society, of teaching the young mind
to think well and wisely by the same unremembered
process and with the same never forgotten results, as
those by which it is taught to speak and converse. Now
how much warmer the interest is, how much more genial
the feelings of reality and practicability, and thence how
much stronger the impulses to imitation are, which a
contemporary writer, and especially a contemporary
poet, excites in youth and commencing manhood, has
been treated of in the earlier pages of these sketches. I
have only to add, that all the praise which is due to the
exertion of such influence for a purpose so important,
joined with that which must be claimed for the infre-
quency of the same excellence in the same perfection,
belongs in full right to Mr. Wordsworth. I am far how-
ever from denying that we have poets whose *general*
style possesses the same excellence, as Mr. Moore, Lord
Byron, Mr. Bowles, and, in all his later and more im-

portant works, our laurel-honoring Laureate. But there
are none, in whose works I do not appear to myself
to find *more* exceptions, than in those of Wordsworth.
Quotations or specimens would here be wholly out of
place, and must be left for the critic who doubts and
would invalidate the justice of this eulogy so applied.

The second characteristic excellence of Mr. W's work
is: a correspondent weight and sanity of the Thoughts
and Sentiments, won—not from books, but—from the
poet's own meditative observation. They are *fresh* and
have the dew upon them. His muse, at least when in her
strength of wing, and when she hovers aloft in her
proper element,

> Makes audible a linked lay of truth,
> Of truth profound a sweet continuous lay,
> Not learnt, but native, her own natural notes!
>
> S. T. C.

Even throughout his smaller poems there is scarcely
one, which is not rendered valuable by some just and
original reflection.

See page 25, vol. 2nd.: or the two following passages
in one of his humblest compositions.

> O Reader! had you in your mind
> Such stores as silent thought can bring,
> O gentle Reader! you would find
> A tale in every thing;

and

> I've heard of hearts unkind, kind deeds
> With coldness still returning;
> Alas! the gratitude of men
> Has oftener left me mourning

or in a still higher strain the six beautiful quatrains, page
134.

> Thus fares it still in our decay:
> And yet the wiser mind
> Mourns less for what age takes away
> Than what it leaves behind.
>
> The Blackbird in the summer trees,
> The Lark upon the hill,
> Let loose their carols when they please,
> Are quiet when they will.
>
> With nature never do *they* wage
> A foolish strife; they see
> A happy youth, and their old age
> Is beautiful and free!
>
> But we are pressed by heavy laws;
> And often, glad no more,
> We wear a face of joy, because
> We have been glad of yore.
>
> If there is one, who need bemoan
> His kindred laid in earth,
> The household hearts that were his own,
> It is the man of mirth.
>
> My days, my Friend, are almost gone,
> My life has been approved,
> And many love me; but by none
> Am I enough beloved.

or the sonnet on Buonaparte, page 202, vol. 2; or finally (for a volume would scarce suffice to exhaust the instances) the last stanza of the poem on the withered Celandine, vol. 2, p. 212.

> To be a prodigal's favorite—then, worse truth,
> A miser's pensioner—behold our lot!
> O man! that from thy fair and shining youth
> Age might but take the things youth needed not.

Both in respect of this and of the former excellence, Mr. Wordsworth strikingly resembles Samuel Daniel, one of the golden writers of our golden Elizabethan age, now most causelessly neglected: Samuel Daniel, whose diction bears no mark of time, no distinction of age, which has been, and as long as our language shall last, will be so far the language of the to-day and for ever, as that it is more intelligible to us, than the transitory fashions of our own particular age. A similar praise is due to his sentiments. No frequency of perusal can deprive them of their freshness. For though they are brought into the full day-light of every reader's comprehension; yet are they drawn up from depths which few in any age are privileged to visit, into which few in any age have courage or inclination to descend. If Mr. Wordsworth is not equally with Daniel alike intelligible to all readers of average understanding in all passages of his works, the comparative difficulty does not arise from the greater impurity of the ore, but from the nature and uses of the metal. A poem is not necessarily obscure, because it does not aim to be popular. It is enough, if a work be perspicuous to those for whom it is written, and

Fit audience find, though few.

To the "Ode on the intimation of immortality from recollections of early childhood" the poet might have prefixed the lines which Dante addresses to one of his own Canzoni—

Canzon, io credo, che saranno radi
Che tua ragione intendan bene,
Tanto lor sei faticoso ed alto.

O lyric song, there will be few, think I,
Who may thy import understand aright:
Thou art for *them* so arduous and so high!

But the ode was intended for such readers only as had been accustomed to watch the flux and reflux of their inmost nature, to venture at times into the twilight realms of consciousness, and to feel a deep interest in modes of inmost being, to which they know that the attributes of time and space are inapplicable and alien, but which yet can not be conveyed save in symbols of time and space. For such readers the sense is sufficiently plain, and they will be as little disposed to charge Mr. Wordsworth with believing the Platonic pre-existence in the ordinary interpretation of the words, as I am to believe, that Plato himself ever meant or taught it.

Πολλά μοι ὑπ᾽ ἀγκῶ-
νος ὠκέα βέλη
ἔνδον ἐντὶ φαρέτρας
φωνᾶντα συνετοῖσιν᾽ ἐς
δὲ τὸ πᾶν ἑρμηνέων
χατίζει. σοφὸς ὁ πολ-
λὰ εἰδὼς φυᾷ.
μαθόντες δέ, λάβροι
παγγλωσσίᾳ, κόρακες ὥς,
ἄκραντα γαρύετον
Διὸς πρὸς ὄρνιχα θεῖον.

Third (and wherein he soars far above Daniel) the sinewy strength and originality of single lines and paragraphs: the frequent curiosa felicitas of his diction, of which I need not here give specimens, having anticipated them in a preceding page. This beauty, and as eminently characteristic of Wordsworth's poetry, his rudest assailants have felt themselves compelled to acknowledge and admire.

Fourth; the perfect truth of nature in his images and descriptions, as taken immediately from nature, and proving a long and genial intimacy with the very spirit which gives the physiognomic expression to all the works

of nature. Like a green field reflected in a calm and per-
fectly transparent lake, the image is distinguished from
the reality only by its greater softness and lustre. Like
the moisture or the polish on a pebble, genius neither
distorts nor false-colours its objects; but on the contrary
brings out many a vein and many a tint, which escapes
the eye of common observation, thus raising to the rank
of gems what had been often kicked away by the hurry-
ing foot of the traveller on the dusty high road of
custom.

Let me refer to the whole description of skating, vol.
I., page 42 to 47, especially to the lines

> So through the darkness and the cold we flew,
> And not a voice was idle: with the din
> Meanwhile the precipices rang aloud;
> The leafless trees and every icy crag
> Tinkled like iron; while the distant hills
> Into the tumult sent an alien sound
> Of melancholy, not unnoticed, while the stars
> Eastward were sparkling clear, and in the west
> The orange sky of evening died away.

Or to the poem on the green linnet, vol. I. page 244.
What can be more accurate yet more lovely than the
two concluding stanzas?

> Upon yon tuft of hazel trees,
> That twinkle to the gusty breeze,
> Behold him perched in ecstasies,
>   Yet seeming still to hover;
> There! where the flutter of his wings
> Upon his back and body flings
> Shadows and sunny glimmerings,
>   That cover him all over.
>
> While thus before my eyes he gleams,
> A brother of the leaves he seems;

When in a moment forth he teems
　His little song in gushes:
As if it pleased him to disdain
And mock the form which he did feign,
While he was dancing with the train
　Of leaves among the bushes.

Or the description of the blue-cap, and of the noon-
tide silence, page 284; or the poem to the cuckoo, page
299; or, lastly, though I might multiply the references
to ten times the number, to the poem, so completely
Wordsworth's, commencing

Three years she grew in sun and shower, &c.

Fifth: a meditative pathos, a union of deep and subtle
thought with sensibility; a sympathy with man as man;
the sympathy indeed of a contemplator, rather than a
fellow-sufferer or co-mate, (spectator, haud particeps)
but of a contemplator, from whose view no difference of
rank conceals the sameness of the nature; no injuries of
wind or weather, or toil, or even of ignorance, wholly
disguise the human face divine. The superscription and
the image of the Creator still remain legible to *him*
under the dark lines, with which guilt or calamity had
cancelled or cross-barred it. Here the man and the poet
lose and find themselves in each other, the one as glori-
fied, the latter as substantiated. In this mild and philo-
sophic pathos, Wordsworth appears to me without a
compeer. Such he *is:* so he *writes.* See vol. I. page 134
to 136, or that most affecting composition, the "Afflic-
tion of Margaret —— of ——," page 165 to 168, which
no mother, and, if I may judge by my own experience,
no parent can read without a tear. Or turn to that
genuine lyric, in the former edition, entitled "The Mad
Mother," page 174 to 178, of which I cannot refrain
from quoting two of the stanzas, both of them for their

pathos, and the former for the fine transition in the two
concluding lines of the stanza, so expressive of that de-
ranged state, in which from the increased sensibility
the sufferer's attention is abruptly drawn off by every
trifle, and in the same instant plucked back again by
the one despotic thought, bringing home with it, by the
blending, *fusing* power of Imagination and Passion, the
alien object to which it had been so abruptly diverted,
no longer an alien but an ally and an inmate.

> Suck, little babe, oh suck again!
> It cools my blood; it cools my brain:
> Thy lips, I feel them, baby! they
> Draw from my heart the pain away.
> Oh! press me with thy little hand;
> It loosens something at my chest:
> About that tight and deadly band
> I feel thy little fingers prest.
> The breeze I see is in the tree!
> It comes to cool my babe and me.
>
> Thy father cares not for my breast,
> 'Tis thine, sweet baby, there to rest,
> 'Tis all thine own!—and, if its hue
> Be changed, that was so fair to view,
> 'Tis fair enough for thee, my dove!
> My beauty, little child, is flown,
> But thou wilt live with me in love;
> And what if my poor cheek be brown?
> 'Tis well for me, thou canst not see
> How pale and wan it else would be.

Last, and pre-eminently, I challenge for this poet the
gift of IMAGINATION in the highest and strictest sense of
the word. In the play of *Fancy*, Wordsworth, to my
feelings, is not always graceful, and sometimes *recondite*.
The *likeness* is occasionally too strange, or demands too
peculiar a point of view, or is such as appears the

creature of predetermined research, rather than spon-
taneous presentation. Indeed his fancy seldom displays
itself, as mere and unmodified fancy. But in imaginative
power, he stands nearest of all modern writers to Shake-
speare and Milton; and yet in a kind perfectly unbor-
rowed and his own. To employ his own words, which
are at once an instance and an illustration, he does in-
deed to all thoughts and to all objects

> add the gleam,
> The light that never was, on sea or land,
> The consecration, and the poet's dream.

I shall select a few examples as most obviously mani-
festing this faculty; but if I should ever be fortunate
enough to render my analysis of imagination, its origin
and characters, thoroughly intelligible to the reader, he
will scarcely open on a page of this poet's works without
recognising, more or less, the presence and the influ-
ences of this faculty.

From the poem on the Yew Trees, vol. I. page 303,
304.

> But worthier still of note
> Are those fraternal four of Borrowdale,
> Joined in one solemn and capacious grove:
> Huge trunks!—and each particular trunk a growth
> Of intertwisted fibres serpentine
> Up-coiling, and inveterately convolved,—
> Not uninformed with phantasy, and looks
> That threaten the profane;—a pillared shade,
> Upon whose grassless floor of red-brown hue,
> By sheddings from the pinal umbrage tinged
> Perennially—beneath whose sable roof
> Of boughs, as if for festal purpose decked
> With unrejoicing berries, ghostly shapes
> May meet at noontide—FEAR and trembling HOPE,
> SILENCE and FORESIGHT—DEATH, the skeleton,

And TIME, the shadow—there to celebrate,
As in a natural temple scattered o'er
With altars undisturbed of mossy stone,
United worship; or in mute repose
To lie, and listen to the mountain flood
Murmuring from Glaramara's inmost caves.

The effect of the old man's figure in the poem of
Resignation and Independence, vol. II. page 33.

While he was talking thus, the lonely place,
The old man's shape, and speech, all troubled me:
In my mind's eye I seemed to see him pace
About the weary moors continually,
Wandering about alone and silently.

Or the 8th, 9th, 19th, 26th, 31st, and 33d, in the col-
lection of miscellaneous sonnets—the sonnet on the sub-
jugation of Switzerland, page 210, or the last ode, from
which I especially select the two following stanzas or
paragraphs, page 349 to 350.

Our birth is but a sleep and a forgetting;
The soul that rises with us, our life's star,
Hath had elsewhere its setting,
    And cometh from afar.
Not in entire forgetfulness,
And not in utter nakedness,
But trailing clouds of glory do we come
From God, who is our home:

Heaven lies about us in our infancy!
Shades of the prison-house begin to close
    Upon the growing boy;
But he beholds the light, and whence it flows,
    He sees it in his joy!
The youth who daily further from the East
Must travel, still is nature's priest,
    And by the splendid vision
    Is on his way attended;

At length the man perceives it die away,
And fade into the light of common day.

And page 352 to 354 of the same ode.

O joy that in our embers
Is something that doth live,
That nature yet remembers
What was so fugitive!
The thought of our past years in me doth breed
Perpetual benedictions: not indeed
For that which is most worthy to be blest;
Delight and liberty, the simple creed
Of childhood, whether busy or at rest,
With new-fledged hope still fluttering in his breast:—
Not for these I raise
The song of thanks and praise;
But for those obstinate questionings
Of sense and outward things,
Fallings from us, vanishings;
Blank misgivings of a creature
Moving about in worlds not realized,
High instincts, before which our mortal nature
Did tremble like a guilty thing surprised!
But for those first affections,
Those shadowy recollections,
Which, be they what they may,
Are yet the fountain light of all our day,
Are yet a master light of all our seeing;
Uphold us—cherish—and have power to make
Our noisy years seem moments in the being
Of the eternal silence; truths that wake
    To perish never:
Which neither listlessness, nor mad endeavour,
Nor man nor boy,
Nor all that is at enmity with joy,
Can utterly abolish or destroy!
Hence, in a season of calm weather,
Though inland far we be,

Our souls have sight of that immortal sea
Which brought us hither; '
Can in a moment travel thither—
And see the children sport upon the shore,
And hear the mighty waters rolling evermore.

And since it would be unfair to conclude with an
extract, which, though highly characteristic, must yet,
from the nature of the thoughts and the subject, be in-
teresting, or perhaps intelligible, to but a limited num-
ber of readers; I will add, from the poet's last published
work, a passage equally Wordsworthian; of the beauty
of which, and of the imaginative power displayed
therein, there can be but one opinion, and one feeling.
See "White Doe," page 5.

Fast the church-yard fills;—anon
Look again and they are gone;
The cluster round the porch, and the folk
Who sate in the shade of the prior's oak!
And scarcely have they disappear'd,
Ere the prelusive hymn is heard;—
With one consent the people rejoice,
Filling the church with a lofty voice!
They sing a service which they feel,
For 'tis the sun-rise of their zeal;
And faith and hope are in their prime
In great Eliza's golden time.

A moment ends the fervent din,
And all is hushed, without and within;
For though the priest, more tranquilly,
Recites the holy liturgy,
The only voice which you can hear
Is the river murmuring near.
When soft!—the dusky trees between,
And down the path through the open green,
Where is no living thing to be seen;
And through yon gateway, where is found,

Beneath the arch with ivy bound,
Free entrance to the church-yard ground;
And right across the verdant sod,
Towards the very house of God;
Comes gliding in with lovely gleam,
Comes gliding in serene and slow,
Soft and silent as a dream,
A solitary doe!
White she is as lily of June,
And beauteous as the silver moon
When out of sight the clouds are driven
And she is left alone in heaven!
Or like a ship some gentle day
In sunshine sailing far away—
A glittering ship, that hath the plain
Of ocean for her own domain.

·   ·   ·   ·   ·   ·   ·   ·

What harmonious pensive changes
Wait upon her as she ranges
Round and through this pile of state
Overthrown and desolate!
Now a step or two her way
Is through space of open day,
Where the enamoured sunny light
Brightens her that was so bright;
Now doth a delicate shadow fall,
Falls upon her like a breath,
From some lofty arch or wall,
As she passes underneath.

The following analogy will, I am apprehensive, appear dim and fantastic, but in reading Bartram's Travels I could not help transcribing the following lines as a sort of allegory, or connected simile and metaphor of Wordsworth's intellect and genius.—"The soil is a deep, rich, dark mould, on a deep stratum of tenacious clay; and that on a foundation of rocks, which often break through both strata, lifting their back above the surface. The trees which chiefly grow here are the gigantic black oak; magnolia magni-floria; fraxinus excelsior; platane; and a few stately tulip trees." What Mr. Wordsworth *will* produce, it is not for me to prophecy: but I could pronounce with the liveliest convictions what he is capable of producing. It is the First Genuine Philosophic Poem.

The preceding criticism will not, I am aware, avail to overcome the prejudices of those, who have made it a business to attack and ridicule Mr. Wordsworth's compositions.

Truth and prudence might be imaged as concentric circles. The poet may perhaps have passed beyond the latter, but he has confined himself far within the bounds of the former, in designating these critics, as too petulant to be passive to a genuine poet, and too feeble to grapple with him;—"men of palsied imaginations, in whose minds all healthy action is languid;—who, therefore, feed as the many direct them, or with the many are greedy after vicious provocatives."

Let not Mr. Wordsworth be charged with having expressed himself too indignantly, till the wantonness and the systematic and malignant perseverance of the aggressions have been taken into fair consideration. I myself heard the commander in chief of this unmanly warfare make a boast of his private admiration of Wordsworth's genius. I have heard him declare, that whoever came into his room would probably find the *Lyrical Ballads* lying open on his table, and that (speaking exclusively of those written by Mr. Wordsworth himself) he could nearly repeat the whole of them by heart. *But* a Review, in order to be a saleable article, must be *personal, sharp,* and *pointed:* and, *since then,* the poet has made himself, and with himself all who were, or were supposed to be, his friends and admirers, the object of the critic's revenge—how? by having spoken of a work so conducted in the terms which it deserved! I once heard a clergyman in boots and buck-skin avow, that he would cheat his own father *in a horse*. A moral system of a similar nature seems to have been adopted by too many anonymous critics. As we used to say at school, in reviewing they *make* being rogues: and he, who complains, is to be laughed at for his igno-rance of *the game*. With the pen out of their hand they are *honorable men*. They exert indeed power (which is to that of the injured party who should attempt to ex-pose their glaring perversions and misstatements, as twenty to one) to write down, and (where the author's circumstances permit) to *impoverish* the man, whose learning and genius they themselves in private have repeatedly admitted. They knowingly strive to make it impossible for the man even to publish[1] any future work without exposing himself to all the wretchedness of debt and embarrassment. But this is all *in their vocation:* and, bating what they do in their *vocation, "who can say that black is the white of their eye?"*

So much for the detractors from Wordsworth's merits. On the other hand, much as I might wish for their fuller sympathy, I dare not flatter myself, that the freedom with which I have declared my opinions concerning both his theory and his defects, most of which are more or less connected with his theory, either as cause or effect, will be satisfactory or pleasing to *all* the poet's admirers

[1] Not many months ago an eminent bookseller was asked what he thought of ——? The answer was: "I have heard his powers very highly spoken of by some of our first-rate men; but I would not have a work of his if any one would give it me: for he is spoken but slightly of, or not at all, in the Quarterly Review: and the Edinburgh, you know, is decided to cut him up!"—*S. T. C.*

and advocates. More indiscriminate than mine their admiration may be: deeper and more sincere it can not be. But I have advanced no opinion either for praise or censure, other than as texts introductory to the reasons which compel me to form it. Above all, I was fully convinced that such a criticism was not only wanted; but that, if executed with adequate ability, it must conduce, in no mean degree, to Mr. Wordsworth's *reputation*. His *fame* belongs to another age, and can neither be accelerated nor retarded. . . .

Index of First Lines of Poems